THE
DERBYSHIRE
COUNTRY HOUSE:1

Maxwell Craven & Michael Stanley

FOREWORD

To all of us who live in Derbyshire and to the thousands of people who visit it every year, this book, when it first appeared in 1982, was a most welcome addition to the existing reference books on buildings in the county.

There has always been a great deal of interest in the large and famous houses (of which Derbyshire has more than its fair share) but no less fascinating are the many and infinitely more varied lesser known houses with which this book also concerns itself.

Until now it has not been easy to discover much about them. Some, alas, have gone forever. Some, happily, are still occupied by the descendants of the men who built them. Many are the homes of people who appreciate something special and are content to deal with the problems that go with living in an old house. Because of the social changes which have taken place in the last seventy or more years many are used for purposes other than those for which they were built. Others still await restoration or conversion.

The awakening of the interest of public opinion in historic buildings and their importance in towns, villages and countryside is one of the most cheerful and heartening things that has happened in the last few years.

Because of the awakened interest, it is less likely now that such buildings are allowed to be demolished or to fall into irreparable decay. Instead they are sought out and appreciated by more and more people who enjoy matching history and architecture, which go hand in hand down the centuries.

The enterprise of the publishers in producing a new, revised and up-dated edition of this publication is to be congratulated. I cannot imagine anything more pleasurable than to set out with this book to hand to explore the neighbourhood with a new eye and I am sure it will be used by many people in this way as well as being treasured as a unique work of reference.

It is therefore with the greatest of pleasure that I write this Foreword and I wish this new, complete edition the success it deserves.

Deborah Devonshire

Chatsworth 2001

Published by

Ashbourne Hall, Cokayne Ave
Ashbourne, Derbyshire DE6 1EJ England
Tel: (01335) 347349 Fax: (01335) 347303
e-mail: landmark@clara.net
web site: www.landmarkpublishing.co.uk

ISBN 1 84306 007 8

DEDICATION: to Carole and Gill

Print: MPG Books Ltd, Bodmin, Cornwall

Front cover: Swarkestone Gatehouse (Landmark Trust)

Back cover: Top left: Sudbury Hall, (National Trust); Middle: Allen Hill (Derbyshire Museums Service); Top Right: Smalley Hall
(FPD Savills); Main photo: The Library, Chatsworth (Trustees of the Chatsworth Settlement and the Duke of Devonshire).

Page One: Chatsworth, early 20th century; **Title Page:** Kedleston, (CLM Porter).

Publisher's Note

The production of this book has been a challenge to say the least, but I hope you, the reader, will judge the work of the authors and the
Landmark production team to have produced a lovely and important book. We would have loved to have gone further and included
more photographs, but space would not allow.

Responsible for this book at Landmark have been: Mark Titterton (overall design); James Allsopp (cover & scanning); Ashley Emery
(scanning); John Shouksmith, myself, Andrew Lewer, Stella Porter (editorial); Diane Riley (general assistance). To Max, Mike and my
team here at Landmark, I'd like to put on record my thanks for a job well done.

Lindsey Porter, September 2001

THE
DERBYSHIRE
COUNTRY HOUSE:1

Maxwell Craven & Michael Stanley

Landmark Publishing

Contents

HOUSES OPEN TO THE PUBLIC

Several houses in this book open their doors to visitors. This list is not intended to be complete, but may be helpful in your planning. Please respect the privacy of houses which are privately owned.

Bolsover Castle (English Heritage)   ☎ 01246 822844

Calke Abbey (National Trust)   ☎ 01332 863822

Catton Hall   ☎ 01283 716311
open: Monday Afternoons
April/October

Chatsworth   ☎ 01246 582204
House, Farmyard &
Adventure Playground
open daily: mid-March/
end October

Elvaston Castle   ☎ 01332 571342

Eyam Hall   ☎ 01433 631976

Haddon Hall   ☎ 01629 812855

Hardwick Hall (National Trust)   ☎ 01246 850430

Kedleston Hall (National Trust)   ☎ 01332 842191

Renishaw House   ☎ 01246 432310

Sudbury Hall (National Trust)   ☎ 01283 585305

Sutton Scarsdale (English Heritage)   ☎ 01246 822621

Tissington Hall   ☎ 01335 352200
open on certain days
only in midsummer

Wingfield Manor (English Heritage)   ☎ 01773 832060

PREFACE

TWENTY YEARS have elapsed since we wrote the original first volume of *The Derbyshire Country House*, and nineteen since it was first published. We originally undertook the project with more enthusiasm than experience; indeed, we were so pleased that someone was willing to publish it that we did not even ask for payment! This was rectified with the second volume which appeared in 1984, and since then the original volume has been completely re-written (with a number of entries transferred from the 1984 edition) and was published by Breedon of Derby in 1991. As all three volumes, despite substantial print-runs, have been long out of print, and in view of continuing demand, we were pleased to accept an offer from the present publisher to undertake a further substantial revision for this new, combined edition.

One inevitable result of publishing a work of this kind, is that, as soon as it is in print, new information starts flowing in; further, after twenty years in which we ourselves have not been idle either in research or in visiting Derbyshire houses, much new or revised information has come to light. Furthermore, the relevant literature, not only of the genre nationally but in local histories and memoirs – good and less good – has also burgeoned, re-inforced especially by a rush of village histories produced to mark the Millennium. This has had to be evaluated and integrated with our research, and we have been especially gratified to have been quoted on a number of occasions, with acknowledgement in the more scholarly works and, regrettably, without that courtesy in many of the local productions (where even some of our errors have entered the canon), although either way it is gratifying.

The present production – effectively the third edition of our original first volume (Matlock, 1982 and Derby, 1991) and the second of our second (Matlock 1984) – is a compendium, consisting of a revised 1991 volume, this time including the notes, which were omitted on grounds of lack of space, forming the first section and a revised 1984 volume, forming the second, but keeping to the compact and formalised format. About four houses have been omitted from both on the grounds that they failed to meet the original criterion that the house must, at some time in its existence, have been supported by a landed estate and about a dozen omitted from both the previous works have gone in. There remain another twenty or so that might have merited inclusion, and the appendix of the 1984 volume of long-vanished seats of which no known illustration has survived, which have had to continue to languish in our files through lack of space. The ten houses relegated to an appendix in the 1991 volume have now been re-integrated into the text of the first section.

Throughout the present work, however, we have gone to some trouble to provide new illustrations where available, although some have had, perforce, to remain the same. Furthermore, in the intervening twenty years, geological terminology has been completely revised internationally, and that has been taken into account in describing the building materials (a unique feature of a book on country houses in 1982) which are included in the main narrative under each seat in the first section and as a separate section at the head of each in the second. The accounts of the early history of estates have also been pruned, especially in the first section, mainly to make space for more information about the houses themselves and their materials.

Where considerations of space have allowed, we have endeavoured to provide more than one photograph, to support the descriptive material in the text. We have also, in places, used good historic photographs, feeling that these are frequently more evocative and instructive than more recent ones. In the case of those taken by Derby's pioneering Victorian topographical photographer, Richard Keene (1825-1894) these considerations are re-inforced by his unmatched talent for landscape photography. He, and his great friend and collaborator John Alfred Warwick, were initiated into this then new art by Canon Edward Abney (of Measham Hall (*qv*) and The Firs, Derby) around 1852, and their mentor was himself a close friend of W. H. Fox-Talbot, Britain's pioneer photographer who was married to a daughter of the house of Mundy of Markeaton Hall (*qv*). One new inclusion, Grangefield, Trusley, is illustrated by a photograph of which the original is a Talbot-type, and cannot be later than 1853; the possibility that it was taken by Abney on one of his peregrinations of the countryside near to Derby with Fox-Talbot cannot lightly be excluded. The views of Radburne and Alfreton Halls were taken by 1854, in the case of the latter, certainly not later, and all three represent some of the earliest topographical photographs ever taken in the county.

Where possible we have tried to say something of the interiors of house and about their settings – landscape, gardens and estates – although photographs of these important aspects are not always readily available, and the space in which they can be used at a premium. Furthermore, some owners are understandably concerned about security, which is a factor of particular relevance with interiors.

We have also, as before, allowed Derbyshire's border to be a trifle elastic. We worked to the pre-1887 boundaries predominantly – those which held constant for the longest temporal period: almost a thousand years – but have also included seats that stand or stood on portions of the county which came into Derbyshire after that date. Thus Beauchief, Croxall, Stapenhill, Mellor and others, all lost to Derbyshire are included, and Netherseal Hall, Overseal House, and others have also found a place as being in parts of Leicestershire given to Derbyshire to replace the lost "islands" of Derbyshire, like Ravenstone (which actually lies substantially south of Loughborough!), Appleby Parva, Measham, Willesley and Stretton-en-le-Field.

However, as of 1st April, 1993, sixteen small portions of Nottinghamshire were added to Derbyshire – in the teeth of opposition east of the Erewash – as a result of a review by a Boundary Commission set up in 1986. The re-arrangement lacks the logic of previous ones, and deprives the Erewash of its natural function as a boundary. Under its terms small portions of the following have been added to Derbyshire (reading from north to south): Shireoaks, Holbeck, Shirebrook, Pinxton, Somercotes, Ironville, Aldercar, Brinsley, Eastwood, Shipley, Cossall, Trowell, Stapleford, Stanton-by-Dale and Sandiacre. In fact we have always treated the third to seventh, tenth, fourteenth and fifteenth of these as being wholly within Derbyshire anyway and, in the event, only one important seat, Shireoaks Hall – a part-ruined house slowly being re-habilitated and firmly within the Smythson family of tower houses – has ended up being transferred from Nottinghamshire to Derbyshire. We have, therefore – at the risk of being accused of inconsistency – chosen to ignore this recent piece of legislative Gerrymandering.

Some seats which were run together previously, like the Hall and Nether Hall at Hathersage, and the Hall and Old Hall at Heanor have, for convenience, been separated for instance, whilst some others – Appleby Manor and Appleby

Hall, Wingerworth and Egstow Halls, Egginton Hall, Rock House and Park Hill and the two seats at Walton-on-Trent spring to mind – have been treated together for reasons which are, we hope, clear from the text. Some of the sites listed in the appendix of long-vanished houses have also been incorporated under main headings where relevant, too.

The time allowed to undertake this revision did not permit the properly keyed foot-noting of all the assertions in the text, so as in the first editions, the sources for the information have been gathered together at the foot of each entry, and referenced to the bibliography, where the format used is explained. Whilst this is not, admittedly, wholly satisfactory, it does at least go some way towards rectifying the omissions of the 1991 volume on this count.

There have been significant changes since we first began our research in the late 1970s. Then, we believed that by making the maximum known about Derbyshire country houses, we would be providing information which would convince local politicians, their officers and others, that the destruction of such buildings, the dispersal of their contents and the ruination of their estates was something well worth avoiding. Further, that better information would at least ameliorate the problem of demolition, highlighted for the nation so dramatically in the 1974 V & A exhibition, *The Destruction of the Country House*. Today the tide has largely turned – only a tiny handful of post-1984 demolitions have had to be recorded here – and the country house is generally a much more secure species. Moreover, it has been a real pleasure to record the return to private occupation of many of the houses which, in the 1980s, were institutions, offices or divided crudely as flats. This is mainly as a result in the enormous increase in prosperity, which has occurred in the intervening period. New, or replacement seats have also appeared: Wootton Hall, albeit just across the Dove in Staffordshire, is being ambitiously replaced by the Hon. Johnny Greenall and Egginton Hall artfully replaced on the original site by Mr. Kevin Ellis are two, not to mention the re-instatement of the lost upper storey of Barrow Manor and others. Sensitive division of larger houses into apartments has followed in the wake of the pioneering work nationally of Mr.Kit Martin and others since the 1980s, although there are still atrocious examples of residential conversion, like poor Duffield Park. A number of houses, seriously decayed in 1982 or 1984, like Alvaston Fields, have also been brought back into use, some institutionally, others as residences.

The use of the appropriate local materials in refurbishment is another tenet dear to us. The opposition of 'environmental' groups to the re-opening of historic quarries – usually disused through the twentieth century's addiction to 'non- environmental' modern materials – has been a distinct disincentive to the proper restoration of Derbyshire buildings of all types; currently a dispute of just this type at Stanton Moor has seen largely unwashed and non-local retired perpetual students of the sort whose ideological *raison d'être* collapsed with the Iron Curtain in 1989, hanging from tree-houses and littering the Peak with the discarded paraphernalia of modern living in order to keep such sites free for fauna whose precarious hold on their habitat is probably more threatened by those who claim to champion them than from any limited and controlled stone-getting. Nevertheless, local stone can be matched closely from other sources, and it is a failing of the architectural profession that they are nowadays geologically illiterate. There are still problems, however, although the majority of them remain, lamentably, the responsibility of local authorities. The County Council's supine destruction of Burnaston House in 1990, and their twenty year neglect of Elvaston Castle – now

to be long-let to a timeshare company of all things – are particularly regrettable, as is Derby City Council's continuing inability to come to grips with the problems of Allestree Hall, a building long on the English Heritage 'At Risk' register and the only seat their predecessors the Borough Council failed to demolish. Other 'problem' houses, like Overton Hall, Ashover, will, in the present economic climate, like as not ultimately find a sympathetic owner. All the houses in this volume were, after all, built as homes, and in the final analysis, that is the best way to preserve them, irrespective of ideology. After all, architecture has been regarded since Classical times (with literature, painting, sculpture and music) as one of the Arts, and one should no more think of destroying a fine piece of architecture than one would burn a painting or smash a bust. Houses are just larger, non-portable, and functional, which adds to the problems of conservation. But their existence is part of the fabric of our national story, a legacy of our forebears' artistic achievements, a monument to the more humble craftsmen and artists – often local men – who actually created them, the glory of our unique landscape and an important element in enriching our daily lives. Hence the continuing need to monitor their progress and fight for them when threatened.

Should any reader be able to correct information given, or provide further information, they are heartily encouraged to let the authors know. Even if no further edition of this book is produced, any amendments will be kept, noted and eventually deposited in a public collection. Nevertheless, even after so many years, there are bound to be errors and omissions, especially as in treating over three hundred houses, not all archival deposits could be examined, and those that were, mainly only selectively. These remain our responsibility, and we would also crave the indulgence of readers privy to information to which we have not had access, or have overlooked. Nevertheless, we hope that, as has happened already, the contents will provoke further research and publication on the country houses of Derbyshire, their proprietors and estates.

Maxwell Craven – Derby
Michael Stanley – Ripon

October 2001

PUBLISHER'S ACKNOWLEDGEMENTS

Publisher's Acknowledgements: Our thanks to Mrs S.M. Barnes, Bearwardcote Hall Residential Home, Mrs N.A. Bird, Mr G. Broadbent, Broomfield College, Mr J. Cartland, Mr C. Chapman, Mr D. Charlesworth, Trustees of the Chatsworth Settlement, Mr C. Clowes, Mr H.L. Cooper, Prof A. Cox, Mr & Mrs M.P. Cust, English Heritage, Exel Computer Systems plc, Fischer's Baslow Hall Hotel, Mr J.W. Lake, Landmark Trust, Nr J.R. Nash, National Trust, Mrs K. Neilson, Mr & Mrs M. Norton, Georgina Oulsnam, Mr & Mrs M. Rudge, Mr & Mrs J.M.W. Pridham, Mr M. Ramsden, Mr A. Rutherford, Mr J. Salisbury, FPD Savills, Mr R.J.G. Shields, Mrs D. Spencer, Mrs F. & Mr C. Stanton, Mr & Mrs L. Staley, Mr J. Stevenson, Mr R.H. Turner, Mr D. Wakefield, Mr B. Walker, Mrs C. Woodruff, Mrs D.C. Woods,

AUTHORS' ACKNOWLEDGEMENTS

Many people have helped us enormously in the preparation of this book and its predecessors. The authors are most grateful for the contributions of all involved, especially to the owners, tenants and guardians of all the extant houses we have visited.

Special thanks are due to the following: Nick Antram, Mrs. T. Bagshawe, the late Clive Bemrose, Alan Bemrose, Drs. Martin and Birthe Kolbye Biddle, John Blackwall, Esq., David Bostwick, Megan Boyes, Peter Brady, Malcolm Burrows, Nick Byrne, James Cartland, the late Maj. J. W. Chandos-Pole, Mrs. J. Chichester, Roy Christian, the late W. G. Clark-Maxwell, David Coke-Steel, Mr. & Mrs. G. Cooper, the late G. T. Copestake, Leslie Cox, Charles Coulson, H. D. Coulthard, Richard Craven-Smith-Milnes, Stephen Croad, Mr. & Mrs. A. Davies, Derby Museum, Chris Drage, the late Capt. P. J. B. Drury-Lowe, David Durant, Dr. D. G. Edwards, Kevin Ellis, the late Sir John Every, Bt., Don Farnsworth, Sir Richard FitzHerbert, Bt., Barbara Foster, Dudley Fowkes, Trevor Fox, David Fraser, the late Anthony Gather, the late Humphrey Gladwin-Errington, the late Charles Harpur-Crewe, Leslie Harris, Philip Heath, the late Jack Henderson, Tony Henniker, Mark Higginson, the late Roy Hughes, P. J. Ibbotson, the late Miss Dorothy Jeffery, D. Jewell, Mrs. M. E. Johnson, David Jones, Lord Ralph Kerr, Pamela Kettle, Derek Latham, Michael Mallender, the late Rosemary Meynell, Mr. & Mrs. R. J. Milward, the late John Morgan-Owen, the late Col. W. H. Olivier, Roger Pegg, Elizabeth & Richard Perkins, D. F. Raybould, Jim Regan, H. I. H. Princess Judith Rhodokanakis-Doukas, John Martin Robinson, Michael Sayer, the late Viscount Scarsdale, Claudia Severne, John Sharpe, the Earl of Shrewsbury, Joan Sinar, Sir Reresby Sitwell, Bt., Ken Smith, H. J. M. Spurrier, Lord Stafford, the late Col. J. R. G. Stanton, the late M. B. B. Stapleton-Martin, R. Starbuck, Esq., Angus Taylor, Richard Theobald, Brig. A. P. Trevor, Gladwyn Turbutt, Mr. & Mrs. Howard Usher, T. D. Vickers, Esq., the late H. J. Wain, David Wakefield, the late Mrs. A. Walker, the late Sir Iain Walker-Okeover, Bt., Sir Charles Wolseley, Bt., the late Miss Theresa Woolley, Joan Wragg, Miss E. M. Wright, and Mrs. V. M. Wright. It is only sad that so many of the above, whose help was so freely given and of such value have been gathered since 1982; we would like to think that this work in some sense stands in their memory.

We have received especial help from a group of friends whose research has helped us immensely: Barbara Hutton, whose meticulously compiled *Derby Buildings Record* surveys – now numbering over 300, and conducted with the help of Mr. & Mrs. Alwyn Davies and others – are compiled under the aegis of the Architectural Section of the Derbyshire Archaeological Society and have added much to our knowledge of the more vernacular seats in the Derby area; copies available for inspection are kept at Derby Museum, Antiquities Office.

James Darwin, formerly a leading light of the Derby Museum City Survey Team, subsequently of the RCHM (E) and now a field officer with the Georgian Group whose encyclopaedic knowledge and research have been invaluable and Edward Saunders whose work on Bakewell, Pickford and Thomas Gardner, not to mention his expertise and experience has been indispensable too. To *Derbyshire Life* we owe a great debt of gratitude to its long-serving and welcoming editrix, Viv Irish and her colleagues, in finding information and lending photographs and also that fine periodical's proprietor, Barry Wood. Likewise, we are eternally grateful to the hard-working staff at Derby Local Studies Library for endless help and assistance, to Peter Day for his aid at the Chatsworth archive, and to the staff of the County Record Office over two decades.

Several eminent architectural and other historians have been of direct assistance to us, have given freely of their valuable time and made constructive comments. Professor Andor Gomme, the publication of whose important work on Francis Smith has just missed the deadline of this edition, has nevertheless been kind enough to share his thought on the houses attributed to members of this family in Derbyshire. Dr. Mark Girouard has kindly commented on matters relating to the Smythson tradition, long after his researches and enthusiasms led him into other paths. Sir Howard Colvin has also most promptly and courteously answered queries and sent information that has come his way, too. Dr. Keith Goodway of Keele was also kind enough to co-present a seminar with us on Emes hosted by the late Capt. Drury Lowe at Locko in 1990, from which much helpful comment emerged. It would also have been impossible to complete this book without the untiring assistance of our old friend Robert Innes-Smith, whose encyclopaedic knowledge of seats and families, unmatched library and general tolerance and support have been sustaining and encouraging over the entire period.

Many of the foregoing have been kind enough to furnish illustrations and, in that connection, we would like to record additional thanks to Mrs. P. J. R. Withington, Alan and Clive Champion and Don Gwinnutt for postcards, John Crossling, Don Farnsworth, Derby Museum, the former Derbyshire County Council Museums Service, the National Monument Record, Nottingham University (by kind permission of Hugh Matheson, Esq.,) Cllr. McGowan, Roger Redfern, Miss T. Spiers, Miss F. Wright, Gladwyn Turbutt and most especially to Frank Rogers, who has repeatedly come to our rescue with new views.

The kindness of the Duchess of Devonshire in being prepared to revise her original foreword is very much appreciated, as is the enterprise of our publisher, Lindsey Porter, in essaying another edition of the book, a gesture we much appreciate – and hope our readers will too – despite the short time available to us to complete the transformation.

We both stand greatly and above all in the debt of our long-suffering wives (and since the earliest editions of this work, children) who for over two decades have driven us, travelled with us and endured some strange situations all over the county in all weathers. Their tolerance, social skills and tact have been beyond compare.

Finally, there are many others who have made various contributions to the compilation of this volume and its predecessors who may have been omitted in error from the list given above, or who have wished to remain anonymous. To them and all the other owners, lessees, tenants and others who have over time welcomed us within their properties and homes, we render our thanks and appreciation.

INDEX OF HOUSES
THIS COVERS BOOKS 1 & 2

THE DERBYSHIRE COUNTRY HOUSE:1

Part I

Detail of staircase, Kedleston, *C.L.M. Porter*

INTRODUCTION

Geology

Derbyshire is a most distinctive county; it occupies a central position in Britain at the southern end of the Pennines and has an irregular outline. Its greatest length from north to south is about 60 miles, measured from Holm Moss to Netherseal, and it is 37 miles at its broadest from Whitwell in the east to New Mills in the west. Four rivers, the Etherow, the Dove and the Trent in the west and the Erewash and the Trent again in the east, form about two thirds of the boundary with the remainder mainly artificial. Prior to the Local Government Board Act of 1888, certain parishes were administratively Derbyshire but were separated geographically. Smisby, Measham, Ravenstone, Appleby, Chilcote, Stretton, Packing and Willesley were lost to Leicestershire in 1888. Subsequently in 1894, 1897 and 1974, other parishes were either lost or gained; Croxall, Stapenhill, Winshill and part of Burton upon Trent were transferred to Staffordshire; New Mills, Taxal and Fernilee were gained from Cheshire; Tintwhistle from Lancashire; Beauchief, Beighton, Dore, Norton and Killamarsh were annexed by Yorkshire. The county boundary now encloses an area of 263,250 hectares (650,000 acres) or nearly 969 square miles.

Derbyshire enjoys startling contrasts in scenery, reflecting its varied geology which has a marked effect on the topography, in turn dictating vegetation, drainage, settlement pattern, industrial raw materials, transport routes and consequently development. This geodiversity, the link between people, landscapes and their culture, a concept binding the interaction between biodiversity, soils, minerals, rocks, fossils, active processes and the built environment, is particularly well illustrated in the county. Local distinctiveness reflects the geodiversity and is manifest in the siting of seats and their use of local materials.

The County lies astride the division between highland and lowland Britain. Northwards of a line from Ashbourne to Long Eaton (Pevsner suggested Ashbourne to Ilkeston but that excludes some Carboniferous outcrops) are the Carboniferous rocks of the southern Pennines. The Dinantian (Carboniferous or Mountain) Limestones of the 'dales' form a central plateau, often referred to as the Derbyshire 'Dome'. The typically grey or white Dinantian limestones, which are the oldest exposed rocks in the county, give wide stretches of open, rolling plateau and are characterised by treeless pastures crossed by numerous drystone walls and dissected by deep, dry dales or wooded valleys. In this 'The White Peak' settlement is sparse and villages are generally restricted to the dales with occasional villages near to springs on the plateau.

Surrounding the limestone plateau, to the north, west and east in a horseshoe formation, the impressive gritstone edges and moors of the Namurian (Millstone Grit) rise to tower above steep shale and sandstone slopes. On Kinderscout and Bleaklow, the peat covered grit reaches just over 610 metres (2,000ft) but declines in height southwards to 300 metres (1,000ft) near Matlock. Scarp features dominate this part of the county with the back or dip slope running eastwards, mainly devoid of settlements and covered with moorland, grassland or heath.

Overlying the Namurian rocks to the east and west are the younger and succeeding Westphalian (Coal Measures) rocks consisting of sandstones and shales, similar to those of the Namurian, repeatedly producing a series of sandstone ridges and shale valleys, cut by busy streams which drain to the main north or south flowing rivers. This structure imposes complex and patchy distribution of settlement and industry, with many minor roads criss-crossing the area.

In the north east corner of the county, the Westphalian dips beneath the prominent scarp edge of the Permian Magnesian limestone plateau forming part of a continuous outcrop extending from Nottingham to the coast of County Durham. At Bolsover the scarp rises to 91 metres (300ft) above the Doe Lea valley. The gently dipping limestone plateau with a maximum height of 182 metres (600ft) is mainly arable, pocked by quarries and cut by narrow dry valleys locally called 'grips'.

The Pennine foothills, south of the White Peak, are mainly composed of Carboniferous sandstones, shales and limestones, and form a well-dissected landscape with heights ranging from 244 metres (800ft) beneath the plateau to 76 metres (250ft) near the lower Dove. Southwards, Triassic sandstones and marls form a belt of undulating landscape, 182 to 61 metres (600 to 200ft) in height, which broadens westwards from Sandiacre, near the border with Nottinghamshire. It is extensively cultivated and supports numerous small settlements and the large sprawl of the city of Derby. The Triassic marls and sandstones extend outside the county boundary south and west as the Midland and Cheshire Plains. Eastwards, in Nottinghamshire, they overlie the Permian to produce the attractive wooded countryside of Sherwood Forest, the real home of Robin Hood.

Between this belt and the hill country centred on Swadlincote, lies the gravel and sand floored Trent Valley, edged by bluffs, mainly on the south, the river sweeps, in large meanders and is prone to extensive flooding. To avoid the inconvenience of flooding the main crossing is Swarkestone Bridge, a medieval causeway of 13th century and earlier in date, spanning the mile wide flood plain with 12 arches, having masons marks carved in their Namurian sandstone structure, and an 18th century bridge over the Trent at the north end.

The Swadlincote hill country is a complex of Carboniferous and Permo-Triassic rocks, well dissected, with heights ranging from 40 metres (130ft) near Stanton-by-Bridge, at the southern end of Swarkestone Bridge, to over 152 metres (500ft) at Pistern Hill. The main settlements are situated in the Westphalian (Coal Measure) area of the South Derbyshire Coalfield around Swadlincote. Dinantian limestones are exposed near Ticknall and Calke with patches of coarse Namurian sandstone surrounding them and in turn, overlain to the south and west by Triassic sandstones.

11

Types of Building Materials

The type of building material and the fabric of the houses is directly related to the geological horizons (beds or strata) on or near which they are seated. The Ashbourne-Long Eaton line is not a real division; it is true that stone buildings predominate north of the line and brick is perhaps more utilised southwards, but further south in the Swadlincote Hill country, stone is again in the majority.

Throughout the county almost every rock type has been worked to provide building materials; all the major, and many minor, beds of sandstone in the Namurian, Westphalian and Triassic have been used for building, walling, decorative and paving stones. Shale and clay horizons within these and the Mercia Mudstones (Keuper Marl) have produced bricks.

Stone slates for roofing were previously worked from the thin-bedded and flaggy parts of sandstone beds within the Namurian and Westphalian. Unusually, stone slate was worked on Bakestone Moor on the Permian limestone and two roofs survive at Whitwell (Stone Roofing Association web site 2001). The name Bakestone derives from the traditional use of thin flat stones heated from underneath to cook oatcakes and similar pancake like food.

The limestone areas have given building and decorative stone, lime for mortars, walling material and cement. The Triassic and river terrace deposits of the Trent and Derwent gravel and sand for concrete.

The original text for the Derbyshire Country House used traditional rock names, which both authors and we suspect most readers, have become accustomed to using. The new introduction above gives the geological purist cause for delight in that rock terms are those in current usage. However in the rest of this volume we have decided to revert to the original rock names introduced by John Farey in 1811, and so Millstone Grit and Coal Measures will be used rather than Namurian and Westphalian. Farey did not introduce the other terms we first used, but we will use Carboniferous rather than Dinantian, and Keuper Sandstone rather than Sherwood Sandstone and Keuper Marl rather than Mercia Mudstones. We trust that most will approve of this author's licence.

The majority of seats described here are stone built or faced and study of the stone has revealed that their builders utilised very local sources of supply. This is not a surprising fact as few places in the county are far from good building stone. All the stone seats generally obtained their building stone from within a three-mile radius, except Kedleston where the stone for the pillars, the portico and other parts of the fabric came by cart from Horsley Castle 7 miles to the north east. Often a quarry on the estate would be opened specifically to supply a building, even in the 19th century as at Alton Manor. This reinforces the fact that few places in the county are far from good building stone and that transport costs have always been a limiting factor even with the advent of canals in the 18th and railways in the 19th century. The pattern of supply and use of local sources has changed little over the centuries.

Brick-built houses on the other hand could afford to purchase stone from further afield, for instance the dressings at Sudbury Hall, are from the famous Hollington quarries (Keuper sandstone) in Staffordshire twelve miles distant; the paving within came from Breadsall (Ashover Grit) 16 miles away.

The sources of stone used for houses earlier than 1800 are generally lost to antiquity. John Farey (1811) listed the free or building stone quarries then working. He provides a clue to the probable source of building stone by inference. Later works noting quarries in work or previously working include: the *Report of the Commissioners for the rebuilding of the Houses of Parliament* (1839), which lists selected buildings with the quarry of supply and those *Memoirs of the Geological Survey of Great Britain,* which include parts of Derbyshire, viz: Green 1887, Gibson 1913, Eden 1957, Smith 1967, Stevenson 1971, Smart 1979, Aitkenhead 1985 and Chisholm 1988. Careful study of these, other archival sources (relatively few building records survive), the building stone used and both topographical and geological maps from the first editions of the mid-nineteenth century to those current, often reveal the position of source quarries, now overgrown, removed by later workings, filled in or afforested. Of the latter, two are worthy of mention; Ball or Bow Cross (one mile north east of Bakewell) working the Ashover Grit, supplied Chatsworth (Watson 1811) and probably Hassop, Churchdale and Ashford. Lees Moor/Lindup Wood (Ashover Grit), north of Rowsley, probably also supplied Chatsworth and certainly Haddon (Clifton Taylor 1972). Other major quarries now extinct, some of which have paled into obscurity, include Weston Cliff, Pistern Hill, Horsley Castle and Stancliffe.

Weston Cliff (now a Ukrainian Centre) on the River Trent and Donnington Cliff (now afforested) on the opposite bank, worked Keuper sandstones (fine grained, buff-pink with a greenish tinge) and probably supplied Swarkestone, Foremark and Melbourne.

Pistern Hill Quarry (three miles east of Swadlincote) also worked Keuper sandstone and supplied Calke Abbey, although the house is much nearer to the Millstone Grit outcrop. Sandstone from the latter furnishes a course, but usable if difficult to work, building stone and surrounds the Carboniferous limestone on which Calke is situated. Melbourne Hall is seated on Millstone Grit sandstone which was used to build the original house. However, the sandstones (probably equivalent to the Ashover Grit further north) here exhibit coarse and finer banding and are not suited to ashlar work, where a flat and even texture is normally required, but more importantly the stone should be 'easy' to cut by saw and hammer and chisel. This fact, and also that Calke had been built (1703) in ashlared Keuper sandstone, which is easy to cut, together with the ashlar fashion of the eighteenth century, would have had a great bearing on the choice of Keuper sandstone for the new facade at Melbourne when it was added in the 1740s. When Calke was repaired by the National Trust in the late 1980s the Pistern Hill site was looked at to supply stone, but only poor quality material was exposed and new stone work had to be obtained from Grinshill in Shropshire of the correct colour match and age.

Horsley Castle Quarry (now overgrown) certainly supplied stone for Kedleston Hall (Clifton-Taylor 1972) and together with Coxbench Quarry (developed later in about 1830 and infilled in 1985) and Morley Moor Quarries probably provided the majority of the stone dressings (smooth ashlar quoins, sills, banding, etc) for the brick houses of the Derby area, e.g. Osmaston Chaddesden, Castlefields, The Homestead and Mickleover Manor. All the quarries worked the Rough Rock of the Millstone Grit series, a medium grain yellow/orange/brown sandstone, which is soft when worked but sets hard and becomes whiter after quarrying (Gibson 1908). It should be expected that Derby's brick houses would have used these local building stones, but when Joseph Pickford's mid 18th century houses were visited in the 1980s to check the building stones used, for Edward Saunders' book (Saunders, 1993), all the buildings visited – Markeaton orangery, The Grey House, Mansion, and Beresford House at Ashbourne, Long Eaton, – used

Keuper Sandstone. Pickford, seems to have prepared stone detailing for these houses at his yard or at least specified Keuper Sandstone for the buildings. William Emes, landscape gardener and his co-worker on some projects, was of Bowbridge Fields now Bowbridge House, also the site of a Keuper Sandstone quarry during the 18th century. Could there be a connection and was Pickford, like the Romans and other builders before and after him maximising profit margins by pre-fabricating commonly used elements? George Myers, Pugin's builder in the 19th century, certainly pre-fabricated and shipped Bath Stone dressings and ornamentation, from his own quarries, all over Britain and into the colonies (Spencer-Silver 1993).

Stancliffe Quarry is world famous for its 'Darley Dale Stone', although this term is sometimes incorrectly used to describe Millstone Grit sandstone from several quarries in the middle Derwent Valley (e.g. Halldale, Peasenhurst, Sydnope, Stanton Moor and Whatstandwell). More correctly the term should only be used for stone once quarried from Stancliffe and Halldale as it is a fine-grained, light buff-light grey sandstone, the Ashover Grit, and was held in the highest regard by architects for public buildings from 1895 to 1939 and prior to 1854, when Sir Joseph Whitworth (q.v. Stancliffe Hall) converted the quarry into a rock garden. Stancliffe Estates Company purchased the quarries in 1897 from the trustees of Whitworth's estate, and re-opened them for stone production. Famous buildings constructed in Stancliffe stone include St. George's Hall, Walker Art Gallery, Liverpool Museum and Lime Street Station, all in Liverpool and the base courses of the beautifully restored Albert Memorial in London, and the equally famous Trent Bridge in Nottingham. Stancliffe Stone should have been used for the rebuilding of the Houses of Parliament as it weathers well in polluted atmospheres and carves beautifully, but Permian Magnesian Limestone was chosen instead with the consequent result of stone replacement after only a few years.

Coal Measure sandstones do not weather well but have nevertheless been used throughout the eastern side of the county north of the Long Eaton line. Generally they are fine-grained silty sandstones, pale buff-grey in colour with a greenish tint, caused by the presence of the mineral chlorite, often with iron staining. Other sandstone horizons which have been worked for building stone include the Crawshaw Sandstone, a coarse distinctive stone, and several sandstone horizons associated with major coal seams, which give them their name; the Silkstone Rock, Deep Hard Rock and Top Hard Rock. Other horizons are near certain seams and are named accordingly such as the sandstone below the Wales Coal, sandstone below the Clowne Coal, sandstone above the High Hazels Coal and the sandstone above the Clay Cross Marine Band. The sandstone below the Clowne Coal is of particular interest as it outcrops below the Permian limestone on which the Hardwick Halls are seated. This sandstone was used to build the Halls and not as stated in Durant and Riden (1979) the Permian Magnesian limestone. They correctly identified the quarry as being halfway down the road from the Halls to the Hardwick Inn where a fine-grained, buff sandstone outcrops, but not a pink Dolomitic limestone, which the Permian is hereabouts; the limestone was used for some window dressings in the new 1591 Hall. The small quarry was reopened/extended in 1997 to supply stone for replacement work on the New Hall to have it in good condition in readiness for the 400th anniversary celebrations of its completion in 1599.

The Ashover Grit is the most commonly used building stone, but other horizons have been worked. The Shale Grit, Kinderscout Grit and Roaches Grit outcrop in the north and

west of the county with the Chatsworth Grit, a buff medium-coarse sandstone, stretching along the Derwent Valley from Little Eaton to the north west of Sheffield. The Redmires Flags is developed locally in east and west Derbyshire. Usually all the Millstone Grit and Coal Measure sandstones are current-bedded, which is seen in the stone by sloping colour banding or variation in grain size, and is a result of the original sands being deposited at the front of a large delta. By measuring the direction of the current supplying the sediment it is possible to determine the source of supply.

Permian Magnesian limestone, here a pinkish-cream fine-grained dolomite, was formerly used as a building stone and was quarried in the Bolsover and Whitwell areas. Used extensively at Bolsover Castle, it was the example of a good weathering stone picked by the Commissioners for the rebuilding of the Houses of Parliament (Barry et al. 1839). The Lower Magnesian Limestone should have been quarried from Bolsover Moor, bur the lack of the correct block sizes promoted the use of Magnesian Limestone from Anston Quarry just over the border in South Yorkshire (Elsden and Howe 1923). This was used for the middle and upper courses and weathered badly in the polluted London atmosphere. However deposits of similar age, but more sandy and hence a dolomitic sandstone, from Parliament Quarry, Mansfield Woodhouse, was used for the lower and still sound courses of the House of Parliament. White Mansfield stone is still available from Gregory's Quarry (Rare Stone Group) off Nottingham Road in Mansfield.

Carboniferous limestone, usually white to grey in colour, has been used to provide coursed rubble and coarse ashlar for the majority of the vernacular houses in the White Peak, but its most important use in house described here was as a decorative stone. Hoptonwood, a buff-grey fine-grained limestone with a small amount of tiny fossil crinoid material scattered throughout, which takes a high polish and is then a 'marble', has been used since the eighteenth century for floors (Kedleston), staircases (Calke Abbey) and fireplaces in most large and small seats. It was exported to all corners of Britain and is best known for its use in Sheffield City Hall, the Bank of England in Threadneedle Street in London and for the grave stones of soldiers killed in action and commemorated in the War Graves Commission's cemeteries in France and Belgium. It has also been quarried as a building stone, unpolished, and was last worked extensively in the 1950s. Derby Dene and Haydene 'Marble', another fine-grained limestone, but darker than Hoptonwood, from Dene Quarry, off Cromford Hill, Cromford was used to floor the new Coventry Cathedral in the 1950s.

The last 20 years has seen blocks won again, but the quality is not as good as previously. New quarries were opened to supply blocks and slabs to the trade in the 1980s; some survive, but Once-a-week Quarry, worked once a week as its name implies, closed in April 2001 after almost 30 years of small scale production.

The interiors of houses have been graced with other decorative 'marbles' from the Carboniferous limestones; Ashford Black (at Hardwick, Renishaw and Bolsover), Black Bird's Eye, Coralline, Crinoidal (ubiquitous for table tops and fireplaces), Duke's Red, Rosewood and Earl Newburgh. Ashford Black Marble is probably the best known of the Derbyshire marbles and was extensively worked from the third quarter of the 18th century into vases, urns, obelisks, thermometer holders, candlesticks, paper weights, clocks and table tops, nineteenth century examples usually inlaid in the Italian 'pietra dura' fashion, in particular from 1860 when Queen Victoria was in mourning following the death of Prince Albert. This inlaying trade virtually died with the death of Victoria in 1901. New small inlaid trinkets can be purchased in Buxton and Tideswell; original inlay also comes on to the market, often at local salerooms.

Cockleshell 'marble', black with white/brown shells in section, used in the fireplace roundles at Bolsover is from above the Dogtooth Rake in the Coal Measures of the Tupton area. It also appears, usually with alabaster and black marble, in other 16th and early 17th century monuments such as Bess of Hardwick's magnificent self-designed-before-I-die tomb in Derby Cathedral and the 6th Duke of Devonshire's grisly monument in Edensor (pronounced Ensor) Church a mile from Chatsworth. There is a great likelihood that the Cavendishes owned the iron workings at Tupton that supplied the marble (not a true marble, but a lime rich mudstone full of molluscs that took a polish) as its use appears to be restricted to Cavendish buildings or buildings in their influence e.g. Bolsover Castle and Hardwick.

Alabaster, the soft, white-cream-brown, massive variety of gypsum, from the Keuper Marl at Chellaston is used in numerous houses, mainly in fireplaces *as at* Beauchief, Aston-on-Trent and Bolsover, but also Sudbury, Chatsworth, and many others. The eight full height columns in the hall at Kedleston are Alabaster, not from Chellaston but Red Hill just over the border in Nottinghamshire. The only use of Alabaster as an exterior finish are the supporting piers for the Golden Gates at Elvaston Castle.

Alabaster has seen extensive use as a decoration in ecclesiastical structures, in particular table tombs and monuments in churches where most, certainly in the 14th to 17th centuries, were made by the Chellaston/Nottingham schools of carvers or alabastermen. John Young's book *Alabaster* (1990) looks in depth at the Alabaster industry over the centuries and lists and illustrates many tombs and altar pieces.

Blue John, a purple-yellow/white plain or striped variety of the mineral Fluorite, is perhaps the best known decorative stone from the county and is common as fireplace roundels, consoles, in laid decoration or ornaments and was used in a pioneering context at Kedleston by Richard Brown of Derby (Craven (1996)). It was used occasionally to glaze windows and one slit window at Birchfield Lodge was removed to Buxton Museum in 1983, where it remains on show, for safe display when the building at Birchfield was adapted to cater for potentially unruly youngsters from Manchester on residential courses. The material is brittle and has to be impregnated with resin before it can be carved, turned or cut. The industry still thrives in Castleton where small decorative ornaments are made during the winter months for sale during the visitor season. The working of Blue John is described in Trevor Ford's recent book (Ford 1999).

History of Building Materials

The three terms ashlar, coursed rubble and rubble represent a range in use by masons and architects. Here ashlar embraces stone blocks more than seven inches. in height, squared and flat-faced, blocks in course and regular coursed rubble, all with or without tooling. Ashlar work usually has thin lime mortar between the blocks but in the best examples the mortar is barely noticeable.

Coursed rubble is defined as squared rubble built in courses. Rubble is random rubble built in courses and uncoursed random rubble in mortar. Dressings, invariably ashlar, are used to define and finish window and door openings, quoins and other ornamental features such as string courses, balustrades and hood moulds. For a much fuller treatment of stone building techniques and other materials used in England, the reader is asked to consult the two excellent works on the subject by Alec Clifton-Taylor. His *The Pattern of English Building* first appeared in 1972 and his book with Archie Ireson *English Stone Building* some 4 years later. Sadly Alec died in 1987. It was always a pleasure to talk to him about houses and their building materials and he very kindly agreed to preface Volume 2 of *The Derbyshire Country House* in 1983.

Any history of building materials must begin with a look at the sources of those materials and how the builders of the time would have accessed them. Derbyshire, if it were possible to view from the air, in the 12th century must have appeared as a sea of trees, oak and ash predominant with beech, birch, hazel, alder, maple and holly surrounding the upland and river valley treeless islands. The reader need only consult the Ordnance Survey maps or Cameron (1959) for reference to villages, hamlets and towns which bear the arboreal prefix to realise the variety of tree cover over the centuries to confer these names. The now ubiquitous sycamore, much beloved of 18th and 19th century poets, was not introduced into the country until the 16th century.

Four main areas were relatively free from trees, the high moors and edges of the North-West, the flood plains of the main rivers Trent, Derwent and Dove, the Permian Magnesian Limestone and Carboniferous Limestone plateaus (all these areas had been cleared during the great felling of the Bronze Age), although in the many 'dales' (from the Norse *dalr*) woodland was still thick. In the remaining wooded areas the two royal forests, the medieval game reserves, Peak Forest (40 sq. miles) and Duffield Frith (old English *fyrthe* – wooded) generally remained 'paled' and intact from the 11th century until the latter half of the 16th century, although by then commoners and lords alike had been making inroads (assarting) both legally and illegally for several centuries. Wood was abundant and was utilised for buildings, fuel, charcoal production, domestic furniture and utensils; it was the universal building material, especially oak.

Forest clearing began in earnest in the 11th century and continued unabated, apart from short periods during civil unrest, until its peak in the 17th century. The early clearing must have revealed stone at outcrop and with the influx of Norman masons, new skills were passed on, and the 12th and 13th centuries witnessed many new stone buildings. Several churches including Steetley, Melbourne, Bakewell and Ashbourne; the Monastic foundations of Darley Abbey (1154), Repton Priory (1172), Dale Abbey (c. 1200) and Stydd (c. 1190); and the keeps of Peveril (1176), Duffield ('new' castle 1178) and Horsley (1180-1203) Castles. Wood was used for roof-timbers probably supporting tile or stone slate roofs. Peveril Castle is unusual in that the 11th century curtain wall and keep were of Carboniferous Limestone whereas, more usually for a new castle, Duffield's 11th century keep was of wood.

The only known domestic stone built house was Norbury Hall (*q.v.*) which was commenced c. 1250. A glance at a map of the county shows that all these buildings were in the south on land already clear or being cleared. The exceptions are Peveril Castle at Castleton, which was erected to protect the important lead mining fields of the north eastern edge of the Carboniferous Limestone plateau, and the elaborate Steetley Chapel in the east. This is by far the richest example of Norman architecture in Derbyshire and one of the most complete small-scale examples in the Norman world. Only 52 feet long and 15 feet wide it was used as a chicken run for most of the 19th century (Stanley 1990). Carefully restored in 1880 to designs by J.L. Pearson with the result that the gable and two outer colonettes of the magnificent south porch are Victorian. The mid 12th century chapel's excellence of design and building probably has its roots in its position by the Whitwell gap, one of the main routes from the Derbyshire/Nottinghamshire frontier into Yorkshire. The Norman stonework is a fine-grained creamy dolomite that shows no sign of weathering. This is similar to the stone chosen for the rebuilding of the Houses of Parliament from Bolsover Moor, which was little used. The Victorian replacement stone is a coarser dolomite, grey rather than cream and already shows signs of weathering after only 10% of the time exposed to the atmosphere compared to the original dolomite. The weathering is probably attributable to the larger grain size of the later stone.

The charters of the monastic foundations reveal the sources of stone used in their building. The Repton Charters (c. 1227) refer to 'Rapendon quarry near Trent' which Frazer (1947) assigns to Quarry Hill Close, which lies to the east of the school overlooking the Old Trent waters i.e. an old cut-off channel. The Close produced a cream Keuper Sandstone which matches with both the stone of the priory remnants, incorporated into the school's west range undercroft (now housing the museum) and parts of the Anglo-Saxon St. Wystan's Church (8th century) adjacent (Stanley 1990). The majority of the stone used in the church is Keuper and originated from Parson's Close to the west of Repton. It is likely that the stone for the Abbey came from the same source, but that the later buildings used stone from Winshill, up river at Burton.

The remnant of Darley Abbey, now a splendid public house with a monastic ambience, is also of Keuper sandstone almost certainly from Allestree. The Cartulary (B33, B48, (.1263) records a gift of a stone quarry in Allestree to the canons from William, son of Joseph of Breadsall.

Dale Abbey utilised Crawshaw Sandstone and the more local Ashgate Sandstone (Dale Cartulary c. 1240 and Stanley 1977). Duffield, Horsley and Peveril castles used ashlar Ashover Grit, Rough Rock and Carboniferous Limestone respectively, all from adjacent outcrop.

The Duchy of Lancaster and Public Record Office Ministers' accounts mention other important quarries, including Rowcliff (c. 1323, 1383, 1483) in Alderwasley Parish, probably working the Ashover Grit of Shining Cliff and the edge running north towards Whatstandwell; Burton Quarry (at ?Winshill) and Bretby Quarry (in the park of Bretby Hall) both worked Keuper Sandstone and are noted for fatal accidents occurring at each, c. 1316. No documentary evidence of quarries in work has been located for the period between 1483 and 1811, when Farey's magnificent *Agriculture and Minerals of Derbyshire* and Watson's *Delineation* were published, except for a reference to 'Brokewalclif' or 'Brodewalclif' in Matlock Manor (probably the old quarrying area on Riber Cliffside, now covered with vegetation) noted in the *Victoria County History*. Both of Derbyshire's famous medieval bridges, Swarkstone (really a causeway and a bridge) and Burton (demolished) were built in stone, a Millstone Grit Sandstone (the equivalent of the Ashover Grit) from Stanton-by-Bridge for Swarkestone (Joyce 1980) and probably Keuper sandstone from Winshill for Burton Bridge. Together with Bakewell Bridge (c. 1300) these bridges, the castles, monastic foundations and parish churches noted above were the only major users of stone until the 15th century when it started to be used for medium as well as large houses.

Timber-framed houses always needed stone for a plinth but the need for an incombustible material for the chimney or the desire to rebuild in a more solid and fireproof material meant that brick and stone were in demand.

Prior Overton's Tower (c. 1437) at Repton is one of the finest and earliest examples of a brick building in northern England. It is surprising to find a brick building, now incorporated into a stone structure, adjacent to other stone buildings especially when the source for the stone was less than a 1/4 of a mile distant. But perhaps by 1440 Repton Quarry had been exhausted and the local Keuper Marl was already in use for tile production. The colour of the brick suggests that local Keuper Marl was used, probably by itinerant brick makers. It is also not surprising due to the abundance of building stone, even in the south of the county, that over a century elapsed before another large seat was built in brick: the first Chatsworth built by Bess of Hardwick between 1552 and 1557 was amazingly brick with stone dressings. Why brick we can only guess, probably a sign of wealth, as Chatsworth abounds with good building stone. Another 30 years and probably for the same reason, Barlborough Hall, 1584, was built with Permian Magnesian Limestone dressings on brick, now stuccoed; perhaps the local limestone quarries could not provide good ashlar blocks at the time, the adjacent Coal Measures could certainly provide good brick clays.

The stability and expansion of the county's economy caused an explosion in house building from about 1560; brick and/or stone at Aston, Brampton, Cutthorpe, Eaton Dovedale, Greenhill, Harthill, Owlcotes and Somersall. The building of seats is contemporaneous with a general increase in building, timber was in great demand. Between 1532 and 1540 some 1,032 oaks were felled in Duffield Frith. The first accurate survey in 1560 of the Frith provides a clear impression of the remaining medieval forest; 59,412 large oaks, 32,820 small oaks, 19,736 decayed oaks, 1 ash and 1 elm. However by 1581 the picture had dramatically changed with only 2,764 large and 3,032 small oaks remaining. Not all of the 107,000 oaks had been used for building, many would have produced charcoal to fuel the iron hearths near Hulland Brook or the lead smelts or 'boles' on the northern fringes of the Frith and perhaps many more to provide fuel to keep the commoners and lords warm; the period 1550-1850 was a mini ice-age with a general lowering of temperatures and the certainty of a 'white Christmas' with winter fairs on frozen rivers.

The 17th century witnessed the continuing general expansion of brick as a building material and several seats were built, probably all by itinerant brick makers; Weston Hall, Sudbury, Shardlow, Risley, Norbury, Green Hall, Croxall, Hungry Bentley, Ashbourne Mansion, Walton Old Hall and Waingroves Hall. In the next century brick making flourished (Farey 1811) even with the imposition of a brick tax in 1784. The size of bricks had been regulated in 1571 to 9" x 4½" x 2", easy to handle, but due to the brick tax by the late 1780s the thickness varied up to as much as three and a half inches. Fortunately by that date all the County's important 18th century brick houses had already been built. Few seats were affected by those other iniquitous taxes on buildings; window tax 1696-1851, glass tax 1746-1846, tile tax 1803-1833 and slate tax 1800-1831. The brick tax was eventually repealed in 1850 and with the repeal of that and the other building material taxes there was a massive increase in building across Britain especially in the expanding towns and cities.

Derbyshire's seats have however been in the vanguard of fashion for glazing. 'Hardwick Hall more glass than wall' is a local saying, which succinctly reinforces the new and imaginative use of glass there from 1591. Rarely, glass of 1545 survives in the parlour at Haddon Hall. Sash windows made their first appearance in quantity in Britain at Chatsworth in 1676 only 9 years before the Elizabethan brick house was replaced. Plate glass, a French invention of

1773, was probably used at Newton Park *(qv)* on completion in 1791.

Sixteenth century glazing required the extensive use of lead cames as only small diamond or rectangular pieces, 'quarries', of glass cut from spun 'crown' glass was available. Glass must have been re-used where possible even in large seats as at Hardwick (Durant & Riden, 1980) where Bess had particular problems due to her estranged 4th husband's (George Talbot, 6th Earl of Shrewsbury) family having a monopoly of glass production. She did circumvent the problem by starting her own glass works under her ironmaster Sylvester Smith. Glass production was probably very localised as it did not travel well; little is known of the early industry and would repay investigation. Glasshouse Common at Whittington almost certainly marks the site of 18th century production.

Lead mining and smelting, a major Derbyshire industry since the Romans, provided much of the wealth needed to build seats especially during the 16th, 17th and 18th centuries. The use of lead as cames, roof covering and piping for both potable and waste water happened very early in the County's houses as did the use of iron. Iron mining from 'bell pits' and opencast workings together with forges are recorded from at least the 13th century; Brampton, Belper, Barlow, Codnor, Chesterfield, Duffield, Eckington, Hulland, Horsley and Heanor are frequently mentioned. The wrought iron hammered from the 'bloom' was used to make window bars and nails at a forge often set up specifically during building, again as at Hardwick.

This very brief history of building materials in Derbyshire would be incomplete without reference to the transportation of the usually bulky and heavy materials. Early references mention the use of sleds and carts pulled by oxen and these methods persisted until the advent of canals in the 18th century when carriage by water boomed. Of course, certain quarries, Repton, Winshill and probably Rowcliff had used water transport for centuries, but canals allowed stone in particular to be exported. Canals also allowed the importation of Welsh Slate and from about 1790 its use in the County expanded but after the tax was lifted in 1831 its use exploded. The railways arrived shortly after that date which, further facilitated the spread of slate and also other exotic building materials which fortunately never ousted the local sources. The research for this volume did reveal several exotic stones including a Jurassic oolitic limestone, probably Ancaster stone from Lincolnshire (brought by river), used for dressings (c. 1791) at Newton Park, and fireplace surrounds at Bradley and Brampton, both 20th century additions. Another oolitic limestone as coping on the balustrade lining the upper drive at Thornbridge, although this was almost certainly brought from Clumber (Notts). Portland stone urns were noted outside at Caldwell and a sundial of Portland near the main entrance at Calke Abbey; fireplace surrounds of St. Anne's (Belgium) marble at Caldwell and Bradley; Pencil-veined Sicilian marble at Birchfield, Morley Manor and Bradley and Onyx at Stanton-by-Dale. Perhaps the most amazing exotic, for its colour, is the bright red Triassic sandstone from Runcorn used at Morley Manor which attractive though it is, seems out of step with the tones of the County.

Perhaps the most pleasing aspect of the Derbyshire landscape is that builders and architects, in the past have heeded their common sense and utilised immediately local materials, which blend imperceptibly into the landscape. The Permian Magnesian Limestone belt from Nottingham to the coast of County Durham typifies this geodiversity. Here throughout the belt cream houses have red pantile roofs with an edge of stone slate to shed the rain water off the roof and away from the walls; they look right and feel right in the landscape.

Only occasionally does one find a brick-house in a stone area *(e.g.* Parwich and Great Longstone), even though it has exquisite proportions and elegance, it still tilts at the senses. Would that present day architects could be persuaded to temper their use of concrete, glass and steel and clad with ashlar or brick. There are many millions of tons of good quality building stone left in the ground just waiting to be sympathetically employed, and the past 20 years has witnessed the reopening of several quarries, all working Ashover Grit. This re-opening has been hard won as the NIMBY (not in my back yard) principle puts the winning of dimensional stone in the same category as aggregate production where the greater quantity means many more traffic movements.

History of Settlement

The topography of Derbyshire, in common with all places wherein man has dwelt and striven, is a palimpsest enshrining the evidences from which the history of his interaction with his environment may be to some extent recovered. At Creswell Crags, in the east of the county, settlers of the Palaeolithic era have left enigmatic traces of their subsistence; later settlements at first scattered thinly but relatively evenly across the county: have left fragments of their habitations which lay undisturbed until antiquaries like Thomas Bateman, of Middleton Hall, followed by modern farming methods, began to erode them irretrievably. Later, the coming of metals – bronze and iron – enabled more successful exploitation of the fertile soils of the lowland zones. The Trent Valley especially, as the main artery of communication throughout the history of the region, is widely scattered with the remains of settlements, villages, lows, cursi, enclosures which, although less evident than the upland monuments to ancient man such as Arbor Low, have under the diligent and more judicious hands of Thomas Bateman's successors, revealed much that is new about the prehistory of the county; excavations such as those at Willington in the 1970s may be taken as an exemplar.

Continuity of settlement is surely one of the most attractive aspects of local history, and it is in the countryside where this is most evident, Willington; indeed, amply demonstrates am emphatic link from the pattern pre-Roman settlement in the Trent Valley to that of the Saxon in the sixth/seventh centuries. The style of dwelling changed from simple hut to *grubenhaus* (sunken floored huts) over a period of more than 500 years and husbandry and cultivation evolved equally gradually. Doubtless at other locales this pattern extended into the later Saxon, Norse and the post-Conquest eras to the present but the presence of a modern village on such an old site unfortunately makes archaeological recovery of such evidence well nigh impossible.

What the Derbyshire sector of the Trent Valley does lack, however, is evidence for that most typical of Roman institutions: the country estate centred on the villa. The story of the seats of an English county further south or west than Derbyshire must begin with this form of land-holding, but villa estates are a rarity in the highland zone of Roman Britain, and none have been positively identified in Derbyshire. The correlation which seems to have emerged between the extent of Roman villa-estates and Saxon and post-Conquest parish boundaries, as first suggested by Prof. H.P.R.Finberg, in his study at Withington, Glos. (*Roman and Saxon Withington* in *Lucerna*, London 1964) and to some extent supported in a

Welsh context by recent interpretations of the Liber Landavensis (Davies, W., *The Llandaff Charters*, Aberystwyth 1979) has not yet been established for Derbyshire. Nevertheless, this pattern doubtless underlies the post-Roman estate holding in the county, reinforced by the relatively late arrival of numbers of Anglian invaders in the region from the mid-sixth century. The vast majority of ordinary settlers, both Anglian and Norse, were undoubtedly preceded by their ruling *elites* – the warrior aristocracies – who may be presumed to have taken over land parcels intact from their dispossessed predecessors, leaving those who came after to inter-marry with the progeny of their predecessors. In support of this, evidence seems now to indicate that the Saxon kingdoms (albeit under different names) and those of their Romano-Celtic coevals – Gwr y Gogledd – the Men of the North – did not all perish in spectacular strife as proclaimed in their poetry, but transmitted their principalities to their conquerors via their heirs (Dark, K., *Britain and the End of the Roman Empire* Stroud, 2000). For all we shall ever know, this may be true of the post-Roman rulers of what later became Derbyshire, perhaps the shadowy kinglets of Elmet in the North and Luitcoit (Wall, Staffs.) in the South and West: as at court, so in country, a likely story of continuity, extending into the relatively well recorded Middle Ages from the migration period or before.

It is important to emphasise this continuity for the study of landholdings in the English countryside, and hence that of the houses supported by that land in order to properly comprehend the speed and extent of the cataclysm. which overtook that tradition from 1918. The swiftness with which punitive taxation, compulsory purchase and modern boundary changes – forms of legislative vandalism – can utterly destroy such an ancient pattern is salutary indeed.

From the evidence of place names (in Derbyshire, admirably dealt with by Cameron, 1959), parish boundaries and settlement patterns, the clearing of new land and the evolution of the panorama revealed in the Domesday Book, penetratingly re-analysed for Derbyshire by David Roffe in 1986, the next stages may be pieced together. Thereafter, charter evidence, and that of the Lay Subsidy Rolls, Pipe Rolls, *inquisitiones post mortem*, wills and inventories amongst other things, greatly aid our understanding, and it is from the Medieval period that the information contained in the pages which follow is traced. Concerning the earliest houses, however, we are largely still in the dark. Only where settlements have been subsequently abandoned, as at Hungry Bentley, can evidence have survived in recoverable form, but apart from an amateurish attempt in front of the encroachments of open-cast mining at Aincurt (Park House North Wingfield) at the turn of the century, little has been done in excavating the earliest post-Conquest homestead sites by local archaeologists.

The earliest seigneurial residences – those of members of the dominant social stratum – in the county were doubtless of wood, even in the upland zone. The surviving cruck-framed outbuildings, for example at Dunston and Hipper Halls seem to support this, and Rosemary Meredith (1981) postulates a timber-framed predecessor for North Lees, well in the upland zone. Strangely however, the earliest remnants of buildings in the south appear to be in stone: the east wing of Norbury Hall and the west wing of Breadsall Old Hall for instance, perhaps a reflection of the opulence of the FitzHerberts and Curzons who built them, as well as the very close proximity of sources of stone. Nevertheless, stone was increasingly employed north of that notional line drawn between Ashbourne and Long Eaton, and Haddon Hall, Padley Manor, Codnor Castle and the predecessor of Wingfield Manor are early examples. The ease with which

the smaller houses, originally the residences of yeomen who grew rich and entered the gentry, could be modified in reflection of the increasing prosperity of their owners has, unfortunately, frequently led to the obfuscation of their earliest building phases, in many cases beyond coherent recall. Many plainly have early cores, Ogston, Romiley Padley (Ripley) and Bradshaw (Chapel-en-le-Frith) halls in the upland area and Arleston House, Longford and Duffield Halls in the lowland are examples, and surviving homestead moats, the majority thought now to date from between 1200 and 1325 (Le Patourel, H.E.J. and Roberts, B. K., in Aberg, 1978), mark the sites of other seats, vanished or replaced (see also the introduction to section II). At first, estates seem to have been relatively substantial, those in the more prosperous south being on the whole larger than those in the north. However, the decimation which resulted from the Black Death, so dramatically recorded for posterity in the *Wakebridge Charters* (Saltman, 1971), gave the free peasants – for example, the earliest Knivetons (descended from the Danish-sounding Humfrid son of Haslac), Alsops and Okeovers – the opportunity to buy more land (plentiful and cheap) or marry daughters of knights, now suddenly become heiresses. Families descended from Domesday tenants, like Brailsford, Harthill, Darley, Meynell (in the senior line, at least), and Bakepuize suddenly and dramatically fail in the senior male line in the mid-fourteenth century. Later families, some now very grand indeed, trace their pedigrees securely back to just this period and no further.

During the period of the Heralds' Visitations – 1569-1662 in Derbyshire – there were many landed families enjoying gentle status. Their estates ranged in size from very modest ones of about 400 acres to 5,000 or more, the smaller ones by this time tending to predominate in the fertile south and east, although a man with a small estate with rights to extract underlying lead or coal in the east or central areas, could aspire to as high a standing of material wealth as one holding several thousand acres of moorland in the north or west of the county. Many of the minor houses, which have survived better in the upland zone through the durability of their building materials and the comparative lack prosperity there, are attributable to this very period when the Visitations were in train. Nevertheless, great estates survived throughout, as at Haddon, Sutton Scarsdale or Drakelow, and new ones began to be formed as great courtiers grew rich, agricultural patterns reacted to improvements and minerals were more intensively exploited. Those of the Harpurs, Cavendishes, Talbots and Eyres, all expanded under one or more of these influences.

In the eighteenth and earlier nineteenth centuries, the economic balance tipped completely in favour of the very rich and the smaller estates began to be swallowed up. The Dukes of Devonshire, for example, commenced buying up these smaller holdings in earnest at this period, and ended the nineteenth century with the most extensive land-holdings in the county. At the same time, the great entrepreneurs, notably the Nightingales, Evanses, Strutts and Arkwrights, began acquiring other smaller estates (and sometimes parts of larger ones, fragmented by co-heiresses, like those of the Talbots and Pierreponts) and building seats: Lea Hurst, Lea Green, Green Hall, Belper, Darley Hall and Willersley Castle.

Toward the end of the nineteenth century came a new wave of industrialists, usually buying more modest estates: the Cammels and Firths from Sheffield; the Grimshaws from Manchester; the Darwins, Leys, Coxes and Swinglers from Derby; the Players and Wrights from Nottingham; and the Basses and Ratclyffes and Grettons (all once allied in trade) from Burton upon Trent are just a few. As with their seventeenth-century predecessors, for example, the Shores, Heathcotes, or Holdens, these business men rapidly shed their mercantile origins (a background never, as is popularly believed, entirely shunned by the English upper classes), intermarried with the established gentry and assumed their places in the social hierarchy of the county. Most of these later arrivals were ephemeral, yet some remain. This all led to a renewed wave of house building and rebuilding, and in a bewildering variety of styles.

The economic cataclysms which have plagued the country during the twentieth century from 1918 quickly cut a swathe through a pattern of land holding perhaps nearly two thousand years old, and rendered the larger country seats especially, increasingly uneconomic. There followed a tide of destruction: Shipley, Chaddesden, Wingerworth, Drakelow, Willesley Halls and both Osmastons – the list seems endless and cannot, regrettably, be considered closed even yet as is most forcibly brought home by the fate of Burnaston House. Whilst landowners were primarily responsible in those earlier years for calling for the pick and hammer (by the sale to the only likely purchaser, in these days the local builder) many houses were left to, or purchased by, local authorities with a view to using them for the benefit of their electors, only for the same beneficiaries to betray the original good intent with shocking celerity. The former Corporation of Derby had the worst record: Chaddesden, Alvaston and Osmaston went in the 1930s, followed by Darley and Markeaton three decades later; indeed, the park of the latter is still being eroded inexorably. The Army also took their toll: they damaged Riber Castle, Farnah Hall and Egginton Hall beyond reasonable hope of repair. There seems to be little to excuse this vandalism: most of these houses came to their corporate owners in acceptable condition; to have kept them thus would have been a manifestation of greater economic sense than to destroy them, and then have to spend six or seven-figure sums in the 1970s and 1980s on new community centres, council offices, clinics, and so on. Lea Green, Nunsfield House in Derby, Bretby Park (until recently), and numerous others, are examples of such uses being found for historic houses, and even so these places are still in danger: anyone who has seen Derby's last surviving great house over the years – Allestree Hall – cannot fail to be alarmed at the poor quality of maintenance being accorded it, and the same goes for at least two houses in the Chesterfield area.

Thus the new uses found for many houses which have escaped the bulldozer deserve study and monitoring, and this is why this volume attempts to chronicle the current status of the seats recorded between its covers. The smaller houses, being a simpler proposition to maintain, even without an estate, have survived much better, increasingly as comfortable and desirable private residences. This role has been enhanced by the ease of communication by car or train which the twentieth century bestowed, not to mention the proximity of large towns in the county, and the cities and conurbations which ring its edges. Also, over the past few decades, proximity to the M1 motorway has improved the desirability of some of the more modest seats to the east. Others, reduced to being farmhouses as the great estates expanded, still successfully fulfil that function, often as not in private ownership. For these, there need be less fear for the future, although the current agicultural recession has resulted in not a few being sold from their accompanying land as individual private residences, as, most recently with Youlgreave Old Hall. For others still seated amid supporting estates, the future (except in unsympathetic 'improvements') will always be threatened to some extent, especially where there is little capital to endow trusts either to maintain them

directly, or to accompany them into the custodianship of bodies such as the National Trust, although again the last two decades has seen some alleviation in the position. Thus the vigilance and vociferous support of all those who care for the embodiment of tradition, of art, of history, in these seats, is urged most strongly.

Some of the houses described below, are even at the time of writing under threat. For those in private hands, it would be improper of the authors to point a finger, but others are publicly or corporately owned, and the fate of Elvaston Castle since 1981 at the hands of the Derbyshire County Council and of Allestree Hall since 1948 at the hands of Derby Borough and City Councils only serves as an awful warning of the fecklessness, mendacity and opportunism of most local authorities.

Architecture, Parks and Gardens

The earliest houses in Derbyshire, as in other parts of the country, were of the open-hall type with a central hearth, in timber or stone according to the availability of materials. An example, although given a thorough-going rebuild in the seventeenth century, is South Sitch, at Idridgehay, a house which is also an example of a timber-framed structure surviving in an upland area in which good building stone abounds and where stone was widely used from an early date. Hasland Manor disguises another within its fabric, too. A variation is found in the medieval wing at Norbury, of stone, where the hall is built over an undercroft with an attached chimney breast. Another, quite remarkable, survival is the medieval aisled hall at West Broughton Hall, which has endured within the structure of a house much rebuilt around its early core. Later still a desire for privacy and the decline of the hall as the focus of the seigneurial life led to the building of cross-wings, and a fine example of such a house survives at Breadsall Old Hall on the very edge of the city of Derby which, although somewhat over-restored in the nineteenth century, survives unobscured by subsequent accretions. Houses which started off in this style and which were overlain with later additions are, however relatively common, although detecting them is ever something of a challenge. However, the survival of the great hall, with its entrance to one side and its screens passage, which persisted later in Derbyshire than in places further south, means that several examples appear in the pages that follow, still marked in instances by their offset entrances. Hazelbadge must have been of this type although all that survives today is a cross wing. Others were old Langley Hall, Romiley Hall, Stanton Woodhouse, Wakelyn Old Hall (with Somersal Herbert, timber-framed), Padley Hall, Ripley (later re-cased intact) and a remarkable later example Whitwell Hall. Even the typical upland Derbyshire stone-built gabled manor house was directly based on this prototype, there being numerous examples, including Beeley Hill Top, Bradbourne, Bradshaw and Cartledge Halls, with Offerton, Unstone, and Hartington Halls having off centre entrances, gabled crosswings, but essentially no great hall, only a large parlour.

The grander type of house also, of course, evolved from the hall-house the great hall being set within defences (which was presumably the case in one of two Derbyshire examples, although all trace of them has vanished). The development for the grandee was not so much in cross-wings, but in having the subsidiary structures set around a courtyard and, as status demanded, to allow the courtyard to expand into two: Haddon Hall is the classic example. It undoubtedly began life as a fortified house, but by the time the present great hall was built in c. 1377, it was placed in the cross range of a twin courtyard house which grew up over several centuries along with the fortune of the Vernons, its proprietors. Codnor Castle, despite its name, a residential rather than a fortified seat of the Lords Grey (whose ancient peerage was happily revived since the last edition of this book), is another Derbyshire example, as was Padley Manor and of course, South Wingfield Manor, also of a non-defensive type. Among these were a number of lesser houses ranged around a single courtyard or part of one: Appleby Manor (also with surviving moat) and the similar pair of Longford and Risley Halls. Indeed, a number of early Tudor Houses were thus disposed: Swarkestone possibly, also Drakelow, Fenny Bentley and Fanshawegate, although not enough survives of any of these to be sure.

South Wingfield Manor, however, as well as being a seat of Lord Cromwell, a great medieval courtier, had the distinction, with Prior Overton's Tower at Repton Hall, of being a precursor of the Midland High House, or tower house. The high tower at the former, at 74ft, was far more impressive than Prior Overton's modest but highly decorative brick affair, but both relate to Tattershall Castle, Lincs., built by the same Lord Cromwell a year or two before Repton (1437) and Wingfield (begun 1439). Tattershall relates to both in concept, but in its pioneering use of decorative brickwork related much more closely to Prior Overton's Tower; neither may have been the work of Flemish artisans, however, despite appearances. These striking and innovative residences, however, set a trend in the Midlands, and Derbyshire has its share, for even before the end of the fifteenth century one had been built by the Reresbys at Eastwood Hall, and another by the Kendalls at Smisby. The concept underwent a revolution with the building of Old Chatsworth, which not only was set around a courtyard, but involved high-rise living of unparalleled luxury, although old Markeaton, almost contemporary with the similar surviving example of Melbury, Dorset, had preceded it by some forty years and both looked forward to Wollaton, Notts., with its centrally placed high storey. Thereafter came Wheston Hall, Buxton Old Hall and Old Hardwick – which doubtless had its inspiration in Worksop Manor, erected for 6th Earl of Shrewsbury by Robert Smythson (died 1614), whose work for the Earl's circle started another boom in such houses: Hardwick, Oldcotes, Barlborough Hall, Blackwall Hall and perhaps Alsop Hall (Girouard, 1983). These houses also inspired a revolution in the plan as well, not least the abandonment of the great hall in favour of the cross-hall, all enthusiastically taken up by local imitators. Smaller tower houses came in the wake of these prodigy houses, too, notably North Lees and Stydd Hall, all culminating in the Little Castle at Bolsover. At this point Robert Smythson handed the baton on to his son, John, who built a second generation of compact high houses and picturesque small seats like Barlborough Old Hall, Repton Park, Swarkestone Stand, Old Wingerworth Hall, Tupton, Holme and perhaps the house embedded in late-seventeenth-century Overton Hall at Ashover. These inspired (if no more) others, such as Brookhill, Highlow, Littleover Old Hall, Old Norton, Cutthorpe and Weston-on-Trent. There was also the enigmatic and substantial seat at Staveley Hall as well, with overtones, especially in its detailing, of the later phases of Bolsover. John Smythson's son Huntingdon completed the romantic ensemble of Bolsover Castle, soon afterwards to become a ducal seat.

By the end of the Civil War a more Jonesian-inspired classicism was beginning to arrive in the area, in contrast to the Smythsons' free adaptations of the works of the continentals Sebastiano Serlio and Wendel Dieterlin. This manifested itself triumphantly and in metropolitan style at Bretby, in a much more relaxed idiom at Beauchief, Hungry Bentley, Mellor, Norbury, Repton and old Swanwick and more sophisticatedly at Willesley and Osmaston-by-Derby. This classicism had spin-offs for the more thorough-going vernacular houses too, especially in the centre and north of the county. Here straight coped gables were still the norm, allied to mullioned windows. Yet houses like Eyam Hall, Bagshaw Hall (Bakewell), Beighton Fields, Glapwell Hall, Park Hall (Barlborough) and old Renishaw were being built with symmetrical (or near symmetrical) ground plans, central entrance halls, and were being embellished with continuous bands over the windows – derived from the entablatures of their grander more strictly classical exemplars – and even cross windows, as their vernacular builders borrowed elements from contemporary architectural trends. Yet some houses, most notably Sudbury, combined the new classicism with old-fashioned elements like stone mullions and transoms, diapered brickwork and outmoded interior features such as long galleries. Sudbury, too, was embellished by the finest craftsmen in the region, who themselves were displaced before the house was complete by their counterparts on a national level, producing fine stucco, frescoes and carving. This impetus seems to have transferred directly from Sudbury to Chatsworth, the first great Baroque house in the county after Bretby, and arguably the finest in the kingdom, then as now. Just as Bess of Hardwick had set standards with Hardwick, so her descendant the 1st Duke of Devonshire did at Chatsworth, and his lead opened the door to a great boom in house building the like of which had not been seen in the county since the heyday of the Smythsons.

The seats of Baroque inspiration form perhaps the largest group covered by this book, starting with Old Kedleston, built for Sir Nathaniel Curzon by Francis and William Smith (of Warwick) in 1700 and Calke, conceivably by William Johnson of Nottingham, now beginning to emerge as an important figure in his own right. Here the craftsmanship was of a high order in the league of Chatsworth, although those who produced it were mainly local men. Yet the example of Samuel Watson of Heanor (1663-1716) at Chatsworth cannot be ignored: local standards were notably high. Robert Bakewell the ironsmith is a significant example of the quality and widespread acclaim that could be reached from a local base (Saunders, forthcoming). Born in Uttoxeter of Derby stock in 1682, Bakewell's career (after an apprenticeship under Tijou and Jean Montigny) was launched through the patronage of Thomas Coke at Melbourne Hall, for whom he had made the breathtaking wrought iron and domed arbour to embellish London and Wise's gardens there. He then moved to Derby, where his screen for All Saints Church – done for a building of 1723-1725 by Francis (1672-1738) and William Smith (1661-1724) of Warwick to designs by James Gibbs – still stands as his other great achievement, after the Melbourne arbour. Whilst the Smiths picked up a whole run of commissions from the gentlemen who subscribed to the rebuilding of the church, Bakewell took his share too, embellishing Wirksworth Hall, Spondon Homestead, Darley, Foremarke, Osmaston-by-Derby, Aston Lodge, Calke, Etwall, Markeaton, Longford and Radburne Halls with screens, gates, balustrades and even tables. Yet his achievement extended well beyond Derbyshire: his work was to be found in Cheshire, Staffordshire, Shropshire Worcestershire, Warwickshire and further afield still, and he worked until blindness set in two or three years before his death in 1752, when he was succeeded by Benjamin (d.1778) and William Yates (1731-1816) father and son, whose work carried the local tradition of wrought iron working down to the end of the eighteenth century.

Fig. I: Houses associated with Francis and William Smith

Date	House	Owner	All Sts Sub	Notes
1700	Kedleston Hall	Curzon, Bt	£50	Replaced from 1758
c. 1713	Etwall Hall	Cotton	£10	Demolished 1955
1722/5	Melbourne Hall*	Coke	£50	
c. 1713	Green Hall#	Hayne	£8-8s	Rebuilt only
1724	Sutton Scarsdale	Scarsdale E	£105	Dismantled 1919
1724	Alfreton Hall	Morewood	£10	Demolished 1964
c. 1725	Locko Park#	Ferne	£10	
1726	WingerworthHall#	Hunloke, Bt. (RC)	-	Demolished 1928
1726	Shardlow Hall	Fosbrooke	£5-5s	Refronted only
1726	Ravenstone Hall#	Cave	-	
1727	Caldwell Hall#	Sanders	£5-5s	Enlarged only
1727	Darley Hall*	Woolley	£10-10s	Demolished 1962
1735	Aston Hall#	Holden		
c. 1736	Aston Lodge *	Greaves	£10-10s	Demolished 1938

In all, Francis and William Smith appear to have been associated with no less than fourteen seats in Derbyshire. These are listed (see Fig. I), along with the subscription of the owner to the rebuilding of All Saints Derby, for there is undoubtedly a correlation between this important event and many of the commissions. Those asterisked (*) also sported Bakewell ironwork. Those marked # are attributed to the Smiths on secure grounds, except Aston Lodge. Prof. Gomme has plausibly suggested that Aston Hall is by Francis or William Smith (junior); Aston Lodge has much in common with it. Unfortunately, Prof. Gomme's important monograph on the Smiths had yet to appear when this introduction went to press; it might be necessary to read the above list in the light of his published remarks.

Nor did the Smiths' connection with Derbyshire end with the death of Francis in 1738; his son William (1705-1747) built Radburne 1739-45 (where Bakewell worked), Catton in 1742-43 and the south front of Melbourne in 1744. William Smith junior's successors were, of course, William and David Hiorne, and the former (died 1776) built the county gaol in Derby to his own severe Doric design in 1754, whilst David was the designer of Foremark Hall (with Chatsworth and Kedleston the only Derbyshire seats to figure in the volumes of *Vesuvius Britannicus*). However, he died in 1758 before work on the house was properly begun; the job was undertaken by his 25-year-old clerk of works, Joseph Pickford.

Derbyshire's building boom had run out of steam (as also happened nationally) by about 1740 (see Worsley, G., *The 1740s: The Lost Decade* (Georgian Group Journal 1991) pp. 21-26), and yet at that date, Palladianism was still largely absent from the county. The builders of houses in the preceding decades, when the style was in its first flush, appear to have been too Tory or too parsimonious to seek architects from Lord Burlington and his circle. Thus, when Foremark was started, based loosely on Isaac Ware's Wrotham Park, only Radburne (1739), Markeaton (1755) and Stoke (1759) Halls could be in any way styled Palladian. Foremark was thus something of a landmark, and it was Hiorne's young contractor, Joseph Pickford, who was to build in this style in Derbyshire, although he was as much a Neo-Classicist almost from the outset, despite the Palladian predilections of his mainly Whiggish clients and on whom now see Saunders (1993). Pickford was born in Ashow, Warwickshire, in October 1734, the son of William Pickford, a mason working on Stoneleigh Abbey nearby and a man from Warwick. On the early death of his father in July 1742, Joseph was sent to live with (and become apprenticed

to) his uncle, also Joseph, in London. Joseph senior had a yard at Hyde Park Corner and was a leading contractor of his day, working with several leading first generation Palladian architects, Cambridge University Library, Horse Guards and Holkham Norfolk being amongst some of his more prestigious assignments. Apart from actually getting his hands dirty helping his uncle, Pickford seems to have undergone formal architectural training, an assertion borne out by the extremely high quality of his surviving drawings. By the time of his uncle's death in 1760 or a little before, he had returned to Derbyshire as assistant to David Hiorne at Foremark. From thence he went to Longford to rebuild the house and provide stables for Wenman Roberts. Here he married Mary, daughter of Thomas Wilkins, the agent, whom he had already met when arranging the getting of alabaster from the quarry at nearby Fauld, in Staffordshire, (for which Wilkins was also agent) for delivery to Holkham. In 1763 he was appointed contractor for the building of the Derby Assembly Rooms, to designs by Earl Ferrers; there is much of Pickford's later style in the detailing of the building. He settled in Derby at about this time, and commenced a wide practice which kept him busy until his sudden death on 11 July 1782. His Derbyshire country houses are listed in Fig. II.

Those places asterisked (*) are those where William Emes of Bowbridge Fields, near Derby (1729-1803) also worked. A leading Midlands exponent of the landscape style of Capability Brown, Emes became much in demand to lay out parks and gardens and worked frequently (not only in Derbyshire) with Pickford, later shadowing the Wyatts after the former's death; indications have been made in the text as to possible other parks by Emes, but they are only suggestions. The table (above) is based on Saunders (1993) with subsequent research.

Pickford, at first, worked in a provincial Palladian style (which quite a few of his Derbyshire clients seem to have preferred) and in the neo-classical. His work over a long period – as clerk of works from 1772 – at Kedleston must have given him splendid insights into Adam's style, and indeed, he made the Scotsman's acquaintance by 1763 when building the Derby Assembly Rooms. It was also at Kedleston that he encountered the Londoner George Moneypenny, senior (died 1809), who carved for him almost exclusively thereafter, Abraham Denstone of Derby (1723-1779) the plasterer, Richard Brown (1736-1816) the Derby marble worker and the latter's cousin, Joseph Hall (1725-1766) as well as John Whitehurst, FRS (1713-1788) who not only made clocks, but engineered cascades,

Fig. II: Houses associated with Joseph Pickford

Date	House	Client	Remarks
1759	Foremark Hall*	Sir Robert Burdett, Bt	To designs of D.Hiorne
1759	Ingleby Toft	Sir Robert Burdett, Bt	Dower house to Foremark
1762-63	Longford Hall*	Wenman Roberts (later Coke)	Reb.House; built stables
1763	Tissington Hall	William FitzHerbert	W.front; firm attrib.
1764	Knowle Hill(*?)	Sir Robert Burdett, Bt.	Banquetting house/folly
1764-5	Ashbourne Mansion	Revd. Dr J.Taylor	Rebuilt; firm attrib.
1763-78	Kedleston Hall*	1st Lord Scarsdale	Various works
c. 1764	Shardlow Hall	Leonard Fosbrooke	Added wings; attrib.
1765-68	Calke Abbey*	Sir Henry Harpur, Bt	Riding school; orangery; Design for new house
1767	Melbourne Hall	1st Lord Melbourne	Various works.
1768	Ogston Hall	William Turbutt	
c. 1770	Locko Hall*	William Drury Lowe	Various addns & Lodges; attrib.
c. 1770	Brookhill Hall	D'Ewes Coke	Refronted attib
c. 1771	Radburne Hall*	Mrs. Pole	Minor alterations
c. l772	Bradley Hall	Hugo Meynell	House conversion from stable
1772	Markeaton Hall*	F.N.C.Mundy	Orange, & offices; firm attrib.
c. 1774	Ashford Hall(*?)	John Barker	Firm attrib.
1777-79	Swanwick Hall	Hugh Wood	
1777	Sutton-on-the-Hill	Richard Ward	Built villa; attrib.
1778	Darley Hall*	Robert Holden	Enlarged Hall
1778-79	Long Eaton Hall	John Howitt	Firm attrib.
1780	Wirksworth Hall	Charles Hurt	Firm attrib.
1781	Draycott House	Thomas Evans	Firm attrib.

hydraulic devices and a variety of innovatory improvements in what was then called Domestic Economy (see Craven 1996a). Whitehurst was a member of the Lunar Society, the Birmingham based association of natural philosophers centred on Erasmus Darwin and Matthew Boulton, whose first house at Soho Pickford was bidding to design and build in 1760. This association brought him much work – including at Radburne, where Whitehurst provided various items, not to mention Whitehurst's portrait and a 'geological' landscape, both by Wright, all these associations without doubt legacies of Dr. Darwin's two years in residence there after he married the widowed Mrs. Pole. That Pickford must have given satisfaction is attested by the fact that he was recommended to others; he never had to advertise. Further, Pickford, Whitehurst and Joseph Wright of Derby (the painter) were freemasons, belonging to London lodges, as were nearly all the Lunar Society members except the ultra-rational Darwin. Pickford's later career benefited from the patronage of F.N.C.Mundy of Markeaton, and the Duke of Devonshire, for whom he built extensively at Edensor and Derby. As he got older, his houses became plainer and the interiors more Neo-Classical. His legacy was that he raised the standard of architecture in Derbyshire very noticeably; the lesser men who followed aped him, and in so doing produced better buildings. We only know of one pupil, however, and one associate: Thomas Gardner of Uttoxeter. He worked as a mason under Pickford in the 1760s, and seems also to have been trained by him. A legacy in 1772 enabled him to set up on his own in Derby (with a local builder, Thomas Freeman). Although the partnership was dissolved in March 1776, Gardner went on to build extensively in the Midlands in a very plain late-Georgian style. He settled in Uttoxeter, and died there in 1804; George Moneypenny carved his memorial in the church. His attested houses in Derbyshire are: Appleby Hall, Appleby Parva (1789), designs for Calke (c. 1792) Doveridge Hall (works, 1777), Sudbury Hall (lodge, 1787) and Willersley Castle (rebuilt after fire, 1792-95). He can also be plausibly credited with Barton Blount, extensions to Markeaton and Hopton Halls, Stainsby House, Park Hill (Egginton), Yeldersley and possibly Ashbourne Halls.

Architecture was more influenced in the northern half of the county by men from Yorkshire and Manchester from the later eighteenth century. These included, notably, Joseph Badger and William Lindley from the former and several from the latter like Richard Lane in the early nineteenth century. Indeed, the latter era marks a time when increasing numbers of architects of national repute worked in Derbyshire: Sir Jeffrey Wyatville, James Wyatt, L.N.Cottingham, Francis Goodwin, Alexander Beresford Hope, A.W.N.Pugin and W.E.Nesfield. The only local men of any stature were Thomas Chambers Hine of Nottingham (1813-1899) and Henry Isaac Stevens of Derby. The latter was born in London in 1806 and worked under William Martin at Bretby, marrying his daughter in 1832. He then settled in Derby, specialising in churches, schools and villas but doing a fair amount of country house work, including the reconstruction of the saloon at Calke and designing Callow Hall, Breadsall Mount and Ash Hall, and his *chef d'oeuvre*, Osmaston Manor. He was latterly in partnership with the Lancastrian F.J.Robinson (1833-1892) and died in 1873. His Derby contemporaries, Giles & Brookhouse were if anything more prolific, but distressingly predictable, as the later Norbury Hall and Eastwood Grange so vividly attest. A later Derby architect, Alexander MacPherson, was most stylish, but Littleover Old Hall appears to have been his only country house, and does not show him at his best.

Parks and gardens in Derbyshire have been insufficiently studied. Although the welcome foundation of the Derbyshire Historic Gardens Group (DHG) just over a decade ago is slowly making inroads on the problem. Nevertheless, the basic research by those best qualified to undertake it has yet, in many cases, to be done. There may be scope for investigation at South Wingfield Manor, and the gardens at Risley were said to have been notable, although only vestiges remained into the twentieth century, and later building has made recovery of evidence difficult. The discovery of the remains of a formal garden at Swarkestone shows that later sixteenth century examples have left traces, and indeed, much is known of the layout at Hardwick, for instance. For the type of garden laid out around the ubiquitous seventeenth-century small manor house, we now have the benefit of work done in the late 1980s in recreating that at Snitterton, and a similar exercise might well be possible at other sites, especially where the house has declined to the status of a farm, and the gardens have been overtaken by pasture as at Highlow Hall. Likewise with parks: Hardwick's parkland seems to have been little touched by later landscapers, and forgotten park buildings of the period still seem to be discovered; recently an example, perhaps a much mutilated hunting stand, has turned up near Pinnock Farm in what had once been the greater park of Sutton Scarsdale, but is unfortunately threatened by opencast mining. More recently the legendary gardens at Bretby have been investigated, and found to be still lurking beneath the current landscape, and the same may apply to poor, benighted, Elvaston Castle where, apart from the incomparable and justly famous work of William Barron, there is some evidence of a late 17th century garden of the type laid out for the owner;'s kinsman Lord Chesterfield at Bretby. Finally there are nineteenth century gardens of some distinction, like that of the horticultural enthusiast Sir Francis Sacheverell Darwin – eldest son of Erasmus Darwin's second marriage to Mrs. Pole – at Sydnope, which may yet be recoverable.

Towards the end of the seventeenth century a new phase of garden design emerged, and Derbyshire is fortunate in having at Melbourne Hall, surviving gardens laid out with the benefit of advice from the king's men, London and Wise, for Thomas Coke, a notable courtier, as a rare intact example, replete with statues by van Nost and others, along with Bakewell's apt and delightful wrought-iron arbour. The details of others of this period are preserved in panoramic estate paintings, notably those of Bretby, Castlefields, Sudbury, and Kedleston. The latter was laid out by Bridgeman, but parks were still then largely enclosed pastural chases. As in architecture, fashion was dictated from the top, and Lancelot (Capability) Brown's new park at Chatsworth set a trend. Although Brown seems not to have worked again in Derbyshire, the beginnings of a new park at Kedleston was undertaken by the head gardener there William Emes, who thereafter worked freelance under Adam who took the task over in 1759-60, before moving on to work on a number of Derbyshire parks in Brown's style (Jacques (1983) Chh. 3-5; *Country Life* 4/1/1990, p. 50ff.). There is no evidence that Emes, the study of whose work has been enormously advanced by Dr Keith Goodway of Keele University, had local origins, for the place of his birth (in 1729) has yet to be pinpointed. Yet he later had family connections with the Chawners of Muse Lane in the parish of Church Broughton and indeed, Emes's son John, who became a silversmith in London, entering into partnership with a member of the Chawner family, long engaged in the same trade, in the 1790s (Craven 1996a). Emes's practice was a wide one, yet he worked at Foremark, Calke, Darley, Osmaston-by-Derby, Radburne, Shipley, Longford, Locko and probably Markeaton, and several others in the county seem to be attributable to him and his link with Pickford has already been touched upon. Allestree, too, is in the Emes manner, but is later; it could perhaps be attributed to Emes's associate John Webb. Emes built himself a neat brick house (probably designed by James Denstone, also responsible for Markeaton Hall) on sixty three leased acres on the Markeaton estate. The house still stands, although by 1800 Emes had removed to grander surroundings at Elvetham Park, Hampshire, one of his sons still described himself as 'of Elvetham Park and Bowbridge Fields in the county of Derby, Esq' long after his father's death.

Just as Brown seems to have eschewed Derbyshire, so also Humphrey Repton seems to have done too; he made a 'Red Book' for Wingerworth, it is true, but the work does not seem to have been carried out in its entirety, and he was also consulted, at least, at Drakelow. However, he rejected a commission at Elvaston, on the grounds that the landscape was too relentlessly flat (it did not have, to use the words of his illustrious predecessor, 'any Capability in it'). He donated six Wellingtonias to Lord Harrington instead, leaving the way clear for the young Scot, William Barron (1805-1891), whose subsequent work there represents something of a triumph, albeit that it is currently under serious threat. The Borrowash based firm he subsequently founded flourished mightily thereafter, and the organization's own list of parks and gardens tackled up to the 1920s runs to fifteen clearly printed pages, and there were few Derbyshire seats the gardens of which did not see some attention from William Barron & Sons between 1855 and 1925.

Other figures demand further research, such as the Revd Christopher Alderson, who went from an incumbency in North-East Derbyshire to Windsor. Sir Francis Chantrey, although one of Britain's greatest sculptors, seems to have been involved in the layout of the gardens at Oakes Park, and in interior decoration at Longford. One wonders if he repeated the experiment elsewhere in the county. Later in the nineteenth century, one finds W.A.Nesfield being brought in at Ogston (and possibly Lea Wood if only by association) and Paxton, quite apart from his enormous contribution at Chatsworth, worked at Burton Closes. The Milners appear in one or two places, too, and further research might establish them in other local seats applying their skills. Two Edwardian gardens stand out only: Shipley Hall and Ednaston Manor; the former was the creation of the owner, working with his gardener, as with his friend Lord Craven and William Milner at Combe Abbey, Warwickshire. By that period, most work in Derbyshire was being undertaken by Barron's but their most inspired period had already passed. The era of great gardens was brought to a close by Sir George Sitwell's eclectic improvements at Renishaw, and the hand of Gertrude Jekyll seems singularly absent from the County's two Lutyens houses, Ednaston Manor and Easton House, Repton (the latter, grand though it is, not qualifying as a seat, having been built for an opulent schoolmaster.)

Thus, as Derbyshire society became more open and fluid in the later eighteenth century, and as communications improved, the architecture and settings of the seats of local grandees and gentry became more up-to-date, and the vernacular tradition withered away, as elsewhere. Nevertheless, the richness of the Derbyshire scenery is matched triumphantly by the variety of the seats built thereon, the wide range of the materials which that scenery reflects, and the skill of the artists and craftsmen who built them, so many of them native to the area.

Moated, Abandoned and Destroyed Sites

The reader will find numerous references to moats, or alleged moats, in the main entries of both sections of this book. Indeed, the original second volume (Matlock, 1984) included a supplementary list of known homestead moats in the county which, taken with those mentioned under the present entries could form the basis of a handlist of such Derbyshire moats, as well as other sites.

Three questions must, at this juncture, be posed and answered, if only in a fairly superficial way, for the sake of completeness. Why are some sites moated and others not? When were moats in vogue? and finally, as a corollary, why did these sites become abandoned? In the main introduction, an attempt was made to explain why seats were (and, alas, are being still) demolished in recent times. Yet the level of destruction in the Middle Ages and later was by no means inconsiderable, and the underlying reasons might, with profit, be identified.

By tackling the second question first, the preceding one might also thereby be answered. Although moats in England can be dated to the later 12th century, such early examples are the exception rather than the rule, and the great period of moat construction seems, from analyses prepared by Le Patourel (1973), Aberg (1978) and others, to lie between 1200 and 1325, after which there was a marked falling-off, few being dateable to the period 1350-1500. Research has also shewn that in nearly all counties studied, over 70% seem to have been of seignurial origin, and only a small number attributable to franklyns and other minor freeholders. 'Most moats,' says Le Patourel, 'Were constructed by holders of one or more manors, in areas where moats were relatively cheap to build' – on claylands and, to a slightly lesser extent on drift deposits. It is not necessarily true that such moats are contemporary with the first seat on the estate, however. Thus, moated sites were in vogue during a period of seignurial prosperity, at a time when direct exploitation of the demesne and ample labour resources manifested themselves together. Prestige was an obvious factor in moat construction, too, as was security – not against organised armed force, but against petty local feuding, banditry and unrest, like the sack of Lord Mountjoy's house at Elvaston by a rabble of armed retainers under the inspiration and leadership of some younger members of the Longford family during the Civil Wars of the 15th Century. These moated mansions were built where it made economic sense – on clay and drift, but not cut into living rock on difficult upland sites. In Derbyshire 67 moated sites have been noted, from field names, extant or recorded remains, and documents. Of these, 43 (64.2%) lie on the lower lands south of the theoretical Ashbourne – Long Eaton line which divides the upland from the lowlands of the County. Of the remainder, that at Holmesfield (SK 322779) lies furthest north, and none at all have been identified in the so-called Dark Peak region to the north west.

The remaining deserted sites are a mixed lot, ranging from the very early *Aincurt* in South Normanton, to latish seats which failed to catch the eye of the topographical engraver, like that of the Draycotts at Loscoe. It will be noted that some castles – Horsley (Harestan), Peveril, Pilsbury, Bakewell and the shadowy ones which seem to have existed in Derby and at Repton – are omitted the text. They have been treated, rightly, as fortresses, not as seats (the first two certainly were, being kept by castellans; the others are too obscure in their history for any certain conclusions to be drawn, except that they were probably adulterine constructions of the period of the 12th century dynastic conflicts and attributable to the Palatine Earl of Chester). Plainly, other deserted sites meriting inclusion, may have escaped the compiler's attention. Nevertheless, it is to be hoped that the present publication will stimulate further research.

The abandonment of the sites is a complex matter. With reference to moats, much could be said: the amalgamation of estates by inheritance or purchase; the desirability, through changing fashion or status, of replacing a medieval seat with a more up-to-date or commodious one on a more favourable site, and the lack of convenience of a moat, limiting the expansion of the house, have all played a part. Similar criteria apply to the other, non-moated, sites, although in many cases lack of adequate documentation prohibits us from finding the answers sufficiently for the compilation of a reliable statistic. It is only through reported hearsay in the 18th century that we know, for example, the first seat at Knowle Hill was destroyed through a whim; in contrast, its successor was demolished as redundant. Of the 168 redundant house-sites known throughout the County, 142 seem to have fallen victim to some form of redundancy; 9 declined in status to the point of extinction; 5 were demolished due to emparkation or other forms of early 'development' – Bess of Hardwick accounted for 3 – 2 were destroyed as a result of civil conflict and the disappearance of 8 others remains a total mystery, obfuscated by the passage of time.

It is possible to see, from much of the foregoing, that the reason for the destruction of seats in earlier times contrast very dramatically with those applicable to the more recent era: whereas redundancy through a variety of reasons accounted for the larger part of the statistic alluded to above, taxation, economics and urban development were the culprits in a later age. In the former instances, houses made redundant were usually replaced nearby or elsewhere; Country houses were still being built or expanded. Today the destruction of seats more often leaves a vacuum, their abandoned sites reverting to nature, being peopled with ruins, or being given up to 'redevelopment', the actuality of which results in the formless brick or concrete morass of inner ring-roads, multi-storey car parks, artlessly designed council housing or office blocks. The days when function in architecture was synonymous with beauty – as typified by the country seat – and such buildings appeared to have sprung from their surrounding landscape in the materials which abounded within its purlieu, to gladden our eyes and refresh our being, seemed, when this book was first written in 1981, to have withered into reminiscence. Thanks, however, to the vastly increased confidence and prosperity which have arisen since the mid-1980s, coupled with the revolution in information technology, enabling people to work from home, seats are once again being built or replaced, despite the reluctance of urban-based planning officials to sanction such positive developments. This revival is typified locally by the building of a new seat by Hon. Johnny Greenall on the site of long-demolished Wootton Hall, Staffordshire, and in Derbyshire by the replacement in the 1990s of Egginton Hall in a similar Regency revival style on the original site, by then forty years vacant. It is sad to think that an age in which more people than ever before in these isles can boast a reasonable standard of living, they should be offered the decayed fruits of 'progress' in the proliferation of concrete ugliness sweeping like an inexorable tide over their environment, sponsored by little men who seem to care nothing for the quality of the life of those whom they represent, and executed for them by planners and the lesser sort of architect who can only institutionalize the vapid and mundane. And yet our less fortunate ancestors occasionally starved amid a smiling countryside set with the jewels which we now, belatedly, strive to document and save.

Note that, throughout both sections of this work, the authors' criterion for a country house or seat is that it had to have been supported, for at least some part of its existence, by a landed estate. There is no doubt scope for another work altogether on the subject of villas – suburban, manufacturers' or gentleman farmers'.

ALDERWASLEY HALL (II)

School

The main front of Alderwasley Hall.   M. Craven

Anciently part of the parish of Wirksworth, Alderwasley Hall sits high on a bluff on the west side of the Derwent Valley, near Whatstandwell. Its earliest holders were the Le Fownes, granted land there in 1284. No trace or description remains of their house, except for the old chapel of St Margaret, largely rebuilt in the first half of the sixteenth century, and sold to the parish of Wirksworth in 1980 after 96 years as a mortuary chapel for the family cemetery; it is now the village hall. In 1884, when it was restored, it lost its later bell turret and a transept. Its replacement is a neat building of 1849-50 by H.I. Stevens. The heiress of the Le Fownes carried the estate to the Lowes in 1471 and their house, described by Wooley as a 'good old seat' and by Pilkington as 'an ancient House', was probably H-shaped and of early Tudor date, like the chapel; 10 hearths were taxable in 1670. The reason for such a supposition is that when the late eighteenth century east range was improved in the 1820s, this Regency addition appears to have been erected directly on to the foundations of the old house, and follows its plan. The house was plundered by Parliamentary forces under Sir John Gell of Hopton on 29 October 1642.

The Lowes, originally from Cheshire, transmitted the estate in 1690 to the Dovedale family of Hurt, and it was transformed by Francis Hurt, closely linked by marriage and business interests to the neighbouring Arkwrights (the Hurt's iron forge in the valley below the house was established in 1764 with a blast furnace added in 1776). Both the Hurts and the Arkwrights were painted by Joseph Wright; the forge could well have been an inspiration, if not the actual setting for his *Iron Forge*. The new work consisted of the addition to the original seat of a new, commodious cast range of seven by four bays and two and a half storeys, of stuccoed ashlar Millstone Grit sandstone, probably Ashover Grit from an adjacent outcrop; the quarry has not been identified.

The central bay is wider, pedimented, breaks slightly forward and boasts a first floor tripartite window capped by a Diocletian; bays two and five on the ground floor have Venetian windows with plain mouldings. It might be tempting to ascribe the house to the Pembrokeshire architect, William Thomas, who at exactly the same time was building Willersley for Hurt's kinsman Sir Richard Arkwright, yet Alderwasley seems a little old-fashioned, and more akin to the sub-Palladian Red Lion Hotel at nearby Wirksworth, and an unknown follower of Joseph Pickford should perhaps be postulated.

The west extension is massive, austere but of two tall storeys over a basement, the five bay sides carrying blank recessed panels above the fenestration to reflect the arrangement of the earlier build; it could almost be by Thomas Gardner, but is too late in date: 1823 on a rain-water head. The rusticated portico is later still, having been added in 1845. The whole was, by 1880 the centre of an estate of about 3,500 acres, and the house was set in a walled deer park of 196 acres a plan of which exists, amended by William Emes; a chain of ornamental lakes embellishing the valley floor is likely to be his work, too. A feature of the park is an eighteenth century deercote, 70 feet square, with colonnaded feeding areas, long in ruins, but recently restored.

The interior is rather plain, but there is a good cantilevered Hoptonwood stone staircase inside the house, but with modern replacement balustrade. The Hurts broke up the estate in 1920 and sold the house in 1930. After 44 years of being run by the Benedictines as a preparatory school for Belmont and a later tenancy of one John James, Alderwasley Hall was taken over in 1974 by the Honormead group of Special Schools. A John Whitehurst II turret clock graces the stable block.

Pevsner, 55; Lysons, 301; Pilkington (1789), II, 301; Woolley, 99; HURT formerly of Alderwasley/BLG (1965) 404; Egerton *et al* (1990) nos. 49-50, 126, 129-30; DRO D126,1056, 2535.

ALFRETON HALL (II)

Demolished

Alfreton Hall before Wilson's addition was built. It was taken c. 1854 and is one of the earliest dateable views of a Derbyshire seat.   *Derby Museum*

The estate at Alfreton was held by a succesion of families from the de Alfretons to the Chaworths (from 1299 Lords Chaworth of Norton) and finally the Suttons of Averham (Notts.) via the Babingtons and Zouches. In 1629 it was all sold to Anthony Morewood of a family of north Derbyshire emergent gentry (qv. Netherseal Hall). He died in 1649, leaving it to his cousin Rowland, of The Oaks (*qv*).

The house at this stage was a fair sized affair assessed at 16 hearths in 1670 standing nearer the church on the site of the later Hall Farm. A letter sent to Francis Smith of Warwick in the Morewood account books provides reasonable certainty for his authorship of the house which replaced the Morewoods previous seat, a supposition confirmed by the appearance of the new house, built 1724-26, when Smith was building Derby All Saints for Gibbs. The new house had two and a half storeys and of seven by five bays with tall rusticated pilasters and top balustrade, leaving little doubt as to Smith's hand. It is of ashlared fine-medium grained Coal

Measures sandstone (probably Wingfield Flags); the quarry source has not been identified.

The dining and drawing-rooms had much rococo stucco work and there was a fine timber staircase. In 1796 the geologist and spar turner, White Watson of Bakewell FLS, supplied a marble inlaid section of Derbyshire strata, probably as part of a fireplace, for two guineas. The Morewood line failed at the end of the eighteenth century, and the estate ultimately passed to the Palmers of Ladbroke, Warwickshire, by a remarriage, their descendants taking the name of Palmer-Morewood. At about this time, too (c. 1796-97), the house was enlarged by the addition of two-storey, two by five bay wings and a tetrastyle Ionic portico at the entrance; the architect is unknown. This also appears to be the period of the stable block, a U-shaped two-storey edifice of ashlar on the north side of Church Street. The central range of three bays, has segmental headed windows with tooled radiating voussoirs and impost bands. Blank arcading graces the five-bay west wing, contrasting with seven bays to that on the east. Some original stalls survive and a room in the east range has a reset eighteenth century fire surround and some panelling from the seventeenth and early eighteenth centuries, all listed grade II.

There is also a contemporary pigeoncote surviving east of the stables, of brick with a pyramidal graduated slate roof, also listed grade II. In 1855, the house was extended yet again, this time to designs by Benjamin Wilson, an architect who came from Sheffield and ultimately settled in Derby. His (east) wing is of two storeys, eight bays with an asymmetrical recessed three-bay focus, and a loggia on groups of four eclectic Doric columns, the entire affair looking like a Renaissance remnant set in a vaguely provincial baroque whole. The range has been equipped with matching pilasters and balustrade to match the main house, which had grown to a quite considerable size in consequence. Later alterations were made to this range in 1898, evidenced by a datestone CRPM/PMPM/RCAPM/CWSPM/1 July 1898 these being the initials of Charles Rowland Palmer-Morewood, his wife and their two sons.

The house had gardens and about 90 acres of parkland, these having been laid out at about the time the house was built by Edward Outram of Afreton and his son Joseph, the latter being the father of Benjamin, the engineer. By 1815, these had been embellished with a Temple of Diana, an obelisk, several moss huts and a grotto built of 'different mineral productions and all that diversity of and colour exhibited by the mineral substances of the Peak'. This grotto was octagonal and had painted scenes within from Izaak Walton's *The Compleat Angler*. The estate by 1883 extended to 4,400 acres.

In 1957 the Morewoods sold up, the Hall and Park being purchased by the Derbyshire County Council for £28,500, four acres of which, and the house, being sold to the Alfreton UDC February 1964. The remaining 523 acres were sold in January, 1966. At this time it had become apparent that the fabric of the eighteenth century house had become terminally weakened by mining subsidence, and despite being listed grade II, it was demolished unceremoniously in 1968, leaving the Wilson wing, currently in use as a WEA and community centre, and the stable block which is now used as farm buildings.

Pevsner (1953 edition) 56; Colvin, 888; Glover II.13; Bateman (1815); Mugliston (1782); Johnson (1968) 187-88; Gomme (2001) 165, 512; DAJ XCI (1971) 146; DRO D517, Morewood a/c book 3; PALMER-MOREWOOD of Alfreton/BLG (1952) 1821.

ALLEN HILL

Matlock   *Demolished*

The Wolley-Dod family at Allen Hill, c. 1894.   *Derbyshire Museums Service*

This long, low house with a straight coped gable to the north was the seat of a younger branch of the Woolleys of Riber Hall (qv). It was of coursed Millstone Grit Sandstone, probably Ashover Grit, with similar dressings under a tiled roof, replacing one of stone slate. The mullioned windows were lower on the ground floor than above, and although all have hood moulds, it may be that an earlier, sixteenth century, house was partially rebuilt in the seventeenth century. The projecting, one storey, gabled porch, built in the same style but of ashlared Stancliffe stone, seems nevertheless slightly incongruous, and may be a later addition. There were contemporary stables, and the dates 1653, 1674 and 1774 appeared in the fabric. The last of this branch of the Woolleys was the antiquary Adam (1758-1827), whose daughter and co-heiress carried the house to the Wolley-Dods of Edge, Cheshire, and Allen Hill was the residence of Charles Clarke JP DL (died 1863) and his widow (one of the other co-heiresses of Wooley) until later in the nineteenth century. On the latter's death it lay derelict for a while before being demolished during World War One. A hydro was built on the site.

Lysons, 207; Walford (1865) 206; CLARKE/op.cit. (1871) 211; WOLLEY-DOD of Edge BLG (1972) 258.

ALLESTREE HALL (II*)

Unoccupied

Allestree Hall, c. 1902.   M Craven

Anciently, Allestree had been divided between the monks of Darley Abbey and the Touchets of Markeaton, although it had no seat before the late sixteenth century. Yet, by the date of the will of Edward Mundy of Markeaton who died in 1607, we find his third son John being left the 'New house in Allestree... builded upon the parcell of land known as The Parcell at Kinder's Farm'. This stood adjacent to Mulberries farm and was completed in 1596. It continued as the seat of younger branches of the Mundys, and in 1713 Woolley recorded that Edward Mundy had 'a good house' there, on which tax was paid on eight hearths in 1670. It was probably timber-framed. It seems to disappear from record after the late eighteenth century.

In 1795, F. N. C. Mundy of Markeaton sold around 130 acres of land in Allestree to Bache Thornhill of Stanton-in-Peak, who wanted a suburban villa within reach of Derby. He commissioned James Wyatt to build him a straightforward gentleman's villa, a plan dated that year and signed byWyatt having survived, an association confirmed by the journal of William Holbech of Farnborough, Warwickshire. Yet the house was not completed to this design, and indeed, a further set of plans by another, inferior hand, exist at Stanton. Whilst the same basic five by five-bay plan with three-bay bow on the entrance front survives, the hall inside the bow goes from a D-shaped plan to an ellipse; the stairs from three sides on a well behind the hall with first floor gallery to a matching cantilevered elliptical plan. In these plans, too, there is an extensive service wing to the west, and this incorporates a tall conservatory with Tuscan pilasters behind the main block on the south side, with underfloor heating. These plans could conceivably reflect a modification by William Lindley of Doncaster, who in 1799 was adding a range of just this size to Stanton Hall for Thornhill (qv). Yet the interior was probably never finished, although a stone near the entrance with JW/1802 cut into it probably marks the exterior's completion by Wyatt himself but to yet another revision of the interior plan: cylindrical entrance hall with rectangular well staircase behind, decorated with a cast-iron balustrade which is repeated within the arches of the gallery above.

As built, the house has a ground floor tripartite window either side of the entrance, the mullions being Ionic half columns with Coade (artificial) stone capitals. The stone is fine grained buff Keuper sandstone, ashlared throughout, but it is of poor quality from quarries in Allestree. Behind the drawing room is a fine dining-room with a Greek Ionic screen at the north end. There is much ornate plasterwork in a rather limp Louis XVI style, some possibly done c. 1830-40, and the fireplaces are all in Carrara marble, with the exception of one in the billiard room behind the diningroom – which may be later anyway – which is in polished Derbyshire crinoidal limestone. The conservatory, as built, was a much more modest affair, subsequently re-built by Messrs. Mesenger & Co. of Loughborough. A U-shaped stable block lay immediately adjacent to the north of the house, where the saloon windows are painted dummies. There is a low-hipped slate roof behind a dwarf parapet.

After standing empty for three years, Thornhill sold it to John Charles Girardot, who appears to have finished the interior, and lived there with his family for 20 years before removing to Car Colston Hall, Nottinghamshire, and selling to William Evans of the Darley Abbey mills family. He added the porch, supported on Tuscan piers, and enlarged the park to about 300 acres and the estate to 6,799 acres, not all of which, however, lay contiguous to Allestree. The pleasure grounds were re-ordered by William Barron & Son 1917-23, and were subsequently municipalized by Derby Council.

On the death of Sir Thomas William Evans Bt in 1892, the whole was inherited by William Gisborne of Lingen Hall, a former New Zealand legislator, and his son Lionel let it in 1902 to the London banker H.H.Raphael,who sat for a local constituency in Parliament, being given a baronetcy in 1911. The collapse of Sir Herbert's parliamentary aspirations in 1914 caused the Gisbornes to sell to Col H.A.Johnson whose family were wire manufacturers at Ambergate. He died in a lightning-strike in the park in 1923, and on the death of his American widow in 1928, the contents were sold, and the house with about 400 acres was sold to the Commercial Construction Company, a director of which was the Derby architect, T.H.Thorpe. They demolished a Wyatt Lodge in the village and built houses on parts of the park, but this work was interrupted by the outbreak of war, when the house was occupied by the Sherwood

Foresters Regiment to 1942 and then the National Fire Service. This caused the suspension of golf, one of the developments in the park in 1928, the club occupying the house.

In 1946 the house and 323 acres were sold to Derby Borough Council for £23,000 although it was not handed over by the Fire Service until two years later, and the deal was finalised in March 1950. Meanwhile the golf club had restarted in May 1948 with nine holes, rising to a full 18 by 1955, and occupying 260 acres of what was now a public park. The Council demolished the west wing (part of the service accommodation) in 1949, and the conservatory had gone a year earlier, but a new one was built in 1989-90.

Despite at least two resolutions put to the Council for demolishing the house in the 1970s, a scheme to make it a natural history museum prompted a programme of long overdue repairs. However, the museum scheme paid scant respect to the high quality interiors, and it was abandoned in 1988. Subsequently, the building was stripped for dry rot treatment; its sale on a 150 year lease to a private developer was wrecked by misguided public opinion, and the last survivor of four municipally-owned houses continues to decay. Public access to the park and the playing of golf, however, continues. The icehouse was restored in 1994.

Pevsner 189; Colvin, 1118; Woolley 11, p.17; Lysons V 203-4; Boyes (1982) *passim*.; DAJ VII (1885) 172-3; Lucas (1995) 41-45; Catalogue of contents sale (J. & W. Heathcote, Derby) 24-27/9/1928, Derby Local Studies Library; GIRARDOT of Car Colston/BLG (1875) I. 175; EVANS, Bt.,/BP (1892) 288 & BLG (1937) 358; GISBORNE of Yoxall /BLG (1875) I. 182; RAPHAEL, Bt/BP (1924) and FD (1910) 1344.

APPLEBY HALL

Demolished

Appleby Parva, which since 1888 has been part of Leicestershire, was held throughout the middle ages by the Applebys, who had a moated seat, probably timber-framed, but with a fifteenth-century gatehouse and bridge of local Coal Measures sandstone, very pretty, which survive, although the old hall mouldered into desuetude in the seventeenth century at the hands of Market Bosworth Grammar School, which had received it from the Dixies, Bts, of that place, as an endowment. Sir Wolstan Dixie had purchased it from one of the heiresses of Francis, the last of the Applebys. A delightful timber-framed farmhouse now graces the house platform, which is largely seventeenth century and listed grade II* but contains fragments of the earlier seat.

The main part of the estate, however, passed from the heirs of the Applebys, via the Heywards to Sir Edward Griffin of Braybrooke, Northamptonshire, who had also acquired other parts of the former manorial estate from the Stanleys who in turn had obtained it from the Vernons. In 1598, the Griffins sold most of this to Charles Moore of Stretton-en-le-Field, of a London mercantile family but claiming decent

from the Moores of Lancashire. The Moores at some stage in the seventeenth century seem to have erected a seat at Appleby, taxed on thirteen hearths in 1662 (when it was tenanted by one of the Kendalls of Smisby), but no further information concerning it has come down to us. They also built a grammar school there, to a design originally commissioned from Sir Christopher Wren, but debased in execution by Sir William Wilson, and it is not impossible to envisage Wilson contributing to the family seat as well. Mercifully, the splendid brick and stone grammar school survives, still as a local authority school.

In 1786 George Moore decided to build anew, and commissioned Thomas Gardner of Uttoxeter, Pickford's old assistant, to design a new seat amid the 3,778 acres the Moores held in Derbyshire and Leicestershire, at a cost of £1,861. The resultant building was one of Gardener's most felicitous, being of two and a half storeys, and in fine quality ashlar of local Coal Measures sandstone. The entrance front was of five bays, the central one framed under a pediment in an aedicule consisting of an attached Ionic Order, with a heavy fluted Greek Doric tetrastyle portico beneath. The cornice was heavy; there was a sill band at first floor level; the fenestration had architraves and there were generous *antae* at all the angles. The south (garden) front was of three bays, the outer ones in wide shallow bows, with tripartite windows of the ground floor echoing a similar one on the first floor of the central bay over another door. There was a single recessed two-storey bay at the north end of the entrance front also ashlared, and a handsome three bay full height brick service wing beyond. Extensions and renovations were undertaken in the mid-nineteenth century by T.C.Hine of Nottingham. Gardner also designed the elegant red brick rectory nearby, which was for sale in July 2001.

The Moores sold up 1920, and the house was reduced in 1927, being ruinous a decade later, and was entirely cleared in 1952 due to mining subsidence. Gardner's elegant and commodious rectory (listed grade II) with its brick stable block remains.

Pevsner (*Leics.*) 48; Colvin, 392; Lysons, V. 5-6; Nichols (1804) II. iv 439 & III. ii 991; Glover, II 24-6; Bagshaw (1846) 223; Moore (1982) *passim*; Building Contract courtesy Aubrey Moore, Esq.; APPLEBY of Appleby/Glover, *loc.cit.*; VERNON/BP (1999) II 2884-8; STANLEY *sub* DERBY, E/*ibid.* I. 815-20; DIXIE, Bt./*op.cit.*(1970) 811; GRIFFIN of Colehurst/BLG (1937) 980; MOORE of Appleby Parva/*ibid.* (1898) I 1894.

Appleby Hall with the entrance front to the left, c. 1905.   *M Craven*

ARLESTON HOUSE (II)

Private

The north front of Arleston House, 1997.   M. Craven

Arleston was in the hands of the Ferrers, Earls of Derby until sold by the Crown in 1294; the Toke family were their under-tenants, and remained so under the Bakepuizes of Barton well into the century following. A moated site (now regrettably ploughed out) 800 yards to the north of the present Arleston House probably marked the site of the Tokes' residence. By the early fifteenth century, the manor had passed to the Bothes (Booths), cadets of those of Dunham Massey, Cheshire, and in his will (1519) William Bothe mentions the chapel at Arleston. This, however, had no connection with the Preceptory at Yeaveley, which had a *camera* at Barrow, which Dr Cox erroneously suggested as being on the site of Arleston House more than a century ago.

The House one sees today is the south wing of what was originally a U-shaped house, the surviving range having a truncated cross wing to the north at the east end. It is on a massive stone plinth of late sixteenth or early seventeenth century date, well buttressed to the west and south, which accords fairly well with the date of c. 1580-1600 put upon the fabric by the surveys conducted in 1991. Above the plinthwork the house is of timber box framing rather more reminiscent of Hereford than Derbyshire and is now missing the hall and entrance range, which must have once lain to the west with a further range to the north.

The gable end of the cross-wing has a bizarre arrangement of windows making a sort of bucolic Venetian window, which is probably a relatively recent phenomenon. Otherwise, most of the north front is windowless, but has a modest entrance. The south front has been clad in eighteenth-century brick and sports five bays of sashes, casements, and one bay blocked, which is probably the result of a reduction and subsequent rebuilding 'lately' carried out in 1718 at a cost of £246, to which the tenant, John Buxton paid John Harpur a contribution of £100. At this stage the cellar was put in or re-lined in vaulted brick.

Within, all is plain and vernacular, a reflection of nearly three centuries as a farmhouse. Three fireplaces have four centered arches. Two ranges of outbuildings form a courtyard on the north side, those on the east side may be on the site of a former wing of the house. The stone is a mixture of coarse Millstone Grit sandstone and Keuper sandstone, both from south of the Trent, probably Stanton by Bridge and Weston Cliff. There is an old tile roof that contains re-used trusses. In the nineteenth century, a small single storey service wing was built out to the NW.

About 1530 the estate was sold to the Beaumonts of Thringston, Leicestershire, who shortly afterwards inherited an estate at Barrow, and sold Arleston on to Sir Thomas Blount of Blount's Hall, at Burton, Staffordshire, who was there by 1542. It is likely to have been his son, John, who built the present house, quite possibly pulling down the Bothes' moated seat and turning the body of its former and presumably detached chapel, into a house, adding at least one cross-wing, for it was assessed for tax on 12 hearths in 1664. Woolley calls it 'a large old hall house'. It was Glover, indeed, who purveyed the story that the house was supposed to have formerly been a chapel. Further, a bell chamber was pointed out in 1846, but cannot now be found; was the house reduced to the east as recently as the nineteenth century? Bagshaw adds: 'On the north side formerly stood a large hall or castle which was taken down some years ago.'

Shortly before 1640, Edward, the last of the Arleston Blounts died, and his second cousin and heir, Sir Henry Blount of Tittenhanger, Hertfordshire, sold it in that year to the Harpurs of Calke, by whom it was at first used as a secondary seat for younger sons, and by the eighteenth century had become a farm. Robert Briggs, of a notable local dynasty, was there in the first half of the nineteenth century. It was sold due to Capital Transfer Tax problems in 1984 and was for sale more than once subsequently. The village of Arleston was nearby (at SK 335297) but was deserted at an early date, the earthworks being ploughed out c. 1976. Today, Arleston House's sequestered canalside location has been hopelessly compromised by the southward thrust of the Derby suburbs.

Pevsner, 84; Woolley 63, p. 102; Glover II 30; Bagshaw (1846) 163; Cox (1877) IV 17 & n.; Usher, H. *Notes on Sinfin & Arleston* MS 7/1989; Hutton *et al, Arleston House* Derby Buildings record (1991) no. 97; RCHM (E) *Arleston House* (York 1991) *passim*; Turbutt (1999b) 18-9, 37 & n.59; D. Misc. 15 pt. 2 (1998) 34-6; DRO D2375 & Harpur-Crewe MSS 63/52/5; BOTHE/DAJ IX (1887) 36; BLOUNT/ Nichols (1804) II iv 523-4, BDEP 54-6 & *sub* BLOUNT, Bt./ BP (1999) I 297-8; HARPUR *sub* CREWE, Bt./*op.cit.* (1923) 618-9.

ASHBOURNE MANSION (I)

Private residence

The garden front of Dr Taylor's house as rebuilt by Pickford, 1966.
Derbyshire Life

Ashbourne Mansion, *2000*.   *C.L.M. Porter*

This impressive house began as a U-shaped edifice of traditional Jacobean configuration, but built for an opulent Ashbourne attorney, Benjamin Taylor, in 1683-84. It was of brick with stone dressings of local Keuper sandstone, quoins, cross windows and tall grouped chimney stacks. Whether the street front was gabled, or had a hipped roof and eaves cornice is impossible to say, for an extensive rebuilding was undertaken in 1763, for Rev. Dr John Taylor, Benjamin's heir. This work can be confidently ascribed to Joseph Pickford of Derby (who built two other houses in Ashbourne) on stylistic grounds, and subsequent circumstantial evidence, a letter from Pickford at Ashbourne to Ralph Sneyd, going a long way towards confirming this.

Pickford refronted the house with a five bay facade, two and a half storeys high, the attic storey being formed by hiding the former attic dormers (or gables) set in the tile roof behind the new work and adding cornice and top parapet above, the latter broken with balustrading over the bays. The fenestration had gauged brick lintels and sits on a sill band on each floor. The central bay is wider, with a broken pediment over, formed by extension of the bracket cornice with gauged brick voussoirs below – almost in the manner of Sir John Vanburgh – beneath which the central panel is recessed to full height with a largish Diocletian above a Venetian window with a tripartite pedimented Doric entrance and portico beneath. In 1769, in building his own house at 41 Friar Gate, Derby, Pickford returned to this formula, but handled it with the increased maturity of nearly a decade, producing a better proportioned and more satisfying result than here.

The other major alteration was the placing between the wings on the garden front of an octagonal music room, domed and entered from the garden through an exquisite Doric portico. Inside, niches flank the door to the hall, and above the bracket cornice, the ceiling is coffered in exuberant rococo plasterwork, probably the work of the Derby plasterer Abraham Denstone the younger. From the centre of the ceiling hung the crystal chandelier which, in 1777 Taylor's friend Dr Samuel Johnson craved to see lit the next evening but Boswell let out that it was the great polymath's birthday that day and Johnson, embarrassed, then refused to 'countenance such extravagance.' In the garden, which was laid out by Taylor himself, is a pretty summerhouse probably also Pickford's work, with a three-arched facade, all in Keuper sandstone.

In the late 1770s, Taylor again improved the house, although perhaps not using Pickford (his former assistant and protege, Thomas Gardner of Uttoxeter might have been

involved, however). The hall was opened out, and a new cantilevered Hoptonwood stone stair installed, rising to the gallery supported on a pair of Roman Ionic fluted columns. The stair rail is supported on an elegant wrought-iron rail decorated with paterae, which may well be the work of William Yates of Derby. Taylor had an estate, partially adjacent, and extensive grounds, in which there was an artificial waterfall, unclogged by Johnson and Boswell after supper one night, when the two were walking in the gardens.

On Taylor's death, the property passed to his adoptive heir, William Brunt alias Webster and was sold to the Dale family on his death in 1843. Shorn of its estate, its was again later sold to Captain Henry ffoliott Powell, who died there in 1872, after which it went into a decline from which it was rescued by Dr Ernest Sadler, when it became the headmaster's house of Ashbourne Grammar School, which it still (with a few boarders) remained latterly under the baleful aegis of the Derbyshire County Council which, sold it as surplus to requirements (along with the Elizabethan School, opposite, in 1993, the house going to an improving owner.

In front of the house, the wrought iron spear-headed railing survived World War Two (they may have been made by an Ashbourne smith), and to its left a typically Pickfordian blind arcade hides the former stables and coach-house. In former times the house was thought to have been the work of Robert Adam – a frequent attribution bestowed on Pickford's houses before their history was more recently unravelled by the work of Edward Saunders.

Pevsner, 63; Colvin 753; Boswell (1905) II. 139; Frith (1920) 70;Saunders (1993) 53, 68-74; 102, 169; DAJ LIII (1932) ; DLC 10/66; CL CXLIII (1968) 730; TAYLOR & WEBSTER/FMG I 234-7; DALE/Glover II. 46; POWELL/ BLG (1937) 1837-8; SADLIER/BIFR 1138-45.

ASHFORD HALL (II*)

Private residence

Ashford Hall, c. 1906.   *Maxwell Craven*

From the Norman Conquest until 1199 Ashford was held by the crown but in that year it was granted, as a result of treaty obligations, to no less a person than Gwenwynwyn ap Owain Cyfeiliog, Prince of Powis. His son, Gruffydd was granted free warren in 1250. After the death of his son Owain de la Pole, it reverted to Edward II, who granted it to his brother, Edmund, Earl of Kent, from whose posterity it passed via the Hollands to the Nevilles, Earls of

Ashford Hall, 1966. *Derbyshire Life*

Westmoreland. They sold to the Cavendish family in the later sixteenth century. As some stage during the medieval period – probably in the late thirteenth or early fourteenth century – a moated seat was built, but no documentary evidence has come to light to suggest by whom, or who lived there. It is presumed that it fell into desuetude during the sixteenth century. The site (SK 197695) survived as a moat, but was ploughed out in the 1960s.

The site of the present hall seems to have come into the leasehold possession of the Barker family in the mid-eighteenth century, and the Lysons tell us that it was built for John Barker (1731-1795). The architect was almost certainly Joseph Pickford, working there c. 1777. The Derby architect had encountered the Duke of Devonshire in the early 1760s, and worked almost exclusively for him in the later 1770s, dealing through John Barker's cousin, Alexander, of Edensor. The latter is clearly described in papers still at Chatsworth as 'at Ashford Hall', so it may be that he lived there until his death as tenant of the Duke, who later sold it to Alexander's Bakewell-based cousins who were agents to the Dukes of Rutland.

The house is of two and half storeys, and five by three bays, the north front only being of coursed rubble, the remaining sides in a fine ashlar of buff, fine-medium grained Millstone Grit sandstone, probably Ashover Grit from Ball Cross quarry, near Bakewell. The south (garden) front was also the entrance, marked by a singularly fine pedimented Ionic doorcase carved on the frieze with the kind of 'snaky handled' urn which is the hallmark of Pickford's carver George Moneypenny (who also worked at Chatsworth) and derives from a pattern book by George Richardson of 1776, to which Pickford was a subscriber. The ground floor windows (now somewhat enlarged to no good effect, regrettably) are set in a blind arcade, with the first floor ones

ornamented with alternating segmental and triangular pediments and blind balustrades below, between bands. Above, the attic windows have architrave surrounds, the central one with an entablature, all under a modillion cornice and top balustrade. The east and west sides have plain fenestration, the north, flat stone surrounds. The roof is pyramidal and slated. The whole is a stripped down version of St Helen's, Derby, (1766-1767) also by Pickford.

To the west of the garden front is a pretty nineteenth century conservatory, carried on a glazed five-bay arcade which may originally also have been part of Pickford's house, and in the garden, to the east, is a distinctive Palladian gardener's cottage, masquerading as a temple, simple Venetian window and giant distyle Tower of the Winds portico *in antis*. Behind the house there is a dignified little coachhouse and stable with a dovecote in the pediment: probably the work of the Chatsworth mason, William Halkesworth. The whole is set in a small but breathtakingly beautiful park through which the Wye runs in a way which suggests the hand of an expert, quite possibly William Emes, who worked elsewhere with Pickford and which makes dramatic visual use of rising ground beyond, although the latter was never part of the Ashford estate; it is said locally that Sir Joseph Paxton laid out the gardens, however.

In 1816 Thomas Barker, the builder's son, died and in 1819 the next heir retired to Bakewell and it was sold to the Duke of Devonshire for £14,000 with 1,000 acres, who let it. It was shortly after this that the south front windows were widened and deepened, and the entrance turned round to the west, which makes a nonsense of Pickford's cool elegant hall, with its Tower of the Winds screen, an order used by Pickford at his own house in Derby (1770) , and published by Stuart and Revett in 1762. Today one emerges almost under the cantilevered stone dog-leg staircase with its plain wrought-iron balustrade. A long, low wing to the north, containing offices was also added. It is worth noting however, that if Pickford's hand is indeed discernable here, he was not averse to planning the gardens as well as the house, as at Ogston (qv).

Throughout the nineteenth century and into the twentieth, the house was occasionally occupied by the Chatsworth estate's agents, although from his marriage in 1835 until his death in 1880, it was the home of Lord George Henry Cavendish, MP, and from 1927 until 1938 by Brig. Hon. G. E. M. Baillie and his wife, a daughter of the then Duke. However, in 1939 Col. W.H.Olivier took the house on, buying the freehold in 1954, and his son Jasper Olivier still resides there.

Pevsner, 66; Colvin 754; Lysons, V. 30-1; Saunders (1993) 146-50, 173; Tarn (1971) 6; Innes-Smith (1972) 44-5; DLC 4/67, 5/69; Sheffield City Libraries Barker MSS D718, 756-63, 773-5; Chatsworth archive, u/c vouchers; CAVENDISH sub DEVONSHIRE, D/BP (1999) I. 837-41; BARKER/BLG (1921) 93 & FMG I 214; BAILLIE sub BURTON, B/BP (1999) I. 435-6; OLIVIER/BLG (1952) 1925.

ASTON HALL (II)

Apartments

Aston Hall, 1996.   M.Craven

Aston was anciently a berewick of the manor of Weston-upon-Trent, held by the King in 1086; another portion was held by Henry de Ferrers. The former was later held by the Chaworths who gave much of it to the Abbey of Dale; the latter by the Babingtons from the earlier sixteenth century, by inheritance from the Tickhills. Ferrers endowed the Priory of Tutbury with two thirds of his lordship at Aston, with more to the Abbey of Chester. At the Dissolution, the latter came to the Bishop of Chester, and from him was transferred by Elizabeth to the Sacheverells who had been the Abbey's tenants since the late fifteenth century. James I in 1603 gave the Sacheverell estate to Charles Paget, who was later attainted, and the Crown sold in 1612 to Anthony Roper. He was an ardent Royalist and was obliged to sell up in 1649 to Robert Holden of Wilne. He had already gained a foothold in Aston by purchasing the former Tutbury Priory estate from the Hunts, who came from Ashover in the 1530s, and had built, before 1540, a capital mansion. This was

through the marriage of Christopher Hunt of Overton with Dorothy, sister and heiress of William Basset of Aston.

It is probable, therefore, that the Holdens in the seventeenth century merely modernized the former Hunt seat, which Woolley described in 1713 as 'an old seat and a good estate', and tax was paid in 1670 on nine hearths, An inventory of 1692 reveals this house had 23 rooms.

In 1735 another Robert Holden built a new house (dated rainwater head H/RE/1735), a double pile in brick with stone dressings of Keuper sandstone from Weston Cliff, which Professor Gomme thinks could be the work of Francis Smith of Warwick. It is of two and a half storeys with cornice, parapet and big hipped tiled roof, of five by three bays, the central bay on the entrance front being wider, breaking forwards and embellished with a Venetian window over the entrance with a neat tripartite affair above. This arrangement is repeated on the garden front, and the windows are all with gauged brick lintels with a single stone keyblock. To the north is a five-bay service wing, with the main fenestration segmental headed, of two storeys and attics in the hipped roof, which looks near-contemporary with the main range. The windows have rusticated stone lintels, which suggests it that it is by a lesser hand than that of Smith. Inside, the hall has contemporary panelling with carved overdoors, and both staircases are good timber originals, the main stair having carved balusters and tread-ends. There are also two eighteenth-century marble fireplaces of some quality and some seventeenth century carved oak has been re-used along with some bolection-moulded fireplaces – presumably from the house's predecessor.

On the failure of this branch of the Holdens in 1791, the heir was a Shuttleworth of Gawthorpe, who assumed the surname and arms of Holden in that year. In 1828 (if we are to accept the evidence of this date scratched on plaster from this phase) the south front was built out on the ground floor and given deep tripartite windows set in Doric pilasters, the slightly recessed centre-piece having four Ionic columns *in antis*, echoing the new porch on the west (entrance) front, a feature virtually identical to that at The Leylands, Derby, suggesting Richard Leaper as the architect. This alteration created a drawing room on the SE and a corresponding dining room with an unfluted Corinthian screen, oddly in timber, both rooms being enriched by exuberant stucco, and an upstairs dressing room acquired a fire-surround in Chellaston alabaster. The entrance, a tripartite affair in the west front, was moved to the north side, and the staircase was, in consequence, moved. At this time, too – certainly by 1846 - it was 'painted stone colour', a hue that gave way to white in the 1920s.

By the later nineteenth century, the Holdens had let the house, first to Reginald Pringle, and afterwards to Major William Dickson Winterbottom, along with the 2,028 acre estate. The latter added a decorative two-storey extension in Arts-and-Crafts manner to the west in 1898-9, possibly by Mack Hamilton. This is of two storeys with attics, a shaped gable pierced by a stack, cupola, and projecting timber framed mullioned and transomed bay windows. The chief space provided thus was a billiard room with an Art Nouveau chimneypiece and bachelors' bedrooms above, reached up a re-assembled earlier eighteenth century oak staircase brought in from elsewhere.

In November 1924 the Winterbottoms moved away on the death of Major W.D Winterbottom, and the Holdens sold the estate, the house eventually going to the Nottinghamshire County Council, who opened it as a Mental Deficiency Colony on 6th April, 1926 and it remained a special hospital, until converted fairly sensitively into separate dwellings after sale in 1995 with 18 acres and a further 24 acres of land on which 'enabling development' could be built. In reality, the profit from erecting houses on 24 acres would probably finance the restoration of three large country houses, and the term is a misleading euphemism, which frequently persuades local politicians to allow the ruination of historic parks. However, in this instance, much of the former park is covered by unsightly ancillary buildings erected from the 1930s, and which are still in medical use in 2001, although their future appears to be uncertain.

The Ballroom (apartment one) as furnished by the Winterbottoms, c. 1910.
RCHM(E)

Pevsner, 69; Woolley, 22 p. 57; Lysons, V. 22-3; Glover, II 68; Bagshaw (1846) 159; RCHM(E) *Aston Hall* (Swindon, 1995) *passim*; Gomme (2001) 469 n., 513; DET 30/5/1995; HOLDEN *formerly* Aston/BLG (1969) 305; WINTERBOTTOM, B/BP (1970) 2682.

ASTON LODGE

Demolished

Aston Lodge & Gates, c. 1904.   M.Craven

The portion of Aston once in the hands of Dale Abbey passed through numerous ownerships before the early eighteenth century when it was purchased by Joseph Greaves, second son of John, of Stanton Woodhouse and Beeley Hill Top. There, probably in the late 1730s, he erected a five by three bay, two and a half storey house which in many respects echoed Aston Hall, although the design was simplified, but it is still easy to discern the hand of an architect like Smith. The central bay on the entrance front broke forward under a simple pediment and had the same plain fenestration as the remainder of the house, like the Hall, with gauged brick lintels with a central keyblock. At the entrance to the small park were massive gatepiers supporting a pair of gates by Robert Bakewell under an ornate, monogrammed overthrow.

Early in the nineteenth century the unpedimented garden

front acquired a wide full length bow to the right of the central bay, itself (later in the century) given a tall segmental headed door with a rusticated arch, so high that the window above had to be shortened, and was turned into a pair of small sashes under an ugly out of proportion triangular pediment. Also in the early nineteenth century a ballroom was added to the left of the garden front, and a four-bay three storey service wing nearly as large as the house was added beyond the bow. Later, at the same time that the garden front entrance was altered, a similar one was provided for the main front, set in a ground floor full width projection plainly inspired by that on the garden front of Aston Hall. The ballroom range was raised to full height on that front only to match the service wing, giving the unfortunate effect of a modest villa swamped by an oversized and brutally plain attached pavilion on either side.

On the death of the second Joseph Greaves, a brother-in-law of Sir Brooke Boothby, of Lunar Society fame, in 1780, it was inherited by the husband of one of his daughters and co-heiresses, Edward Sneyd of Byonby Lodge, Staffordshire, but Mrs. Greaves remained in residence until the first decade of the nineteenth century, when it was sold to George Redmond Hulbert, whose executors sold in 1820s to James Sutton of Shardlow who rebuilt it, perhaps with the help of Richard Leaper of Derby, as at the Hall. They retained it until about the period of World War One, when the supply of tenants who had occupied it throughout their period of ownership dried up. Amongst these had been William Drury Holden in the 1820s, Charles Hope, of the eminent Derby family in the 1880s, and the antiquary Charles Eyre Bradshaw Bowles a decade later. It stood empty for a time, and was demolished after World War One, the shell allegedly being shipped to the USA, although no confirmation of this unlikely tale appears to be forthcoming. The stables survive, unsympathetically converted into flats. The Bakewell gates, which are of exceptional quality, were purchased by the Borough of Long Eaton, and now grace a municipal park there.

Lysons, V. 22-3; Glover, II 69; Briscoe (1900) 234; GREAVES of Aston Lodge/BLG (1833/7) I. 386 & IV 105; Derbyshire Now! 5/1994 p. 49.

Haddon Hall from the west. *M. Craven*

Haddon Hall, the Lower Courtyard. *C.L.M. Porter*

Flower Lilies. *J. Lake*

Smalley Hall. *FPD Savills*

Statue of Flora, Kedleston Hall.
National Trust Photographic Library/M. Antrobus

Marble Hall, Kedleston Hall.
National Trust Photographic Library/N. Mackenzie

Sudbury Hall, south front. *National Trust Photographic Library/A. Butler*

Wingfield Manor. *English Heritage/A. Tryner*

Remains of Tower, Wingfield Manor. *J. Allsopp*

Bolsover Castle. *English Heritage/J. Bailey*

Opposite page Chatsworth. Top left: the west front; top right: the Dining Room; bottom: The Painted Hall, all photographs: *Devonshire Collection, Trustees of the Chatsworth Settlement and the Duke of Devonshire.*

Opposite page: top left: Baslow Hall. *Fischer's Baslow Hall Hotel*; top right: Foremark Hall. *M. Craven*; middle left: Mickleover Old Hall, garden front. *M. Craven*; middle right: Callow Hall, entrance front. *C.L.M. Porter*; bottom: Hartington Hall, west front. *C.L.M. Porter*;

Stubbing Court. *David Charlesworth*

Norbury Manor. *M. Craven*

Above: Medieval doorway at Norbury Old Hall. *J.A. Robey*

Below: Tissington Hall, The Hall. *Derbyshire Life*

Somersall Hall, Somersall Herbert. *FPD Savills*

Calke Abbey, south front. *National Trust Photographic Library/R. Truman*

Calke Abbey, Drawing Room. *National Trust Photographic Library/A. von Einsiedel*

BAGSHAW HALL (II*)

Private residence

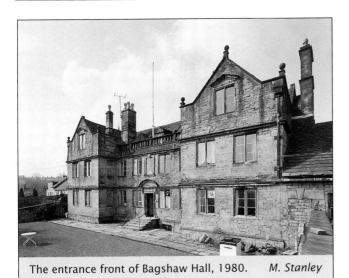

The entrance front of Bagshaw Hall, 1980.   *M. Stanley*

Bakewell, even today, abounds with minor seats and villas, and at first glance the history of this distinguished, if rather old-fashioned building seems to start in the 1684 when the man after whom it is named – Thomas Bagshawe of Ridge Hall, Chapel-en-le-Frith – erected it. A rich attorney, he appears to have purchased the site during the Commonwealth, but from whom remains unclear.

The house itself is a typical H-shaped Derbyshire manor house, of ashlared buff Millstone Grit sandstone, probably Ashover Grit from Ball Cross quarry, with its main front situated high up facing east across the river and over the roofs of the houses lower down the steep slope upon which it is set. Bearing a datestone of 1684, it is of two storeys and attics, with two bays in each of the projecting wings, and five in the central section which has a central entrance with a simple classical segmental pediment riding on a string course from which all the ground floor fenestration hangs. The window over the entrance alone has an architrave surround (in this instance with a keyblock), and somehow this element looks a generation later. All the remaining windows are large two-light mullions, those in the attics each being ensigned with a triangular pediment, rather reminiscent of East Anglian practice of the century before. Above these, the gables, set in a stone slate roof, are slightly depressed into a parapet, and decorated by miniscule ball finials whilst the centre section has a balustrade resting on the string from which the first floor windows depend, transforming it into a rudimentary cornice rather neatly, if naively; it effectively hides the attic dormers. A low wing runs off to the north, and at the so the-west corner is the remnant of a much older range, sixteenth century in all probability, but containing traces of earlier fabric in coursed Carboniferous Limestone rubble with low mullioned windows and dressings of Millstone Grit. It is possible that this is a fragment of a previous house, and the site may indeed mark that of the former capital message of the medieval manor of Bakewell, perhaps degenerated by Elizabethan days into little more than a courthouse.

The medieval manor was held by the King in 1086, but was granted to the Gernons in fee by Henry II, from which family it passed way of heiresses the Botetourts, Swinbournes, Helions, Tyrells and Wentworths, the latter selling in 1502 to the Vernons of Haddon, from whom it descended to the Earls of Rutland. The hall may have been the residence of their stewards, of whom, for instance, William Savile died in Bakewell in 1658. How it became alienated to Bagshawe is unclear. Bagshawe's heiress brought it to William FitzHerbert of Tissington, whose heirs sold it to the Barkers of Darley and Ashford *(qv)*. From them it passed by sale back to the Dukes of Rutland, whose tenant at the turn of the century was a representative of another family of local solicitors, Herbert Brooke-Taylor, then Town Clerk of Bakewell. By 1948 it had become the Conservative club, which organization bought the freehold in 1982. Most of interest within has unfortunately, long since vanished, but the through hall gives access to the original staircase, and several original fire-surrounds remain.

Pevsner, 76; Tarn, (1971) 5; FITZHERBERT, Bt./BP (1999) 1066-69; RUTLAND, D./ *op.cit.*2482-87; BAGSHAWE of Ridge/Vv. 1569,1662.

BARLBOROUGH HALL (I)

School

The entrance front & service wing of Barlborough Hall by Keene, c. 1860.   *M. Craven*

Barlborough is one of a most important group of Midland high houses and within that category, one of a number of seats associated with Robert Smythson and the circle of the Earls of Shrewsbury. Aptly summed up by Mark Girouard as an 'exciting, odd and romantic' house it was built 1583-4 (date on porch and great chamber fireplace respectively) and is firmly attributable to Smythson. It was built for Francis Rodes, from 1585, a justice of the Common Pleas and a protege of Lord Shrewsbury. Rodes was also a cousin to the Hewetts of Shireoaks Hall, Nottinghamshire, and a son in law of Henry Sandford of Thorpe Salvin Hall Yorkshire, both, like Shrewsbury's astounding Worksop Manor, houses attributable to Smythson. Rodes himself was the scion of a very old but rather obscure gentry family long seated at Staveley Woodthorpe *(qv)*, although he was obliged to accept detail changes to his arms and a radical alteration to the tinctures, which rather suggests that there was some doubt as to his legitimacy.

The house is of brick, covered with later stucco, with dressings of Permian Magnesian limestone. It is almost square in plan, of two tall storeys over a high basement, with four canted D section towers carried up above the parapet, two each on the north and south fronts. Each front is different in detail if not in articulation and is garnished with inset portrait medallions, as at Wollaton. The towers, as at Worksop and Hardwick *(qv)*, are inset from the corners and topped with a fanciful crenellation of alternating pylons and merlons. The chimneys are carried up within the walls, and until 1875, when they were removed, made for a restless skyline where they emerged above the leads. The fenestration is mullioned and transomed, generous of glass, and on all levels suspended from a moulded string course.

The entrance portico, forming a rectangular projection on the south front, has a modest and rather old-fashioned door ensigned by a large paired and fluted Doric order supporting frieze and entablature rising proud of the string course, the columns enclosing the arms of de Rodes, with those of his patron, Shrewsbury below the 18-light mullioned and transomed window above, and the Royal arms above that. The whole projects above the plain battlemented parapet and is embellished as the towers. To echo this feature the north front is centred on a more modest rectangular V-shaped projection with a full height window, whilst the east and a west fronts have a wide canted bay a piece. The whole is a grander version of Heath Old Hall over the county boundary in southern Yorkshire of c. 1585 and demolished in 1961, undoubtedly by the same hand.

The centre of the house once boasted a central courtyard with the unusual feature of a corridor running right round within the walls overlooking it and adjacent to it on each floor. This is echoed in a plan by Smythson for Slingsby Castle, Yorkshire of c. 1588 (but not built) made for – significantly – Sir Charles Cavendish of Bolsover. The plan of Barlborough is also enfiladed right round just within the exterior walls, whilst the more central interior walls are quite remarkably thick and massive although poorly constructed: can they represent the vestiges of an earlier tower-house on the site? If there was a previous building, it could conceivably have been put up by John Selioke who purchased the estate (1,020 acres; a moiety of the original manor) in 1534 from Stephen Constable of Catfoss, Yorkshire, (ER). He was a member of a burgeoning family of old minor gentry with business interests in London, an ancient seat in remote Hazlebarrow (*qv*) and lands in Norton. He further purchased another moiety of the manor from the Wingfields, co-heirs of the Goushills, who had inherited their portion from the de Hathersage family in the thirteenth century. It is less likely that the Constables had a house at Barlborough, for they were based in a remote part of Holderness, but in 1518 they let their portion – significantly – to Nicholas Hewett of nearby Wales, Yorkshire, a man on the make. De Rodes's connections with his family may indeed account for his decision to acquire the estate.

Inside, the house boasts a hall and an impressive Great Chamber on the *Piano nobile*, but oddly, no long gallery. The Great Chamber has stone Doric pilasters and a fine two-tier chimneypiece; at one end there is a generous newel staircase toplit by a lantern. There is nice heraldic stained glass by Willemont of London, 1831. Generally, the awkwardness of the detailing suggested to Girouard that Smythson had provided a set of drawings but had left the details to an executive mason, and he opines that the house is ultimately a disappointment. In 1671 tax was assessed on 11 hearths, and in 1697 the courtyard was covered over and filled with a substantial staircase, and other alterations included additional outbuildings to supplement those built in 1639. In 1825, the house was re-orientated, the entrance henceforth being on the east front at basement level; some Georgian sashes were also inserted. There is also priests' hole in a first floor room in the south front.

Allegedly a curse was placed on Judge Rodes to the effect that the estate would never pass from father to eldest son, a legend which no doubt grew up with the benefit of hindsight, and a stone relating to this, mainly of a genealogical and armorial nature, in the west court illustrated this, although two successions from father to son did occur, in 1675 and 1856. The Rodes's were created baronets in 1641, but the

senior line died out in 1743, and the title became dormant (with the line in which it was vested by then domiciled in America, where there are today numerous descendants). Thereafter the estate descended via the Heathcotes, Reastons, Hatfields and Gossips to Rt Hon Godfrey Locker Lampson, MP, PC. In 1883, the estate extended to 2,293 acres, and in 1935, Locker Lampson's widow sold the house to T.J.Garlick of nearby Park Hall. He sold on to a Catholic body in 1938 along with the fine 300 acre park, and a prep school to complement Spinkhill (Mt. St Mary's) College was founded in the year following, which still flourishes. The outbuildings are listed grade II and the formal garden, pleasure grounds and park are also grade II. There is also allegedly a Grey Lady who walks a corridor looking for her bridegroom to be who is alleged to have been killed *en route* for his wedding. A gatepost of Coal Measures sandstone exists on the west side.

Pevsner, 81; Lysons, V.43-44; CL VIII (27/10/1900) 528-34; Locker Lampson (c. 1941) *passim.*; McArdle (1979); Girouard (1983) 120; RODES/BDEB (1838) 448, BLG (1972) 960-1 & DAJ XXIV (1902) 64 f; LOCKER LAMPSON/FD (1929) II.200-1.

BARLBOROUGH OLD HALL (II*)

Private residence

Barlborough Old Hall, 2001.   N. & C. Chapman

An intriguing rubble-built H-shaped house built (or at least started), on the site of an older capital mansion in the later sixteenth century, and rebuilt early in the next by the Rodes family of Barlborough Hall. The design the house ultimately assumed has been attributed by Girouard and others to John Smythson, and was plainly intended to be an ornamental and romantic villa, perhaps castellated, with two small towers on the west front in the angles of the returns of the gabled projections. These, however, appear not to have been completed – or were, but were later taken down – and since at least 1780 have terminated in lean to roofs. The south front is almost symmetrical, with five two-light mullioned windows on the lowish upper floor with a pair of six-light mullioned and transomed ones between the outermost bays. If only the entrance had been centrally placed, symmetry would, indeed, have been the result. Yet it appears almost beneath bay two, but such is the state of the building stone that it is not impossible to imagine that symmetry was indeed what once pertained, nor does the interior at this point seriously contravene such a postulate. The four straight coped gables all end in stacks originally stone, but now brick, very reminiscent of the south front at Brookhill Hall *(qv)*. Neither west gable has any fenestration except for a pair of cross windows at ground floor level on the south- west one. Doubtless, given the later history of the building, both have been quite rebuilt, and indeed, this same gable had been constructed at kneeler level in eighteenth-century brick. The south-west angle also may have been the springing point for some kind of ornamental architectural feature, now lost. The north-west gable in 1780, if a view by S.H.Grimm is to be trusted, had attached to it a lower service range, perhaps of a later date than the house. The north front is (or was) not unlike the south, but with two low doorways with depressed pointed arches between bays two and three and three and four. Either they are original (one has been recently renewed) or they represent a later adaptation into multiple dwellings. This side has a plain stone staircase echoing a similar one running towards the south wall.

Like so many buildings by John Smythson and his father, it is very subtly planned, and changes in floor level have survived to emphasize the point. There are one or two fine Sheffield school plaster overmantels, one with a bravura cartouche of the arms of John (later Sir John) Savile of Bradley impaling those of his wife Jane, daughter of Richard Garth of Morden. Savile was a distant kinsman of Sir John Rodes's second wife, Dorothy, daughter of John Savile of Wakefield. Yet this armorial carries the house back into the sixteenth century, for John (later Sir John) died in 1607, and the first of two dates on the fabric is three years after this (the other is 1633).

It is thought, indeed, that the house was probably originally built not long before 1583, and that John Savile was then Sir Francis Rodes' steward, a position he may have held until around 1594. Thereafter his career took off, and he also acquired the Methley estate in Yorkshire, where his posterity resided. Thus, whether Savile bought the land from Sir Francis Rodes and built the Old Hall, or was merely a tenant, it would seem that the property by 1610 – the date on the porch, clearly added later to the main fabric – was back as part of the Barlborough Hall estate. It is possible that it was then thoroughly rebuilt and given a more distinctive

profile for a member of the family – perhaps Sir John Rodes's widowed step-mother or one of his half-brothers. This also led to some interior re-ordering, the best bedroom, for instance, appears to have been switched from the hall chamber to the parlour chamber. The central section contains solely the neat great hall with a great chamber of outstandingly intimate proportions above.

In 1670 the house was occupied by a Scots freebooter called Alan Lockhart – possibly another Rodes steward – who was assessed for tax on 12 hearths, but the house had been alienated by 1723. Thereafter it appears to have been divided into two, and renamed Crosshouses, although a century later it was back within the Barlborough Hall estate and was at sometime thereafter divided into four as 2-8 Church Street. By 1970 it had been empty for some time and had fallen into a state of dereliction, but a decade later it was acquired for restoration by the Derbyshire Historic Buildings Trust, a Herculean task which had been partly completed (the interior left to be finished by a purchaser) by January 1984. Unfortunately it failed to sell for some time before finally being acquired at a price below the cost of acquisition and conservation, by David Bostwick then of Sheffield Museum, who embarked on a careful restoration of the interior. It has since been sold again. The building stone used in the house is complex: there is coursed rubble of Coal Measures sandstone, probably that above the High Hazels Coal, adjacent. The west elevation is of Millstone Grit sandstone (non-local). The dressings are all of Coal Measures sandstone except parts of the doorway to No.6 Church Street, which is of Permian Magnesian limestone. The roof, originally of stone slate, was later pantiled. Purchased in 1995 by Nigel and Catherine Chapman.

Pevsner, 73; Sinar, J., *Report to the DHBT* (1981) *passim.*; Girouard (1983) 276; Clay (1939) 83 & pl. 96; SAVILE of Methley, *sub* MEXBOROUGH, E/BP (1999) 1912-13; RODES/as previous article.

BARTON BLOUNT (II*)

Private residence

Barton Blount, c. 1899 before rebuilding.   *M. Craven*

The manor of Barton was held from before 1086 to about 1380 by the family of Bakepuize, whose name was added to that of the settlement thereby. Their seat was moated, had a chapel, and stood close to the village, now long since deserted. The estate passed to Sir Walter Blount whose posterity were created Lords Mountjoy of Thurvaston in 1465. It was at about this time the house was remodelled. Although there was no license to crenellate, the surviving entrance, or gatehouse, suggests that it was defensive in character, although the architecture rather suggests that such things had become at least in part ornamental. Nevertheless, a memorable raid by the neighbouring Longfords on Elvaston – another Blount seat – during the Wars of the Roses might suggest that the house was at least fortifiable, and with good reason. In 1560 when the sixth Lord Mountjoy sold much of his interests in the Midlands and retired to the West Country, the Barton estate – by now called, often as not, Barton Blount – was alienated to John Merry. The last of this recusant family, John, died without issue and his sister and heiress brought it to Henry Simpson, allegedly the son of one of Merry's grooms. In 1700 Merry Simpson took the tonsure and declining fortunes forced the sale of the estate to Sir Nathaniel Curzon, and this family soon afterwards sold to the Listers of Armitage Park, Staffordshire. In 1774 it was purchased by Samuel Crompton, an opulent Derby banker, whose town house was the Friary. In 1808 his posterity sold on to the Bradshaws of Holbrook, from whom it passed, in 1959 to E. S. Wilmot-Sitwell and later to Sir H. Waring, Bt., (ex info M. Mallender) from whom it was bought by Basil Mallender in 1925. The latter family sold in 1981 to Mr. & Mrs. J. Pratt, and it has since been again sold in 1995 to Mr & Mrs Faulkner.

This catalogue of a complex ownership is best recited before describing the evolution of the house, simply because the building is equally complex. The Merrys, being Royalists and Catholic, had the misfortune to preside over the destruction of the medieval seat by fire at the hands of a detachment of Sir John Gell's troops in 1646. All that remained was the gatehouse. After the Civil War, a makeshift dwelling of two ranges was made out of the ruins of its predecessor behind the gatehouse. Judging from a view dated 1730, the outer shell of this was either made to match the decorative cornice the medieval work – machicolations would be to flatter what remains – or was a surviving remnant. Eight-light mullioned and transomed windows and a spindly tall chimney leant a jaunty air. Behind this, and enclosing a three-storey tower, probably another survival of the late medieval house, the Simpsons built a U-shaped brick house with stone dressings, the east front being of five bays and two storeys divided by a simple string course under two gables, with a four-bay section between. On the west were two projecting wings of two bays each under a gable. However, after the Simpsons left, it became only a second residence under the Curzons and Listers. The coming of Crompton saw vast improvements to both house and estate. The moat was filled in and much of the house was dismantled, to be replaced by a new, plain and dignified classical edifice which left only the old west front, suitably modified by the removal of the gables.

The architect for this work was almost certainly Thomas Gardner of Uttoxeter, and the work in local Keuper sandstone was probably done in the mid-1780s, after the death of Pickford (in 1782), for the latter was part of Crompton's circle in Derby and would have been the logical choice had he been living. Further, comparison with Appleby Hall (qv) not only underlines the basic similarity of the two but suggests that they were built within a few years of each other.

The main (east) front is on two storeys and five bays, with a very modest, almost mean, pediment over the central bay,

which breaks slightly forward. There is a first floor sill band and the ground floor windows reach almost to terrace level; the cornice is oddly high over a blank frieze and there are *antae* at the angles. On the north (gatehouse) front, the facade flows round the medieval fabric which was raised to the height of the new cornice and crenellated; like the remainder of Gardner's work, it has been refaced with smooth ashlar in Millstone Grit sandstone, and although the frieze runs across it, the medieval features lower down have been faithfully reproduced. Beyond the south end of the entrance front, another range in brick has been set back, but has an extra half storey above, explaining the height of the main cornice. The panelled brick stacks of the previous house have largely been suffered to survive. Inside, however, there is good plasterwork, a large hall, with a two arched screen and a cantilevered well staircase behind graced with carved tread ends, stick balusters and a wreathed rail. Either side of the marble drawing-room chimney piece are the dials of the wind vane by John Whitehurst I, and the clock made by the same eminent Derby maker which graces the offices was made in 1826 for the Derby Gaol, and brought to the house by Basil Mallender. Behind the gatehouse is a rib-vaulted Gothick hall and window – perhaps by Gardner, but more likely early nineteenth century.

The Bradshaws added an incongruous brick Jacobethan full height bow to the south front in the later nineteenth century, but most subsequent alterations were Mallender's. He laid out the gardens, rescued the stone urns from St Mary's Gate House, Derby (which grace the garden), and Bakewell ironwork from the same source, from Osmaston Hall (qv) and also some wrought iron from Wollaton, the latter dated 1771. He also incorporated a surviving fragment of moat into delightful gardens, graced with appropriate brick walls and buildings. Rain-water heads dated 1741 (on the main fabric of the house) are probably Mallender importations. Ten hearths were taxed in 1664, and the house was still moated when Woolley wrote in 1712 "a handsome brick house and a chapel…moated about". The stables and garden structures are grade II.

To the north of the house the medieval chapel and parish church of St Chad still stands. Probably ruinated during the Civil War it was rebuilt in 1714 by Samuel Taborer of Normanton-by-Derby, with pinnacled pilasters at the angles and a generous entrance to the south below a curly pediment. By 1835 the round-headed windows had been replaced by lancets, which were again renewed in 1854. The blocked north doorway may be medieval, and the church certainly features in the Domesday Book. Despite its status, it remained the Hall chapel, and most of the records of its parishioners appear in the registers of Sutton. It ceased to be a parish church under the Mallenders, who beautified it with altar rails by Horrabin of Derby.

Pevsner, 84; Woolley, 74 p.112; Lysons, V. 46-47; DM 8-15/4/1774; BLOUNT, B./BDEP (1883) 54; CROMPTON of Flower Lilies/BLG (1937) 518; BRADSHAW of Barton/op. cit. (1894) 209-10; MERRY of Barton/V.1611; WARING, Bt./BP (1999) II 2938.

BASLOW HALL

Restaurant/Hotel

An example of the longevity of the traditional, gabled, north Derbyshire style of house; built as recently as 1907 for Revd Jeremiah Stockdale on land purchased from the Duke of Rutland. Two storeys, two prominent projecting gables, porch with segmental pediment, the gables with five light mullioned and transomed windows, the whole built in local ashlared Millstone Grit Sandstone [CG] in the Arts and Crafts manner of Percy Currey of Derby, much more apparent inside. In 1913 the house was sold to Sebastian Ziani di Ferranti, by whom it was sold again in 1930 to Sir George Kenning. It was then purchased by another budding motor car vendor, T.C.Harrison, eventually passing in 1957 to Mr and Mrs. Clixby. It was converted into a hotel 1982 and into a restaurant by Mr. & Mrs. Max Fischer in February 1989.

Baslow Hall.   *Fischers' Baslow Hall Hotel*

Pevsner 86; DLC 9/69; KENNING/BP (1956) 2537; ZIANI DI FERRANTI/Gayre (1978) 361.

BEAUCHIEF HALL (II)

Corporate headquarters

Beauchief Hall, 1981.   *M. Craven*

The extra-parochial district of Beauchief (now transferred to Sheffield) came into being through the founding, between 1172 and 1186 of the Abbey of *Bello Capite* – hence, Beauchief – by Robert fitz Ranulph, alias de Alfreton for the Premonstratensian canons, an order founded by St Norbert 61 years or so before. It was believed that de Alfreton was a murderer of St Thomas a Becket, but although (amongst his known assassins) le Breton and FitzUrse had Derbyshire connections, his name does not normally appear amongst the four knights. Nevertheless he plainly intended to honor the murdered archbishop, to whom (with the Blessed Virgin) he dedicated the Abbey. Indeed, an alabaster reredos depicting the assassination was removed from Beauchief by a Foljambe (one of whose ancestors had dedicated it) and taken to Osberton Hall, Nottinghamshire, where it was recorded in 1833. At the Dissolution, the Abbey and its 600 acre estate became the property in April

1537 of Sir Nicholas Strelley of Strelley, from whom it descended in 1657 to Edward Pegge, an opulent Ashbourne attorney. The house he inherited was probably fairly large, doubtless an adaptation of the former Abbot's lodging, as at Repton and Darley Abbey, on which he paid tax on 14 hearths in 1670. A fine Jacobean staircase in oak survives from it, unless it was brought in subsequently from elsewhere. It is, of course, quite possible that there was no previous seat (if one allows that the stairs were an importation), for the present house was completed in 1671 (dated) and the tax may have been computed on the partly completed edifice; further, both Pegge and the Strelleys had chief seats elsewhere.

Pegge's house is of two storeys raised on a high basement, of seven bays by five and with cross windows (mostly timber replacements of stone originals) suspended from string courses on each main floor. The returns are of five bays each. The structure is ashlared, with quoins and parapet in Coal Measures sandstone (probably Greenmoor Rock from an outcrop in the park), and the hipped roof was once dormered, with a top lantern and rooftop balustraded promenade. The grounds were, a generation later, laid out with a complex of formal gardens and parterres, two enclosures lying before the entrance front, with wrought iron gates (perhaps by John Gardom the elder) and palisades. An avenue led the to the ruins of the Abbey chapel, suffered to remain, partly as eyecatcher, partly (restored by Pegge) as chapel, and partly as cottage. On the *piano noble* of the hall are several main rooms, of which the finest is the dining-room which contained an early Jacobean chimney piece of some size carved with figures and scenes in Chellaston alabaster, and which was given to Pegge by Adrian Mundy of Quarndon Hall, a younger son of the Mundys of Markeaton: can it have been from old Markeaton Hall when that house was being modified after the Civil War? It is now in the entrance hall, surrounded by original panelling, which also survives in two other ground floor rooms, although partly repositioned. The main staircase (perhaps of c. 1700) has been rebuilt, although the secondary one is original.

The house descended through a number of female lines, but these successors retained the surname of Pegge. It was rebuilt with four canted bays along the entrance front, an odd balustraded portico over the entrance and above it an awkward piece of stone ogiform cresting, dated 1836; however, Glover records most of the changes in 1833.

Doubtless at this time too, the dormers were removed, and the parterres landscaped away, leaving the odd stone forecourt to be ramped and bridged with a complexity of flying staircases rising to a perron at the entrance. All this tends to obscure Edward Pegge's datestone, which is inscribed:

Eben - ezer
Haec Domus ergo Deus stet honoris grata columna
Nam domus et domini conditor ipse Deus
E.P. Maii 17 1671

The stables appear to be eighteenth century, redone in the early nineteenth century Jacobethan style, of two storeys, with four shaped gables, the larger of which contains a clock and dovecote over.

In the later nineteenth century the house was let to the Wilsons, Sheffield manufacturers with a penchant for the chase, and they ultimately purchased the house and the 1,541 acre estate from the last of the Pegge-Burnells, in 1923. Part of the estate remained with the Pegge-Burnell heiress and descended to the Craven-Smith-Milnes's of Winkburn Hall, Nottinghamshire (*cf* Dunstone Hall) by whom it was sold for building. On the death in the 1950s of the last and most redoubtable Miss Wilson, the house became the centre of a golf course but was more recently occupied by the De La Salle Company, who have since been succeeded by a more reclusive concern.

Pevsner (*Yorkshire, West Riding*) 476; Glover, II. 94-95; VCH II. 63-69; Cox I. (1877) 73-80; Anon (1824) 334-337; DAJ XIV (1892) 122; CL CLXXX (25/12/1986); STRELLEY/DAJ XIV (1892) 72-118; PEGGE, *see* CRAVEN-SMITH-MILNES of Hockerton/BLG (1969) 439; WILSON/*Who's Who in Derbyshire*(1934) 192.

BEELEY OLD HALL (II*)

Private Residence

It is to be presumed that this house rests on the site of the original capital messuage of the Beeley family, and is a tall house of three storeys and attics, with a two storey porch and lower projecting wing, all probably dating in its present form from the early seventeenth century. It is built of Millstone Grit Sandstone, coursed rubble, probably Ashover Grit from the adjacent outcrops at Lime Tree Wood or Lindup Wood across the Derwent valley, with a stone slate roof. The windows are mullioned, the lower ones with transoms also. Adjacent outbuildings are dated 1791. The ancient manor passed to the Cheneys and thence to Vaux, the latter selling it in 1560 to Edward Deane, whose grandfather (of Longstone) was frankpledge for Beeley in 1473. The Deanes were in possession in 1611, but it is not known for how long they held it thereafter. Eventually, however, the property passed to the Dukes of Rutland, and by purchase in the last century, to those of Devonshire. Latterly it was the

Beeley Old Hall, 1967.

Derbyshire Life

property of Prof H.R.G.Greaves, who died in 1981, leaving the house to the National Trust under whom it is tenanted, but not open to the public.

(1971), 32 Pevsner 86; Tarn (1971), 9; Lysons, V. 32, Alcock (CBA 42) 106; DAJ XLV (1923) 1 f.; DLC 10/67; BEELEY/*ibid.*; DEANE/V 1611; VAUX of Harrowden,B/BP (1999) II 2873-5.

BEELEY HILL TOP (II)

Private residence

Beeley Hill Top, 1968.   *Derbyshire Life*

Pevsner in 1953 dismissed this delightful small gentleman's house as: 'Irregular early seventeenth century house with gables', which hardly does it justice. It seems to have been built by James Greaves in about 1603-04. The arms of England as at first adopted by James 1 done in bravura Sheffield school plasterwork in the main bedroom on the first floor fixes the period of building fairly precisely; the same room boasts a foliate frieze and coffered strapwork ceiling which elements are part and parcel of the arms, although the style is old fashioned for the date. The same room has Jacobean oak panelling, a feature found elsewhere in the house, although nowhere is the plasterwork comparable to that in this one room. Strangely, the fireplace over which it stands is modest and plain, of local stone. This is Millstone Grit sandstone, probably Ashover Grit on which the house stands, or possibly Chatsworth Grit from Hellbank Plantation nearby. The house itself is more or less L-shaped, with two storeys, attics, straight coped gables and contemporary outbuildings, all of coursed rubble. The fenestration is largely of stone mullions – three and four-light – one or two windows having transoms as well; some also have hood-moulds and the east wing has fenestration suspended from string coursing. Indeed, the south part shows every sign of including older work, for this is not the first house on the site. The west front is rather marred by the insertion of a single Georgian sash. The west portion of the attractive outbuildings is probably late medieval.

The site was originally named Greaves, from which the family took their name, and where they had been settled under the Beeleys of Beeley since the early thirteenth century. They ultimately sold the manor in 1687 to the Saviles of Blaby, although the latter had been living there since the hall itself was sold by John Greaves (died 1673) in 1664 to the Earl of Rutland, who sold it on to George son of William Savile of Bakewell (*qv* Bagshaw Hall), his steward, who paid tax on ten hearths there in 1670, which figure confirms that

the house has been since reduced, by the demolition of the south range, probably in the 18th century. When the Saviles, who were cadets of those of Thornhill, Yorkshire, became extinct in 1734, their heir, John Gilbert of Locko, sold the estate piecemeal in 1747, most of it going to the Duke of Devonshire, under whose regime it became a tenanted farm. Since the war it has been the residence of Mr. Rupert Turner.

Pevsner, 86; Tarn (1971), 9; Lysons V. 32; DLC 3/68; DAJ XIII (1891) 220-222; GREAVES/DAJ XLV (1923), BLG (1833/37) I. 386, IV 105, V. 1662, SAVILE/V.1662.

BEIGHTON FIELDS PRIORY (II)

Private residence

The early history of this site is difficult to unravel. Beighton appears in the will of the Saxon grandee Wulfric Spot not, as some commentators have said, as part of his legacy to the Abbey of Burton, but as an element of the inheritance of his heir, Morcar. After this, which took place in 1002, there is a lacuna until 1086 when the Domesday Book records two manors, one held by Lewin under Roger de Bulli, and another belonging to Roger de Poitou. The first descended or was granted, to an ancestor of Sir Gervase de Bernake, from whom it descended ultimately by marriage to Ralph, fourth Lord Cromwell, who held it from Welbeck Abbey, to which foundation it was probably granted by one of Roger de Bulli's descendants, the Lovetots of Blyth, Nottinghamshire. The other manor was held by Walter de Furneaux of Charlton-in-Lindrick (Notts) in 1279, from whom it descended via the FitzHughs to the Fiennes, Lords Dacre of the South, by whom it was sold in 1570 to Francis Wortley. By 1649 it was in the hands of the Pierreponts, and passed from them to Earl Manvers.

Beighton Fields Priory, c. 1903.   *J. Darwin*

This house plainly belongs to the first manor, and was said to have been at some stage an hospice for sick monks from Welbeck Abbey, although it was more likely a grange of that community, although another house in the parish actually rejoiced in this title. It was also said that there were monks' cells were still to be seen in the fabric of the present seat.

At the Dissolution, it seems to have come to the Hewitts of Killamarsh, who settled it on a younger son. The heiress of the last of the family, Mary, daughter of John Hewitt of Beighton, married in 1665 the recusant Henry Bowdon or his son, and is typical late seventeenth or early eighteenth century work. Whilst plainly incorporating some earlier fabric, the house is of two storeys in coarse ashlar, with attics under end gables, which are plain, straight and coped, each containing two bays with three in the central section, which boasts a generous entrance with bolection moulding and a segmental pediment on rather ill-articulated brackets. The fenestration has architrave surrounds, and is separated by a plain band, with quoins at the angles. The roof has two dormers at the front, ensigned with triangular pediments, but they differ in size and position, suggesting that one is a replacement or an afterthought.

In 1831, Bruno Bowdon had only 56 acres, and it was by this time let to William Potter, a farmer describing himself as a gentleman, succeeded by Henry Potter. By 1895 it was the home of C. H. Stones, a solicitor. In 1925 it was in the hands of James Frederick Robertson, and 40 years later, those of N. V. Craig. Mr and Mrs J.M.W. Pridham purchased the property in 1968 and are the current occupants.

Two moated sites in the parish may reflect the original division of the area into two manors, both with seats: Castle Stead, traceable in 1895 (SK 446837) and another surrounding a farm of twelfth century origin at SK 444832.

Pevsner, 87; Lysons, V. 47-8; Glover, II. 84; Bagshaw (1846) 590; Cox (1877) I. 83-9; FITZHUGH, B/Clay (1913) 73-5 & BDEP 207-8; FIENNES sub SAYE & SELE,B/ BP (1999) II 2554-8; HEWITT, Bt./BDEB 260; BOWDON sub GREY de RUTHIN,B/BP (1956) 970-2; PIERPOINT sub MANVERS, E/BP (1931) 1607-8.

BENTLEY HALL (II*)

Hungry Bentley   *Private residence*

Bentley Hall c. 1900; the entrance front.   M. Craven

Two Saxons, Wulgeat and Ulfkell, held Hungry Bentley in 1066 but, by the time of the Domesday Book, the entire manor was waste – hence, no doubt the soubriquet "Hungry". It was then (1086) part of Ralph de Bakepuize's holdings under Henry de Ferrers. As late as 1397 it was held in dower by Joan, Lady Bakepuize. The family who held under them were the Bentleys, but the last of this family became involved in Babington's Plot (1586) and paid the

ultimate penalty, the modest estate being seized by the Crown in consequence. It was granted, by James I, to Thomas Browne of Shredicote, Staffs., for a consideration of £2,600, and the older part of the present house was apparently built by him soon after 1612-14, replacing its predecessor which had stood within the nearby moat (SK 178380), closer to the deserted medieval village. Mention of a chapel is probably a red herring, the reference being to the medieval one at Alkmonton.

The main, north front, which is also the entrance, is of two storeys with attics and three bays. It is of brick, the Keuper sandstone dressings probably from the Clifton-Norbury area or from Hollington, Staffordshire. The gable is very wide and oddly low, above the brick facade with its very regular quoins marching up to its eaves. There is a visible suggestion that the tile roof has undergone some alteration, and it is not beyond the bounds of possibility that it was originally shaped, with a central feature, as at the (admittedly later) Hellaby Hall, near Rotherham, and, more importantly, Lady Cooke's house in Holborn, as so memorably recorded in 1619 by John Smythson, and attributed by Girouard to Inigo Jones. This drawing records a three-bay, three-storey town house, with the central bay canted through two storeys, topped with a balcony entered from a round arched door which reaches up to the 'Dutch' gable. In sort, Hungry Bentley Hall looks like a provincially developed form of precisely this concept, for the disposition of the elements is arrestingly similar, although the fenestration is simplified from the house at Holborn. At Bentley Hall, the ground floor windows are six-light mullion-and-transom ones, with cross windows above and two-light mullions above that. It is not clear where the entrance to Lady Cooke's house was, but at Hungry Bentley, the ground floor of the central bay has been cut away, and is supported instead on barbarous Doric columns with titanically exaggerated capitals.

The window above, in contrast, is delicately decorated with arched heads, with carved keyblocks, below an entablature, cornice and elaborate strapwork balcony. If there once was a doorway giving access on to the flat top of this canted bay, it has long since been bricked up, and no vestige of its is visible. The fenestration depends from continuous string coursing, a common enough phenomenon locally, but which Girouard suggests derives from the 'stripped down' classical vocabulary introduced into the county by Robert Smythson at Hardwick. It again echoes the detailed cornicing between the floors at Lady Cooke's house. Inside, few original decorative features remain, after centuries as a tenanted farm, and its plan is by no means suggestive, until one realizes that there must have been another wing, presumably on the site of the present west one.

At some time in the two decades or so after the Civil War, the west wing was replaced (perhaps as a result of destruction by fire) and from the road presents an essentially blank wall with pilasters and, in the centre, a large swagger Baroque doorcase with an open scrolly pediment. It bears all the hallmarks of the maverick West Midlands sculptor and architect, Sir William Wilson, and it may well be no coincidence that at precisely this period he was working at Sudbury Hall, nearby.

The estate was sold by the Brownes (who moved to Chesterfield, and trading prosperity) to the Wilmots of Chaddesden in 1749, and under them became a tenanted farm. If the postulations made above are indeed not too wide of the mark, it may be that under their regime the facade was simplified, the stimulus perhaps being some structural instability, or the desire to reduce maintenance costs. The house "had lately been improved" in 1846 – how is difficult to determine – and the estate was sold again to

Lord Vernon in 1860, passing some 18 years later to S. W. Clowes of Norbury Hall (qv), with 1,040 acres, at which time the house was reported as once again 'fast going into decay'. This point, of course, is another at which modifications to the roof might be postulated, but if so it is strange indeed that larger, standard bricks are not in evidence. Woolley, in 1712, described it as having 'a good large park…and seat…an old house and also a very good new brick and stone house, built by the late Thomas Browne.' The park was still noted as being 'large' in the earlier nineteenth century, but Lord Vernon seems to have put it all down to tillage. The tenants under the Wilmots were the Oakden family. It was sold in 1981 by Arthur Barker, a former Littleover butcher, for £75,000, although he had purchased it only in 1975, when it was a farm with 160 acres, for £15,000 more. The 1981 purchaser was Mr McMurty and it is now the home of Mr & Mrs. Michael Copestake.

Pevsner, 161; Woolley 83, p.122; Glover, I 121; Anon (1839) 100; Bagshaw (1846) 313-4; Cox (1877) II 363-4, III 996-7; Bulmer (1895) 273;Girouard (1983) 258; Cooper (1999) 196; BENTLEY/V.1569; BROWNE/Glover II 295; WILMOT of Chaddesden, Bt./BP (1999) II 3037-9; VERNON, B/ibid. II 2884-8; CLOWES of Norbury/BLG (1952) 474.

BIGGIN HOUSE

Biggin-by-Hulland

see BLACKWALL HALL

BLACKWALL HALL

Kirk Ireton   *Private residence*

Blackwall Hall, Kirk Ireton c. 1905.   M. Craven

The early history of this site is quite unclear; at the time of the Domesday Book, it was part of the Royal Manor of Wirksworth, and after the division thereof, the portion that descended to the Hollands included at least that part of Kirk Ireton in which Blackwall lies. Like the Bentleys of Bentley (qv), the Blackwalls of Blackwall emerge upon a freehold estate, from which they plainly took their name, as early as about 1414, certainly by 1506. In all probability, they gained land and freedom as a result of the depredations of the Black Death. At an early date they fixed their seat and farm on the edge of a spectacular slope facing south, with the road almost touching the north wall of their house.

The present edifice contains old fabric, most of it being concentrated in the north range, which looks sixteenth century, and parts may be even older, but frequent renewals have obfuscated its history on the ground. In this part, however, are two and three-light mullioned windows, some with rudimentary mouldings, and it is possible that it was originally L-shaped as the east wall of the newer part looks associated, and contains two early windows, now blocked. The house is built a mixture of ashlar and coursed rubble of local, in parts, red-stained Ashover Grit, with similar dressings and a stone slate roof.

Shortly after 1670 (when tax was assessed at four hearths only), the present west range was added, and that to the east rebuilt to match, giving the south front a twin gabled aspect with recessed centre. Later still, probably around 1800, the central part was filled in to make an entrance hall between the two gabled ranges with a modest timber dog-leg staircase with simple Regency handrail on stick balusters. Above it a landing was created, dropping in level to match those of the older, north, range at the rear, at which point there is a depressed ogiform fanlight as one passes through the thick old rubble wall, with gothicky astragals.

The exterior of this infill ends in a pretty shaped gable, making an odd contrast with the larger straight coped ones of the seventeenth century house. Above the entrance is a segmental headed window, which matches the simple vernacular Venetian ones installed at this time under each gable on both ground and first floor; the attics have segmental headed sashes. Most of the interior was reordered at this time, with early nineteenth century fire surrounds and a pair of elegant niches in the drawing-room. The original staircase, probably of the stone newel type, was also doubtless removed at this time; it may have occupied part of the present large, L-shaped kitchen. There is also a low wing to the NE of indeterminate date and a range of seventeenth century outbuildings.

In 1838, the male line of the Blackwalls failed (although not that of a cadet branch, which still flourishes in Wales as the Blackwall-Moulsdales of Bryndyffryn), and the sole heiress married Revd Charles Evans, vicar of Hulland, the son of a Cornish parson. At this time a further modification to the house included a very 'churchy' porch added to the front door, approached from a pleasing, rather Jacobean, perron. The Evans Blackwalls (Charles Evans' son assumed the surname and arms of Blackwall by Royal Licence in 1871, but his posterity dropped the Evans) are still living at Blackwall to this day, a record amongst the minor gentry of the County only surpassed by the Longsdons of Little Longstone (qv). The family let the house for nearly 20 years from 1959 to 1978, retiring to their other seat, the elegant Biggin House, Hulland, and extensive renovations were undertaken in the 1970s. It is now the seat of Mr & Mrs. John Blackwall.

Biggin House was built following the marriage of John Blackwall (1715-1802) in 1746, or shortly thereafter, (dated rainwater head 1747) on an adjoining estate acquired through marriage with the Mellors of Idridgehay and originally vested in the Ashbourne family. Although old-fashioned for its date, it is an elegantly proportioned five bay two storey ashlar house with a vernacular Tuscan doorcase with giant pilasters of the same Order at the angles supporting a deep Doric frieze, all quite tall and ending abruptly in a pair of end gables with stacks rising through them, the shafts forming a recessed blind arch beneath. There is a later two storey apsidal extension to the west and a Regency service wing to the north. It rather looks as if it was intended to be wider, and to have had a parapet, but all was, for some reason, left unfinished. It has an unexceptional interior and stands in a miniscule park. After the death of Blackwall's son in 1838, it was tenanted as a farm, but became the residence of Miss Evelyn Blackwall in the twentieth century until her death in 1957, when it was sold. It was sold in July 1978 with 13 acres to H. McGhee for £57,000 and is on the market for only the third time in June 2001.

Pevsner 90, 260 ; Lysons, V. 174, 194, 301; Glover, II. 121; Bagshaw (1846) 395; Bulmer (1895) 393-4; Tarn (1971) 46;DLC 5/73; BLACKWALL of Blackwall/BLG (1972) 68-9.

BLADON CASTLE (II)

Newton Solney   *Private residence*

Bladon Castle, Newton Solney, c. 1904.   *M. Craven*

This extraordinary confection forms an eye-catcher atop a ridge on the south-west side of what was once the park of Newton Park House (qv). It began as a modest piece of quasi-medieval brick curtain walling, probably designed by Francisco Bernasconi, who was building the house at Newton Park for the opulent brewer and attorney Abraham Hoskins at the same time: 1792-95; the folly was actually completed in 1795. Hoskins's grandfather was a former Mayor of Stafford with romantic notions about his lineage. The building was, from the first, quite reasonably dubbed 'Hoskin 's Folly'. In 1801-05, Hoskins decided to enlarge it, and to transform it into a dwelling, and to this end he employed Jeffrey Wyatt (later Sir Jeffrey Wyatvllle). He provided the building with a full height canted bay with two mullioned and transomed windows, adding living quarters behind. To this he added a much extended curtain wall, two pairs of octagon towers, an arcade of Tudor windows and a round tower behind the wall. The side of the edifice which boasts a sham gatehouse has a wing added c. 1890 The whole is in brick with dressings of Keuper sandstone from an adjacent outcrop; the roof is slated.

In 1836, Abraham Hoskins, junior, sold Bladon Castle to the Earl of Chesterfield, whose tenant was G. Kettle. He reduced the accommodation c. 1840. About 1860 the tenancy was taken by Repton tanner Francis Holbrooke (qv Repton Grange) who later managed to acquire the freehold. He was succeeded on his death in 1882 by his son Francis William, who died within four months of his father and then by his 17-year-old grandson, Francis George Seymour Holbrooke, who lived there until his death in 1937, and it was sold on his widow's death a year later. It subsequently failed to find a tenant or purchaser, and fell into considerable decay but was eventually sold to a restoring owner in the 1960s, and is now again a residence.

Pevsner, 288; Colvin, 1130; Bagshaw (1846) 257; DAJ XCII (1972) 90; DLC 4/81; Holbrooke deeds, private collection; HOSKINS/DAJ *loc. Cit.*; CHESTERFIELD, E *sub* STANHOPE, E/BP (1956) 2054-7.

BLADON HOUSE (II)

Winshill [Parish of Newton Solney]   *School*

Originally Bladon House was a modest three bay villa in neo-Greek style, built by 1827, when it was the home of Robert Chaplin, architect of the Baths at Ashby-de-la-Zouche, whom one must presume built it for himself. Yet by 1834, he had removed back to Ashby, and it was let to Mrs. Clara Bailey as a 'respectable' school, which it remained until acquired by the Burton brewer John Gretton (died 1869) as a home for his son of the same name. He not only built a church for Winshill in 1869, but immediately set about rebuilding the house, probably using the same architect, Edwin Holmes. The two storey villa was transformed into a seven by three bay double pile house with rusticated pilasters at the angles, top balustrade and a very prominent rough-finished roll-moulded band between the floors, the fenestration, large plate glass sashes in plain surrounds, being set on a thinner but similar band.

The central bay on the west front breaks forward under a tablet between a pair of flat-toped piers above the bold modillion cornice with a prominent portico, also balustraded, supported on two pairs of Doric columns. In front is a stone terrace with a wide flight of steps up to it guarded by a pair of couchant stone lions. The garden front is of only five bays, the central one narrow with an entrance under a plain pediment, flanked by wide tripartite windows, those below also pedimented. The end bays break forward with, again, narrower windows, the parapet being pierced with balustrading over the bays. The SE boasted a filigree arched conservatory set at an angle to catch the south light. Inside, there is a spectacularly wide and deep hall set off by a grand stone and cast iron balustraded staircase, with the remaining rooms equally lavishly fitted out, with much high quality joinery. The whole rather resembles a scaled down version of demolished Wootton Hall, Staffs., not so far away.

Gretton (father of the 1st Lord Gretton) lived there until he acquired Stapleford Park (Leics.) in 1894, when it was occupied first by his sister, Frances, and from the turn of the

The entrance front to Bladon House, c. 1902. *M. Craven*

42

century by his second son, Maj. Frederick Gretton until his death in 1928. After requisitioning in World War Two, it was made available as the HQ of the Staffordshire Yeomanry, but later on was sold as a school, which it remains. When Winshill became part of Staffordshire in 1894, the estate was transferred to Newton Solney parish, and remained largely in Derbyshire.

The garden front to Bladon House, c. 1900.   *M. Craven*

Pevsner (*Staffs*) 88; White, F. *Directory of Staffordshire* (1834) 320; Bagshaw (1846) 231; Information courtesy Sir Charles Wolseley, Bt; CHAPLAIN/Colvin 244; GRETTON, B/BP (1999) I 1222.

BOLSOVER CASTLE (I)

Part ruinous; open to public

Bolsover Castle: the Gallery Range in 1991.   *J. Sharpe*

Viewed at a distance from the west, Bolsover Castle is reminiscent of a German *schloss* guarding the valley and with its small town clustered around its foot. Indeed, Girouard says that Bolsover '... is like nothing else in England'. better still, it has suffered no significant alterations to its original fabric except the unroofing of its major ranges, done in 1750-52 by the Countess of Oxford, the daughter and heiress of the last Duke of Newcastle to hold the estate. Essentially,

the Castle is the most perfect and fantastical expression of the chivalric revival which marked the later part of the age of Elizabeth 1. It has its conceptual roots in the sham castles which were a feature of the pageants of the sixteenth century, as do certain other houses of contemporary date; Repton Park *(qv)* may be another example. Sir Charles Cavendish, for whom John Smythson, the son of the builder of Hardwick, built Bolsover, was responsible for houses and plans of houses which echoed, ever more overtly, the Gothic-romantic chivalric ambience. The link which brought Cavendish together with Smythson was the fact that he was the third and youngest son of Bess of Hardwick and stepson of her last husband, George Talbot, sixth Earl of Shrewsbury, for both of whom Robert Smythson had worked extensively.

Bolsover was once a Royal castle of twelfth century date built on a site originally granted to William Peverel, but which was lost by the latter's heirs by forfeit in 1141. It had a chapel from *c.* 1199-1235. After several changes of ownership, it was in 1553 granted to the same George Talbot who later married Cavendish's mother. Sir Charles at first acquired it by lease from his step-brother, the seventh Earl, later buying the site, and began building in 1612.

His original intention seems to have been to erect a hunting lodge on the site of the twelfth-century keep, the resulting edifice being that known today as the Little Castle, a most apt name. It is a single high rectangular stone block with decidedly medievalizing profile; the result is a typical, if late, example of the Midland High House. There are three storeys over a vaulted basement, the top crenellated, with small turrets at the angles, a large cupola or lantern, a stair tower to match and a forest of interesting chimneys punctuating the leads . The fenestration is largely of mullion and transom cross windows, but the entrance, in a projecting full-height bay, is crowned with a balconied window set in a classical aedicule with rusticated columns supporting a triangular pediment, the whole deriving from a drawing John Smythson made of similar feature on Arundel House in London (on the same visit on which he drew Lady Cooke's, *cf.* Bentley Hall), and another, similar, graces the east front. A wildly romantic and castellated outer courtyard lies before the Little Castle, which thus stands complete in itself. The building is of Permian Magnesian limestone (from Bolsover and Bolsover Moor) and Coal Measure sandstone from below the Wales coal from Shuttlewood, ashlared throughout.

Inside, the ground floor, like the basement, is vaulted in stone, although more elaborately, and the hall is loftier than the parlour, allowing in turn, a higher room on the floor above, a typically Smythsonian arrangement. One modest room on the first floor is also vaulted in local polished limestone: the Marble Closet. On the uppermost floor there is an octagonal lobby beneath the lantern, with bedrooms grouped around it. The master bedroom is below, with two smaller rooms *en suite* known, from their decoration especially the frescoed ceiling, as the Heaven Room and the Elysium Room. The staircase in stone, is built around the central core the house (wherein lower down, are elements of the various offices and service accommodation) and ascends to the stair tower on the leads. There are a number of subsidiary stairs with communicatory functions as well. Girouard considers the plan to have been very strongly

Above left; One of the inspired chimney-pieces in the "Little Castle", Bolsover Castle, 1992.   J. Sharpe
Above right: The entrance to the "Little Castle"; photographed by R. Keane, c. 1890.   Derby Museum

influenced by the builder's father, Robert, who did not die until the house was fairly well advanced, in 1614.

Sir Charles Cavendish also died before completion, in 1617, being succeeded by his elder son, Sir William, who finished the house close to the intentions of his father. The detailing throughout is wonderfully thought out and superbly executed; nowhere is anything truly repeated, yet there is a true unity of concept, probably that of Sir Charles as much as that of his architect. The painted and decorative schemes are superb in their way, with painted and carved panelling of considerable variety, carved pendants and otherdetails. Unfortunately, much was destroyed in the eighteenth and nineteenth centuries, a good deal of panelling and some original furniture being taken by Revd John Hamilton Gray of Carntyne, vicar of Bolsover, in the nineteenth century, when the Little Castle was being used as a vicarage, and installed in his Scottish seat. It mainly came to Charleton, Fife, where it is today, via his heiress.

The greatest glory of the Little Castle, however, is its fireplaces. All are hooded, and convey an impression of Gothic without departing from the vocabulary of the classicism, being derived mainly from Sebastiano Serlio's *Book of Architecture*. Each one is a miniature architectural masterpiece in itself, and each is smothered in a riot of contrasting local polished limestones and alabaster. Their date seems to be c. 1619-21 (from the heraldry and one dated example). It is unknown who carved them, but Derbyshire was not without expertise in carving and polishing its own marbles, and the suggestion that foreign workmen were imported to do the work seems less than likely. One innovation is the placing of one fireplace in the corner of a room, the first use of this practice in England, continued at Chatsworth in

some smaller rooms and a convention still glimmering when Joseph Pickford installed a similar arrangement in butler's pantry at his house in Derby in 1769.

The next stage in building began when Sir William Cavendish, as Lord Lieutenant of Derbyshire from 1628, decided that he needed a Derbyshire seat as well as one in Nottinghamshire (at Welbeck). This took the form of a separate range, canted round at the northern end and built to the south west. It was originally of two storeys and attics over a basement. The southern-most four bays on the west side had straight gables with paired stacks sprouting from the apices. The section nearer to the Little Castle was equipped with large Dutch gables. This range was later rebuilt c. 1635-42 with an extra storey, when the roof to the east lost its parapet in favour of more Dutch gables, and those on the west were also altered. This range contained the hall (later the dining-room) and additional accommodation for guests; its skewed effect was dictated by the curving alignment of the old outer bailey wall, which was followed in building the range, the windows of which are of the cross type under plain attenuated hood moulds. There are two rather bizarre features on this build: the decoration of the masonry with projecting square studs, some initialled and dated (suggesting 1629-30 as the building date), and a row of attached half columns, without capitals or bases, which divide the bays, also applied to the later gallery range. These have been compared to cannon barrels lying in sand, half uncovered by a receding tide, which seems apt; no source for them has yet been identified.

Immediately the Terrace Range was completed, a further range was begun to the south, called the Gallery Range. This continued the earlier work over 11 bays, again divided by

44

'cannon barrel' half columns and of one storey over a much higher basement, containing kitchens and offices. The cross windows are capped by what Girouard calls 'shattered' pediments with knobbly rustication within and extremely vestigial cornices under them, giving them an 'eye brow' effect. They appeared first at Cavendish's house at Slingsby Castle, Yorkshire – also by John Smythson – and reappear at Staveley (qv). The central entrance aedicule is a wildly developed form of the same, rusticated more conventionally, and is reached via a high perron. The range is topped by a battlemented parapet, groups of two crenelles being divided by finials at regular intervals. The inspiration for the detailing here was not Serlio, but Wendel Dietterlin's *Architecture* of 1593, a work full of surreal detail which Smythson was not slow to plunder and evolve into new elements in his own peculiar style.

While his house was growing in size, so was the list of Sir William Cavendish's honours. As early as 1620 he had been made Lord Ogle of Bothal and Viscount Mansfield; eight years later he was made Lord Cavendish of Bolsover (with the distinctly geographically incorrect addition 'in the County of Nottingham'!) and Earl of Newcastle under Lyme, the latter being raised to a Marquessate in 1643. Thus the Terrace and Gallery range can be seen as logical growths to the seat, concomitant with his increasing status. He ended up (in 1664) as Duke of Newcastle, and Bolsover in consequence became a great ducal palace. Newcastle was fiercely loyal to his Sovereign during the Civil War, and lost an immense fortune thereby, parts of Bolsover being dismantled, especially the gates, walls and parts of the buildings themselves. However, his memory lives on through his achievements in equestrianism, and this is summed up in the penultimate addition to his seat, the riding school and stable range, which completed the outer courtyard on the line of the medieval defences. The seventeenth century fountain garden was restored by English Heritage in 1999-2000.

In 1635-42, at the same time as alterations were made to the Terrace range, and after John Smythson's death in 1634, the riding school was built, probably, as Girouard cogently argues, by his son, Huntingdon Smithson (as he spelt his surname). The riding school itself is roughly central, and the highest part of the work, of five bays, with a central rusticated swagger doorcase with open segmental pediment. There are three lower bays to the left (harness room, etc) and

seven to the right (forge and other offices); the whole range is topped by dormers with stubby Dutch gables. George Vertue attributed this work to Samuel Marsh, the post civil war Cavendish architect, but the assertion is contradicted by too many other factors. Yet after the civil war, Marsh did work at Bolsover, beginning in 1663 and more or less coinciding with Newcastle's elevation to the Dukedom. This was the addition of a further suite of state rooms on the east of the gallery range, finished in 1666. The grand entrance, in the mid-European Baroque style which Marsh so indelibly stamped upon his work at Nottingham Castle (also for Newcastle) has the new Duke's coronet proudly displayed above his arms; the rest of the work is uncompromisingly classical, and echoing none of the eclectic motifs of Smythson. A planned chapel, which Smythson ultimately failed to add to his build was not gone ahead with; the family stayed loyal to the Smythsonian side chapel at the parish church, (dated 1618). The gardens, John Smythson's delightful Venus Fountain (after 1628), are listed grade II*. In 1670, the Duke was assessed on 36 hearths, which seems positively modest.

During the Civil War, Bolsover was surrendered by its garrison to Parliamentary forces in 1644, and in 1649 the Council of State ordered its partial demolition. The Marquess went into exile, but his brother, Charles, bought it back in 1652. After the death of the second and last duke, it passed via the heiress to John Holles, Earl of Clare, created Duke of Newcastle on inheriting. His heiress brought it in 1711 to her husband Edward Harley, Earl of Oxford and Mortimer; later she unroofed the majority, probably in 1742-50 to provide materials for the new Oxford wing at Welbeck, the family's Nottinghamshire seat. However, recent research has established that the remainder was used regularly during the eighteenth century as an occasional retreat, and kept furnished and in good repair. From Oxford it passed to William Bentinck, 2nd Duke of Portland, under whose son it was noted as empty by a visitor in 1789. The Little Castle from 1829 became the rectory, but after 1882 fell, once again, empty. In 1883 their Derbyshire estates ran to 5,074 acres. The house was presented to the the Ministry of Works in 1945, and has since undergone much restoration. It is open to the public.

The gallery range in 1634 was the scene of the presentation of *Love's Welcome*, a masque by Ben Johnson, before Charles I and his Queen.

Bolsover Castle in all its glory, with the "Loyall Duke of Newcastle" in the foreground, c. 1636.   *Private Collection*

Pevsner, 92; Colvin, 640, 904; Lysons, V 51-4; Ford (1839) 466-86; Burke (1952) I 204, (1855) II 199; Tipping (1922) I 348; Faulkner (1975) *passim*; Girouard (1983) 205 f.; Worsley (1999) 5-17; CL XV (1903) 98 & XVI (1904) 198-207; DLC 6-7/64; *Journal* of the Georgian Group XI (2001) 169-84; Renishaw Hall muniments, Bolsover Castle drawings, 1630s; TALBOT *sub* SHREWSBURY,E/BP (1999) II 2604-13; CAVENDISH *sub* NEWCASTLE, D/BDEP 109; HOLLES *sub* NEWCASTLE, D/*ibid*. 281; OXFORD & MORTIMER,E/*ibid*. 265; PORTLAND, E/BP (1999) II 2285-90.

BOTHE HALL (II)

Sawley   *Private residence*

Bothe Hall, Sawley, entrance front, 1995.   *M. Craven*

The history of Bothe Hall is closely bound up with that of the church, both going back to a grant of 822 of the estates at Sawley to the See of Lichfield, wherein Aethelwald, Bishop of Lichfield, appointed one of 19 newly created prebendaries to Sawley. Due to the fluidity of the English-Scots border in the eleventh century however, the manor, priest and two churches (one at Sawley, the other at Wilne) were in 1086 held by the Bishop of Chester, rather as Melbourne *(qv)* was held by the Bishop of Carlisle. In 1255, Roger de Weseham, Bishop of Lichfield assigned the churches of Sawley and Wilne *cumearum capellis* to the treasurer of the Cathedral, who was henceforth always ex-officio Prebendary of Sawley.

The Manor thereafter remained attached to the See. Dr Cox was of the opinion that three major residences pertained to the church at Sawley by the fourteenth century: The Bishop's Mansion, the Prebendal residence and the vicarage. The vicarage was instituted in 1266 by Prebend Alan le Breton under the mandate of the Dean and Chapter of Lichfield, and the vicar (Hugh de Scoter) was to have the 'manse outside the churchyard, and sufficient material for building a hall, a chamber and a kitchen to the said manse'. However, it would appear that no appointment was made after 1432, and as it is known that the Prebendaries were in residence at Sawley from 1474 onwards, it would seem that the office of vicar lapsed. The question is whether the prebends took over the vicarage house, or stuck to the Prebendal residence. Bothe Hall, previously the "mansion place" known as Chantry House, takes its name from William Bothe, Bishop of Lichfield and Coventry 1447-52 who granted a lease of three lives to his brother Roger. This lease ended in 1550 with the death of Agnes, Mrs. William Mordaunt of Oakley, Beds., daughter of Roger's grandson of the same name. He was the son of Robert, whose younger brother John was Prebendary of Sawley, as was Roger, junior's, brother Charles. An new lease for 99 years was granted without delay to Geoffrey, son of Edward Edmundson of Sawley. Indeed, his father may have been a tenant of the house as early as 1539. The Edmundsons were there until 1627, when Thomas, Geoffrey's grandson, probably died, and a new lease was granted to Sir Edward Leech of Shipley, who sub-let to the Hill family from whose heiress the Hackers of West Bridgeford inherited the lease; Richard Hacker paid tax on ten hearths in 1670. The were succeeded by Dorothy Fosbrooke, widow of Leonard of Shardlow, who

died in 1727, who was succeeded by a branch of the Holdens of Aston who lived there until 1808, although sometime before 1771 Joseph Parkinson, a local landowner had purchased the freehold. From 1808 the then Prebendary, Revd. Spencer Madan, occupied the house, but in 1865 William Parkinson, a lace manufacturer had it, succeeded by his grandson William Parkinson Bennett, JP, "farmer and landowner", his widow living on there until at least the Second World war. The freehold has changed a number of times since, most recently in August 1998, when it was sold for £300,000, and an extensive restoration followed.

The dating of the two and a half storey three by three bay house is problematical. The house is of ashlar with a slate roof set on a stone eaves cornice. The rear (N) elevation contains some mullioned windows of indeterminate vintage, with varying levels in evidence, two superimposed sashes breaking through the wide plat band. The general appearance of the fabric suggests a mid to late seventeenth century date with a late eighteenth century rebuild. The hearth tax return rather suggests that a somewhat larger building was replaced by the present more modest structure later in the century, retaining some of the earlier fabric. The plinth moulding, the irregular banding and some unexpectedly thick interior walls might suggest its predecessor might have been a tower house of the Tupton Hall type, although even this could have been a rebuild of an earlier structure. Some of the tooled ashlar of which the house is built, is irregularly laid and looks like old work. The central eighteenth-century fluted entrance doorcase and rather unexpected Regency staircase suggests that the house took on its final form c. 1800. It is said that some of the fabric of the house in its former guise is built into the fabric of the Church Farm.

Pevsner, 314; Woolley 24, p. 58-9; Lysons, V 247-8; Cox IV (1879) 378-84, 387-94; Reedman (1979) 15-16, 33; BOTHE/*Reliquary* VII (1866-7) 19, DAJ IX (1887) 36, & BDEP 59-61; FOSBROOKE of Ravenstone/BLG (1952) 895-6; HACKER of East Bridgford/Thoroton (1791) I 299 & n.a, V. Notts. 1663.

BOWDEN HALL (II)

Chapel-en-le-Frith   *Private residence*

Bowden Hall, Chapel-en-le-Frith, c. 1910.   *M. Craven*

The origins of Bowden are somewhat obscure, but by 1477 one Nicholas Bowdon (sic) was of Bowden Hall, and in all probability this family had held their freehold estate there from at least the time of the Black Death. The Bowdons, gradually increasing their estate (*qv* Beighton Fields), lived in what (in 1833) was described as 'an ancient mansion', which they sold to Sir Simon Degge of Derby in 1680. The trustees of the last Degge sold in 1765 to Robert Hibberson, whose descendant James, reversing the trend of over a century when it was tenanted as a farm, was living there himself in 1833, described as a 'farmer and gent'. In 1836, the house – which was probably no more than a traditional H-shaped small manor, having been taxed on eight hearths in 1670 – was sold, with the estate, to John Slack(e), a kinsman of the Slackes of Slack Hall (qv). In 1844, he demolished the old house and built the present pretty seat, which was designed by Richard Lane of Manchester. It is delightfully situated in a bold acclivity and the main front is of five bays, with a central two-storey porch projecting between two straight coped gables, one of two bays, the other of one, with prominent kneelers. The porch has a four-centred arch, with full mouldings, and there is a similar window above with a hood mould. To the left of the entrance is a ground floor canted bay with terrace windows. It is of ashlar throughout of millstone grit sandstone, probably Kinderscout Grit, with similar dressings. A rear Georgian wing with flat roof is of coursed rubble of the same stone. The roof is Welsh slate.

The house remained in the ownership of the Slackes and the Barnes-Slackes until at least World War One, although for most of the time it was tenanted: Joseph Wainwright, a Wormhill quarry owner was there from 1890 until 1900, when he moved into Hargate Hall, which he built for himself; he was followed by Robert Parsons Earwaker, a son of a Manchester merchant, and though the period between the wars to at least 1941 it was occupied by Francis Alexander Lander. Since this time, the house has been somewhat reduced in size, mainly at the rear.

Pevsner, 125; Colvin, 596; Lysons, V 73; Glover II 247; Bagshaw (1846) 464; BOWDON of Bowden/*Reliquary* VII (1866-7) 70, Glover, II. 338, FMG III 1034 & *sub* GREY de RUTHYN,B/BP (1956) 970-2; DEGGE/Le Neve (1873) 231; SLACKE/BLG (1898) II. 1853-4 & Derby Local Studies Library MS 8271, peds. 84, 87.

BRADBOURNE HALL (I)

Private residence

The entrance front of Bradbourne Hall, c. 1931.
Derbyshire Museum Service

In 1086, Bradbourne was one of the numerous holdings of Henry de Ferrers, in succession to one Aelfric. It seems to have come to the family which took their name from the place from Sir Geoffrey de Cauz (qv Brampton Hall) early in the thirteenth century,and their seat was at a moated site in Hulland, called The Hough. In 1548, however, a capital messuage at Bradbourne was held by Michael, third son of Sir Roland Babington of Normanton-by-Derby and he was succeeded by his son, Henry. From them it ultimately came to the Buxtons (later spelt Buckston), of whom, Henry, first of Bradbourne, or his son George (d. 1631) probably built the house.

The fabric undoubtedly seems to contain early work, and the garden front is distinctly higher at the right than the left-hand bay, of three storeys and attics, with low mullioned windows; on the entrance front this feature is disguised by a gabled addition of 1929, a two-storey canted bay with high mullioned and transomed windows. To the left of the higher range on the right of the garden front – the gable of which is *ad hoc* in the extreme, and which links to its neighbour via an awkwardly placed two-light mullioned window which is part of an ancient stair tower – are two gables, both topped by stacks, that to the left being slightly lower than its twin. Below them, the fenestration, mostly two-light mullions, blocked and open, is scattered across the elevation in a seemingly haphazard and random fashion, probably the result of quite two rebuildings. The left bay is lower, and stands at right angles to a yet lower range which extends further with a single-storey bay. From this front, terraces descend to the ha-ha (or dry moat, adapted as such). The entrance front is simpler, more unified. To the right of the modern bay, which is high in contrast, as might well be expected bearing in mind what lies behind it, there is a three-bay, two-storey house, with quoins, quite symmetrical under two linked attic gables, straight, and coped, as are all the others. The plain rectangular entrance has a two-light mullioned window above, and is flanked by windows of three lights on the ground and first floors. Behind the left gable, the high roof of the recent extension rides across the house to its ridge. The high end of the house – perhaps originally a tower – was set back at the NW angle, and the twentieth century part was in essence an effort to fill in the void at the W end of the entrance front and to produce a fairly unified façade matching in width that to the rear.

Nearly all the windows have short, plain hood moulds. It was, like Bowden Hall.(qv) taxed on eight hearths in 1670 It is all built coursed rubble of carboniferous limestone with dressings of millstone grit sandstone; the roofs are of stone slate and slate. The estate was 271 acres in 1829.

The house is said to be on the site of an 'old pagan altar', presumably (if such did indeed exist) Roman. It is said, too, to have been haunted in times gone by and both Catholic and Anglican exorcisms were held, one having been conducted by Revd. R. F. Borough (qv Hulland Hall) at which the chalice was knocked by an unseen agency from his hands! Francis Brett Young's *Cold Harbour* is also said to have been inspired by the house.

At the beginning of the last century, the Buckstons removed to Sutton-on-the-Hill and after a period serving as the vicarage, it was let, Albert Hartshorne, FSA being in residence in 1895. In 1844 a fireplace carved from stone from Standhill, a local quarry giving high quality stone, was installed in the dining room. The 1929 extension was added by the then owner, L. W. Hodson.

Bradbourne Hall, the garden front, 1890s.   M. Craven

Inside is a little vernacular plaster-work and a 'good simple Jacobean staircase'. It was sold in 1965 and in 1984 it was the home of Mr & Mrs. Edward Harrison.

Pevsner 104; Woolley, 142, p.209; Lysons, V 59; Bagshaw (1846) 357; Bulmer (1895) 330; DA 16/4/1965; BABINGTON/V. 1569; BUXTON/Glover, II 155-6; BUCKSTONE of Bradbourne/BLG (1965) 94.

BRADSHAW HALL (II)

Chapel-en-le-Frith   *Private residence*

Bradshaw Hall, Chapel-en-le-Frith c. 1903.   M. Craven

Originally, Bradshaw Hall was an L-shaped stone built gabled manor house of sixteenth century date. It has – or had – mullioned and transomed windows without hood moulds, straight coped gables, oak panelling and an early newel staircase. In about 1619, the owner, Francis Bradshaw – in the event the last of his family to live there – added a matching wing to make a U-shaped house, enclosed within a wall and built an impressive – almost triumphal – arch rather in the mould of that at Highlow Hall *(qv)* through it, which is the only aspect of the house in which the language of Renaissance classicism manifests itself. It is dated 1620, the house, 1619. Later in the century, the space between the projecting gables was infilled with a two-bay wide gabled feature, which preserved the recession of the house's centre. In 1635, however, Francis Bradshaw died, and his posterity, having inherited an estate at Eyam from the Staffords, removed there and built Bradshaw Hall there *(qv)*, now a decaying ruin. Thereafter it was let, the tenant in 1670, Edward Ash, paying tax on 12 hearths which rather suggests that the house had by then reached its greatest extent. It is built of millstone grit sandstone, probably Roaches Grit (an Ashover Grit) from an adjacent outcrop, in coursed rubble; the roof is stone slate.

In the mid eighteenth century the estate passed via the Jennens and Galliards to the Bowleses and it is said that 1753 was the date of the demolition of the right gable – probably part of the earliest phase of the house - and its replacement with a single-storey extension containing a kitchen. The estate was a mere 300 acres in 1881 when C. E. B. Bowles restored the house (describing it in the Archaeological Society's journal of 1903), but he never lived there, the tenants being the Lomas family, who remained there until beyond 1925. It was, however, the subject of a disastrous 'restoration' in the early 1960s which stands as an object lesson in how not to undertake such a demanding task, and a shocking indictment of the planning policies of the Peak Park Joint Planning Board at that time – and for some time afterwards, it has to be said.

The Bradshaws were at Bradshaw by the late twelfth century, and their first seat there was built by John de Bradshaw between 1215 and 1222; it was certainly there by 1225, presumably upon roughly the same site as the present edifice. The Lancashire Bradshaws, equipped by Sir Bernard Burke in the nineteenth century with a long and spurious pedigree, were thought by C.E.B.Bowles to have actually been cadets of the branch; more plausibly, there were two families which took two similar place names as their own.

Pevsner 104; Lysons, V 73; Glover II 248; Bagshaw (1846) 464; Bulmer (1895) 146; *Reliquary* II (1861-2) 145-50; DAJ XXIV (1902) 1 f.; BRADSHAW/DAJ XXV (1903) 1f. & *sub* BRADSHAW-ISHERWOOD of Marple/BLG (1952) 1362; BOWLES of Abney & Bradshaw/*ibid.*(1894) I 203.

BRADSHAW HALL

Eyam   *Fragmentary ruin*

Parking one's car in the centre-of-village car park at Eyam, it is impossible not to notice the ruined remnant of a stone house wall complete with multi-light mullioned and transomed window, weed-grown and forlorn. This is, however, all that remains of one of the two important seats in the village, Bradshaw Hall.

One of the moieties into which the manor of Eyam was divided on the death of Humphrey Stafford in the sixteenth century was that bestowed upon Anne, the co-heiress who married Francis Bradshaw, son of the builder of Bradshaw Hall, Chapel-en-le-Frith (qv) in 1565.His mother-in-law wrote in her will (dated 5/6/1560) that her executors were to 'Dystrybute and equally devyde...[the estate] to my sayd children'. Her portion included lands at Bretton and Foolow with messuages and lands at Eyam 'including ye auncient mannor house'. This implies that Bradshaw Hall represented a much more ancient seat, that of the Staffords, into which

The remains of Bradshaw Hall, Eyam in 1983.   *M. Craven*

Bradshaw moved, and to which, ultimately – perhaps more by common usage than vain intention – his name came to pertain.

In 1635, his descendant, George Bradshaw, set about building himself a new, grander and more modern seat, but work was suspended on the onset of the Civil War, during the course of which, in 1646, he died. It may still have lain unfinished (for want of adult heirs male) when the family fled to Brampton from the village on the outbreak there of plague in autumn 1665. It was never re-occupied as a seat, the habitable portion (taxed on 7 hearths in 1670) being let to tenants as a farm and thereafter as a tenement wherein dwelt 'three or four families'. But before the end of the eighteenth century it was converted into a barn, the majority of it being abandoned completely, falling rapidly into desuetude. There was still a carved armorial on the south wall in 1859. The Smiths of Ecclefechan, the Bradshaw family's ultimate heirs, disposed of the freehold to the Wrights in 1883. Much of what remained in the twentieth century collapsed in 1962.

Peter Furness, writing in 1862, said of it:... '*it was intended to be hung with tapestry, which came to the place but was never put up, and that an old man who was born in this part of the hall informed him that when a child he saw the tapestry lie in a heap in a corner of the chamber where it rotted away.*' One suspects that what was seen was the unusable portion of a larger quantity of tapestry, the better part of which was rescued by one of the Wrights of Eyam Hall, very close by (qv) and incorporated it into his house as best he could – hence the puzzling but endearing chaos which greets one's eyes when entering the tapestry room there to this day. Apparently there were also fowls roosting under collapsing Jacobean chairs.

Pevsner, 214; Lysons, V 163; Wood (1859) 177-8; *Reliquary* II (1861-2); DAJ XVI (1894) 138-9; BRADSHAW/ V.1662; SMITH of Ecclefechan/BLG (1875) II 276.

BRAILSFORD HALL (II)

Private Residence

This surprisingly large brick house of 1902 has an irregular, two storey front, with four asymmetrical coped gables, and a seven bay wing. The windows are mullioned and transomed, and the Jacobean effect just about comes off; the dressings are of Keuper Sandstone from an adjacent outcrop. The Brailsford family (descendants of one of only two Derbyshire sub-tenants of non-Norman origin in 1086) built

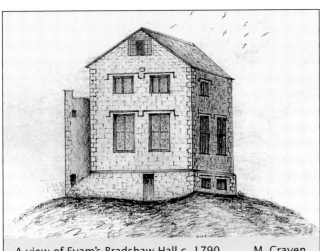
A view of Eyam's Bradshaw Hall c. 1790.   M. Craven

Brailsford Hall, 2001   M. Titterton

when the Derby suburb of Oakwood was being built in the early 1980s with some Roman remains beneath.

The other branch of the de Dunes held Upper Hall, now Old Hall, until c. 1264, when Joan, daughter and heiress of Hugh, son of Robert de Dune, brought it to Henry son of Ralph de Curzon – undoubtedly a kinsman of those of Kedleston, but his precise relationship to them is unknown. By 1392, Cecily, heiress of Thomas de Curzon married Sir William Dethick and two centuries later it passed from the Dethicks to Sir John Harpur, the last man to use it as a seat. Until very recently, however, it remained in the Harpur-Crewe family, but after having been abanboned before the Civil War, it became the rectory, one of the incumbents being Revd John Heiron, the non-conformist divine who was ejected from the living in 1662. After that it became a hunting lodge, then a farm, and a school. In the later eighteenth century, after some time as the village shop, the pathetic remnant became an inn, even being the venue for auctions, as in 1815, the advertisements for which confirm that it was known as the 'Old Hall Inn'. In 1833 Glover reported: 'Plenty of original furniture remaining... the ivy creeps up the walls and hangs luxuriantly around the ruined mansion'. The bracket of the inn sign is still visible in a photograph taken by the Derby photographer Richard Keene in 1859. Woolley wrote of it that it was an 'Old decayed building' and there is no clue in the hearth tax returns as to its size in the later seventeenth century.

the first hall, the site of which was marked by a moat east of the rectory, which was ploughed out some time before 1949. After the manor passed via Basset of Cheadle to the Shirleys in the fifteenth century, this house must have been allowed to decay.

In 1771 William Cox, an up-and-coming lead merchant, bought part of the Brailsford estate from 5th Earl Ferrers, to whom his father had been tutor, and proceeded to adapt a rather neglected farm house as a seat. His son rebuilt it c. 1810, possibly with the help of Richard Leaper of Derby, in a thoroughgoing Regency style: two storeys, plain parapet hiding the irregular hipped roof of the farmhouse, five bays (those to the left somewhat lower and all with cast iron jalousies) and an off-centre Tuscan portico. The Cox family sold it to the Strutts of Bridge Hill House, who built the present house, probably to the designs of Maurice Hunter of Hunter & Woodhouse of Belper in the late nineteenth century. It was let from 1902 to Col. H. C. Holland, from 1897 Chief Constable of Derbyshire. It was later seriously damaged in a fire and was rebuilt between the wars with an extra gable and a parapet on the entrance front. Having re-occupied it, the executors of Col. G. A. Strutt sold it in May 1936 to Cecil Dalton, by whose son R. G. Dalton it was sold in 1980 to Charles Clowes, a local property developer.

Pevsner 105; Lysons, V 65; Glover, 11.138; DET 16/11/2000; COX/Glover II 163; STRUTT of Belper/BLG (1952) 2441; HOLLAND/Kelly (1911) 362.

BREADSALL OLD HALL (II*)

Private residence

The manor of Breadsall was held from Henry de Ferrers in 1086 by one Robert in succession to Siward. Robert was the ancestor of the family of de Dune of Breadsall, and the manor was divided between two branches of the family c. 1200. One branch held the manor or moiety of Breadsall Nether Hall, which was practically a separate village. By 1269 this was held by Henry de Chaddesden, passing shortly afterwards to first Lord Ferrers of Groby, who probably abandoned the seat, and the village appears to have followed, perhaps as a result of the Black Death. Vestiges appeared

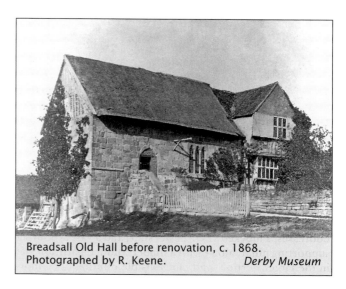
Breadsall Old Hall before renovation, c. 1868.
Photographed by R. Keene.   *Derby Museum*

At first sight, the present building, thoroughly re-stored in 1877, when it again became a farmhouse, consists of a stone south front with a three light mullioned window with trefoil heads cut from one slab of stone at the left end over an undercroft, and a gabled and attenuated cross-wing at the east end, which is half-timbered and thoroughly suburban in appearance. The west end is a coped straight gable, with a four-centred arched entrance breaking through a string course and above it is a four-light window matching that of the south front. The entrance is approached up a flight of stone steps. The stone work – tooled ashlar throughout of Millstone Grit sandstone, probably Ashover Grit from an adjacent outcrop – appears uniformly recent, and the roof

Breadsall Priory as it was originally built. From an engraving of c. 1760.

M. Craven

is tiled. Yet it was not always thus.

Keene's photograph shows the south range longer, with the window distinctly nearer the right and the self same four centred arch we now see rebuilt in the west end to its left. The thatched roof was supported on old stone walls, and the west gable had timber studding above eaves height. The east gable was jettied, and the first floor oversailed rising from a jetty in a cove to a simple light mullioned and transomed window in the lowish straight gable, infilled with brick above the window; the rest is timber-framed, and the west-offset ground floor window, a timber ten-light mullioned and transomed one carried on brackets, still survives. The roof, at this time, was tiled over the gabled cross-wing. The east front of the present house is of old stone, with a chimney flue and a small high single-light window, and traces of the same string course visible on the south front. There is also a two centred relieving arch to accommodate a first floor doorway, long since blocked; another door occurs lower, and the face ends in a brick section with outbuildings of indeterminate date beyond.

The north side of the gabled part is brick with modern fenestration, but old stone reappears on this side of the main range, and there are traces of former chimneys. A blocked window and door are visible and a relatively modern sash obtrudes. Inside, the undercroft is a twin celled affair, garnished with a vast stone trough, which Mrs. Barbara Hutton has suggested might have been for pig curing, and there are two chamfered four-centred arched stone doorcases, a blocked stone newel stair, and a vast cylindrical supporting pillar, along with a timber studded partition wall in the larger portion, and much visible plinth-work. Above is an open hall, the inside of the west wall being studded in timber with two blocked round headed doorways, with a later door between them, presumably the traces of the screens passage. The former fireplace is against the north wall. The ornate window in the south front has straight reveals with chamfered arrises terminating in pyramid stops, and the east wall is also studded.

Mrs. Hutton has concluded that what remained in c. 1859 was a complete secondary dwelling, with hall, solar crosswing and service end built against the west wall of an earlier, probably larger, house itself most likely taken down by the Harpurs when they abandoned the seat and turned it into a rectory, or possibly when it later became a pub. The bulk of the remaining fabric must be of earlier

fourteenth century date, although the timber cross-wing, Mrs. Hutton thinks, is somewhat later, perhaps built in the mid-sixteenth century. Most likely it was rebuilt c. 1580 when the Harpurs inherited it. The whole edifice, plainly recased in 1877, poses many problems of interpretation and more research is required. An inventory or two might shed more light on the available accommodation in the crucial periods of the sixteenth and seventeenth centuries.

Nothing is known concerning the extent of the park or estate at present. Eventually, the house was given to the parish, and was administered by the PCC as a village hall meeting room, with the cross wing rented out as a residence, but it was sold for restoration in February 1998. A substantial late Regency house in the village, now called the Manor, was built for a Harpur incumbent by Thomas Cooper of Derby c. 1836 as a rectory, and is now the seat of Sir Richard and Lady Morris.

Pevsner, 108; Woolley 52, p.86; Glover, II 156; Bagshaw (1846) 280; Bulmer (1895) 712-3; Hutton, B. *Breadsall Old Hall* DBR (1991) *passim;* Sheppard (1996) 213 pl. 212; DM 1/6/1815; DUNE /Glover, II 179; DETHICK /V. 1611 & DAJ VI (1884) 1 f.; HARPUR/Glover II 217 & *sub* HARPUR-CREWE,Bt/BP (1923) 618-9

BREADSALL PRIORY (II)

Hotel

In the years between 1255 and 1266 a priory of Augustinian canons was founded in Breadsall by either Richard de Curzon or his son, Sir Robert, of Breadsall Upper Hall *(qv)*.It was never a large affair, and was in consequence dissolved in 1536 by Henry VIII, from whom it was leased by one Lawrence Holland of Belper, who farmed there and built a farmhouse on the site. In 1552 the Crown granted it to the Duke of Suffolk, by whom it was sold immediately to Thomas Babington of Dethick. He sold it in 1553 to Thomas Hutchinson and by 1573 it was the property of John Leeke of Hasland. He sold it fairly soon after that to Sir John Bentley, who erected the house. Bentley built a very tall E-shaped house, probably before the end of the sixteenth century, with straight coped gables six- light mullioned and transomed windows throughout, except over the central entrance , above which a large panel of his arms necessitated an attenuated light. It was in ashlar throughout, of millstone grit sandstone. There was a string course between the first and second floors, and the entrance front faced east. Miraculously, and in spite of all later accretions, the bulk of Bentley's fabric survives, albeit much hidden. In Blore's engraving of 1791, a large octagonal dovecote is visible to the north, made up of four timber stages crowned with a lantern. Interestingly, a dovecote is mentioned at the priory as early as 1291, and this strange erection may well have been a pre-Reformation successor, but it had vanished by 1802. There was a lower two-storey range to the west and a large complex of outbuildings beyond. A thirteenth century wall in coarse sandstone, most likely Ashover Grit from an adjacent outcrop, and an arch were found in the basement and survive, and other remains were excavated by

Breadsall Priory in 1991.   M. Craven

Sir Francis Sacheverell Darwin in the 1840s beneath the floor of the drawing-room to the right of the entrance hall.

On Bentley's death in 1622, the house passed via his heiress to Sir Gervase Cutler, and from him, similarly to Sir Edward Mosley of Ancoats, 1st Bt (of the first creation), from whom it descended to Sir John Bland of Kippax, Yorkshire. He sold it in 1702 for £1,675 to Thomas Leacroft of Wirksworth who passed it on to one of his partners in the lead smelting business, Andrew Greensmith of Steeple Grange. On the extinction of his line in 1788, it was again sold, to Mrs. Hannah Greensmith Beard of Lincoln widow of the heiress's son, and in 1799 it was purchased for £3,500 by Erasmus Darwin, eldest son of the eminent Lunar Society luminary, whose tragic death by suicide followed within eighteen months. His father thereupon moved in from his house at 3, Full Street, Derby, dying within a month of so doing. The locals to this day claim that the frequent changes of ownership and failures of male heirs is due to Bentley having 'disturbed the bones of the monks', but Glover's story of the finding of the stone sarcophagi of these long dead worthies was disproved to Dr Cox's satisfaction in the 1870s by Miss V.H.Darwin, who had been responsible for the sale of the estate (with 122 acres) on the death of her father, Sir Francis Sacheverell Darwin (eldest son of Dr. Darwin's second marriage) in 1859. The purchaser was Francis Morley, a Nottinghamshire hosier who paid £13,000. From him it passed in 1884 to Henry J. Wood and thence to R. R. Rothwell in 1892. He installed electric light and a large three manual hydraulic organ built by Alfred Noble, removed in 1975 and later broken up. In 1897 the estate was sold for £12,000 to Sir Alfred Seale Haslam, an ex-Mayor of Derby knighted by Queen Victoria on the platform of Derby station when she came to the town to lay the foundation stone of Royal Infirmary in 1891; he was a son of the bellfounder, William Haslam who had revived

(with another son, Edwin) the art of wrought-iron smithing from the1850s. The Haslams extended the estate to 828 acres. On the death of Eric Haslam, Sir Alfred's surviving son, in 1967, house and estate were purchased by Charles Hapur-Crewe of Calke in order to consolidate the Harpur holdings in Breadsall, but he failed to find a role for the house which was eventually in 1974 let to Mr David Cox, to be converted into an hotel which opened in 1976; a golf course followed in 1977. On Charles Harpur-Crewe's death in 1982, Cox purchased the freehold. In 1988 it was again sold, to Whitbreads, who later re-named it the Marriott Breadsall Priory hotel, adding a lamentably gimcrack 60 bedroom extension and over-restoring the original interiors in 1989-90, quite ruining its ambience.

Under the Greensmiths, the only alteration seems to have been to infill, at ground floor level only, the space between the south gable and the central one, giving the resulting room an unsightly lean-to roof and door in the northernmost bay, but containing a new entrance, with a range projecting yet further in front of the north gable. These additions had sashed windows under rusticated stone lintels, quoins and a band between the floors. A view of 1857 also reveals that the south gable was, in effect, a gabled tower, like that at Cutthorpe Old Hall (qv) with, beyond, a single wide gable facing south and set back, the coping running from its apex horizontally to the top of the tower which, from the disposition of its fenestration, plainly held the staircase. The wide south gable had two large 18-light mullioned and transomed windows on the ground and first floors.

Sir Francis Darwin, in 1836, also built a chapel at the lodge gate, which was served by the rector of Breadsall as required, but this had already fallen out of use in 1846 and had been mostly demolished by 1880. The rockery in the grounds, laid out by Darwin and Joseph Heathcote his gardener, was composed of pieces of gothic tracery and other architectural fragments of the Priory, excavated by Sir Francis Darwin, who was a keen antiquary. These were confusingly joined by fragments of the crocketed pinnacles of All Saints', Derby, which he acquired when that church was undergoing renovation. Items of this rockery, which was cleared away 1909 when T. H. Mawson laid out new pleasure grounds and a rose garden, still lurk in forgotten corners of the site. Sir Francis Darwin had also excavated in order to find a secret passage, said to have run 1.5 miles south to the church and – even less credibly – a similar distance north to Horsley Castle; needless to say, he was successful in disproving its existence.

In 1860-1, Francis Morley rebuilt the house, to the designs of Robert Scrivener of Hanley, Staffordshire, who rebuilt Darwin's extensions in a fairly thorough-going gothic, the north-east projection becoming a dining-room, and the central part a new entrance hall, into which Haslam later installed a large neo-Gothic door which his firm had made for the 1851 exhibition; its wrought-iron fittings are undoubtedly the work of his brother Edwin. The fenestration is mainly mullioned and transomed, with trefoil headed lights, although some are plain, with short hood moulds. Behind the south gable, however, in 1861, Scrivener built a large square three-storey tower, with bartizans at the angles linked by crenellation, and a tall octagonal stair tower on top, with cross arrow slits, machicolations and further battlements, although the latter have since been removed. On the south range, the large gabled return was replaced by a Victorian replica, with a large ornate ground floor canted bay with another beyond containing a billiard room fronted by a Gothic loggia. All this work was in millstone grit, in this case Rough Rock from Horsley Castle, Coxbench or Morley Moor quarries; the roof is slate. The grounds were re-landscaped by William Barron & Son at a cost of £4,000.

After Haslam took over, he too decided to enlarge the house, adding a two-storey wide bay over a loggia on the south front behind the gable, containing the very Edwardian Wedgwood Room and an oak panelled smoking room beyond it. There is a matching wide gable beyond that, with a two storey square bay over a basement. This included a fine billiard room in Moorish style, and the architect may well have been Percy Heylin Currey of Derby c. 1900-04, who shortly afterwards wrote the house up for the Archaeological Society's *Journal*. All the surviving pre-Reformation work was carefully exposed and conserved. Most of the interior, however, is unexceptional, although of good quality. The hall, flagged in Hoptonwood until recent changes, has a two-arch Gothic screen with deep-cut foliated capitals, leading to a good oak stair. The plan is a trifle untidy, due to the complex evolution of this most interesting house. Today, new mahogany doors, simulated eighteenth century panelling, fireplaces and overdoors, give the interior a slightly contrived atmosphere.

Scrivener's Jacobethan stable court now houses a golf club and, added to its south side, is a country club, full of deal furniture, bars and jacuzzis. The general effect is rather sad.

Pevsner, 108; Woolley 52, p.87; Lysons, V 66-8; Glover, II 15203; Bagshaw (1846) 280; Cox III (1877) 67-78; Bulmer (1895) 712; Redman (1998) passim; King-Hele (1999) 325-6, 330, 341; DM 14/1/1802, 28/3/1860; *Building News* 1/11/1861; DAJ XXVII (1905) 127-37, 138-49; DLC 1/38, 1 & 2/67; BENTLEY/V.1611; CUTLER/V. Gloucs. 1682; MOSLEY, Bt. *sub* RAVENSDALE, B./BP (1999) II 2362-66; BLAND, Bt./BDEB 65-6; GREENSMITH/FMG III 1214; DARWIN of Elston/BLG (1965) 187; ROTHWELL/*ibid.* (1952) 2204; HASLAM/FD (1905) 640 & (1929) 1897.

BRETBY PARK (II)

Divided as residences

At the time of the Domesday Book Bretby was held by the King as a berewick of his manor of Newton Solney; previously, it had been part of the extensive holdings of Algar, Earl of Mercia. It had come, by the end of the thirteenth century to the Segraves, and John de Segrave had a license to crenellate in March 1301. Little is known of the resulting Castle, although a moat on the corner of Bretby Lane and Bretby Road, Bretby (SK 293231) marks the site. Bretby Castle passed to the Berkeleys via the Mowbray Dukes of Norfolk, and was last lived in by John Mee, the agent to the Berkeley estate in the later sixteenth century, who later took a lease of it. Another moat at SK 278227 may mark an even earlier seat.

Thereafter it was purchased by the Stanhopes of Shelford, Nottinghamshire, and Philip, 1st Lord Stanhope (later Earl of Chesterfield) obtained Royal consent in 1610 to enclose a park. The house he proceeded to erect some years later was spectacular in the extreme. The main range, only one room deep, faced south, of two storeys and attics, and nine bays, the centre ones being part of a sumptuous classical centrepiece which broke forward under a lanterned tower. At either end, a pair of long ranges enclosed a *cour d'honneur* each ending in a giant segmental pediment. There was a profusion of ornamental stacks, and shaped attic dormer gables, and the whole was isolated by a screen of 'massy iron gates', a feature repeated across the ride which divided the site, where a second courtyard with offices on either side provided the termination of the formal drive to the house from the village. At the east end of the main range was a later (1696) chapel, of which, 'The architecture was Grecian, or of the Ionic Order, very light and handsome. Within was a rich lining of cedar, the altar piece of Italian marble, was remarkably fine; there was also an organ in the gallery; and at the east of the chapel stood a very large and venerable cedar.' This was the description printed in *The Topographer* in 1790; what the author did not know was that the gardeners' bill for the tree survived, and that it had been planted in February 1677, making it one of the earliest in England. It was finally felled in February 1953, for some time before having had its branches supported by chains attached to the trunk.

The architect for this magnificent palace was said to have been Inigo Jones, but proof for this is lacking; certainly it was some one highly competent and indeed perhaps from the continent, probably France. It cannot be without significance that when, in 1670, Lord Chesterfield wanted to make alterations, he chose the Frenchman Louis Le Vau. At that time the house was assessed for tax on a colossal 68 hearths. Within, all we know is that there was a hall and large staircase, painted and hung with many excellent paintings. The rooms were, for the most part, 'magnificent, with painted ceilings (by whom?), rich tapestry and noble pictures.' The fenestration was probably of casemented cross type, for in 1698 Celia Fiennes wrote: 'None of the windows are sashes which in my opinion is the only thing it wants to render it a complete building.' The house was completed by 1639 when a masque by Sir Aston Cokayne was given; it was said to have been constructed from the materials of the Castle, but Woolley saw the ruins standing in 1712, so the story is unlikely to be literally true.

As important as the house, however, were the formal gardens, parterres, water features – which included a water clock and arcade not to mention an hydraulic organ which played *Lillibulero* - and park. These gardens were by another

Bretby Hall as replaced by Sir Jeffrey Wyatville; the photograph was taken by R.Keene, c. 1861.　　　*M. Craven*

Frenchman, M. Grillet, and are drawn in the famous view by Kip. Woolley waxed lyrical about them too: 'The very large park is stored with several sorts of deer and exotic beasts... but the gardens, fountains, labyrinths, grooves (sic) green houses, grottoes, aviaries, but more especially the carpet walk and situation of the orange trees, waterworks before the summerhouse which is built of marble over which is written – MEIOR SOLO QUAM IN ALTRO ACCOMPAGNECTO – better alone than in all company.' The water works, which included canal, lakes (still extant) and spectacular fountain constructed in 1684-1702 are also the work of Grillet, who was working at Chatsworth at about the same time. Bretby supplanted Shelford as the Stanhope's chief seat after the Civil War, during which the latter was destroyed, and even the former was taken by Sir John Gell in December 1643 and looted. Nevertheless, from the middle of the eighteenth century, it was little used, and the Lord Chesterfield of the day was persuaded, by a mendacious steward, who wished to make a killing from the materials, that it was much decayed and should be demolished. This ghastly act of vandalism began in 1777, and was completed in 1781, during which time the inherent strength of the fabric became apparent, to the discomfiture of the instigator of the vandalism. Indeed, within 36 years, it was felt the house should be replaced and James Wyatt was commissioned to prepare designs in 1812-13. These were freely adapted by Sir Jeffery Wyatville, although it would appear that his contribution was confined to the east front, and most of the building was adapted from Wyatt's plans and construction directed by the Earl's local architect, William Martin, father in-law of H I Stevens, who was also articled to him, and trained by Wyatville. Nevertheless, the house was left unfinished on the Earl's death in 1815.

Taken with a Jacobean range, south-east of the previous house, and probably a surviving office range, the building was to form a courtyard. It is built of Keuper sandstone from Burton. The main front is to the east, of nine bays, the central three forming a castellated projection with angle turrets, and with very massive drum towers at the angles, all over three

storeys, except the latter feature, which had one extra; most of the ashlar work is oddly, if strikingly, tooled. A single bay marked the return on either end, that on the north being plain, of three storeys, and that on the south being a one-bay version of the central projection, with a straight parapetted facade and crenellations running all along behind. The north front, which is undoubtedly Martin's work, is 14 bays, and of three lower storeys , three groups of four bays being broken up by one bay square turrets with quatrefoil windows above the parapet string course, and battlemented throughout, but with plain rectangular sashed fenestration with brusque hood moulds, as on the east front. The south front was intended to be 11 bays, including the turreted return bay of the east front, with a similarly embellished carriage entrance with a shallow oriel above dividing two groups of four bays, of two storeys this time, and with paired lancet windows with quatrefoils in the spandrels; the entrance projection had an extra story.

However, this had proceeded only as far as the entrance by 1815, and it was terminated by a screen wall which conceals the earlier building. The space between the south and west wings was intended to be filled with a Chapel, but, again, this was never built, and the west is marked off by the seventeenth century range, much altered, and offices, presumably by Martin, although various other Wyatts worked here, latterly Thomas Henry Wyatt, who made alterations before 1850.

Inside, the decoration is almost entirely classical, the only really interesting rooms being the music room in the south east tower and the circular saloon with chimney pieces in statuary marble by Richard Westmacott. Furniture was supplied in 1816-19 by Thomas Tatham of Mount Street. The interiors were unfinished in 1828, and Samuel Beazley's sumptuous Gothic *Lady Chesterfield's Boudoir,* the design for which was exhibited as late as 1838, was probably never built; there is no sign of it now. He probably designed it somewhat earlier for part of the finished south wing. It is much closer to the eighteenth century in feeling than to the more scholarly form of gothic one might expect in 1838, and is very rococo being 'all over cosmetic of cusped panelling'.

The park was re-landscaped in a similarly picturesque style, by whom is not clear, and the competent William Martin from 1805-15 built a series of agreeable estate buildings, of which his home farm was the crowning achievement. This consisted of three linked courtyards, elaborate marble dairy, hen and pheasant rearers and other up-to-the-minute refinements, and was considered sufficiently remarkable to be included in Farey's *Agriculture and Minerals of Derbyshire* a year or two later, from whence the article was lifted by Stephen Glover in 1831. Most of this was left to decay after World War Two, and was cleared in 1960-67. Disraeli, a frequent visitor said of the products of the dairy (part of which survives, built into a dwelling), when writing to Lady Chesterfield 1878. 'You have fed me to the last with unrivalled delicacies, not the least of which was the produce of your unrivalled dairy. I will back Bretby butter against Paris.' Four years earlier, on 31 March 1871, he had written: 'I long to see the farm again with its room full of cheeses'.

The sixth Earl, who succeeded as a child in 1815, later laid out a racecourse in the park, but in the mid-nineteenth century the house and park passed via an heiress to the Earl of Carnarvon. Having a vast seat at Highclere already, the house was left by the Earl in occupation of the widowed Lady Chesterfield, and in 1915 the house and park were sold to J.D. Wragg, MP, a local businessman, the park extending to 1,220 acres. Lady Chesterfield had retained the estate which, however, had been reduced from 50,207 to 3,942 acres by 1910 when much of what remained was sold as freehold farms and building land. Wragg was sufficiently well-heeled to undertake some improvements, and called in William Barron & Son in 1924 to re-landscape the gardens, but he must have over-reached himself, for it was sold a year later, in 1925, to Derbyshire County Council to become a hospital and it was opened as a childrens' TB hospital in 1926. Much of the park was sold to J.C. Sanders of Stenson and became farmland. The hospital was later turned over to the treatment of orthopedics and taken over in 1954 by the Regional Hospital Board and was summarily closed in 1997. It was then purchased by a development company and converted into apartments, which went on sale (work then not being finished) in June 2000, a development marred by tasteless 'enabling development' on the east side of the house.

It has been long suspected that the parkland concealed much of Grillet's exciting seventeenth century work. And local and national pressure was brought to bear in the planning process which followed the sale of the hospital, resulting in an English Heritage sponsored archaeological investigations which triumphantly bore out the prognostications and it was duly added to the National Register of Parks & Gardens in 1998.

Further continuity with the past remains in the completion in 1989 of a new seat called Bretby Park, by Richard Perkins, the son of one of Sir Herbert Wragg's daughters by her first marriage. To him descended a portion of the original estate as purchased by Sir Herbert's father, and he set about adding to his property to rebuild a small estate. Starting in 1985 he began to rebuild the old so-called Dower House, a strange castellated two-storey, three-bay house, with a three-storey, tower-like projecting central bay entered through a four-centred arch, and formerly mullioned windows; it looked seventeenth century, but was probably one of William Martin's confections.

It was utterly transformed under the inspired hand of Digby Harris. Using the shell of the old house, and turning it into a five-bay centrepiece with a central Palladian entrance with attic *oeuil-de-boeuf,* and Gibbs surround to the doorcase, higher cross-wings were added at either end, with hipped roofs. On the garden front these have open pedimented breakfronts containing each Venetian over a Wyatt window, and there are quoins at the angles. The entrance front is similar but plainer; the cross wings have two plain bays, with the first floor windows much deeper than those on the ground floor, in contrast to the centre section which, on this side, has round headed ground floor windows with a stone band at impost height. Of pale pink brick laid to Flemish bond, the house has stone dressings mainly of Macclesfield gritstone, with limited use of *ersatz* substitutes where such could be done economically yet without detriment to the whole. The interior is surprisingly ornate for the later twentieth century, with good stucco cornicing, fireplaces and a Tuscan screen in the low ceilinged hall. The staircase, an exceptionally pleasing cantilevered one in stone, has a very striking wrought-iron rail designed by the architect and made by Paul Dennis of Defynnog, Breckonshire, is lit by a curved Venetian window on the mezzanine, with a blank balustrade below it. The entire interior is subtly planned and executed with a satisfying assuredness. Nor does it strike one as pastiche, but is in the best tradition of neo-Classical revival.

Pevsner , 109; Colvin, 116, 1131; Woolley 112, p.149; Kip (1715) I pl. XXVI; Lysons V 241; Glover, II 158-162; Burke II (1855) 103; Cox (1877) III 442; Wain (1964) *passim;* Hill & Cornforth (1966) 223; Clemenson (1980) 116; Harris (1985) 30; Usher (1997) 6-8; Topographer II (1790) 162; *Burton Mail* 26/12/1963 & 13/2/1969; DLC 7-9/50, 2 & 3/70, 8/75; DET 7/3/1997; *The Knot* (Newsletter of Derbys. Historic Gardens Group) 1 (1/1999) 1-2; *Journal of the Georgian Group* XI (2001) 196-7; SEGRAVE, B & NORFOLK, D. *sub* MOWBRAY, SEGRAVE & STOURTON, B/BP (1999) II. 2021-7; BERKELEY, B/*ibid.* I 254-8; CHESTERFIELD, E/*ibid.* (1956) 2054-7; CARNARVON, E/*ibid.* (1999) I. 505-7; WRAGG of Bretby/ BLG (1972) 979.

BRIZLINCOTE HALL (II*)

Stapenhill   *Private Residence*

Brizlincote Hall, 1981.   M. Craven

For much of the middle ages, Brizlincote was part of the holdings of the Abbey of Burton upon Trent, but under it was held, from early in the fifteenth century by the Hortons of Catton (qv). They built a moated seat slightly to the north of the present house, and remains of the earthworks are still visible. In 1540, 18 months after the Dissolution of the Abbey had been completed, the estate was granted to William, 1st Lord Paget, who in January 1546 obtained a licence empark and crenellate the house. Unfortunately, we have little indication of its appearance, and by the time of the Hearth Tax it appears to have been unoccupied, and does not appear. It is, indeed, possible that the crenellation was never carried out, although Woolley described it as 'a large stone house that was set in its moat on a bleak ridge'. It was sold, in 1560 to John Merry, merchant and tallow chandler of London who had just purchased Barton Blount (qv) from James Blount, 6th Lord Mountjoy. He made Brizlincote over to a younger son, and for the following century it rested with a cadet branch, members of which were just as fanatically recusant and Royalist as their kinsmen at Barton. The estate was seized by the Parliament in 1650 and more was sequestered in the year following, although John Merry's wife Anne was suffered to remain there with her children. After the war, Anne died (in 1660) and the son, Gilbert, went and resided elsewhere in the county, leaving the house apparently empty.

Thus matters rested until the executors of Gilbert Merry sold the manor and estate in 1708 to 2nd Earl of Chesterfield. Apparently, a new house was begun without delay, for Lord Stanhope, the Earl's eldest son, was living at Lichfield, and needed a seat near his father. Thus was brought into being one of the oddest houses in an age of Baroque eclecticism.

The house, an integral part of the vast landscape concept at Bretby, was built of remarkably small wire-cut red bricks – 'the brickwork is very curious', wrote Woolley – and liberally dressed in Keuper sandstone, probably from Burton upon Trent. It is of two main storeys and five by four bays. The south east (entrance) front has a central doorcase with a particularly sinuous scrolly pediment enclosing a monogram, apparently PDS (thus: Philip Dormer Stanhope), but now mutilated. From the pediment runs a string course, from which (formerly) sashed fenestration depends, each with a pulvinated frieze, all the windows being surrounded by an architrave slightly shouldered at the upper end. The windows on the first floor, beneath a bold modillion cornice, are capped by alternating segmental and triangular pediments, and there are quoins at the angles. The really startling aspect of the house however is the enormous segmental pediment which spans entire front on each side, beneath which the attics are lighted by three sashes and two oeiuls-de-boeuf at the ends. Above rises a hipped roof terminated by a fine pair of panelled stacks. Had the entrance front alone enjoyed such a Crowning feature, little surprise would be occasioned, for Hopton Hall (qv) has a similar embellishment, but at Brizlincote each front has one, producing an effect, when viewed from a distance, like a giant upturned coal scuttle.

Over the front door is the motto NON IGUARA MALI, MISERI SUCCURRERE DISCO AD 1714. Over the door on the opposite front, which in all respects resembles the other, is written: HOMO HOMINI LUPUS, which is a motto usually associated with the Wolseley family of Wolseley Park some 11 miles distant, and with no known direct connection with the Stanhopes. The date seems to suggest not so much a finished date (the house cannot have taken seven years to build) as the date of its next occupant taking up residence, for in January of that year Lord Chesterfield died, and the

son for whom the house was built succeeded. That son was the illustrious Phillip Dormer, later fourth Earl of Chesterfield, and the date was that upon which he also happened to come of age; it is not impossible that it was his first independent residence. The monogram over the door rather supports this. Local legend would have us believe that the second Earl actually designed the house, and indeed, its engaging combination of correct detailing and overall eclecticism rather suggests the hand of an informed amateur. Yet Lord Chesterfield had no personal track record for architecture. On reflection, the whole building bears the inescapable imprimatur of the memorable Sir Thomas Parkyns of Bunny, Nottinghamshire, – the wrestling baronet – who, not content with remodelling Bunny Hall with precisely this form of brash innocence, also rebuilt most of the buildings on the estate and a good many in the village of Bunny, too, but Professor Gomme suggests William Gilks of Burton may have been involved. Parkyns was also of a character to match that of Lord Chesterfield, albeit nearly 30 years his junior, and although not directly connected by blood or marriage, shared interests may have brought them together. Certainly he must stand as a prime candidate for its authorship.

In 1728 the third Earl died, Philip Dormer Stanhope went to London and the house was let to a kinsman, Philip Barnes of Hartshorne and Derby, whose wife, unkindly dubbed 'Blowzabella' by Lady Jane Coke, presided over the County Assembly at Derby. After the Barnes family died out in the later eighteenth century, it was tenanted as a farm, first by the Nadins who farmed 42 acres only, apparently, then the Startins , and later by the Lomas family, of which Mr A. Lomas was able to purchase his farm there from the break-up of the Bretby estate in 1923; his descendants still own it.

Pevsner, 100; Woolley 113, p. 151; Lysons V 69; Coulson (1982) 7; Gomme (2001) 73 n., 242n; *Burton Mail* 21/9/1979; *Journal* of the Georgian Group XI (2001) 197; HORTON/DAJ III (1881) 72; PAGET *sub* ANGLESEY, M/BP (1999) I 171-8; MERRY/Vv. 1611, 1662; CHESTERFIELD, E/BP (1956) 2054-7; BARNES/Derby Local studies Library MS 6351 & Box 57B; CARENARVON, E/BP (1999) I. 505-7.

BROCKSFORD HALL (II)

Doveridge   *Divided as residences*

Brocksford Hall, entrance front, c. 1965.   R. Evans

56

A stolid and imposing diapered brick house with stone dressings, Brocksford Hall – named after the neighbouring brook – is, like Thornbridge Hall *(qv)* an exercise in what might be termed 'Arts-and-Crafts Jacobethan' but, unlike the latter, is far more conventional in outline, being more akin to contemporary Morley Manor in this respect. It is of two storeys with attics, and both fronts, whilst superficially symmetrical, are to some extent irregular in their details. The main south front is broad, with a central gabled bay and two further ones at the ends, that to the east being somewhat larger. There are two bays recessed between the west and central bays, and one wide one between that and the east end bay, the fenestration being stone mullioned on the first floor and with transoms on the ground floor. The end bays have full height canted bays as well. A joky little timber portico protects the egress from house to garden to the right of the centre bay, and set back to the east is a full height one bay link with a cleverly canted ground floor parapetted screen connecting the house to a pyramidally roofed square tower. The steep slated roof has two dormers and a number of slim, high brick stacks. The whole is set on a terrace marked by a generous stone balustrade.

The entrance front consists of a two storey porch with oriel and top parapet, in which the Smith arms are carved. Either side are straight coped gables with strapwork enrichment over the mullioned windows on the first floor. To the left is a further gabled bay, slightly recessed with a double transomed window lighting the staircase, and at the east end a much larger gable – wider and higher, with a full attic window and with the fenestration below it divided to create the illusion of two bays. Beyond, a half-timbered gatehouse leads into a fine stable and service court.

Inside a spacious entrance hall is richly panelled and a wide oak staircase of earlier eighteenth century date, with turned balusters, swept rail and carved tread ends, leads up to a galleried landing with a three arched screen, also in oak. All this fine joinery came from Fenton Old Hall, Staffs., although much more is contemporary with the house, built in 1893 to the designs of John Douglas of Douglas and Fordham of Chester.

The client was Charles William Jervis Smith, JP, who was descended from a sixteenth century Bishop of Lichfield and Coventry, and whose Newcastle-under-Lyme based forebears had married the heiress of Nicholls of Great Fenton, which explains the presence of so much architectural salvage from the family's former seat, then not long demolished. After Smith's death, his son, R. B. Smith sold the house to Sir Harold Nutting, 2nd Bt., whose Mastership of the Meynell made a seat – or, rather, a hunting box – in the area essential. Come the Second World War, the house was unoccupied. Eventually a preparatory school founded by J. Gibson Roberts in Birkdale in 1942, moved in and remained, doing the house remarkably little harm, until closure in 1995. Mr. Roberts's tenure lasted until about 1970, the last headmaster being Revd. Robert Clarke. The house was subsequently acquired by a property company and re-developed by 2000 as individual dwellings.

Pevsner 198; DLC 5/67; DET 13/1/2000; SMITH of Great Fenton/BLG (1898) II 1366; NUTTING, Bt/BP (1999) II 2135.

BROOKHILL HALL (II)

Pinxton   *Private residence*

Brookhill Hall, Pinxton; the entrance front   M. Craven

The original capital mansion at Pinxton was that built by Ralph le Poer c. 1235, who was granted one quarter of a knight's fee there by Robert de Alfreton, probably on marriage into that family. His daughter and ultimate heiress brought it to Robert le Wyne c. 1278. A moat marks what was later called Wynne's Castle (SK 459569) and find scatters range from green glazed ridge tiles of c. 1250 to sherds of c. 1380. Sir William Le Wyne sold to Sir Alfred de Solney of Newton who abandoned the site, before his heirs, the Longfords, in turn, sold to the Sacheverels from whom it ultimately descended to the Cokes of Trusley.

The earliest fabric today seems to be c. 1630 and appears to a be pair of parallel ranges in stone, joined by straight coped gables from the apices of which sprouted slim stacks, all rather Smythsonesque in feel. Oddly, only three hearths were taxable in 1670. Some additions were made in 1742, perhaps including an outshoot at the south west end of the range, of a single storey, latterly with three sashed windows. It is perhaps not without significance that d'Ewes Coke acquired the collection of Smythson drawings now in the RIBA drawing collection from Lord Byron in 1778. In 1770, Coke, who had married an heiress, greatly expanded the house. Truncating the westernmost of the two ranges, he built at the north-east end a five-bay three-storey brick range with a centre and end gable echoing that to the left, remaining from the original build, which accordingly had its chimney cropped at this end to match the small ball finials topping the other two, which were originally depressed into a parapet over the single bay linking sections, and the fenestration was sashed (now casements) under gauged brick lintels.

The south-cast front, being part of the un-shortened seventeenth-century range, was given a two-storey five-bay sashed facade with architrave surrounds, over the original tall basement, and with a parapet over, which may be an alteration of an original feature, perhaps crenellated. Within is a new cantilevered Hoptonwood stone staircase with slim wrought-iron balusters, quite plain and conceivably by one of the Yateses of Derby, carrying a slim mahogany rail. Downstairs, the doorcases have glyphic entablatures above, triangular pedimented overdoors, and there is much modillion cornicing of high quality. At the same time

57

handsome seven-bay stable block was built with a central projecting Palladian tower topped by a pyramid roof, lanterns and a Whitehurst turret clock of contemporary date, looks strikingly like a scaled down version of the central range of the Markeaton Hall stable block, by Pickford (qv). It was converted into residences by Mary G.Cawthorne in 1977. The ground floor boasts segmentally headed fenestration set in a blind arcade relieved by a stone impost band, much like the loggia of 41 Friar Gate, Derby, and thus suggesting the hand of Joseph Pickford of Derby who, with Joseph Wright, was in the circle patronised by Coke and his cousin Daniel Parker Coke. If so, then the interior detailing of the house itself falls into place, and the artfully contrived landscape park with its modest lake may be the work of William Emes. Wright's painting of c. 1781 of D'Ewes Coke, his wife and D. P. Coke in the park and looking at plans on a table may relate to this. All the ashlar work and dressings are in Coal Measure sandstone, probably that above High Hazels Coal; there is some pebble dashing, seventeenth and eighteenth-century brick and stone slate on the roof.

The remainder of the interior has much early seventeenth century panelling (mostly moved, one feels), a fine oak chimney piece in the dining-room of earlier date removed from Kirkby Hall, Nottinghamshire, the heiress of which place the Cokes had married, some late seventeenth-century panelling (now painted) and one or two fireplaces with bolection mouldings. Later work, including the odd porch, was done by Col. W. L. Coke and is dated 1898. He also altered the roofline on the entrance front, to no good effect. The last of the family here was the composer Roger Sacheverell Coke, although by the time of his death in 1973 the house was in parlous state and the heir, Gilbert Darwin, sold it with 8 acres in October 1974, to a Mr. Meeks, a haulier from Kirkby-in-Ashfield for £28.000, but not the estate. The owner in the 1990s, Mr. Trevor Cookson, completed the rehabilitation of the building. It was again for sale, in August 1997 with nine acres.

The Cokes were the proprietors, in the first decade of the nineteenth century, of the Pinxton porcelain factory, which employed William Billingsley for a time, and there are several views of the house and park on these wares, some in Billingsley's hand.

The park and canal pond, Brookhill Hall, c. 1902
M. Craven

Pevsner, 111; Thoroton (1791) II 245, 298; Bagshaw (1846) 660; Bulmer (1895) 676; Smith (1994) 153-6; DLC 10/68; le POER/Thoroton (1791) III 283-4 & BIFR 959-61; le WYNE/Jeayes (1906) nos. 1863,1866; SOLNEY/DAJ XLIX (1927) 317-28; SACHEVERELL/V.1611; COKE of Brookhill/BLG (1965) 147; DARWIN sub KINDERSLEY/ibid. (1952) 1436.

BURNASTON HOUSE (II)

Etwall   *Dismantled*

Ashton Nicholas Every Mosley (1792-1875) was the son of Ashton Mosley – himself a son of Sir John Parker Mosley, 1st Bt (of the third creation) of Rolleston Hall – and the widow of Sir Edward Every of Egginton, Bt, who lived at the Egginton Hall dower house, Park Hill (qv). In 1820 he married a wealthy Yorkshire heiress, Mary Theresa Stables, of Hemsworth and four years later had acquired a modest estate in the parish of Etwall, called Conygree Hall, which centred on a seventeenth century farmhouse, built by Thomas Brailsforth before 1633. He thereupon set about building a villa. His architect was Samuel Brown of Derby (1756-1838) in whose hand are the plans and elevations of the house, now in the Harpur-Crewe MSS at the Derbyshire Record Office (DRO).

The house Mosley built was delightfully well proportioned exercise in post-Soanian classicism: compact, convenient and contemporary. Its south (garden) front was of six bays and of two storeys under a low parapet panelled discreetly over the bays, with the upper floor windows sitting on a band; the whole was faced in fine ashlar of Keuper sandstone. The end bays broke back slightly on the ground floor and by a whole bay above, the parapet over the resulting low pavilions being an echo of that above. The ground floor fenestration, carried down to terrace level, was set in a series of blind panels. On each rendered return, the windows were tripartite, in shouldered tapering architraves, which give almost a slight Egyptian flavour. To the north ran a partly colour-washed brick two-storey service wing, perhaps eighteenth century, which might have been a legacy of Conygree Hall. Beyond that lay a handsome brick two-storey stable block of eight bays, with a central pediment with a pair of oculi below, later converted into a dwelling. The home farm lay beyond to the north-east. A pretty gabled lodge of c. 1890 stood by the gate on to the lane, brick and bargeboarded.

The house, renamed by Mosley Burnaston House (in which township it lay), was sited on a low knoll overlooking the flood plain of the Trent, with a burst of trees to its west and north, making a delightful and unforgettable ensemble. Inside there was excellent, restrained plasterwork a little old fashioned for the date, perhaps, and a good cantilevered Hoptonwood stone staircase with a mahogany rail supported on elegant cast-iron balusters cast in Derby by Messrs. Weatherhead, Glover & Company, as with other houses by Brown.

A.N.E.Mosley's elder grandson, Arthur Rowland, was the last of the family to live at Burnaston House, although latterly he had let it to George Darcy-Clark c. 1908, and to a school from 1916. On his death in 1923, his brother Godfrey, a Derby solicitor, inherited, himself moving to Calke Abbey the year following, when his wife, the senior daughter and co-heiress of Sir Vauncey Harpur-Crewe, came into that estate. In 1936 it was purchased by Derby Borough Council with 382 acres of the estate for £21,500 in order to lay the park out as an aerodrome, which was opened by Rt Hon Sir Kingsley Wood in 1938. The house became clubhouse and terminal building combined, and continued in this role until the opening of the East Midland International Airport in 1968.

At this point, the aerodrome was down-graded to club flying mixed with some industry operating from redundant hangers. The house was sold to Mr Stanley Fisher, who occupied the service wing with the intention of restoring the remainder, at this stage in sound condition. However, it

Burnaston House, by R. Keene, c. 1860.

RCHM(E)

gradually decayed to being a ruinous shell, and the harsh winter of 1981-82 led to the collapse of a major portion of the facade. Two applications to demolish were defeated at public enquiries, with various conservation bodies and enthusiasts backed by the County Council's Conservation section pitted against the South Derbyshire District Council and the applicant. In the mid-1980s, English Heritage, with local help, tried very hard to find a restoring owner, believing against the odds that the house was capable of restoration. In 1987 it was bought by Mr J. Keck, who set about adapting the house into a retirement home for the elderly. However, a combination of the Derby City and Derbyshire County Councils, with government help, succeeded in attracting Toyota to the site, to desecrate the Trent Valley with a vast car manufacturing plant, and the entire estate and several neighbouring farms were compulsorily purchased for immediate demolition, the house being repurchased for £1,250,000. Numerous representations from the usual conservation groups including Derby Civic Society and other lovers of the building were to no avail, and this time County Council's Conservation Section suddenly decided that the house was of 'insufficient importance', and its fate was sealed through the whims of expediency and compliance.

At the 11th hour, however, Mr. Kevin Ellis of Gainsborough Properties, a Derby development company, stepped in and in March 1990, proceeded to dismantle the house systematically, numbering the stones, and palletting the materials. The highly laudable intention was to re-erect the entire building, including service wing and stables on a new site within the parish. This plan foundered in the summer of 1990, when the Etwall Parish Council objected to the plan on the grounds that this fine house would spoil the view of those living in Sutton Lane. This caused a long delay, and by the time the District Council had given consent, the option on the land which was to form the new park of the re-erected house had expired and the owner chose not to renew it. After discussions with Derby City Council about resiting it in Markeaton Park on the house platform (qv), it was sold to the proprietors of a golf club near Tokyo, where it was to be re-erected as a clubhouse; an offer for a similar role from a club in Texas was not taken up. In the event, all these schemes fell through, and the house still awaits a site and a well-off, sympathetic owner. The whole sorry tale is an example of the sheer vulnerability of the county houses of this sort even today when faced with massive vested interests, political pressure on local authorities, and gross Nimbyism.

The timber framed Old Hall at Burnaston, once the seat of the Brownes, situated in the village, was purchased from the Mosley estate by William Smith, a local farmer, and demolished around 1888, being replaced by a three gabled house in brick with moulded brick decoration, rather in the outline of its predecessor, probably to designs by Alexander MacPherson of Derby. It was sold in 1892 to Thomas R. Dearle, and was later the residence of Maj. R. O. Feilden.

Lysons, V 162; White (1857) 210; Tilley II (1893) 75; Bulmer (1895) 747; *Official Programme of the Opening of Derby Airport 7/6/1939* (Derby 1939) 70-1; Henderson & Robinson (1979) 49; *Burton Mail* 16/11/1985; DET 4 & 8/9/1998; *Derby Trader* 22/3/1989; DRO Harpur-Crewe MSS 84/27-29; MOSLEY *sub* RAVENSDALE, B/BP (1999) II 2362-6; DARCY CLARK/Briscoe (1900) 360; BROWNE/ *Reliquary* XV (1874-5) 92 f.

BURTON CLOSES (II)

Bakewell   *Institutional use*

In 1845, a modest estate immediately south of Bakewell, and on the edge of the town, was purchased from the Duke of Rutland by a Quaker stockbroker, John Allcard. Born locally at Leek (Staffs) with a wife from Sheldon, he became exceedingly opulent running to a London town house in Upper Brook Street. He immediately engaged Joseph Paxton to lay out the grounds and to build him a house. Burton Closes, as it was called (from the name of the land upon which it was built, once a freehold of the Burtons of Bakewell, yeomen who went on to gentility after they had left the area), is a highly romantic essay in Tudor Gothic,

Burton Closes as extended, showing the later turret and the east front, 1987.
J. Sharpe

extensions and alterations. Those parts of the interior not embellished by Pugin himself were turned over to J. G. Crace and George Myers. The surviving turret clock is signed Roskell/Derby, the short-lived successor firm to the last John Whitehurst.

Allcard died in 1856, being succeeded by his son, William Henry (1808-1861), an alderman and twice Mayor of Warrington, but important to the lover of railways as the whilom locomotive engineer of the Grand Junction Railway. An ex-apprentice of Robert Stephenson, as a young man he drove the first locomotive at the opening of the Liverpool and Manchester Railway in 1830, going on to found a locomotive manufacturing concern, which supplied the motive power for the Paris-Rouen Railway. He died only five years after his father, and the house and estate were sold in 1866 to Smith Taylor-Whitehead.

In 1888 he made further extensions, including a new dining room decorated by the Craces, transforming a middling villa (albeit a richly decorated one) into a sizeable seat. The architect on this occasion was J. B. Mitchell-Withers. Paxton's grounds, now regrettably covered with 1960s box-like modern housing, fell away from the house in a series of terraces, with a pleasure ground to the east, parkland to the south and a Wellingtonia avenue to the west.

In 1902, Taylor-Whitehead sold to Alexander Campbell-Blair, the Duke of Rutland's agent, who enlarged the estate to 138 acres, but its decline had begun by the end of the 1930s, the removal of the Ford Maddox Brown window being symptomatic of this. During the war it was unsympathetically treated by the RASC, the Dutch Army, and later by prisoners-of-war. A part demolition was made in 1949 and by 1953 the interior was recorded as derelict, the entire service range being pulled down and an absurd block of flats, was built on the site in 1972. Also in the 1940s, the tower lost its conical cap. In 1972, when the flats were being built, the Colebrook housing association of Sheffield obtained planning consent to convert the remaining interiors as flats, to the lasting detriment of the work of Crace and Pugin,

called admiringly by Pevsner 'A virtual epitome of early Victorian visual taste'. As built, it consisted of two main ranges at right angles, east and south. The latter focused on a stone belfry tower of three stages with a conical cap over a robust porte-cochere flanked by a pair of pinnacled straight gables. To the left, are two further canted bays and a long ornate conservatory, behind which is an intimate and satisfying *cour d'honneur*, mainly gabled with a gothic castellated entrance. The east range was a riot of straight gables, oriels over bay windows, attic dormers and angled projections, with steep pitched roofs topped with barleysugar twist chimney stacks, the whole being largely of two storeys with attics. In the building, Paxton was, as at Edensor, assisted by his protege, John Robertson. It is built of ashlar throughout of Ashover Grit from the quarry at Bakewell Edge. The roof is slate.

The lavish interior was decorated by A. W. N. Pugin who ' ... took on the job of fitting out a large house near Haddon' in 1847-48, and was generous with gothic detailing and rich colour schemes. There was a good timber main staircase, much Minton tiling and stained glass by John Hardman, although there was also a stained glass window of the archangel Uriel by Ford Maddox Brown, criminally sold off in 1939, but more happily installed at Tansley Church in memory of the vicar, Rev. Brodie Mais, by his son, the well known writer, S. P. B. Mais, in 1914. Pugin also designed the decorative iron and brasswork also made by John Hardman and his son, E. W. Pugin, was working at the house in 1854 when T. D. Barry was called in to make architectural

Burton Closes; fireplace, 1979.   *M. Craven*

especially as it was done insensitively, and it was a certain recipe for the deterioration of the fabric yet further, despite cosmetic repairs. An application to demolish was made April 1982 and pressure for a viable restoring use forced the owners to place it on the market, but an unrealistically high price of £180,000 in July 1983 proved prohibitive for the Derbyshire Historic Buildings Trust, who were the potential purchasers most favoured by the planning authority, the Peak Park Joint Planning Board. A repairs notice was at last considered, and the price fell by £40,000. Finally, it found a buyer and has since returned to rehabilitation as an old folks home. A pretty gate lodge survives on the main A6, and the house is listed grade (II) – one of the first (with Snelston Hall) Victorian Country houses in the County to be so listed, in 1951, although it must be said that the accolade afforded Snelston no protection whatsoever (qv) and precious little to Burton Closes which, had it remained intact, would have been one of the more important early Victorian houses in the region.

Pevsner, 77; White (1857) 479; Bulmer (1895) 306; *Journal of the Bakewell & District Historical Society* XVII (1/ 1990) 13-15; Stanton (1971) 206; ALLCARD/Walford (1871) 15; TAYLOR-WHITEHEAD/FD (1905) 1333 & (1910) 1573.

CALKE ABBEY (I)

Ticknall   *National Trust/Open to public*

Calke burst on to the consciousness of the nation in March 1984 when it was announced that it was to be accepted in lieu of Capital Transfer Tax in excess of £8,000,000, after a similar offer had been rejected in November 1983, and that the house and land were to be transferred to the National Trust. It opened to the public some five years later after a colossal restoration programme not only of the fabric, but also to the immense and chaotic collection of family treasures from the Victorian drawing-room to the piles of neglected personalia found decaying quietly in its deserted rooms.

At the time of the Domesday Survey, the land at Calke was part of the village of Ticknall, the latter being sokeland of the manor of Repton, itself in divided ownership. However, in c. 1115-20 Richard, third Earl of Chester gave Calke to the Augustinian Canons, who founded a priory there dedicated to St Giles. Yet a few years later, Richard's widow had founded another priory at Repton, on the site of the venerable Saxon double house destroyed by the Danes in 874, and it took over the foundation at Calke in c. 1172. The resulting cell of St Giles at Calke was dissolved, along with Repton, in 1538. The cell itself was let to one John Priest, and his widow carried it to Richard Blackwall (of the Blackwalls of Blackwall-in-Peak, qv) in 1546. On her death in 1549, their daughter brought it to her husband, William Bradbourne, a member of another Peak District gentry family.

In 1573-75 the lease was bought by Richard Wendesley of Wensley, MP, who also acquired the freehold interest from the Beaumonts of Gracedieu Abbey, Leicestershire. Shortly thereafter he 'did build divers edifices thereupon and did inhabit and dwell upon the same'. Yet in ten years Wendesley had sold up to Robert Bainbrigge, MP, a Derby lawyer to whom Wendesley had mortgaged the property. This must have suited Bainbrigge, an extreme protestant, for the church at Calke was a peculiar, and outside episcopal jurisdiction, enabling him to worship there in his own, Puritan, way. In 1622, his second son Robert sold Calke to Sir Henry

Harpur for £5,350, and it has remained in the hands of this illustrious family ever since.

Sir Henry Harpur was the third son of Sir John, of Swarkestone (qv) whose father, Richard, a junior scion of an old family long seated in Warwickshire and Staffordshire, married Jane Findern, a great heiress, acquiring thereby estates at Swarkestone, Findern, Potlock, Littleover, Stanton-by-Bridge and elsewhere. Sir Henry's elder brothers were seated at Hemington, Leicestershire, Breadsall Upper Hall (qv) and, of course, Swarkestone; an uncle held Littleover, Twyford and Findern with parts of Willington and Repton. Many of these came ultimately to Henry's grandson, Sir John, on the failure of the senior lines, and from this promising start the Harpur family estates in Derbyshire, Leicestershire and Staffordshire rose to a total of over 33,000 acres by the beginning of the twentieth century.

Sir Henry Harpur, created a baronet in 1626, probably did more building work, for by 1662, the house was taxed on 23 hearths, making it nearly as large as Swarkestone. A three-bay arched loggia at ground floor level to the east and west of the inner courtyard probably survive from this period, and inner corner stair towers adjoining may well represent survivals from Wendesley's building. The present house still has signs of its older core, with thick, angled walling, irregular spacing of window bays and similar anomalies still visible to those prepared to seek them out. In 1988, repairs to the north wall of the house revealed two blocked three light mullioned windows with hollow chamfers and no less than three blocked doorcases each corresponding to the partition of the space behind of the present house, latterly staff accommodation. Beneath, Mr. Philip Heath excavated a well-moulded plinth and established that the re-used fabric at this point represented a different floor level from the present, but one which closely followed that of the internal courtyard loggias. Plainly, although the function of the three doors must be a matter of speculation, the whole would appear to be a re-use of the 1620s build, despite the hollow chamfers, which are quite in tune with the architectural conservatism in the region at this period. Inside, some seventeenth century fireplaces survive, one very fine and tall, of Jacobean date, and said to have come from Swarkestone Hall; this is quite possible, although the Harpur arms in the centre panel seem later in style and bear a baronet's escutcheon – which could only relate to Calke. Other anomalies, like the lack of right angles on the interior walls on the inside of east range, were rationalized out of existence in the 1840s.

As soon as he came of age in 1701, Sir John Harpur, 4th Bt, began to rebuild the house in a very grand manner, still around the central courtyard, but with three storeys and with substantial projecting pavilions at the angles, each containing a self-contained suite of rooms. It is of ashlar throughout, like its predecessor of Keuper sandstone from Pistern Hill, just 3 miles away. Yet for all the plenitude of records, no name obtrudes to suggest who the architect was, although all the craftsmen are named. The high-quality joinery was by Messrs Whelpdale and Leech, carved by one Wright, the painting was by Jonathan Reading of Derby (died 1746, having also worked at Sutton Scarsdale, qv), the plasterwork, which is generally modest, was by Petty Dewick of Ashby and the ornate plumbing and rain-water goods were by George Braseby. It is likely that William Johnson of Nottingham had some input into the building, but there is insufficient evidence to claim for him the overall design. The house seems unsophisticated in its relationship to the fabric, which remained, from its predecessor, especially the position of the entrance in the centre of the south front to the centre-line of the courtyard behind it. Yet the giant order

The entrance Front, Calke Abbey.   *C.L.M. Porter*

which graces the angles is an adaptation of a highly sophisticated composite one published by Philibert de l'Orme before 1648 and unknown previously in England. The pilasters support a richly detailed and beautifully executed cornice beyond which lay a flat, leaded, roof, but with no parapets as built. Between the first and second floors is a string course. The east front is rather featureless, despite the addition of a Regency iron balustrade at *piano nobile* level spanning the ten bays between the projecting pavilions, on this elevation of two bays only each. The south, or entrance front, is of 13 bays, the three at each end breaking forward as part of the angle pavilions. The entrance itself was through an open segmentally pedimented door at *piano nobile* level again, the three central bays being ensigned by the giant order, with two bays beyond on either side, ensuring some movement to the façade. James Gibbs designed a fine flight of stone stairs to this entrance in 1728-29 at the same time as Richard Jackson was doing unknown work, but Gibbs's steps did not survive the alterations of 1808 in this form. Today the central three bays are masked by a giant Greek Ionic tetrastyle portico topped by a plain pediment, all standing on a lesser portico of paired square Doric pillars. No external steps remain, some iron ones approaching the main portico from the sides having been dismantled some years ago. This addition was one of a number of fairly extensive alterations carried out by William Wilkins the elder, who died in 1815. The west front is of seven highly irregular bays between three-bay pavilions, the return on the northwest being partly re-entrant, probably reflecting anomalies from the fabric of the previous building, the west wall of which is identifiable with that which can be seen today. The north side, against rising ground, has in effect no lower ground floor, and is irregular, the seven-bay central section being flanked to the east by a pavilion of three bays (of which two are blind) and to the west by one which was subsequently altered and extended to provide a laundry.

Inside, the entrance front hides a full height saloon on the *piano nobile*, dignified and richly decorated, although largely the work in its present form of Henry Isaac Stevens of Derby (1806-1873) who was employed to remove anomalies and undertake alterations in 1841. This was reached through an arcaded oak screen with a Corinthian order from the staircase, an extremely handsome one with two turned and carved balusters per tread and carved tread ends, sited to the east side of the so-called centre-line of the front, with another stair, rebuilt in stone and sealed off by Stevens, to the west: this now functions as the staff stair. The main stairwell is topped with some fine baroque plasterwork, and one or two rooms remain of this period. More arresting today are the three rooms created by Wilkins, the dining-room (1793-94), the drawing-room and the library. Of these the dining-room is the most delightful, with a pronounced neo-classical decorative scheme and a recess behind a screen of Greek Ionic scagliola columns in which the contemporary sideboard is visible and a pair of service doors are not. A fine long case clock by John Whitehurst of Derby FRS with a days of the week dial and a musical movement stands in the lobby behind. The library was redecorated and altered by Stevens, so retains little of its original ambience. Entrance to the house is now via a hall created by Stevens through the under-portico.

Beyond the house itself, stables were built in 1712-16 by William Gilks of Burton upon Trent, topped with a handsome cupola sporting a highly ornamental weathercock by Robert Bakewell of Derby and replaced by him in 1750. The stables are in brick, unlike the house, with Keuper sandstone dressings, and lie higher up upon the north side. Like the main house, though, they are equipped with highly decorative rainwater goods in lead sporting the Harpur boar crest. The facade is of 13 bays, with a central three-bay breakfront under a pediment, all with quoins, cornice, sill band, and the windows are of the original cross casement type ensigned with stone keyblocks. There is a central rusticated arched entrance to the courtyard behind the subsidiary entrances are at bays three and ten. Converted, it would on its own make no mean seat. Behind are a variety of other associated buildings, mainly added during the eighteenth century.

It is not known what Richard Jackson was doing here c. 1720s but there were three attempts to replace the house in the eighteenth century, perhaps inspired by the drastic approach of Lord Scarsdale at Kedleston (*qv*). Sir Henry Harpur, 6th Bt came of age in 1760, and was elected MP for

Derbyshire a year later, dying in 1789. He employed Joseph Pickford of Derby to renew all the sash windows, repair the roof and add the very simple but elegant riding school behind the stable block. The latter has a roof based on a pattern in a contemporary handbook by Francis Price (the *British Carpenter)* which he was to use again at the Trinity Hospital, Leicester, and an ambitious gauged brick Diocletian window at the north end. The pretty orangery of 1778 is almost certainly also a design by Pickford, and elements of it are paralleled at Markeaton and Ashford Halls *(qv).* It had a five-bay front with full height segmentally headed windows, with a string course at impost level taken over the fenestration, like the loggia at 41 Friar Gate, Derby, and was top-lit by a glass dome set between two hipped roofs. Pickford's greatest triumph at Calke, however, never came about. When the National Trust were making an inventory of the house, they found an unopened packet containing a set of eight architects' drawings for a quite new house – aggressively Palladian, with an ornate central block with a giant portico and pyramidal roof connected by colonnaded sweeps to elegant three-bay pavilions. This was a clear attempt to upstage Kedleston from the hand of a man who was even then helping to create it and who had cut his teeth with his mason uncle at Holkham. The drawing and handwriting makes it certain that this bold design was Pickford's yet, on arrival at Calke, it was put into a draw and not even opened.

Another design was drawn up for Sir Henry Harpur's son, the 7th Bt, by Thomas Gardner of Uttoxeter, Pickford's pupil, but this plainly represents a rebuild of the 1701 house with an attic storey above the cornice and a plain pediment. Wilkins in 1794 proposed an even more modest rebuilding with a domed semi-circular portico where later he installed the present one. Yet only Pickford's design represented a grander concept which, if completed, would have been a wonder indeed.

The gardens were laid out as the house was building by George London and Henry Wise with work extending to 1713, and Charles Bridgeman appears to have done more in 1721, which work was embellished by Robert Bakewell ironwork. In 1776 William Emes of Bowbridge Fields created a new walled garden, as well as removing all traces of the original gardens. Emes frequently worked with Joseph Pickford and indeed the orangery turns out to be an element of Emes's plans. Emes also transformed the park, enlarging it to some 500 acres so that earlier commentators remarks about the situation of the house as 'ill-chosen' and 'desolate' became superfluous, as any visitor today beholding its lambent beauty can see for himself. The park was enlivened by lodges designed by Wilkins, a grotto, cascade and Gothick bridge (1809-10), a Chinese temple on an island in a pond (1747) and a gazebo. The grotto, cascade and bridge were the work of the estate's favourite architect in the Regency period, Samuel Brown, of a Derby family of stonemasons, who also designed numerous cottages in Ticknall and Stanton-by-Bridge, estate farms, and who probably built the new church which stands on a knoll on the south of the main house of c. 1823-25. In 1795-1805 the park gained another less common feature: a tramway engineered by Benjamin Outram, which ran from lime kilns in Ticknall through the park to Ashby-de-la-Zouch; although it ceased to run a century or so later, its course is still clearly visible.

At their maximum, the contiguous Harpur estates in the counties of Derby, Leicester and Stafford vied for size and importance with those of the Duke of Devonshire, although the total was reduced to 12,300 in the early 1970s, and is less than 4,000 today. The family themselves assumed the surname and additional arms of Crewe (of Steane, Northamptonshire) by Royal Licence in 1808, the fourth baronet having married the heiress of the last Lord Crewe of Steane at about the time the house was built. It is clear that Sir Henry Crewe was after a revival of the barony, a happenstance which never achieved reality, for the Harpurs were hardly a family given to life at court or paying a close part in politics. He died disappointed in 1819 (he fell from his coach-box in London), and thereafter his posterity stayed even more at home. On the death of Sir Vauncey Harpur-Crewe in 1924, the property passed to his elder daughter and her husband Godfrey Mosley, previously of Burnaston House *(qv),* who at last plumbed it, and on their death, to the elder son of the younger daughter, Charles Jenney, who, like the brother who succeeded him on his unexpected death in 1981, assumed the surname of Harpur-Crewe. Charles Harpur-Crewe it was who finally installed electricity at Calke in the 1960s.

When Charles Harpur-Crewe died, there was found to be a colossal amount of duty payable on the estate, and in November 1983, the government rejected an *in lieu* offer in settlement. However, after a vigorous campaign, the treasury altered the rules and reversed its decision in the 1984 budget, and with a £4,000,000 grant from the National Heritage Memorial Fund an *in lieu* arrangement was finalized and this unique house was saved for the nation, restored by the National Trust at enormous expense and opened in 1989 to the public. One of the great attractions of the house is the contents which, although not in any way outstanding artistically, have been preserved almost by default down to the last lead soldier. Charles Harpur-Crewe's brother retained apartments in the house, and was succeeded by his unmarried sister Airmyne Harpur-Crewe on his sudden death during his High Shrieval year, in 1992. She died in 1999 whereupon the estate devolved upon a distant kinsman, Andrew Frederick Johnson (a US citizen), a descendant through two female lines of the Repton Park branch. Even the baronetcy is only dormant and not extinct, for an entire line of descent from William, youngest son of the first baronet, blossomed in the local area before spreading far and wide in the mid-nineteenth century.

The Orangery following restoration.   C.L.M. Porter

Colvin, 168, 403, 410, 753, 888, 997. 1054; Pevsner, 119; Woolley, 117 p. 155; Glover, II. 187; Lysons, V. 70; Pilkington (1789) II. 77; Colvin (1985) *passim*; Cox, (2001) *passim*; Gomme (2001) 518; Kitching (1995) *passim*; DAJ CII (1982) 102-106; CL CLXXIV (20/10/1983) 1062 f & (27/10/1983) 1162 f; (HARPUR-) CREWE Bt./BP (1923) 618-619; JENNEY of Ditchingham Lodge/BLG (1952) 1379.

CALLOW HALL (II)

Mapleton   Hotel/restaurant

In 1848 the Derby architect Henry Isaac Stevens designed an ambitious Jacobethan house to go on a moiety of a former estate which lay between Ashbourne and Mapleton. The client was John Goodwin Johnson, whose like-named father (died 1838) had been an opulent Ashbourne attorney who had adopted the surname of a Wirksworth heiress. He married a daughter of Francis Beresford of Ashbourne by an heiress of the Doxeys, which had added to the estate upon which there appears to have been a previous house called The Callow.

Callow Hall, which has several features in common with Stevens's Ash Hall *(qv)*, was of two storeys with attics, and a symmetrical three-bay south front with a small shaped gable enclosed by larger straight coped ones, with a bowed window between. At the angle of the east return there was planned a largish tower with a bulbous top and the offices beyond; to the south an arcade was to connect an ornate iron conservatory and a small pavilion with a turret to the house. As built, however, it was lower, plainer and altogether more pedestrian. The tower was reduced in scale to a thin rather Teutonic-looking affair, the bow became an oriel

and conservatory extension vanished entirely. The windows are all mullion and transom ones and suspend from a string course on the ground floor and have hood moulds above. The east, entrance, front is lower, irregular, with the first floor windows obtruding into stone coped gablets and is marked by a muscular porch, rusticated and topped by a balustrade and ball finials. There is a larger gable to the right with eight-light mullioned and transomed windows. Inside, there is a reasonable profusion of oak panelling and a good if rather predictable staircase. The setting and small park are, however, very attractive. It is built of rough-faced ashlar of Carboniferous Limestone with dressings and porch of Keuper sandstone and a slate roof.

Johnson died around 1871, and it was inherited by the Buckstons of Sutton and Bradbourne, Johnson's sister Mary having married Rev. Henry Thomas Buckston. They proceeded to let the house to the Harcourt-Cappers, from 1901 Frederick Henniker, who died there in 1908, and then the Claypon Woods before it was ultimately sold to Alderman Arthur Frederick Longdon MBE of Derby, (1860-1938) a tape manufacturer whose father Frederick had been Mayor of Derby in 1865. On his death, the son, R.A.F.Longdon, sold it to George E.Gather OBE (1900-1975), a director of Richard Cooper Limited, a firm of Ashbourne corset manufacturers. It was eventually sold in November 1982 for over £100,000 with 42 acres, the buyer being Mr. David Spencer of Ashbourne, who subsequently opened it as a hotel and restaurant, with self-catering units and fishing. The cellars were apparently used to store War Department archives during World War Two, and a TV series called *The Mallens* was filmed there in 1980.

Lysons, V. 296; DLC 5/66; BUCKSTON of Bradbourne/ BLG (1952) 298; HENNIKER, B/BP (1999) I. 1374-5.

The south front of Callow Hall.   C.L.M. Porter

CARNFIELD HALL (II*)

South Normanton Private residence/Open by appointment

Carnfield Hall C. 1910, showing the 1698 front entrance and Jacobean gallery.
Private Collection

Prior to the mid-fifteenth century, Carlingthwaite – as Carnfield was then called – was part of the estates of the Babingtons of Dethick. From them, an estate of just over 500 acres was settled upon Richard Page by virtue of his marriage with a Babington, and their son William sold in 1502 to Hugh Revell who was the third son of Thomas, of Derby, sergeant-at-law, allegedly a scion of the Revells of Newbold Revell, Warwickshire. His eldest brother John was the founder of the Revells of Ogston *(qv)*.

By the time of Hugh's grandson, Thomas, there appears to have been the nucleus of the present house on the site, for it is mentioned in 1563 when it was let to Anthony Eyre, a member of the Derbyshire family of that name then living in Yorkshire. It would have appeared to have been timber framed (traces of which remain in the fabric of the present house) and consisted of a great hall connecting two cross-wings of three bays each at that time. However, its building history appears by no means simple. Today the entrance front – which faces nearly east – goes some way to confirm this impression: a three-bay recessed facade lies well back between two projecting three-bay wings. However, in the 1690s Robert Revell rebuilt this front, raising the centre section to form an additional storey, topping it with a bare-looking cornice, and installing classical windows with eared architrave surrounds and keyblocks. The gables were also raised and oddly paired, as once at Norton House (garden front *qv*), and a new entrance was graced with a bolection moulding with a segmental open pediment supported on console brackets. The house is built of Coal Measures sandstone (Top Hard Rock) in coursed rubble, the dressings are a mixture of Permian Magnesian limestone and a coarse sandstone under an old tile roof.

Yet all the other fronts lack this rustic unity and betray the true antiquity of this most complex and fascinating edifice. The north front is short, and most of the northeast gable stands proud of it like a baroque corner pavilion, with a vast partly quoined chimney breast in the angle. If the 1563 account of the crosswings having three bays is correct, then this range and its twin attached chimney breasts must post-date that time; indeed an early seventeenth century

rebuilding seems everywhere apparent. Between the chimneys are a miscellaneous trio of sash windows, at least one superimposed upon a blocked mullioned and a multiply transomed one, with another blocked light evident. The chimney breast tucked into the rear of the entrance front is quoined along that edge, supporting the supposition that the north-east projection must be later. The west front consists of an irregular pair of gables at the north-west corner, both straight coped with quoins below, at the angles, the range to the left being two storeys with attics, its pair being fractionally lower yet containing two full storeys (that on the top having a taller mullioned and transomed window) over a semi-basement. Some quoining at ground floor level suggests that one end gable pre-dates the other. Beyond these, the house recesses again, and a further wing projects in ranges of diminishing size with small mullioned windows and at least one blocked archway. The south front rises from this longish two (low) storey wing to the full height of the main build where quoins at the angles establish the fact that the wing must represent services tacked on, again later in the seventeenth century, although multiple small alterations have left anomalies upon it, including three early nineteenth century sash windows with plate glass. At the west end of the main part of this front is a three-storey gabled projection followed by tall, later windows lighting the south staircase, and another protruding chimney breast with quoins. The windows here appear to be mainly eighteenth century. Thomas Clark worked here in the 1720s but little evidence survives.

Inside, one enters via the hall, with a plain compartmental ceiling, lined with Jacobean panelling and with a fine carved oak fireplace and overmantel of similar date. Much more ornamental is the chamber over this, which has full height panelling, a Sheffield School plasterwork frieze and cornice, a bolection-moulded fireplace and a Jacobean overmantel with arcaded compartments. This is approached via the north stair, another fine Jacobean affair with a square section bulgy newel and turned balustrade. The first floor room at the north-east angle has a very interesting fireplace with leafy pilasters enclosing lozenge panels, and the frieze atop the panelling is richly, if unsophisticatedly, carved. Elsewhere there is a profusion of oak panelling, even in the corridors and there is exposed timber studding, including on the south staircase, which is itself hardly less imposing than that on the north, but with slimmer balusters and more elegant carved newels. In short, the interior is surprisingly spacious and noble, somewhat exceeding the aspirations of the Revels themselves, ever plagued by the symptoms of decline.

The park was once quite pretty (until coal mining and industry supervened) sporting a fine avenue of beeches and a herd of deer right into the present century. There is also a fine stable block, and 120 acres of demesne survived until early in the present century too, the park occupying 25 acres thereof. The estate, however, was ever very modest, being some 1,200 acres at the time of the refronting of the house (1693-99), and the tax was paid on 15 hearths in 1670, betokening a reasonably spacious house even before rebuilding.

Edward Revell, grandson of the Thomas who let to

Anthony Eyre, died in 1639 leaving an illegitimate heir, Francis Adamant (or Adiman) alias Revell. What with his Royalism in the Civil War and disputes with other claimants, the estate suffered by the time his son Francis (died 1681) took over after a long minority in 1666. His father had, however, had a regrant of the family arms with due difference: a *bordure compony or and sable*. This second Francis also left a grandson who was unable to produce a legitimate heir. This was Rev. Francis Revell, who had the livings of South Normanton and Youlgreave, but had children by at least two mistresses. One of these was the sister of the dubious Derby banker, John Heath, and her eldest son by him, Col Tristram Revell (alias Heath) inherited, but disputes with various people who felt they had a better claim obliged him to sell a reversion of the estate to a kinsman, Sir John Eardley Wilmot in 1741.

The estate duly fell to the Wilmots on Revell's death in 1797, but they fared no better over it. The Wilmot's solicitor was one Joseph Wilson of Alfreton, who more or less engrossed the estate by guile and by the time he became bankrupt in 1840 was well in residence at the Hall. He was arrested there on 13 April 1840, and died in gaol on 3 July following. These misfortunes did not, however, lead to the loss of the Carnfield estate, for his daughter and heiress brought it to her husband Thomas Radford, of the Smalley family, and they had regained possession by 1853. Their son, Vaughan Hobbs Radford sold up in the Edwardian period to William Lucas of Dronfield whose grandfather had founded a firm of Sheffield tool manufacturers, and dying childless, his trustees sold in 1947 with 1,000 acres to the then tenant, Mrs Melville Watson, who died in 1949, after which it was the home of a L. N. Darbyshire. From the 1960s, however, it was effectively empty and decaying, although a garden centre was established adjacent in the 1970s.

In 1987 it was finally purchased by James Cartland, who has restored it at vast personal expense, but with restraint and characteristic good taste, and in 1990 he opened it to the public for the first time. It is to be hoped that a three century decline has at last been reversed.

Pevsner, 122; DAJ XCI (1971) 141 f.; RCHM (E), *Carnfield Hall* (York, 1988); REVELL/Vv.1569, 1611, 1662; RADFORD-NORCOP/BLG (1952) 1893.

it incorporates slight traces of earlier timber framing yielding a dendrochronological date of around 1583. Beyond the gable on the south-west corner is another, lower, gable uncoped, with similar fenestration, an extremely plain entrance with a miniscule two-light mullioned window above which appears to represent a slightly later extension to the houseplace incorporating two small chambers. Beyond again, is an old, low wing of two builds, the furthermost part being nineteenth century, and various outbuildings, like the house, with stone slate roofs. The string course between the floors observed on the west front has been carried right round in an attempt to establish some kind of stylistic unity. The straight parapeted part on the west seems to be the latest feature, having much in common with Newton Old Hall *(qv)*. The south-west corner would appear to be a trifle older, with the south-east corner older again, and probably sharing a genesis with the bulk of the stacks on the west front. The house is ashlared throughout in Coal Measures sandstone, probably Greenmoor Rock, with dressings similar, from a local outcrop.

The interior, which may have started out with an open hall plan, is surprisingly rich, although some of what one sees today was brought from demolished Greenhill Hall, Norton *(qv)* in 1964. The magnificent plaster ceiling in the parlour – a classic of the Sheffield School genre – is partly from Greenhill Hall, although it includes a fireplace with a relief of the Fall of Man with, above, the motto 'Whatsoever dost take in hande thinke of the ende and seldom shalt thou offend' from vanished Attercliffe Hall in Yorkshire. The plasterwork in the north bedroom is, according to the RCHM, all from Greenhill Hall, too, but the barrel vaulted best bedroom appears to be original. A fine cruck barn adjoins.

The original hall – thought by some to be the house now known as the Grange – was acquired by John Wolstenholme, whose father or grandfather settled at Horsleygate Hall from Lancashire c. 1450. In 1556, Alice, the heiress brought it to Thomas Burton of the Dronfield family, and one suggestion is that the present Hall was built as her dower house in c. 1585. Their posterity, who seem the likely creators of the bulk of the house, also rebuilt the Grange nearby and eventually let the Hall to a cadet branch of the Wolstenholmes, the main branch of which family had removed to London in the mid-sixteenth century and gone on to a baronetcy. In 1670 a Mrs. Wolstenholme paid tax on

CARTLEDGE HALL (II*)

Holmesfield   Private residence

Local tradition has it that this charming house was built in 1492, but although parts of it certainly look older than the early seventeenth century date, which appears most likely for the bulk of it, this date has to be rejected; indeed, it may refer to the nearby Cartledge Grange. Indeed, it is the very irregularity of the house than enhances its picturesque appearance combined with its surprising lowness. To the road one sees only a pair of massive projecting chimney breasts topped with diamond section paired stacks, with a lower parapet running in between and a five-light mullioned window on each of the two storeys in the centre – 20th century insertions – over the lower of which the string course is cranked. Behind each chimney are straight coped gables, and on the south is another of the same build with a three-light mullioned window above a pair of six-light ones with transoms. Thus far the house appears to be of, say, late sixteenth century date but

Cartledge Hall, Holmesfield in 1982.   M. Craven

eight hearths there which probably represents the house much as it is today. Later in the eighteenth century, however, it degenerated into a farmhouse, subdivided by 1851 and owned by the Waterfall family of Sheffield, followed from 1851 by the Blands and from 1896 George Greaves, whose grand-daughter sold to Basil Doncaster. In 1875 tenant Mark Spittlehurst, farmer, had allowed the master bedroom to become 'a roosting place for fowls' and although his successor, another farmer called Elliott made efforts to reinstate it, the house continued to decline.

In 1892 it had been let to the writer and Bohemian free spirit Robert Murray Gilchrist (died 1917), who divided the house into three to accommodate himself, some relations, and his friend George Garfitt. Isabella Gilchrist died in 1947 and the house swiftly became completely derelict, but was restored by Basil Doncaster, upon whose death in 1959 his good work was continued by his son Richard. Since 1980 it has been the home of Ashley Turner, Esq. who has continued the work of conservation.

Pevsner, 246; DLC 1/66; RCHM (E) *Cartledge Hall and Outbuildings* (Swindon, 1992); Deeds etc (ex. Pers.comm.. A. B. Turner, Esq.); WOLSTENHOLME, Bt./BDEB (1838) 578-9; BURTON of Dronfield/Glover, II.288.

CASTLEFIELDS

Derby   *Demolished*

The west front and gardens of Castlefields, c. 1730.
Derby Museum

In 1713 William Woolley wrote: '... beyond is Castlefields, where Mr Boroughs builds a very good house (with a curious garden and a paddock for deer) and has a very good seat;' which fixes the date for the erection of this tall three-storey brick house with stone dressings as in the years up to that date. The architect's name is unknown, but Abbott's Hill, also in Derby, was very close to it in many respects; the mason Roger Morledge is known from this period in Derby, and it could be he, or perhaps even the father of Richard Jackson of Armitage, Staffs., who built the Derby Guildhall in 1731 and was working earlier at Calke *(qv)*.

The west facade was of seven bays, the central three slightly recessed, with quoins at the angles, architrave surrounds to the windows and a segmental pediment to the entrance. The Bucks' engraving of Derby from the east (1728) rather suggests that each main front was similar, in which case it would have appeared with two-bay angle

pavilions, like indeed a miniature version of Calke – which may, of course, have been what the client, Isaac Borrow may have sought to achieve. The entrance front looked west, and on either side were two service wings, gable end to the west, extending back towards the river Derwent on to which the house's garden front looked. Stables, offices and a dovecote were placed to the north. All was in brick probably with Millstone Grit sandstone dressings, probably Ashover Grit or Rough Rock from the Coxbench area, with a flat roof.

The demesne was part of the ancient commonality of the Borough, and derived its name from the ephemeral adulterine castle thought to have been erected in the 1140s by the Earl of Chester during the war between Stephen and the Empress Matilda *(qv Repton Hall)*. To the west lay an enclosed garden decorated with formal parterres near the house. Down the north wall of this ran a thoroughfare later to become Traffic Street, and between it and the Derwent Navigation ran Siddall's Lane (now Siddall's Road) an ancient way to the pastures to the south. The park also lay to the south with some estate beyond; the rest of Mr. Borrow's land was at Hulland Hall *(qv)*. The park may have been landscaped at some time: Hutton says: 'Great care has been taken to secure it from the eye of the traveller. The premises abound with well disposed clumps, nearly perfect. No situation can be ill, which has Derby on one side, the fine river Derwent on another, the spacious London Road on a third and a beautiful park on the fourth.' In fact, the London Road turnpike was only driven along the western boundary of the park in 1738, travellers to the Capital having previously had to travel via Osmaston Road and Swarkestone Bridge.

In 1803, Capt Thomas Borough (he had changed the spelling of his name some years before) purchased Chetwynd Park, Shropshire, and retired there. The Castlefields estate was gradually sold off in parcels, one of the earliest being a chunk west of the London Road on which the Derbyshire General Infirmary was built in 1806-10. The last parts were disposed of in 1856. The house itself first was let to Baroness Grey de Ruthyn (later Marchioness of Hastings) then to Henry Moore, a silk throwster, until 1832 when Mrs. Bateman had it. It was offered for sale in 1833, apparently without success. From 1836 it lay empty for a year or so, and was demolished in 1837-38. The aptly named Park Street was pushed through in front of the house, Siddall's Lane was widened, as was Traffic Street, and the entire area became covered with artisans' dwellings and factories, all the result of the coming of the railway to a large site at the south end of the park. On Siddall's Road some outbuildings remained in use until at least 1895, one as a school, but today no trace remains of this fine house, bar the odd place or street name.

Woolley, 16, p.31; Hutton (1791) 306; Chetwynd Park Account Book (Private Colln.); DAJ I (1879) 92, II (1880) 28, IV (1882) 144; DM 5/6/1833; BOROUGH of Chetwynd Park/Glover, II 581-84, BLG (1937) 197, HASTINGS, M. *see* LOUDOUN, E/BP (1999) 11. 1765.

CASTLETON HALL (II)

Youth hostel

An unexpectedly pleasing, but in detail rather quirky, early eighteenth century seat which sits unobtrusively right in the centre of Castleton. The main front is of two lowish storeys stretching across seven bays and made of curiously small ashlar blocks almost giving the effect of bricks of Carboniferous Limestone. The central three bays break slightly forward under a cornice and parapet supported by pilasters topped by capitals composed only of metopes and guttae betraying a complete lack of understanding of classicism by the local mason who must have built it. Likewise the central fenestration has large slab-like triangular pediments resting on a thin unrelated cornice on to which terminates the large keyblocks carved from the entablature which merges to form the architrave. This arrangement pertains on the first floor, where the windows (today rather fussy casements, but once paned sashes) are headed with three odd rusticated blocks and all have aprons. The outer bays have simpler windows with flat architraves and modest keyblocks, being separated by a band. All these dressings are of Millstone Grit sandstone, probably Shale Grit. The whole was described aptly by Pevsner as: 'comically ignorant'. The pitched roof is set off by panelled stacks, and a three-bay range of much less pretension – conceivably a remaining portion of the previous house, much rebuilt subsequently – stands at right angles at the right. This too is built of small stone blocks, but here merely brought to course. Inside, most of the pretension that it must have had has been lost to nineteenth century decorative ideas and twentieth century imperatives. Today the facade has been rendered in a most unsatisfactory manner.

The previous house must have been a much more modest affair, Richard Ashton paying tax on but four hearths there in 1670. Its enlargement was probably the work of his kinsman, Robert Ashton around 1700, whose posterity endowed it with the title of Hall, although their estate was modest and lay outside the village rather than contiguous to the house. Robert's nephew was arraigned for murder, however, and the house was advertised to let in June 1742, its contents having previously been sold. The tenant and later proprietor was Micah Hall (1725-1804), a local attorney, and the Halls – who had important interests in the

nearby Blue John mine and were related to the Derby spar turner, Richard Brown – remained there until the mid-nineteenth century. Joseph Hall left two daughters: Josephine, who brought it to her husband Charles Lombe, and Eliza Louisa, married to William Cameron Moore of a mill owner of Bamford. Henry Charles Buxton Lombe, Josephine's second son, thereafter sold it to his cousin Joseph Hall Moore by whom it was let (and later sold) to the YHA after a contents sale in 1929.

Pevsner, 123; Tarn (1971), 21; Lysons, V. 71; DM 3/6/1742; Ashton/V.1662; MOORE of Bamford/FD (1929) II.1387; LOMBE *sub* EVANS-LOMBE/BLG (1969) 776.

CATTON HALL (II*)

Private residence

A seat has existed at Catton for a very long time, Amaury de St Amand being in possession there from at least 1284, his father having married Ascelina, daughter and co-heiress of Robert de Albini of Bedfordshire to whom it had descended from an heiress of de Ferrers. His great grandson, Sir Almaric, second Lord de St Amand (a creation by Writ of Summons of 22 March 1313) exchanged Catton for Harlington, Bedfordshire, with Ralph son of Reginald Pyrot in 1336 in order to consolidate his holdings in the south Midlands. In 1404, however, the estate was obtained by Sir Roger Horton of Coole, by Nantwich, in Cheshire, and his male descendants held it until the death of Eusebius Horton in 1823.

The earliest vestiges of the first house lie in the chapel, a building of 1892 replacing two earlier ones, the medieval one having been destroyed in the earlier seventeenth century. This had its origins in the late eleventh century, for about 1100 Nigel d'Albini had granted it to Tutbury Priory, but it later became attached to the house for all practical purposes. Later it was deserted (like the lost village of Catton), then demolished. The Hortons later built a new one which was mentioned in 1650 by the Parliamentary Commissioners as being '... lately consecrated for the convenience of Mr Horton's famelye.' This was accidentally destroyed by fire in 1744, and was not replaced for 148 years, during which time a curse was said to have operated whereby no son would succeed his father until it was rebuilt. The present Norman font was rescued from the river where it was doubtless thrown when the Commissioners caught up with the royalist Hortons in the Civil War. Pieces of medieval masonry also abounded in the gardens at one time, and the stable clock now chimes the hours upon a bell cast in the sixteenth century by Newcombe of Leicester which may or may not have had a similar origin.

The only other possible fragment of the former house is thought to be a remaining gatepier, but an inventory of 1625 survives showing it to have been of moderate size, a fact supported by 15 hearths having been assessed for tax in 1662. Unfortunately it failed to catch Woolley's eye in 1713, and he merely mentions a seat here. However, in c. 1740 Christopher Horton commissioned designs for a new house from William Smith, who proposed a seven by seven bay house of two and a half storeys measuring 62 feet by 65 feet on the ground. The contractor was to have been one of the Trubshaws of Great Heywood (Staffordshire) – Richard (died 1745) or his son Charles Cope – and a revision of the design by one of them also exists. In the event, a third design was proposed, larger at 93 feet by 70 feet and nine by six bays. This was also by William Smith of Warwick and is

Castleton Hall, 1997.   C.L.M. Porter

Catton Hall.   K. Neilson

dated 26 January 1741, and this is the house that was built. The contractor in this case was one of the Pickfords, probably William, father of the Derby architect Joseph, who was working on Stoneleigh Abbey, Warwickshire, with Smith at the time, and actually built the kennels there.

The house as built is of three storeys in brick over a stone faced basement and from a distance looks very large and dignified, although a trifle old-fashioned for its date, harking back, with its hipped tiled roof, to William Smith the elder, although a low parapet proclaims the true date. The dressings are all of Keuper sandstone. The former entrance front, on the south, is of nine bays with keyblocks and a band between the principal floors, the central entrance aedicule being a stone one with Tuscan columns supporting a triangular pediment on a metope frieze. The central three bays break slightly forward, a similar arrangement pertaining on the west front of seven bays. To the north, the house is deeply recessed, and there is an office wing in Queen Anne style of 1907 by T.G. Jackson. In 1829 the house was 'turned round', putting a new entrance into the six-bay east front, and converting the former hall to a dining-room. This, as one would expect with Smith, has plenty of fine rococo plasterwork both on walls and ceiling, and carved overdoors. It led to the main staircase, a rather old-fashioned one with turned balusters on a string under a chunky rail upswept at the angles. Here, too, the ceiling of the stairwell is richly stuccoed, as are two other principal rooms. The general effect is all very sumptuous and agreeable, effectively showing how Smith could guarantee 'value for money' over more fashionable architects like Gibbs. The kitchens were fitted up in the regency period with 'steam boilers, Stoves etc'. by John Harrison, a Derby iron founder who was exploiting improvements made to domestic apparatus of various kinds by William Strutt, FRS. These were all swept away in 1907, however, when the new wing was built. The property is set in a fine park which dramatically used the Trent for effect, and may be by William Emes.

In 1823 the heiress of the last Horton brought the property to Sir Robert Wilmot 3rd Bt of Osmaston (qv) who adopted the surname and arms of Horton additionally to his own the same year. His wife was a great beauty for whom her husband's first cousin Lord Byron wrote the famous lines:

She walks in beauty, like the night
Of cloudless climes and starry skies
And all that's best of dark and bright
Meet in her aspect and her eyes.

the manuscript of which is still at the house. This lady's aunt, Mrs. Christopher Horton, had earlier created a scandal by morganatically (and bigamously) marrying Frederick, Duke of Cumberland, one of George III's brothers.

The Wilmot-Hortons became extinct with the death of the sixth baronet in 1931, but as he was not himself descended from the Hortons, the estate went with his predecessor's heiress Mrs. Henry Tufnell, whose daughter brought it to Henry Anson, who had also assumed the additional surname and arms of Horton in 1899. On the death of his elder son in 1951, the estate came to his sister's son, Mr. D. W. H. Neilson, whose eldest son and daughter-in-law now occupy the main part of the house, the remainder having been converted into three other residences. The house was re-roofed in 1999, and opened to visitors on Monday afternoons from June 2001.

Colvin, 407, 902; Woolley, 130, p.168; Cox III (1877) 363-64; Usher (1881) 178; Summerson (1970) 157-163; Gomme (2001) 475-78, 519; CL CXXVII (17/3/1960) 566 & (24/3/1960) 624; DLC 3/1969; DET 14/6/2001; Staffs. CRO, D260/M/E379-98; HORTON of Catton/Glover, II 205 & DAJ III (1881) 67-72; WILMOT-HORTON, Bt./BP (1931) 2492; ANSON-HORTON *sub* NEILSON of Catton/ BLG (1972) 676-77.

CHADDESDEN HALL

Demolished

Chaddesden was the seat of Erneis de Chaddesden in the last years of the twelfth century and the Chaddesden family flourished there until the manorial estate was divided via their heiresses between the families of Herberjour, Lawrence, Sacheverell and FitzHerbert. The most important moiety descended via the Herberjours to the Plumptons and was sold by their heirs, the Cliffords to the Curzons of Kedleston from whom it was purchased in Elizabethan times by the Newtons (*qv* Duffield Hall, Mickleover Manor), from which family it was ultimately acquired by the Lowes of Locko. The other moieties fragmented into minor freeholds, several of which were ultimately acquired by a Derby draper of Nottinghamshire extraction called Robert Wilmot. These he increased out of the spoils of the Reformation in 1539. As his immediate progeny are described as 'of Chaddesden' rather than as 'of Derby' it must be assumed that they resided there, although it is not until the will of Robert Wilmot of Chaddesden in 1639 that we can be sure. In this he says that he was '...building a new house at Chaddesden' and this seat remained until 1727-28 when it was replaced. The cellars of this house were not so long ago (1988) stumbled upon by accident, and there is circumstantial evidence to suggest that this was largely a timber-framed seat – perhaps along the lines of Wakelin Old Hall, Hilton, of a similar date (*qv*) – and that it is known that timber from the house was incorporated in the new music room at Etwall Lawn. Robert also provided timber-framed almshouses at Derby (1619 rebuilt 1834 and demolished in 1936) and Chaddesden (in 1634, demolished in the 1960s).

Chaddesden Hall, c. 1900.

D. Gwinnett

Sir Edward Wilmot 1st Bt, (so created 1759, the recipient having been physician general to HM Forces) was the son of Robert Wilmot, who is the one who decided to replace the old house in 1727-8, shortly after having come into his inheritance (he was paying for the bricks in the latter year). He built a typical four-square house, tall, of three storeys over a basement with a seven-bay front facing west towards the lane. The central section of three bays broke forward under a cornice and panelled parapet – a sort of Castlefields (qv) in reverse. It was of brick and stone; the Rough Rock, Millstone Grit sandstone, (from Horsley Castle quarry) with gauged brick lintels and skinny rusticated pilasters at the angles. The general style of the house might suggest an attribution to Richard Jackson, as it has much in common with Hopwell Hall (which Prof. Andor Gomme has suggested may be by Jackson) and Walton-on-Trent (qv).

Around 1790, the 2nd baronet decided to enlarge the house and added a lumpish portico in matching style, rebuilding the breakfront with a single large tripartite window with a slightly under-scale Diocletian over, and rebuilt the corresponding section on the garden front to project quite considerably, again in matching style, but with a large uncompromising tripartite window. A pretty three-bay two-story pavilion with a pediment was added to the north. A less handsome one to balance it on the other side was added as a ballroom by Sir Henry Wilmot VC in the 1870s. The interior appears to have left no record, but the whole was set in a pleasant landscaped park, a portion of which remains today for public recreation. If it was laid out contemporary with the rebuilding of the house, it may be that, yet again, William Emes was responsible, but this is by no means certain.

After the death in 1901 of General Sir Henry Wilmot, VC, 5th Bt, the estate passed to his nephew, on whose death in action in 1918, the house was closed up, and was sold and demolished in 1926. Subsequently, much of the park was acquired for building, and the remainder was leased in 1936 by Quinton Estates of Birmingham to Chaddesden Parish Council, which lease was later transferred to the County Borough of Derby for 99 years at £250 per annum. Later the Derby City Council acquired the freehold for £11,000, including a total of 60 acres.

Woolley, 51, p.83; Lysons, V. 260; Hutton (1791) 309; Binney *et al* (1982) 18; Henderson & Robinson (1979) 72; Fearneyhough (1991) 20-27; Cholerton (1999) 28-32; Catton MSS, Derby Local Studies Library; WILMOT of Chaddesden, Bt/BP (1999) II. 3037-39.

CHATSWORTH

Private Residence/Open to public

The west front from the approach road from Edensor.
C.L.M Porter

In 1066 Chatsworth and Langley (a 'lost' place-name, but part of the same manor) were held by the homonymous (if not eponymous) Chetel, and thereafter the manor appears to have been held by a branch of the de Edensors (kin to the Shirleys) until c. 1330 when Sir John Leche, who was surgeon (or 'Leech') to Edward III, was granted the estate. How it had come into the King's hands is not now apparent. Nor did the Leches get their name from Sir John's profession, for the family is met with not so far away at Pinxton where three of this name witnessed a charter there c. 1216-35. The estate then went through 11 generations to Francis Leche who married Bess of Hardwick's sister and sold the estate with the house and park to John Agard, a scion of the Agards of Foston Hall (qv) who had taken a lease of Cromford and made a fortune in lead dealing. He died without surviving issue and it was sold on for £600 to Sir William Cavendish in 1549, who nearly two years earlier had married Mrs. Richard Barlow of Barlow, daughter of John Hardwick of Hardwick and the ultimate co-heiress of her brother: this of course is the woman known to most of us as Bess of Hardwick; she was William Cavendish's third wife; he was her second.

Cavendish held most of his land around Cavendish in Suffolk, but was persuaded by his forceful new wife to sell all of them and remove to Derbyshire where she already held some land and had expectations of more. Immediately she began to build, although the old Leche seat was not immediately demolished, for in May 1560 the roof of the 'holde howse' was under repair: six days' slaters' work at 6d a day. When it ultimately came down is unknown, although its site was a little to the north of the present house. Whether Queen Mary's Bower, nearby, which is a moated feature to the north-west of the house which bore a structure as early as 1610, is the reused site of an even earlier seat of the Edensors is unclear; conflicting claims abound, but no solid evidence is available. Although a relatively small feature, the likelihood certainly exists.

Bess of Hardwick's Chatsworth was built over a period of 15 years; the first plans were drawn up by Roger Worth in 1551, and after a long lacuna in the accounts, record the finishing in 1576. Mark Girouard suggests that the house expanded with their builder's fortunes: Cavendish died in 1557, whereupon his widow married a courtier, Sir William St Loe of Tormarton Court, Gloucestershire, in 1559; he died in 1564 and in 1567 she married George Talbot, sixth Earl of Shrewsbury – a very grand catch indeed for the daughter of a minor gentleman. The house Bess built was the epitome of the Midland High House: four-square, of the three, four and five storeys, battlemented, with towers and many chimneys all built around a courtyard. In keeping with Bess's extravagant character, it was largely brick in an area rich in building stone, although there appear to have been plentiful stone dressings, probably of Ashover Grit from Ball or Bow Cross. The only views of it to survive are all of the west front, although Wilson's painting after Siberechts suggests that the east front was similar. The centre of the facade was marked by an in-built gatehouse, slightly higher than the rest of the house, enclosed by V-shaped towers with a wide segmental archway topped by a bay of mullioned and transomed windows, and an array of heraldry' carved in relief. Either side again were four bays in four storeys (in contrast to the central feature's five) but with the end of the long gallery at a mezzanine level at the south end and a balancing feature to the north, all with bands between the floors over the window heads. The huge, ten-light gallery windows were also pedimented. The south-east and south-west angles were marked by square five-storey towers, with a similar pair carrying staircases near the north-west and north-east

angles, but inset by a bay, a felicitous idiosyncrasy foreshadowing the arrangement at Hardwick 30 years or more later. The battlements were in fact merlons, or something very like them, which also anticipates a feature of high houses built for members of Bess's family and their circle in Derbyshire by the Smythsons whom, however, had yet to appear on the scene. A most notable feature was that the grandest suites were on the third floor (for the family) and the fourth (for state use), an arrangement, which was very nearly unique at the time. Again, this was to become a hallmark of the houses with which Bess was associated.

The long gallery, across the south front, was taller than either adjoining floors, but built on a mezzanine between them. It is reasonable to assume, too, from the layout of the present house, that the great chamber was reached by a staircase direct from the great hall. Girouard suggests that an extra floor may have been added after Bess's fourth marriage in 1576 when the interior was being completed. In addition to the substantial and decorative outworks to the west, visible in Wilson's painting, a hunting stand was built on the hill to the east-north-east of the house in the 1580s, very possibly to a design by Robert Smythson. This is a four-storey, decorative affair in ashlar, with four grouped dome capped towers, three good rooms with decorative plasterwork, mullion and transom cross windows with diamond panes, and sill bands; fortunately, it survives. In the *Wonders of the Peak* (De Mirabilibus Pecci) Hobbes eulogises Chatsworth thus:

As to the astonished seaman's startled sight
The City of Venice 'midst the waves appears
Unlooked for; thus 'midst many a mountain's height
The Devonian Hall its towers uprears.

He was, of course, a long-time Chatsworth resident. Charles Cotton, too, has some lines which throw some light on the Elizabethan House:

On Derwent's Shore stands a stupendous Pile,
Like the proud Regent of the British Isle.

The forenamed outward gate then leads into
A spacious court, whence open to the view
The noble front of the whole edifice
To a surprising height it seems to rise.
Even with the gate-house, upon either hand,
A neat square turret at the corners stand;
And to the lodge admits, and three steps more
Sets you upon a plain and level floor,
Which paves the inner court, wherein doth rise,
Another fountain of a fine device,
Which large limbed heroes with Majestic port,
In their habiliments of war support.
Hence cross the court, thro' a fine portico,
Into the body of the house you go...

...and so on in McGonagallesque vein.

From this one can gather that the interior was as richly ornate as one might reasonably assume, although the descriptions of the fountains, terraces (a large one graced the south front apparently) and parterres are more specific, suggesting that the author saw a good deal less of this interior than of the outside! The old house saw Mary, Queen of Scots within its walls in 1570, 1573, 1577, 1578 and 1581.

Chatsworth passed, on Bess of Hardwick's death, to her second son, Sir William Cavendish KB, created Lord Cavendish of Hardwick and Earl of Devonshire. His great-grandson, William, fourth Earl of Devonshire, re-solved to modernize the old seat and commissioned William Talman to rebuild the south front, which work began 12 April 1687. Devonshire was then in the political doldrums, and probably felt that he would have plenty of leisure to concentrate on these works. Yet in 1688, he was prime mover in the so-called Glorious Revolution, which role ultimately led to his elevation to the Dukedom of Devonshire and Marquessate of Hartington. His rebuilding began to take on the aspect of an adaptation of the old house as a ducal seat, and Talman proceeded to rebuild the east front too, a move prompted by the replacement of the original staircase which led off the Great Hall on the east front, opposite the old west entrance, in 1689. This led logically to the replacement of the Great Hall itself, and the natural consequence of that was that Talman was ordered to rede-sign the whole east wing, which was completed in 1696, two years after Devonshire received his Dukedom.

The south front is of 13 bays, two tall storeys being carried over a high basement, with a frieze decorated with Cavendish knots marking the three-bay projecting end pavil-ions, and the punning family motto: *Cavendo Tutus* over the central seven. Above this is a muscular cornice topped by a balustrade and urns. As with Elizabethan Chatsworth, the window heights are greater on the upper storey, for this was, after all, only a rebuilding of the old house, and the dispo-sition of state rooms is in fact a penumbra of that which went before. The end pavilions are divided into bays with a stop-fluted giant Ionic order, but the centre is quite plain except for the complex perron and stair to the terrace below, by Wyatville of 1837, replacing a curvy one by Talman which had been decorated with a wrought-iron balustrade by Jean Tijou. The fenestration is in architrave surrounds, con-nected to bands above each storey by massive keyblocks, those on the pavilions decorated by carved stags' antlers. The fine ashlar work was of the same stone used by Bess of Hardwick's masons, with Chatsworth Grit from Beeley Moor.

The east front was originally much more workaday, of 11 bays with a frieze decorated with Cavendish knots. Incon-gruous projections marked the second and tenth bays, dis-guising spiral staircases still doubtless clad in their sixteenth century fabric of their original angle towers, and these were enlivened later by Wyatville with paired giant pilasters. He also altered the balustrade to match that on the south front. However, by the time this phase had been completed, rela-tions between the Duke and Talman had deteriorated to such an extent that the architect was given his marching orders. Furthermore, the two fronts marked the limit of Devon-shire's architectural ambitions at this time: the old Eliza-bethan west front still dominated the Derwent valley.

Whether the building of a massive terrace below the west front actually presaged the latter's replacement, or was merely part of the embellishment of the surroundings, linked to work on new parterres by George London – decorated by Talman's chaste bowling green temple – is difficult to say. After Talman left, the terrace's exotic frostwork grotto was completed by his mason Benjamin Jackson. However, in 1700-03 the monumental west front was put up to one of a set of three proposals, signed by the master mason John Fitch. Thanks to the fall of the site from east to west, the semi-basement of the south front here becomes a full ground floor, with two storeys above, and contains the Duke's original rather modest entrance. The ground floor is rusti-cated and forms the plinth from which springs the giant Ionic order which ensigns the nine bays, as pilasters in the outer ones and as attached columns supporting a pediment in the three-bay centre which breaks modestly forward. The frieze and balustrade run round from the south front but the former is exuberantly enriched under the pediment, itself crisply carved by Samuel Watson of Heanor, a man of sensational talent who scarcely moved outside his own county except to serve an apprenticeship in London under Charles Oakley. The garlands below are the work of Henri Nadauld, a refugee upper-class Huguenot who turned his

The south and east fronts about eighty years ago. This view is lost now by the yew trees which have grown up between the statues.

C.L.M. Porter

Chatsworth, the Library.   *Devonshire Collection, Chatsworth*

than those at the west. They were linked by a full height bow of five bays divided by a later giant Corinthian order of pilasters (replacing rusticated ones) all rising beyond the height of the remainder of the building. Here also the fenestration was segmental-headed with oval attic windows. All this was unfortunately rebuilt later by Wyatville as a rectangular projection with more orthodox fenestration. Throughout, the new house, as such it had become, was built in fine ashlar, and sported the earliest sash windows outside London, which on the west front at least are divided with bronze glazing bars supporting bevelled glass panes -a most exquisite refinement. Despite the three architects who contributed to the building, the short time in which it was done and the height of the edifice (giving it a false appearance of compactness), Chatsworth displays an astonishing unity of style, and is thus pictured by Siberechts in 1707 in its formal setting, with Talman's 13-bay orangery and Elizabethan outbuildings between it and the north front.

Inside there is craftmanship of the highest order. The great Painted Hall, on the site of the Elizabethan Great Hall on the east range is approached via a Doric entrance hall contrived by James Paine in the late 1750s from the former kitchen, but which has been subsequently altered by Wyatville. The painted Hall is richly frescoed with the *Life of Julius Caesar* by Laguerre and Ricard, 1694, although the effect lacks the conviction of the carving of Watson which was done to compliment it. The stairs are the third flight in that position, put in to the designs of W.H.RomaineWalker in 1911-12 along with the gallery. Beneath the stairs is the Grotto, a triumph of Watson's carving in stone: above, one at last encounters the great staircase. Beyond the grotto too is the rather bizarre Oak Room full of early eighteenth century German carving, looking rather incongruous, and thence one approaches the most dramatic room in the house, the Chapel. It is a full two storeys in height and one is immediately arrested by the superb reredos in Chellaston alabaster designed by Caius Gabriel Cibber and carved by the matchless Watson; *Faith and Justice,* behind the altar, are by Cibber himself. The cedar panelling has limewood carvings in the style of Grinling Gibbons, probably also by Watson, whose work at Chatsworth was for generations assumed to be by the former, such is its richness and competence. The reredos had also columns of Ashford Black marble, and local stones are to be found throughout the house; White Watson was reflooring the lower floors in them in the 1770s. The walls and ceilings are by Laguerre, upstaged by the painting of *Doubting Thomas* over the reredos by Antonio Verrio.

Beyond the chapel is the west staircase with a wonderful *Fall of Phaeton* by Sir James Thornhill on the ceiling, and balustrade by John Gardom of Baslow, a pupil of Tijou. The stairs lead to the State Rooms via two connecting rooms, and also give access to the sumptuously baroque Sabine Room, by Thornhill. The five State Rooms are enfiladed in the new formality of their period, but look back to Bess of Hardwick by their appearance on the top floor, their presence dictated by the constraints of the piecemeal nature of the first Duke's rebuilding scheme. This enfilade is extended by the device of hanging a sumptuous mirror at the east end. The State Dining Room has a very fine ceiling by Verrio, the remainder being by Laguerre and Ricard, here much superior to their work in the Painted Hall and Chapel. Here too the carving

hobby of carving into a profession after coming, pennyless, to England. Like Watson, he left a local dynasty ensconced nearby.

The entire west front is superb, massive, dignified and (like the south before it) quite un-English; the main derivation is not so much J.H.Mansart but Vaux-le-Viscomte, by Le Vau, according to John Harris, endorsing the opinion of Sir John Summerson. The question which remains unsolved is: who designed it? Sir James Thornhill used to be favoured, but his work lay within, in fresco; Thomas Archer had always been a strong contender: he almost certainly designed the attractive cascade house, and later built the ingenious north front. Harris suggests that Talman might at least have had some influence on the final design before being bundled off the site, and it might not be too fanciful to see the hand of the redoubtable Sir John Vanburgh in it, for he stayed 'four or five days' with the Duke in 1699, and one doubts if he stayed there purely for social reasons. Geoffrey Beard, indeed, remarks of Castle Howard (begun by Vanburgh shortly afterwards). 'The stone carving really belongs in spirit to the work of William Talman at Chatsworth' and not only did Henri Nadauld work on both, but Vanburgh actually replaced Talman at Castle Howard. Thus the mystery endures.

Following the completion of the west front, a colonnade with gallery over were added to the inside of the south front, overlooking the courtyard, with its enriched Talmanic facades, in 1703-04, and then work started on the north front. This *tour de force* by Thomas Archer completed the eclipse of the Elizabethan mansion, but in order to do so, Archer had to disguise the non-alignment of the ends of the east and west ranges, which he overcame using an 11-bay three and a half storey facade having its three east end bays wider spaced

The "Great Stove" at Chatsworth, by D. Burton & J. Paxton. Photographed by R. Keene 1858/59.

M. Craven

is less by Watson, and mainly from the hands of Joel Lobb, William Davis and Thomas Young, men from the capital. Wonderful furniture in these rooms has been supplemented by pieces from Chiswick (by Kent), Wanstead and Devonshire House, London.

The State Apartments lead to the head of the Great Stairs via a doorcase of titanic proportions in Chellaston alabaster carved by Cibber, some of whose statues can also be seen here. The stair rail is by Tijou himself, and the ceiling is the *Triumph of Semele* by Verrio. The scheme for the stair well walls was never realized, and what remains is anonymous. On the east front of the upper floor is the library, originally the Long Gallery, another survivor from the old house, with a rich plaster ceiling by Edward Goudge, but otherwise remodelled by Wyatville. It was, of course, Wyatville who greatly extended the house at the sixth Duke's behest to the north, starting in 1820. This effectively produced a new suite of state rooms, including a ballroom-cum-dining room, with chimneypieces embellished by figures from the hand of Richard Westmacott, a sculpture gallery (containing all manner of riches) and orangery, besides bachelors' bedrooms, offices and the notable Belvedere topping the theatre, itself once over a swimming pool, in all an extension of almost 600 feet, of ashlar cut from Ashover Grit from Stancliffe. Wyatville also altered the family rooms in the main house, below the state rooms on the south front, with decorative work in some by the Victorian decorator J.G. Crace.

As rebuilt, the house seems to have had some highly state-of-the-art plumbing, by which Celia Fiennes was most struck, writing that the bath room she used had blue and white marble walls and a marble bath (which sounds as if it might be chilly in winter) and which "...was as deep as one's middle on the outside and you went down some steps into ye bath big enough for two people. At ye upper end are two cocks to let in one hot ye other cold water to attemper it as persons' please."

Outside, the most striking feature is the magnificent stable

court by James Paine, 1758-63. Its west front is of nine bays set in heavily rusticated blank arcading, with higher corner pavilions decorated with broken pediments and pyramidal roofs; the centrepiece is also massively rusticated and banded, with four giant attached Tuscan columns with rusticated sections. Above is a pedimented aedicule containing the fourth Duke's arms (with Boyle, Earl of Burlington in pretence – whose shade must rejoice at such a Palladian *tour-de-force*) carved by Henry Watson of Ashford, son of the incomparable Samuel, and a cupola above containing a fine turret clock: essentially all forming a great bruising triumphal arch leading through to an impressive courtyard with more rustication and an open arcade all round. The contractor was the accomplished James Booth of Stoney Middleton.

The gardens were laid out afresh by George London and Henry Wise, the King's gardeners at the same time as the house was rebuilt; the cascade was by Grillet (*qv* Bretby) and the charming cascade house by Archer, behind which, in the woods is the striking aqueduct built for the sixth Duke. The other notable piece of waterworks is, of course, Sir Joseph Paxton's Emperor Fountain, finished in 1843, placed in the canal and fed by the Emperor Lake; it has the highest throw recorded, of 267 feet. In 1761 Lancelot ('Capability') Brown was called in to help Paine landscape the 1,300-acre park for the fourth Duke, whose own ideas were incorporated. Paine built a new bridge at the south end and the marvellously Palladian mill, now romantically ruined. The mason for this work was William Halkesworth, the estate foreman, who also worked with Joseph Pickford of Derby who was called in to rebuild the weir above it in 1774. Pickford went on to build a new vicarage, near the north-west gate of the park, the north lodge (1782; now converted intro a residence and the arch blocked) and the stunning Edensor Inn of 1777, now somewhat altered and extended, and used today as the estate office.

Pickford's vicarage did not last long, because in 1838 the village was removed to its present site by the sixth Duke, and it was demolished along with all but one remaining cottage, protected by an outstanding freehold. The new village was the work of the Duke's former head gardener Joseph Paxton and the Derby architect John Robertson, a collaborator of J.C.Loudon. The exception is Edensor House of 1839, by Decimus Burton, and the uncompleted octagonal stables which may have been started by Pickford and curtailed by his death in 1782, or could just as easily be by John Carr of York, taken on shortly before by the Duke to build in Buxton. Had they been completed, they would have been most impressive; unfortunately, no records relating to the structure have come to light. Paxton's greatest work at Chatsworth was the Great Stove, or conservatory (1836-40) a structural precursor of the Crystal Palace, in the design of which he was undoubtedly assisted by Decimus Burton. Paxton also relaid the gardens starting a decade earlier; the conservatory, a very elegant and innovative building was, however, demolished in 1920; the foundation walls remain and the space is now a maze. Paxton also built the forcing wall, planted the pinetum and 100-acre arboretum, and finished the Baslow Lodges, begun by Wyatville in 1837. His own rather opulent Italianate house at Edensor, Barbrook, was demolished in 1954.

Modern improvements include the Greenhouse by G.A.H.Pearce of 1970, and a lifetime's work on behalf of the present Duke and Duchess reshaping and in places restoring the gardens and grounds, a triumphal continuation of a distinguished tradition. At the end of the nineteenth century the estate was 89,462 acres, but death duties payable when the present Duke succeeded caused considerable reduction to 35,000. During World War Two, Chatsworth was used to house an evacuated girls' school. Of the family itself, little need be said, so enduring is their fame and so well known their history as great political hosts, patrons of the arts and conservators of this unique and important house and its environment. It has few, if any, rivals in the British Isles.

Colvin, 77, 99, 144, 198, 225, 248, 365, 371, 725, 753, 943, 952, 1023, 1132; Lysons, V. 149; Pevsner, 126 ff.; Glover, II, 220 f.; CL VII (1900) 800-5; XXI (1907) 832-838; CXLIII (1968) 140-9, 220-3, 280-4, 496-510, 554-5; CLIV (1973) 1668-2; DLC 8/56; Devonshire (1982); Thompson (1949); Wood (1973); Girouard (1983) 116-7;119; Brighton, T., *Samuel Watson, not Grinling Gibbons, at Chatsworth* Burlington Magazine CXL (Dec. 1998) 811-818; PRO Ward 9/129; Chatsworth archives; AGARD/V.1611; DEVONSHIRE, D./BP(1999) I. 837-41.

CHURCHDALE HALL (II)

Ashford   *Private Residence*

Built on a small estate purchased by the Dukes of Devonshire from the Earls of Westmoreland early in the nineteenth century and built in 1831 at a cost of £448-19s, when it was the residence of the Duke's agent, Samuel Smithers. The architect was John Price of Derby (1795-1859), who also designed Lea Green (*qv*). It is of ashlar, Millstone Grit Sandstone, probably Ashover grit from Bakewell Edge, with dressings similar; it is L-shaped and remarkably low for a nineteenth century house in a charming, Jacobethan style with ashlar surrounds and hood moulds to the casemented windows, some of which are mullioned. It has coped gables on the entrance front, which started off as three wide bays under deep-coped gables, the coping being extended to form a parapet. There is a ground floor canted bay to the left and an odd, quasi Tudor portico which looks as if it is too high

for its purpose, but in fact the roof forms a balcony for the central first floor window. This was almost certainly an afterthought of c. 1842, when the three irregular right hand bays were added by John Robertson, who increased the ceiling heights in his portion, and added pillar finials capped by balls on his ground floor mullioned and transomed bay which exactly match those topping the portico. The slated roof is punctuated by ornate chimneys. The returns are of three bays, each under a neat gable, similarly coped, and an irregularly placed ground floor canted bay has its parapets forming triangular semi pediments with finials. The symmetrical garden front is of five bays, two eared gables at the ends and a similar central one all breaking slightly forward with a battlemented bay between. There is a modest service wing to the left of the garden front. It was soon let to a succession of tenants, including Messrs. Offley Shore, Haworth, William Fenton, Sladen, Walthew and Fairholm. In the 1920s the 10th Duke resided in the house with 17 acres of grounds, and he remained there until his death in 1950. Five years later it was sold to David Russell, who was farming there 20 years ago. In 1996 it was the home of P. Pathe Esq.

Churchdale Hall: the entrance front.   M. Craven

Pevsner, 66; Colvin 781; Catalogue of the Derby Mechanics' Institute Exhibition, 1839, 130/3; DM 15/7/1840; DLC 12/1966; SHORE of Norton/BLG (1875) II., 1257; DEVONSHIRE, D/BP (1999) I 837-41.

CROXALL HALL (II*)

                       Private residence

At the time of Domesday, Croxall was held under Henry de Ferrers by one Roger who, S.P.H.Statham argues with some conviction, was a kinsman of Hubert, ancestor of the Curzons. Both held jointly at Fauld, in Staffordshire, and it was the Curzons who succeeded to Croxall within a generation. By marriage to heiresses of Camville and Brabazon they swiftly added Edingale (lying partly in Derbyshire until the last century) and one of the manors at Twyford (*qv*) to their holdings. Richard de Curzon, who married the Camville heiress (who also brought land at Clifton Camville), was the elder brother of Thomas de Curzon of Kedleston, and it was at this point, 1205, that the latter estate became detached, leaving Richard's heirs, the elder line, at Croxall.

The present house, of brick with dressings of Keuper sandstone, has its origins in the sixteenth century, with at least one further phase of building around the middle of the century following. It was originally a multi-gabled E-shaped

Croxall Hall c. 1875 by R. Keene   M. Craven

house in brick with stone dressings, with its main front facing approximately south across what was once the park. It is of two storeys with attics, the first floor being the principal one with a predominance of mullioned and transomed windows, whereas those on the ground floor are lower and merely mullioned. Moreover, the attic storey is grander than such a description might imply, for the rooms are loftier, and the window on the south-east gable is a six-light mullion, canted round the angle. The centre of the South front is marked by a tall gable – like the others, straight and coped – with a pair of ornamental brick stacks rising through it, flanked by three other plain gables on either side, those next to the end ones recessed, giving a striking and dignified effect.

The west front is generally similar, although less grand, and it is to be presumed that the east side was too, but it was removed in the nineteenth century probably in 1868 when Potter of Lichfield was carrying out alterations and improvements. The bay nearest the main south front is probably original, having its main floor at second storey level, but north thereof the levels change, and a gabled projection with projecting mullioned and transomed bays marks the position of new formal apartments. This extension is bereft of attics, and is therefore lower, but is marked by tall brick stacks similar to those on the earlier part of the house. Inside, the dining-room chimneypiece bears the date 1658, which may mark the completion of a later phase of construction, and the majority of panelling which is not of nineteenth century date is of a period with this chimneypiece. However, much of the original work has been replaced.

Sir George Curzon, the last of the line, died in 1622, whereupon the estate of some 2,000 acres passed to Hon Sir Edward Sackville, KB, son of the Earl of Dorset. His descendants enjoyed the Dukedom of Dorset from 1720, but in 1785, the third Duke sold Croxall to Thomas Prinsep (1731-95) an 'eminent agriculturalist' from Staffordshire, whose cattle contemporary commentators much admired.

His son died in 1814, whereupon it all passed to his sister's son, Thomas Levett-Prinsep of Whichnor Hall. For much of the nineteenth century, the two estates, divided only by the Trent, were run as one, and Croxall, the east wing removed, was mainly occupied as a farmhouse. However, the 1868 alterations were brought about by expanding requirements, and it was once more occupied by a member of the family. From 1880, however, it again reverted to the role of farmhouse, albeit an impossibly grand one. From 1927 it was let to Col. Percy E.F.Chirnside, who had married the sister and heiress of Nicholas Poyntz Charlton of Chilwell Hall, an estate then in the process of being turned into a piece of outer suburban Nottingham. They remained there into the 1950s, and it was then the residence of Joseph Rose until

his death in 1980. It was subsequently on the market in 1981 and July 1989 with 21 acres. In April 1999 Mr & Mrs A. Staley acquired the Hall and are the current owners.

Pevsner, *Staffordshire*, 111; Glover, II 330; Lysons, V. 92; Woolley, 128; DORSET, D., *sub* SACKVILLE, B./BP (1999) II.2490-1; LEVETT-PRINSEP/BLG (1952) 1517 & 2083; CHIRNSIDE *formerly* CHARLTON of Croxall/*op.cit.*431.

CUTTHORPE HALL (II*)

Private Residence

A charming house which seems to have grown piecemeal from the later sixteenth century, although there is evidence of an older core. Built of coursed Coal Measures Sandstone, probably Wingfield Flags or Sandstone. above Kilburn Coal, with similar dressings, it has two storeys; the garden front has seven irregular bays, some mullioned windows and has a gable on the right hand bay. The main front has, on the other hand, been Georgianized, all under a stone slate roof. Within, there are three very good oak panelled rooms; some decorative plasterwork of c. 1600 and a gallery or chapel in the attic with a flueless fireplace of stone which may have been intended as a priest's hole. Interesting outbuildings lie near an early seventeenth century dower house of two storeys and attics, gables and mullioned windows (II). The house may have been the Linacre Hall of the Linacre family, who certainly held it into the sixteenth century, when it passed to the Foljambes. In 1614 it was sold to a branch of the Heathcotes, Chesterfield municipal oligarchs. The family, (a younger branch of which later held Littleover, *qv*) later inherited Barlborough Hall and assumed the surname and arms of Rodes. It was sold c. 1790 and was tenanted with 250 acres, by William Bowes Wright (1764-1839) of the Great Longstone family who had two wives and a mistress. His widow married the French General Francois-Joseph d'Henin, a prisoner of war whom her husband had befriended. Wright, then a Captain in the Derbyshire Yeomanry Cavalry, managed to take sixty prisoners at Langley Bridge whilst helping to put down the Pentrich Revolution. It was occupied by F.J.Butcher between the wars.

Cutthorpe Old Hall in 1982.   M. Stanley

Pevsner, 162; Lysons,V 85; Glover II, 336; LINACRE/ V.1569. FMG II 837-8; FOLJAMBE of Osberton/BLG (1972) 338-9; HEATHCOTE/Heathcote (1899) 42-3, 57-8; WRIGHT of Great Longstone/BFR 645-7.

DARLEY HALL (II*)

Darley Abbey Demolished

Darley Hall: the entrance front as rebuilt in the 1840s. *M. Craven*

The Darley Hall estate first surfaces in the twelfth century as the patrimony of a local grandee, Hugh, Dean of Derby. This he gave to the fledgeling convent of St Helen, Derby to create Derbyshire's greatest monastic house, The Abbey of St Mary, Darley. At the dissolution the Abbey was 'asset stripped' by Robert Sacheverell before being sold on to Sir William West. In 1574, however, the Wests – not an indigenous family to Derbyshire – sold the estate to Peter Bullock, the son of Robert, a prosperous local yeoman. It is unclear who built the first seat here: Sir Henry Sacheverell, whose nominee Robert was; Sir William West, or one of the Bullocks. Probably it was West, for Bullock purchased amongst others the 'Abbye howse'. Nor do we know what this residence looked like, for even Woolley, whose son had pulled it down and replaced, failed – perhaps out of modesty – to describe it. In all probability it was a rebuilding of the lodgings of the Augustinian Abbot of Darley, doubtless a relatively comfortable house.

The estate stretched to the north side of Bridge Gate, in Derby, to the south, and almost to Duffield to the north, whilst the east was dramatically punctuated by the Derwent, with the ancient trackway running north from Derby below the scarp to the west at a lowish level to debouch into the courtyard behind the house itself, which it passed to the east. This road was not removed to the present Duffield Road alignment until turnpiked in 1756. The actual boundary between the old Liberty of Darley and Derby town was the line of the old Roman Rykneld Street, leading by a bridge over the Derwent, of which the foundation may be perceived under water, to the old Roman fortification at Little Chester.

The grandson of Peter Bullock, John, purchased an estate at Norton (*qv*) and the vicissitudes of the Civil War caused the family to let the house to a Derby merchant, grown rich upon the strife, Thomas Goodbehere. He died in 1658, and Sir William Bullock retained it until his death in 1666 when it was sold to Roger Allestrey MP, second son of William Allestrey of Alvaston Hall (*qv*) a direct descendant of a

villein given his freedom by the Abbot of Darley in 1141, and whose posterity still live in Derby. Roger, son of Sir William Allestrey, the elder Roger's son, eventually sold to William Woolley, (died 1716) the historian of the County, in 1709. He had made a fortune in trade in the capital, and his son (also William) decided to build a new house. According to Wilfred Holden, writing in the 1930s and using family muniments now largely unavailable, Woolley found his architect in Francis Smith of Warwick, from 1723 to 1725 the contractor brought in by James Gibbs to build All Saints' church, Derby (now the Cathedral), and the house, which was built in 1727, originally displayed most of his architectural characteristics, as a drawing of 1758 shows.

A brick house with dressings of local Keuper sandstone, it appears to have been of three storeys over a basement, and of seven by five bays. On the east front the end bays broke forward and were enclosed by giant Doric pilasters in stone. The central three bays were divided from bays two and six by rusticated pilasters, with a central entrance marked by a Gibbs surround under a triangular pediment, although the drawing of 1758 shows it plain, with segmental pediment, which suggests that the west doorcase was substituted for the one shown in 1750 during the rebuilding of 1778. The fenestration had gauged brick lintels with stone keyblocks, and there was a top cornice, parapet and hipped tile roof.

On both west and east fronts Robert Bakewell of Derby supplied wrought-iron balustrading, that on the west only being ornamental; its present whereabouts is not known. The west front also broke forward at the ends much as on the east. Inside a fine timber well staircase was situated in an inner hall with a decorated stucco ceiling, separated by a screen from the entrance hall, and adorned with three turned balusters per tread, a fine carved handrail and tread ends. Ornamental stucco-work also graced the entrance hall, and three main rooms, as one might expect in a house by Smith; there was a rain-water head marked W W A 1727 on the west front.

Darley Hall in c. 1904. *M. Craven*

The east front of Darley Hall of 1728.   *Derby Museum*

William Woolley was Mayor of Derby in 1722-23, and was thus in the thick of the shenanigans surrounding the rebuilding of All Saints' church, and must have come into direct contact with the Smiths, unlike most of their other clients in Derbyshire at this time, who were nevertheless all subscribers to the new church. Woolley however, a profligate fellow, died in 1732, leaving his widow encumbered with debt. She eventually placed the estate on the market in December 1748 '...with new built capital mannor HOUSE', but failed to attract a buyer. It was eventually sold in November 1754 under a decree in Chancery with a paltry estate of 76 acres (the remainder having been sold earlier to Alderman John Heath, a banker of dubious repute) after Mrs. Woolley's death and was snapped up at a bargain price by Heath.

In July 1775 the house and estate, now reunited with most of those portions sold before 1754, was leased by Heath to Robert Holden of Aston with the proviso that should he wish to 'improve' the house, he should employ or consult Joseph Pickford of Derby, who frequently occurs as a collaborator of the Heaths at this time. He, like Holden, was a friend of Joseph Wright, ARA, who painted both (and the Heaths). In 1777, Holden did indeed decide to extend the house, and Pickford duly carried out the work, the year following to a total of £4,000. He added ranges of approximately similar dimensions on the north and south fronts, of two storeys only and five bays. The latter provided a new suite of rooms with breathtaking views down the Derwent Valley to the towers and spires of Derby, then mainly unsullied by the fires of industry. The west and east fronts were also simplified, and the roof was altered to a flat one, although to no good aesthetic effect. The real achievement of Pickford's south

front (the north was offices and bachelors' rooms) was its simplicity and lack of ornament combined with the excellent proportions and harmony of its elevation: the hallmark of all Pickford's later work. The new rooms were loftier than the old, with elegant stucco cornices, fine carved marble chimneypieces, probably by George Moneypenny, and carved dados ornamented by blind frets. He also turned the house around making a new entrance hall on the west front, and a dining-room out of the old hall on the east. One of John Whitehurst's ingenious weather vanes was installed on the roof, registering on a large dial in the staircase hall; this survives in Derby Museum. Whitehurst also supplied one of his flushing water closets (a three-seater) on the ground floor, and may well have designed other domestic economy improvements as at Clumber Park.

But in March 1779, disaster struck: the Heaths went massively bankrupt, ruining many in Derby, rich and not-so-rich alike. To his horror, Holden discovered that before assigning him the lease John Heath had previously mortgaged it to Boldero and Company, a London Bank, for £8,000 as security for a loan. As a result of a Chancery decision, Holden agreed to buy the estate from the assignees (chaired by another banker, Thomas Evans) for £7,000 – a much greater cost, for the valuation included an assessment of the extensions Holden had made to the house, for which he had already paid Pickford! At the same time that Pickford was extending the house, the parkland was being landscaped by William Emes, who is known from a private diary still in the family to have dined (with Pickford) at Darley at this time. Evans also conveniently detached from the deal part of the village, on which he built a cotton mill.

Worn out by these fiscal disasters, Holden died in 1780,

his son leaving the estate to his cousin, Robert (1769-1844) in 1808. He set about undertaking further improvements including the addition of a library in 1814. The Holdens retired to Nottinghamshire in 1835 and the estate was sold to the only other freeholder in Darley Abbey, Samuel Evans. Evans' grandfather's large cotton mill by the Derwent which he had acquired out of the Heath bankruptcy had meanwhile made him extremely opulent and he had gradually built the present well-preserved mill village to house his work-force. In 1835 Evans' seat was Darley House *(qv)*, but he now removed to the Hall, making further improvements. Of these the most notable was the building of an arcaded loggia protecting the entrance and linking the projections on the west front with an ambitious domed conservatory, all perhaps the work of H.I.Stevens. His successors also replaced the entrance lodge from Duffield Road, equipping it with elegant gatepiers and chaste wrought-iron gates probably by Edwin Haslam of Derby.

Here Evans' family remained until the death of the last Mrs. Evans in 1929. Her heir, Lionel Curtis, offered the house and 40 acres of park (which had been open to the public since the 1880s) to the Borough Council and they purchased the remainder of the parkland. The 66 acres thereupon became a public park since amalgamated with those areas remaining of Derwent Bank and St. Helen's House parks (the former carved from the latter in 1811) and the whole is still one of the finest in the area. Meanwhile, the house became the Derby Central School in the 1930s, and a Whitehurst turret clock was added (with dubious aesthetic value) to the parapet of the south front in 1950, the gift of the daughter of Alderman W. Hoare, an ex-Mayor of Derby. In August 1958 the school moved out, and the building was shut up. A DoE grant of £14,000 was offered to the Council for repairs but this was refused, and demolition began 13th March 1962 following the issuing of a perfectly spurious dangerous structures notice; an act of lamentable municipal vandalism, for without the distinguished house the fine park is like a headless mannequin in a shop window; lovely, but lamentably incomplete. One room on the former SW angle was suffered to remain, now the most architectonic ice-cream parlour in the region, along with the stable block of c. 1730 (added to in the early 19th century) and the ice house also survived for a time.

Colvin, 753; Pevsner (1953 Edn.) 108; Woolley 22; Hutton (1791) 312; Holden (1936) 63-64; Gomme (2001) 158, 524; DLC 6/70 p.63; Terrier Map & elev. 1755, Derby Local Studies Library; DRO D769 p.46; Drury Lowe MSS, Nottingham University Library DrP/7.1, 8/4; DM 16-23/12/ 1748, 4/11/1754; DDT. 24/4/1930; BULLOCK of Darley/ V.1611; WOOLLEY/Woolley xiv; HOLDEN *formerly* of Aston/BLG (1969) 305; EVANS of Darley Abbey/BLG (1937) 358.

DARLEY GROVE

Darley

see The GROVE

DARLEY HOUSE

Darley Abbey   *Demolished*

Darley House was a fairly substantial seat built mainly of brick with some sparing Keuper sandstone dressings built shortly after the Evans family acquired part of Darley Abbey and established their cotton mill there in 1782. The architect may have been Joseph Pickford (who, however, died the same year) or his *eleve* Thomas Gardner of Uttoxeter. William Strutt, FRS may have had some input too, for the Strutts and Evanses were doubly inter-married, and Strutt himself was an amateur architect of some versatility. The client was Thomas Evans, the banker-turned-cotton spinner who built the village of Darley Abbey. Its main east (entrance) front was of seven bays and it was of two and a half storeys, with plain but generous fenestration, a low parapet and hipped roofs. The south elevation was of three bays but another range of equal size lay to the west but stepped forward giving this elevation a further three bays. In the angle was a later single-storey extension containing a ballroom, faced in grooved ashlar, perhaps the work of Alderman Richard Leaper. Inside, the rooms were largely plain, but generously proportioned; there were eighteen bedrooms, reached via a cantilevered Hoptonwood stone staircase was graced with a plain cast-iron rail from Harrison's

Darley House at Darley Abbey, c. 1909.   *J. Darwin*

Foundry. This concern also produced patent ranges and heating apparatus to the design of William Strutt – designs which owed much to the ideas of John Whitehurst the elder – which were tried out in Darley House and in modified form were installed in St Helen's House nearby when Strutt purchased it in 1803.

The house was set in a small ornamental park on the northeast edge of the village, and after the family moved to Darley Hall in 1835, the house was occupied by two unmarried daughters of William Evans, whose widow had entertained Coleridge there. The poet wrote to a friend in 1796:

'Perhaps you may be so fortunate to meet with a Mrs. Evans whose seat is at Darley about a mile from Derby. Blessings descend on her! Emotions crowd on me at the sight of her name; we spent five weeks at her house – a sunny spot in our life.' The young widow offered Coleridge the post of tutor to her children at a salary of £150, but the rest of the family talked her out of it.

On the death of Elizabeth Evans, the last survivor, the house was let to the banker Col. James Charles Cavendish, VD, who remained there until his death in 1918. Thereafter it became a school which fell victim to the recession in the early 1930s, leaving the house empty, whereupon the Evans's trustees sold it in 1931 with 23 acres to Derby County Borough Council and they regrettably demolished it in 1934, and houses were built over the park.

Evans MSS, DRO; Sale documents, 27/1/1931, Derby Local Studies Library; Glover, II 383; EVANS of Darley Abbey/ibid.; CAVENDISH/ (1931) 770.

DENBY OLD HALL (II*)

Demolished

Denby Old Hall, 1964.   RCHM(E)

Denby was held at the time of Domesday by an un-named knight under Ralph de Buron; other evidence suggests that this was in fact Sir Patrick Rosel of Cotgrave and Rempstone, Nottinghamshire, and indeed in the reign of Henry I Denby was the holding of Patrick de Rosel, son of Sir Patrick. The Rosels held it down to the 1440s when their male line failed and the heiress married Laurence Lowe, a Cheshire gentleman from the Macclesfield area and a Serjeant at Law. During this period the Rosels had a capital mansion at Denby, the site of which may have been marked by a moat with house platform some 50 yards north of the later Old Hall measuring 58 by 80 feet. Some authorities have, however,

seen this as the site of a parker's lodge relating to nearby Park Hall (qv). However, the emparkation related to the Rosel house, not to Park Hall, which became detached from the ancient manorial estate by gift of one of the Rosels to Lord Grey of Codnor, and the sheer proximity of the moat to the house under consideration, also suggests that it marked the site of its predecessor. However, the matter is beyond proof, for the site was obliterated by railway sidings and coal yards in the early years of the twentieth century.

The house which was finally demolished – quite inexcusably – in 1966 was basically two separate builds, being a seventeenth century range added to a very modest two-gabled house from the later part of the previous century. Bearing in mind that the Lowes were really quite an opulent family, in must be supposed that the Elizabethan range had been, in its turn, an extension to an older edifice perhaps built when the moated site was relinquished, possibly when the Lowes took over. The older surviving part consisted of twin straight uncoped gables over two storeys, the elevation at the entrance front being punctuated by four-light mullioned windows one above the other either side of a two-storey porch which latterly had a flat top, but was originally probably gabled. The range was constructed of roughcast Coal Measures sandstone, probably Crawshaw Sandstone or Wingfield Flags from an adjacent outcrop, but with dressed quoins at the angles and a massive attached chimneybreast to the north.

In 1563, the senior line of the Lowes died out, and it was inherited by Jasper Lowe of a younger branch, which had purchased Park Hall, thus reuniting the two moieties of the estate. However, his posterity sold it in about 1628 to Robert Wilmot (of the Chaddesden family), consolidating at Park Hall instead. Wilmot's heiress married Thomas Robey of Castle Donnington who built (or rebuilt) the south range by 1660, for the impaled arms of Robey and Wilmot graced this build in confirmation. The newer part had its showfront to the south, with its wall exactly in line with that of the older wing and of similar thickness. Further, its lower courses showed some evidence of being of a similar build. Thus it could constitute a reuse of part of an earlier fabric. This part was of two storeys and four widely spaced bays of mullion and transom cross windows (later replaced by paired sashes in the old apertures). The end bays broke emphatically forward, and straight bands over the windows were emphasized by a straight coped parapet above, behind which was a hipped tiled roof, doubtless added in the late 18th century, when the rear appears to have been totally rebuilt, possibly in a reduction of the house. The entrance, replacing that in the older west wing, was through the right-hand projection, and was marked by an arched doorcase within a deep moulding joined by a prominent keyblock – all rather old-fashioned for the 1660s when this range presumably took on its later form. Above this entrance was the armorial, well carved and carefully hatched, on a stone plaque over which the string course was slightly raised. The quality of carving and the general appearance of this suggest that it was a replacement for the original, which could easily have become weathered, and hence the awkwardness of its fit beneath the string course. The quality of the stonework of the parapet suggests that it was itself a later addition and the rather eclectic nature of this front suggests a somewhat earlier date, with its slight overtones of John Smythson's minor houses. It may be, too, that this range was intended to be extended (to replace the earlier build, the work not, in the event, being done. The position of the new entrance, close to the previous one, both of which incongruously survived, rather suggests that an E-shaped facade was originally planned. Parallels could also be made with the entrance front of Tissington Hall *(qv)*. There may also have been an intention to provide a through hall, but nearly all the original interior walls seem either to have not been built or to have been taken out, for by the 1960s, all were partition walls. Further, apart from the west end, the rear of the house appears to have been a rebuild in cottage style of c. 1800, and the hall latterly boasted a plain but elegant Regency timber staircase. The rear wall was also in brick, and goes some way to confirm that a grandiose scheme – doubtless to be paid for out of the profits of coal extraction – was either curtailed or never realized, whether it was one of c. 1630 or 1660.

The interior of the older part was a simple four rooms to a floor in plan, although the central dividing wall across the range oddly aligned with the centre of the entrance, which suggests that it predated it. There were some timber-studded walls at the rear and a simple staircase. The later part had a fine parlour to the west of the hall, panelled in mid-seventeenth century style with fluted Doric pilasters punctuating it; there is, however, some reason to believe that this fine oak panelling had been reset at some stage. There was one surviving early eighteenth century fire-surround remaining by the 1960s. Another, ripped out during demolition, revealed a much older one behind, massive, stone, with chamfered surround. The substantial coarse ashlar remnant of a further structure immediately to the west of the house may have represented the vestiges of a later stable block rather than a fragment of the larger extent of the house.

In 1763 the Robey heiress married a Strelley of Oakerthorpe, and from them it passed in the early nineteenth century through heiresses to the families of Parker, Harris and Gregory. This process reduced still further the already depleted estate, and each heir was less well off than his predecessor, constant sales being made to make ends meet; the Lowes (by then the Drury - Lowes) thereby gained through purchase. The house at the same time gradually declined into a farmstead and imperceptibly decayed, as coal mines burgeoned around it. In the early twentieth century it was farmed by tenants called Evans, but their fields gradually succumbed to coal extraction, and they left, too. Thereafter this delightful and fascinating house was divided as cottages, finally becoming untenanted sometime after World War Two. When it was demolished the site was removed by opencasting.

Little is known of the grounds, save that there was a fine sundial dated 1714 the very year in which Woolley described it as: 'A good old house', and on which tax had been paid a generation earlier (in 1670) on 13 hearths, also suggesting that it had also been reduced.

Pevsner (1953 Edn.) 110; DAJ XXVI (1904) 1ff.; RCHM(E) survey, 1/1966; Fryar (1934) 54-55; Woolley, 41 p. 73; LOWE/V.1569,1611, 1662 and *sub* DRURY-LOWE of Locko/BLG (1965) 458; ROBEY/DAJ XXVI (1904) 18; STRELLEY/*op. cit.*XIV (1892) 72.

DERWENT HALL

Derwent   *Demolished*

Derwent Hall before rebuilding, by R. Keene, 1858.

Private Collection

Derwent was anciently part of Hathersage, and the bleak uplands of the Dark Peak seem not to have encouraged the establishment of an independent estate until a farmhouse there was inherited from the Barbers by the Balguys of Hagg. Henry Balguy (1648-1685), whose father was a cadet of the Balguys of Aston, thereupon purchased Derwent Hall in 1672 and, with nearby Rowlee, an estate was forged. Unfortunately, it is difficult to discover anything about the Hall that he purchased. The house had four hearths in 1670, and probably formed the nucleus of the later hall, which bore the entirely convincing date of 1692, bearing in mind the conservatism of north Derbyshire architecture. This suggests that Henry Balguy's like-named son actually built the house to form an H-shaped dwelling, of coursed rubble with dressed quoins and other details.

Derwent Hall as rebuilt, c. 1910.   M. Craven

This house, built in coarse ashlared gritstone (probably Shale or Kinderscout Grit from an adjacent outcrop), faced south, and had a four-bay recessed centre of two storeys punctuated by regular six-light mullioned and transomed windows under continuous bands on both floors. The straight coped gabled wings had cross windows on the inside of the returns, and eight-light mullioned and transomed windows, with three-light attic mullions above ensigned by cranked hood moulds. The east and west sides were of five bays, of which three on the east were low two-light mullions which seem to have marked the remnants of the original house which was probably L-shaped. The 1692 windows were of the cross type on the first floor over a ten-light window below with an enhanced transom; the roof was stone slated. In front of the entrance, with its massive ashlar surround and single prominent keyblock, stood pretty rusticated gatepiers, with a further pair to the east giving on to the garden.

The grandson of the builder, Henry Balguy (1700-1770) sold up in 1767 and went to live in Alfreton near his kinsmen, the Morewoods. The purchaser was the Bennet family, but by 1816, John Bennet had tenanted it as a farmhouse, but not before putting in tapestries saved from the fire at Worksop Manor. Shortly afterwards in 1831 it was sold to John Read (1777-1862), who used it as a summer residence, later as his house, and from him it went by sale in 1846 to the Newdigates of West Hallam and Arbury, Warwickshire, again becoming a farm. Read made some cosmetic alterations and laid out the gardens. In 1876 it was sold to the Duke of Norfolk, who vested it in a younger son, later 1st Viscount FitzAlan of Derwent. Between 1878 and 1880 it was extensively rebuilt and enlarged by J. A. Hansom. This entailed extending the east front in ashlar by a further two full height matching bays with two more lower ones beyond. Gabled dormers, five in number, were added and seven single-storey projecting bays were also added: a rectangular

one to the oldest section, with another to its north, and a considerable canted one attached to the lower part. This latter portion had its first floor windows in gables, and attached to its north was a large Roman Catholic domestic chapel, the east end of which ended in three lancet windows with hood moulds under a quatrefoil. Inside it was richly decorated. The house itself was smothered in pastiche Jacobean panelling, much with arcaded sections, and a new, richly carved oak staircase appeared. An overmantel dated 1634 from old Norton Hall (qv) was installed, but was removed in 1920 to the Cutlers' Hall, Sheffield. The estate was built up to 1,274 acres, and the grounds laid out afresh.

Between 1932 and 1938 it was let to the YHA, being opened in the former year by Edward, Prince of Wales, but nemesis was approaching. In the 1920s it was decided to expand the reservoir provision in the upper Derwent Valley, in a joint project sponsored by the Councils of Sheffield, Leicester and Derby. This involved deep flooding following the construction of the Derwent Dam, and the planned drowning of the villages of Derwent and Ashopton. The house and estate were therefore sold to the Water Authority in 1924, and was vacated in summer 1943, and Charles Boot dismantled much of it, carrying many fixtures and fittings away to embellish Thornbridge Hall (qv). Some of the panelling was purchased from him by Derby Corporation and was used to decorate the Mayor's Parlour in the new Council House, then under construction. One pair of gatepiers were removed to Woodthorpe Hall, Holmesfield, another erected at the entrance to Ladybower dam. Thereafter, the shell gradually disappeared beneath the waves, finally disappearing from sight in 1945, although the spire of the village church lingered longer. Excessively dry spells which have heavily depleted the reservoir in 1976, 1989, 1990 and 1996 have failed to reveal any recognizable vestiges.

Lysons, V. 178; Builder (27/8/1881) ii; DAJ XVI (1894); CL XXI (1907) 198-205; Transactions of the Hunter Archaeological Society V pt. 6 (1945) 279-284 & VI pt. 3 (1947) 126-130; BALGUY of Duffield/BLG (1952) 98 & Vv 1569, 1662; READ of Ipsden, Bt./ Foster, Baronetage (1882) 525; FITZALAN of Derwent sub NORFOLK, D/BP (1999) II. 2090-2101.

DETHICK MANOR HOUSE (II)

Private house

The barn at Dethick Manor House; all that remains of The Babington's great house. Taken in 1982.   M. Stanley

The only remnant of this once impressive house is a large barn at Church Farm, Dethick, with massive angle buttresses, stone-surround windows with flattened arches and displaying at least three blocked-off doorways. Parts of the fifteenth/ sixteenth century farmhouse seem also to contain vestiges of the original house, as the latter was undoubtedly large and built around at least one courtyard: an inventory taken in May 1560 reveals at least 42 rooms. It is built of Millstone Grit Sandstone ashlar probably RE from an adjacent outcrop, with a stone slate roof, although much of what is lost probably included timber framing. Glover makes the unlikely claim that a secret passage was dug from the house to Wingfield Manor where Mary, Queen of Scots was a prisoner, by the conspirator, Anthony Babington of Dethick, using his own mining workforce 'on the advice of Francis Rolleston of Lea' – this in the 1580s. Unfortunately, such a feat would be difficult enough today, and impossible then, the topography being against it. George, the conspirator's brother sold to Wendesley Blackwall, but it was deserted when the civil war forced his Royalist grandson to sell in the 1650s to the republican Nathaniel Hallowes; furthermore, at this time the locals were quarrying its stone for their own houses.

The Dethicks probably built the first house on the site, their heiress bringing it to the Babingtons. The Hallowes family sold out in the present century to J.B.Marsden-Smedley. It has for many years been farmed by the Grooms, Mr. Simon Groom, the son, being a media personality of some local renown.

Pevsner, 196; Lysons, V.20; Glover *Notes*, (1843) 9; DETHICK/Vv 1569, 1611; BABINGTON/*ibid.* & BLG (1952) 82; HALLOWES of Glapwell/*op.cit.* (1875) 1.567; MARSDEN-SMEDLEY of Lea Green/BLG (1965) 636.

DOVERIDGE HALL

Demolished

Doveridge Hall showing the garden front, c. 1904.   M. Craven

The ancient manorial estate of Doveridge was given by Henry de Ferrers to the Priory of Tutbury before 1086, and remained in their hands until the dissolution. In that time it was farmed in fairly small parcels, no one landlord really emerged to dominate and take over from the Priory, the property of which came directly into the hands of the crown. In 1552, however, the manor was granted to Sir William Cavendish, husband of Bess of Hardwick. He granted it to his eldest son, Sir Henry Cavendish, who also held Tutbury Castle. It is believed that he built a seat at Doveridge, and it is interesting to speculate upon what this house would have been like. It is known that in 1662 tax was paid in respect of 11 hearths, and it presumably occupied the site of the plain three-bay two-storey farmhouse now called the Old Hall, occupied in the eighteenth century by the Sadliers and in the nineteenth by the Mynors. With connections with the Earl of Shrewsbury and a mother like Bess one might have expected him to have employed Robert or John Smythson and indeed, there are characteristics of the latter in the last phase of building at Tutbury; would that a view of the original Doveridge Hall might surface somewhere! Woolley in 1713 called it a 'Good old seat', which is rather unsatisfying, if typical of him.

In 1611, Sir Henry settled the estate on his natural son, Henry Cavendish, whose posterity were to hold it until the early part of the twentieth century. Rt. Hon. Henry Cavendish PC (I) was in 1755 created a baronet of Ireland whither he had gone with his kinsman the third Duke of Devonshire who had been appointed Lord Lieutenant in 1737, and where he served as Teller of the Exchequer. In the later 1760s he returned, and resolved to build a new seat on a new site, letting the old to a descendant of Queen Elizabeth's faithful courtier, Sir Ralph Sadleir, whose descendants had settled in Ireland in 1669. Possibly it was in Ireland that Cavendish and James Sadleir became friends.

To design his new seat Cavendish employed another man he met in Ireland, Edward Stevens ARA (1743-1775), a young protege of Sir William Chambers: it was to be his first (and, unhappily, his last) major building project. He employed his friend Joseph Pickford of Derby as contractor and work began in 1770. The house was mainly in brick and was one of the few large Palladian houses in Derbyshire. However, there were Keuper sandstone dressings, and the south (garden) front – the real show-front – was faced in this material. This was of two storeys over a lower ground floor made taller by the park sloping away to the Dove, and consisted of nine really very cramped bays, the central five being under a pediment and separated by attached Ionic half-columns supporting a deep frieze. The central four columns and three bays were more closely set than the outer pair, giving a strange, restless effect to the otherwise flat facade. The windows on the *piano nobile* under the pediment were topped with alternating triangular and segmental pediments with blank balustrading below, three central round headed openings were made in the rusticated lower ground floor in the centre, and there were bands between the floors.

The north front, by contrast, was

83

well proportioned, of five bays with a pedimented three-bay breakfront over a rusticated ground floor with tripartite entrance. The end bays on the *piano nobile* were marked by deep tripartite windows pedimented over the central light, almost identical to those used by Pickford on the garden front of Hams Hall, Warwickshire, and proposed by him for Calke in the 1760s, and it is worth wondering whether Pickford actually designed this front – or modified it as it was building – for the whole effect is quite unlike the south front and very much in his style. There were low hipped tile roofs. Stevens went away to Italy whilst building was in progress, where he was in touch with Joseph Wright ARA and where he died in 1775, having exhibited his plans for Doveridge at the Royal Academy in 1771, but these have since vanished, so we cannot now compare them with the finished result.

However, by 1776 two single-bay two-storey pavilions were added, connected by single-storey three-bay links. Like the house, these had hipped roofs, but unlike it, they were almost certainly built by Thomas Gardner of Uttoxeter and Thomas Freeman of Derby – for a while partners from 1772 – and who certainly built the stable block to the north-east of the house in the same year. As it does not take a year to build a stable block, the fact that buildings were 'Now carrying on' for Sir Henry Cavendish at Doveridge when their partnership was dissolved in March 1777 goes a long way to confirm their involvement with the wings, rather than, say, Pickford himself. With regard to the interior, there is little known except that there was a quite grand top-lit staircase in the middle of the house with a cantilevered stone stair with a pretty wrought-iron rail, no doubt by Benjamin or William Yates of Derby. No other record has survived, except that the upper floor of the west pavilion was in the nineteenth century converted into a ballroom, reached at *piano nobile* level by a glazed passage.

In 1792, Sir Henry's daughter-in-law, Sarah, nee Bradshaw, was created a Peer of Ireland as Baroness Waterpark, with remainder to her issue male by her husband, Sir Henry Cavendish, 2nd Bt. In the later nineteenth century, however, 4th Lord Waterpark let Doveridge to Frank Addison Brace, who later purchased the house, although Lord Waterpark retained the estate of 1,704 acres, and in 1891 was living nearby at West Lodge. At about this time too the house was sold to 1st Lord Hindlip who, as an Allsopp with a lineage stretching back to an early Hanoverian Derby businessman and thence (putatively) to a cadet branch of the Alsops of Alsop-en-le-Dale, was anxious to assert his Derbyshire credentials. Yet, after his time his successors preferred Hindlip Hall, Worcestershire, (from which the first Baron had taken his title) and Doveridge lay increasingly empty. The 3rd Lord Hindlip put it up for auction in April 1935 and Messrs. W.S.Bagshaw of Uttoxeter managed to obtain £4,000 for it and a portion of the very attractive park. The parts of the latter nearest the village were sold as building plots, and the hall was purchased by a local contractor who demolished it in 1938. Only the stable block, a lodge, the bailiff's house, and the part of the park down to the river remain today, and looking at it one is tempted to ascribe or attribute it to William Emes. Indeed, there is always this temptation with unattributed landscaped parks in southern Derbyshire if they are of late eighteenth century date, and caution is certainly due. In this case the presence of Pickford, who worked in parallel with Emes so often during the 1770s, is suggestive, but much more research is required.

Colvin, 331, 781-2; DLC 8/1972; Woolley, 78, p. 118; Lysons V. 129; DM 3/1/1777; Saunders (1993) 24, 171; Wedgwood MSS, University of Keele, 31141/11; WATERPARK,. B/BP (1999) II. 2957-8; HINDLIP, B./ *op.cit.*I. 1415-16; BRACE/FD (1929) I. 203.

DRAKELOW HALL

Demolished

Drakelow Hall before rebuilding, c. 1898.   M. Craven

Drakelow was one of the larger and more important seats in Derbyshire and was in the hands of one of the very oldest of families until early in the twentieth century: the Gresleys, descended from Nigel de Stafford – a genuine 'Baron' of William the Conqueror – who held it in chief and who was ancestor also of the Longfords, FitzNicholases and Staffords of Egginton (*qv*), Eyam (*qv*) and Bottoms (*qv*). They took their name from Church and Castle Gresley nearby, where in Henry I's reign they founded an Augustinian Priory, (dissolved in 1536) dedicated to St George, and where at the latter place they had their earliest seat. At neither do any vestiges remain, and even in Camden's time (1610) the castle was 'A mere ruin'. The manor and Priory were granted to Henry Criche in 1543 and thence came to the Alleynes (*qv*).

The first seat at Drakelow was probably marked by a moat in the north-west corner of the 500-acre park about 700 yards east of Warren Farm at (SK 234201). The later house may have had later medieval origins, but its earliest fabric can only be ascribed to a house known to have been built in the middle of the sixteenth century. In 1662 this was recorded as having 23 hearths taxable, the same number as Calke and, indeed, it may well have been, like Calke, a courtyard house. A date of 1723 on a rain-water head may have marked a phase of rebuilding – although little which could be ascribed to that era survives in photographs, most of the early classical work evident being Restoration interiors of a high quality. The house also showed clear signs of late Georgian work, and may be related to a design '...for an intended alteration at Drakelow' by John Westmacott, son of the sculptor Richard the elder, of 1806. As nothing seems to be known of John Westmacott after that date, it is possible that his plans were carried out by someone else, or that an entirely new scheme was launched shortly afterwards. This may also relate to the eighteenth century Trellis Dining-Room – a breathtaking masterpiece of *trompe de l'oeuil* by Paul Sandby of 1793, partly preserved by the Victoria and Albert Museum and created out of the former Great Hall of the sixteenth century house erected by Sir Thomas Gresley, with a barrel-vaulted roof. Anna Seward, Erasmus Darwin's

84

friend from Lichfield, wrote of this room (1794): 'Sir Nigel hath adorned one of his rooms with singular happiness. It is large, one side painted with forest scenery, where majestic trees arch over the coved ceiling. Through them are glades, tufted banks and ascending walks in perspective. The appropriate side exhibits a Peak Valley; the front shows a prospect of more distant country, viewing with the beauties of the real one admitted opposite through a crystal wall of windows. Its chimneypiece formed of spar and ores and shells represents a grotto. . . (before the scene are) little wicket gates that, half open, invite us to ascend the seeming forest banks.'

Girouard has tentatively related this room to the frescoed Casino at Swarkestone (qv) by Samuel Brown who worked in Derby and extensively for the Harpurs; it may well be that the remodelling which plainly took place at this time was undertaken by Brown. It is also known that a further extension was added in 1840. This scheme, illustrated in an engraving published by Stephen Glover, was for a comprehensive rebuilding which was probably never fully completed. Finally, the house was remodelled – largely to bring some unity into a rather haphazard ensemble – in the 1870s, but again, the name of the architect is not known. The only description of the house from more than a century ago is that of the dour Belper Presbyterian minister D.P.Davies (1811): 'The house is a large irregular pile of brick building, whitened over, but not presenting any thing remarkable.'

The east (entrance) front was latterly of three bays with a two-storey projecting porch enclosed by octagonal turrets capped with small ogiform domes (replacing carved knights holding lances with banners, according to Glover's engraving). Between, a canted oriel window, the lights divided by transoms and having depressed pointed arched heads, all with an ornate balustrade above. Below it, the entrance was equipped with a projecting Roman Ionic portico with a pulvinated frieze and an open, rather muscular, segmental pediment above with a cartouche of the arms of Gresley. The space between the pinnacles was filled by an eclectic Dutch gable containing an *oeuil-de-boeuf*. This work was undertaken 1901-04 by Sir Reginald Blomfield, with Gregory & co. undertaking the extensive interior re-panelling, George Jackson & Sons the stucco and carving was by W. Aumonier & Son. Part of the house, and all the south front, was two and a half storeys high, with the attic windows marked by two-light mullions suggestive of a gabled house 'modernized' with a parapet. This was until it was crenellated – part of the 1840 rebuilding – but it was changed to a balustrade by Blomfield. To the north of the entrance front was the main 1840 addition: a two-storey link connecting with a hexagonal turret in the return, created by a higher extension with a projecting ground-floor bay with mullioned and transomed fenestration topped, like the remainder of the wing, by crenellations: in all a picturesque and stylish addition. The original intention was to have had a five-bay gothic orangery here, like the remainder, with crow-stepped battlements.

The south front was spectacular, if faintly unsatisfying. It consisted of seven very widely spaced bays and was two and a half storeys high, again looking as if a multi-gabled house had been adapted with an extra storey and a parapet. One bay in from the south-east end was an attached chimneybreast supporting a cluster of four brick stacks, all decorated with different patterning. A similar pair flanked the central bay marked by a full height canted bay with a balustrade. The fenestration to the east was of eight-light mullion and transom type, but to the west was marked by paired sashes in the original apertures. This would appear to be part of the 1806 build and ran around on to the west

front, also three bays wide. Yet the south-west end bay was a stylish oriel matched by one at the south-east angle, both parts of the 1830 scheme to unify this front. Thus the Elizabethan house must have occupied the same plan. Yet the oldest photographs show an attached chimney breast and clustered shafts inside of the south-west oriel, too, so the various nineteenth century alterations actually destroyed the symmetry of the facade, for this was partly removed and truncated above the roofline. Contrary to Davies' remarks, the whole house appears to have been of ashlared Keuper sandstone from an adjacent outcrop; had it been encased thus in 1830, it is highly unlikely that the south front would have been left with polyglot fenestration. The 'whiting over' may have obscured the true nature of the materials from Davies' eye; one doubts if he saw it close to.

Inside, the house was quietly magnificent. The hall and adjoining rooms were remodelled by Blomfield. The former was richly panelled with a fluted Ionic order flanking the fireplace and the doors, with much carved fruitwood decoration from the hand of Aumonier. The plaster ceilings were of high quality, and decorated with deeply moulded fruit and flowers. Other rooms, like the canted-ended music room were panelled in oak with pilasters and bolection mouldings. The parlour, and other rooms, however, were 16th century panelled oak and some of the linenfold wainscot is now in Netherseal Old Hall (qv) having travelled there via Netherseal Hall, the family's second seat (qv). The parlour itself had a richly wrought over-mantel with a variety of motifs of the period, and a Victorian fireplace oddly decorated with the arms of families not particularly closely related to the Gresleys: in a photograph one can recognize FitzHerbert of Norbury, Babington and others; local but incongruous. Was it carved for another house entirely? Elsewhere there was further linenfold work, and two staircases, each equally massy, in oak with pendentives, bulgy balusters and newels.

The gardens also were magnificent, although their true nature is unclear before the beginning of the twentieth century. Humphrey Repton is said to have advised Sir Nigel Gresley on the landscaping before 1793 according to Peacock's *Polite Repository* of that year but no Red Book appears to have survived. Before the south front was a high terrace with a series of others, seemingly rich with former parterres, going down in three great stages to a canal, with higher parts on either side emphasized by ornamental trelliswork, perhaps in a conscious effort to ape the dining-room, the work of Francis Inigo Thomas (1866-1950), a friend and collaborator of Blomfield's, in 1900-02. The park itself, as at Catton and Doveridge, making dramatic use of the river, nevertheless looks eighteenth century. Parts of it survive,

The entrance front as rebuilt in 1902. Photographed by C.B. Keene, c. 1912. *M. Craven*

85

including the early eighteenth century stable block (listed II); great gates of 1902, but consciously neo-baroque in feel, lead still out of the park and once afforded entry to the house. A garden pavilion by Blomfield survives (dated 1902) and a pretty thatched *cottage orne'* lodge has since been reconstructed as a two-storey building, perhaps in the late nineteenth century.

The Gresleys received one of the first baronetcies in 1611, and remained at the house until 1931, when declining agricultural receipts, the depression, and diminished family fortunes forced them to sell up, when the contents were sold in 2,229 lots over seven days. The AA planned to turn the park into a three-mile motor racing circuit in 1932, but the money ran out. The estate was sold in January 1933, being the 707 acres contiguous to the house and park, for the remainder adjoined Netherseal Hall, which had, by this time, become a separate estate. The Gresleys moved to the south of England, and the last baronet died in 1978 when the title became extinct.

In 1934, Clifford Gothard, a brewery director, purchased much of the land and the house (which had for two years been in use as a country club) was pulled down. The entire porch and entrance bay was, however, acquired by Sir John Thorold, 13th Bt., and used in the rebuilding of Syston Hall, Lincs., 1934-35. By 1939 Mr. Gothard had re-assembled much of the original demesne. All this went for nothing, however, when in 1948 the newly-nationalized electricity authority, using the Big Brother tactics which one has come to expect of such conglomerates, compulsorily purchased 744 acres of land, obliterating everything to build a power station of titanic proportions. The Gothard family managed to retain what was left, but the CPO tore the ancient heart out of the estate, leaving them with the Georgian brick dower house and 512 acres, for sale in 1991. Only the gates and their rebuilt lodge remain from the historic hall.

Woolley 119, p.157; Lysons, V. 170; Davies (1811) 367-8; Britton & Brayley III (1802) 397-8; Colvin (1985) 51-52; Fellows (1985) 35-40, 162, 168; Henman (1986) 54-56; DLC 9/74; CL XI (1902) 368-375 & XXI (1907) 378-384; *Architectural Review* (1904) 20-25; GRESLEY, Bt./BP (19670) 1172.

DUFFIELD HALL (II)

Corporate headquarters

Duffield Hall c. 1895 showing the south and east fronts.　　　M. Craven

To Duffield fell the distinction of being the capital of Henry de Ferrers' 114 Derbyshire manors, and at Duffield he built, on a site going back at least to Roman times, a Castle. By the time his descendants the Ferrers Earls of Derby had rebuilt it in stone c. 1177 and extended it in the mid-thirteenth century, it was one of the largest in England. Yet the last Earl of Derby of this creation lost everything in the wars against Henry III, and in 1266 it was forfeited by the crown and given to Prince Edmund Plantagenet, Earl of Lancaster, being shortly afterwards entirely dismantled. Duffield remained part of the Duchy of Lancaster estate (with one small gap) until 1628 when Charles I, seeking to raise money, sold and granted the huge manor of Duffield out in smaller units, thus creating at least three major estates within Duffield itself, let alone in outlying parts like Holbrook, Makeney, Belper, Windley and Heage. One of these was the so-called Rectoral Manor, held by the Pyndar family; another was Duffield Park (qv), held by the Chaloners and the Wilmots and a third was that of Duffield Hall.

It does not take long inside Duffield Hall to divine that it contains the core of a house older than that which one sees on the exterior: c. 1660s with Victorian additions. The second staircase at the south end is a nice example of vernacular oak work with wiggly splat balusters and a former exterior timber studded wall forms part of the well of the main stair, although it is now plastered over. Yet we cannot identify this house specifically in the records of the Duchy's estates, nor can we point to a family which held it from the estates' Commissioners. In 1628, however, it was granted (in return for a fine of handsome proportions) to Thomas Newton of Chaddesden and Horsley, a descendant of Welsh Princely stock whose ancestors had come into Derbyshire in the fifteenth century. He does not appear at once to have built a new house, perhaps because of the uncertainty of the times before and during the Civil War, although some accounts suggest that the house dates from the 1630s. However, a close examination of the fabric suggests that the present house was erected by his son – another Thomas (1631-1709) – perhaps anticipating his marriage in 1671.

The new house was somewhat old-fashioned for its time, but perhaps less so when one bears in mind the architectural conservatism of the area. It was built in ashlar Ashover Grit from Duffield Bank - of two piles, with a three gabled six-bay front, and three full storeys in height with cramped attics above lit by miniscule oculi. The entrance was a simple affair, central with a depressed pointed arch leading into a modishly square hall with the new oak with twisted balusters on a string staircase off to the south-west. There were three clusters of three chimney stacks, the upper parts built in brick, and the south front was of two bays and two gables (as the east front, straight, coped and topped by slim finials) with the southern-most chimney breast between them. On the ground and first floors there was a band over the windows, which were probably of the mullion and transom cross type. The rear, now cleared of its Victorian extension, suggests an affinity with Eyam and Wormhill Halls, with the gables depressed with a parapet in between.

In 1664 it was taxed on seven hearths. In c. 1685 Thomas Newton for some unknown reason sold to the Coapes, Henry Coape (of an old family originally from Shatton in Hope) being described as 'of Duffield' at his death in November 1691. His son, also Henry, seems to have indulged in some rebuilding in the early eighteenth century, in which the house was refenestrated with sashes, and which saw the addition of a plain two-storey flat-roofed wing at the south-west side of the house. The last Henry Coape died in 1776 and the house and modest estate passed via his daughter and heiress to Henry Porter, a Nottingham entrepreneur who assumed the surname and arms of Sherbrooke (of Oxton, Nottinghamshire). He removed to Oxton Hall, leaving Duffield to his nephew Thomas Porter Bonell who died in 1797. His widow, in the first decade of the nineteenth century, managed to engross the sites of both Bradshaw's and Potterell's almshouses, expanding the park. On her death Duffield Hall was inherited by Col. Charles Henry Colville of Lullington Hall (qv), who occupied the house, although his son remained at Lullington, letting it to John Bell Crompton (1785-1859 and Mayor of Derby in 1828) who eventually acquired the freehold. He ultimately sold on 19 July 1860 to Rowland Smith, MP (1826-1901).

Smith, a scion of the famous Nottingham banking family, and which also produced the Lords Carrington (briefly Marquesses of Lincolnshire), needed a seat near the railhead of Derby through his election as MP for Derbyshire. His confidence was underscored by the fact that he resolved to rebuild the house in 1870-71. The architect is not known, although the name of Thomas Chambers Hine had been canvassed on stylistic grounds, and the fact that he built for the Smiths in Nottingham makes the attribution the more attractive.

One of Smith's objectives was to considerably increase the size of the house in order to meet the criteria for entertaining of the age in which he lived. A secondary factor was a desire to restore the house to something resembling its original appearance. And whilst the two were to some extent exclusive, he did achieve a happy compromise. The entrance front he embellished with a projecting canted bay with a parapet to form a larger dining-room, and he built a matching projecting porch embellished with his arms (impaling Somerset, Duke of Beaufort) and elephant's head crest. To the north he added a new range, of two gables, which projected a bay's depth beyond the original facade, but which (like all other additions for Smith) was in matching, if slightly embellished style. To the south, the early eighteenth century extension was removed and replaced with a two-storey canted bay with a further gabled bay beyond with two others on the (west) return. This effectively formed a ballroom, and also on the west, which had a high rectangular projecting ground-floor bay, was a pretty conservatory with underfloor heating and lavish use of Minton tiles.

To the north of the house was a lowish vernacular, perhaps Regency, stable block since converted into a residence, an earlier gabled coach house, and a pretty gate lodge. The five-acre park lay within a ha-ha to the west and the Derby-Sheffield road (now the A6) to the east. Inside, the hall was equipped with Victorian oak panelling, incorporating a screen of triple depressed arcading, and all the seventeenth century panelling was gathered together into the study, where it remains, some of it cobbled around the bolection moulded fireplace to make a gawky looking overmantel.

Smith died in 1901, and his son in 1917, surviving his own elder son and heir, killed in action in 1914. Thus the house and estate came to the second son of Col. Granville Smith, Rev. R.A.Smith, who in 1919 sold to Andrew Hingley the elder, a rich timber merchant in the village. He let the house and immediate grounds of 21 acres to Miss D.W.Gardiner, proprietrix of St Ronan's School for Girls, which admirable institution remained there, mainly under the tutelage of Miss Gardiner's successor Mrs. E.M.Melbourn, until its much regretted closure on 17 July 1970. In April 1944, Mrs. Melbourn had purchased the freehold from Mr. Hingley's

trustees, and on 13 December 1972 the house and land were sold by Mrs. M.W.K.Wrigley, Mrs. Melbourn's heiress, to David M.Adams Developments Limited. In the year following, the house and much less land was sold on to the Derbyshire Building Society for conversion into their Headquarters. By this time the house was in a sorry state, having lost its roof-leads, been vandalized and having been with remarkable rapidity overtaken by creeper. The Building Society called in George Grey & Partners of Derby, and had them demolish the south-west wing entirely, including the conservatory; an un-necessary act of vandalism in view of the vast new buildings erected contiguously to the house to the north and west. However, the house itself was sensitively restored for George Grey by Mr. Edward Saunders and opened in 1977; it now presents a pleasing sight from the A6 (which was widened at the same time, the boundary wall losing its ornamental ball finials in the process of recession). Fortunately, 2 years on, artfully planted trees have hidden the gross bulk of the Society's administrative buildings. The rest of the former school's grounds were developed with the usual banal brick dwellings much loved by 1970s entrepreneurs; in visual terms, a serious loss to the village.

Pevsner, 202; Woolley, 56 pp. 90-2; DLC 4/1975; Architecture East Midlands No.75, 3-4/1978 25-33; NEWTON/V.1611; COAPE of Duffield/BLG (1937) 56n & sub SHERBROOKE of OXTON/BLG (1965) 776; COLVILLE of Lullington/BLG (1937) 458; CROMPTON of Flower Lilies/op.cit.518; SMITH of Duffield/BLG (1965) 804.

DUNSTON HALL (II)

Sheepbridge   *Private residence*

Dunston Hall, Sheepbridge.   NMR

Dunston Hall stands on a portion of the ancient and extensive Manor of Newbold, held by the King in 1086, and later granted to Welbeck Abbey. Dunston itself, however, became detached and was held by Matthew de Hathersage who gave it to Lenton Priory, in Nottinghamshire. At the Dissolution it was granted to Francis Leake and by 1600 it was owned by Richard Milnes, an Alderman of Chesterfield and Mayor there in 1625, and who was a son of the Milnes family of Ashford in-the-Water. He it was who built the first house there, and it forms the core of the present seat.

This pleasant unpretentious house has an irregular five-bay facade on the entrance front, under four straight coped gables. The centre bay, containing the entrance, under a nineteenth century gothick porch with four-centred arch and bulbous finials, lies slightly to the left of the actual centre-line of the building and this bay, with the two to the left of it, are of two storeys. This part indeed seems to contain the oldest work, and as it stands appears to be a rebuilding of 1828. The upper windows, three-light tallish mullions with curt cranked hood moulds, sit on a sill band; those below are graced with four centered arched heads and have three lights with decorated mullions. To the right of the entrance the building is of three lowish storeys but is overall of the same height. Each bay here is directly under the gable (which is not so to the left) with three-light mullioned windows under cranked hood moulds on the third storey. The first floor windows are of four lights, and the sill band carries on by cranking over these, whereas it had run under those on the south end of the house. These windows seem *almost* perched upon a pair of canted bays at ground floor level, and the entire facade, which is terminated with fine ashlar quoins, seems to have been refaced in ashlar – Coal Measures sandstone, probably Deep Hard Rock or Silkstone Rock – at the same time as the gothick work was done or later. This part is also marked by a central four-shaft chimney stack and appears to be, in effect, an eighteenth century house tacked on to the original build, and later modified to suit the nineteenth century scheme; the roofs are slated.

Internally little remains of the original work, and the staircase appears to be of nineteenth century date. Outside, there is an interesting cruck framed building renovated in 1981. The grounds have largely been lost to later building and the estate to industry. The traditional date of 1597 is when Richard Milnes acquired the house, and it is possible that he either inherited it or purchased it from Michael Eyre, a descendant of the Eyres of Holme, of whom Roger, four generations before, had married the heiress of a branch of the Whittingtons of Whittington who had themselves inherited it from the knightly family of Bakewell.

In 1787 the last of the Milnes died, bequeathing it to Rev. William Smith (who thereupon assumed the surname and arms of Milnes additionally to his own), husband of the heiress of Robert Mower, whose wife was the aunt of the George Milnes who had died in 1787. After the death of Smith, his son died leaving the house and modest estate to his sister, wife of Rev. C.A.A.Craven, whose son assumed the additional surnames of Smith-Mimes and had a grant of arms, but who was forced to sell, withdrawing to Winkburn in Nottinghamshire where his posterity still reside. The house at Dunston was let, however, in the early years of the twentieth century, to Ernest Dixon Fawsett. It was most recently for sale in December 1974 (a year after it had previously been on the market) with an asking price of £40,000.

Pevsner, 150; Lysons V. 83; EYRE of Holme/ V.1569; CRAVEN-SMITH-MILNES of Hockerton/ BLG (1969) 439.

EASTWOOD GRANGE

see EASTWOOD HALL

EASTWOOD HALL (II)

Ashover   Ruinous

Eastwood Hall, 1982.   M. Stanley

Ashover is a large parish which, by the seventeenth century possessed several small estates, each with a seat. The process whereby this came about was lengthy and involved, and the barest outlines will be found under the entries relating to some of these houses Eddlestow *(qv)*, Goss, Overton, Marsh Green and Stubbing Edge Halls. Ashover was held at the time of Domesday by one Serlo under Ralph *fitz* Hubert; previously Serlo's two manors had been held by Leofric and Leofnoth (Levenot), and it is interesting to note that a family deriving their surname from the latter subsisted within the parish until the seventeenth century – conceivably descendants of the Saxon Lord.

Serlo's great grandson, Serlo de Pleasley, whose brother was ancestor of the Glapwells of Glapwell *(qv)*, left two daughters and co-heiresses, Matilda and Sara. The latter's heiress (by Hugh de Stivinton) married Ralph de Willoughby, who inherited a share of the estate; Matilda married John d'Eyncourt who also left two daughters, married to Isidore de Reresby of Rearsby, Lincolnshire and Thrybergh, Yorkshire and William de Musters, respectively. In due course, the Reresbys added to New Hall manor (whereon they built the New Hall, later Eastwood Hall), part of the Munsters' share and all the Willoughby's share.

It is not, however, clear when the Reresbys first built a seat on the site, but by the middle of the fifteenth century a

Eastwood Grange, Ashover, c. 1910.   M. Craven

remarkable early example of the Midland high house seems to have been erected. This appears to have originally been a free-standing five-storey tower, of fortified appearance (although no licence to crenellate was applied for, and none granted). The east front had the highest part at its south end, with a lower, three-storey part connected forming the east front proper. This consisted effectively of five bays marked by miniscule two-light mullioned windows with a string course above. The central bay was deeply recessed, but with an infilled porch at ground level – possibly a later addition. The whole was built of coarse squared stone brought to course, with ashlared quoins at all the angles probably all in Ashover Grit (appropriately) or Chatsworth Grit both outcropping nearby, giving a powerful aspect. So ruinous is it today, however, that we can form only a hazy idea of what sort of skyline it would have had. There are no surviving obvious signs of earthworks, and the assumption has to be made that this was a possible hunting lodge, owing much to the Prior's lodging at Repton of 1437-38 (qv).

Sir Thomas Reresby married Mary Monson of South Carlton, Lincolnshire, and set about spending her money – to the tune of £2,000 – in rebuilding the house to make a more comfortable residence of it. He added a new range to the south-west and carried this to the north-west angle, adding a short service wing to the north and a parlour range of only one storey to the east of that face of the high tower, lit by six-light mullion and transom cross windows under straight hood moulds and quoined in a matching style to the older work. The interior was, apparently, richly plastered. Yet not many years later, Sir Thomas had made the house and estate over to trustees in an attempt to discharge his debts, to some extent caused by over-extravagance in building. It was, however, too late and in 1612 it was mortgaged to Samuel Tryon, although Sir Thomas resided in the house during his High Shrievality in 1613-14. Shortly afterwards, however, Tyron foreclosed and in 1623 sold to Rev. Emmanuel Bourne, whose ancestors came from Whirlow, near Sheffield, but who was then rector of Ashover. The Reresbys were to go on to a baronetcy earned through loyalty to the Crown during the Civil War (granted 16 May 1642) but the third baronet repeated the extravagance of Sir Thomas, of Eastwood, his ancestor, and gambled his remaining estates away, dying in poverty and obscurity, depriving his successor of any chance of marrying, and the line terminated on the death of the fourth baronet in August 1748.

Emmanuel Bourne took up residence in the house, but took a rather naive 'A plague-on-both-your-houses' attitude during the Civil War, resulting in the estate and house being pillaged by foraging Royalists in 1643 and, more seriously, by the forces of Sir John Gell of Hopton, Bt, the Parliamentary commander, in 1646, when his refusal to provide sustenance for the troops resulted in the house being fired, and it has remained a mouldering ruin ever since. Bourne, disgusted, removed to Chesterfield, but after the war his successors built a new residence, Marsh Green Hall, nearer the church (qv.)

In 1762, the ruined Hall and some land was sold to the governors of Queen Anne's Bounty to augment the living of Brimington. Another part of the estate, which lay on the northern edge and marched with that of Eddlestow, was sold by 1870 to William Chesterman JP who built in that year a

largish Jacobethan seat with shaped and straight coped gables, projecting bays full of plate glass and a square tower topped with bartizans, one projecting as a stair tower. The architect was Joseph Brookhouse of Derby, who also built the hill-top gatehouse nearby. He landscaped the grounds, taking full advantage of the site on the south slope of the hill on which it lay, and provided his guests with a golf course behind and above the house. It was later sold in the 1930s to Sir George Kenning.

Pevsner, 68; Lysons, V. 16; Lugard (1924) 17-21; Emery (2000) 459 n.18; RERESBY of Thrybergh, Bt./BDEB 438; BOURNE/Glover II 57; PLEASLEY & WILLOUGHBY *sub* WILLOUGHBY D'ERESBY, B./BP (1999) II 3031-3034.

EDDLESTOW HALL (II)

Ashover   *Private residence*

Eddlestow Hall, Ashover, 1982   *M. Stanley*

This seems to represent the site of the original manor house of Ashover – presumably seat of Serlo de Pleasley (qv Eastwood Old Hall) – known in times past as Old Hall Manor. The oldest part of the present house is in the fabric of what is now a barn behind, containing two large and ancient fireplaces. The main house is mainly of late sixteenth or seventeenth century date, but in plan the house is quite untypical, being a single five-bay two-storey range without cross-wings or projections (apart from a good two storey projecting porch with straight coped gable). It is conceivable that, with the barn, Eddlestow contains the shadow of a much earlier courtyard house later reduced and rebuilt. The present main range has had its fenestration Georgianized, although to the rear some mullioned windows survive. At either side are lower, vernacular two-storey wings, irregular in outline and in detail. The building is in ashlar Ashover Grit from an adjacent outcrop, with stone slate roofs now regrettably covered in a black bitumastic treatment. The interior is today largely plain.

This part of the Domesday estate was that which passed to the Musters family in the thirteenth century. In 1337 it was again split, part going to the Reresbys of Eastwood, and the rest, including Eddlestow Hall to Ralph de Wynfield. The heiress of this family married into the Rollestons of Lea and it passed from them to the Peshalls of Weston-under-Lizard in the later sixteenth century. Sir John Peshall was created a baronet on 25 November 1611 – one of the first creations – but the penalties of loyalty to the Crown in the Civil War forced its sale to Thomas Cowley of Marsh Green; the family thereupon moved away, and the title became extinct in 1712.

Cowley's son-in-law Thomas Gladwin thereafter inherited the estate, and his son William later endowed his brother Thomas with it, and he promptly let it. In the century following, the heiress carried it to Dr Henry Bourne of The Spital, Chesterfield (qv), of the Eastwood Hall family. The Bournes sold in 1808 to John Milnes of Ashover and by 1816 Eddlestow was occupied as a farm, the tenants in the late nineteenth century being the Shaws. Today it is still a farmhouse, and one with an interesting a history as any in Derbyshire.

Pevsner, 205; White (1857) 670; Lugard (1924) 16; ROLLESTON/V.1611 & BIFR 991; PESHALL, Bt./BDEB 406; BOURNE & MILNES/Glover, II. 56-57; GLADWIN sub GLADWIN-ERRINGTON of Hinchleywood/BLG (1952) 766.

EDNASTON MANOR (I)

Private residence

Ednaston Manor, 1987.   J. Sharpe

William Goodacre Player, a Nottingham tobacco magnate, purchased part of the Ednaston estate in 1913. He commissioned Sir Edwin Lutyens to design him a seat, and the result, Ednaston Manor, is a most impressive house, and dignified in Lutyens' grand classical manner. The house is chiefly characterized by its high hipped tiled roofs, its rhythmically recessed elevations, each front being quite different, and its perfect proportions. It is built of brick, with courses of Flemish bond separated by ones of stretcher bond, and finely judged stone dressings of Millstone Grit sandstone, the fenestration being casemented, yet glazed to look like early sashwork without being in any way pretentious or bogus. The deep eaves are of timber. With its tall sturdy brick stacks the entire ensemble has great power without in any way appearing to threaten.

The entrance front faces west, enclosed by a circular courtyard strongly reminiscent of that placed before St Helen's House, Derby, by Joseph Pickford, but here penetrated radially by three main gateways with two garden gates on the axis of the facade itself. This front is of five bays, three wide and two less so, divided by stone pilasters terminating in capitals carved with chaste trophies all inset into the eaves cornice, itself interrupted over the centre bay by a plain frieze with a keyblock from the window immediately below all under a plain triangular pediment. Below this is the doorcase in an eared stone surround capped by an open swan-neck pediment carrying a baroque cartouche, itself left with a pounced ground where one might have expected Mr. Player's armorial bearings: *argent a pale azure between two saffron flowers leaved and slipped proper* to appear.

A stone band runs from the doorcase to be broken by the very tops of the ground floor windows which have gauged brick lintels. Beyond the five bays, there is another, blank, bay, recessed, forming the returns of projecting ends on the north and south fronts. Two dormers grace the roof inward of two stacks.

The south (garden) front is softer, less monumental. Five bays, the end ones only flanked by pilasters, are recessed a bay deep between projecting wings two bays wide and ensigned by further pilasters, inset from the angles, with another pair in the returns flanking a ground floor window under a stone niche, all the pilasters being plain with capitals carved as monograms again inset into the eaves cornice. A central entrance is graced with a broken triangular pediment framing a carved trophy with the window above omitted on the south. Apart from ground floor keyblocks and a flat stone band, the east front is devoid of ornament. The north, which contains the service accommodation, is unexpected and has no less impact than the others. As with the south, the end bays of the east and west fronts form plain classical projections, but the recessed centre, again of five bays, takes the form of two steep and wide straight coped brick gables graced by a low ellipse of rain-water goods. Neat outbuildings extend back from the projections.

Inside, the rooms are spacious yet by no means lofty, the scale is rich but not intimidating. Much use is made of stucco panels and decorative arches. Timberwork is of high quality including the second staircase (and hardly less magnificent than the main one) being an impressive essay in William and Mary mode with three turned balusters per tread. The main stair, placed off the hall in the manner of Francis Smith, is of Hoptonwood and decorated with a delicate wrought-iron rail and balustrade made to Lutyens' design by Messrs Taylor, Whiting and Taylor of Derby, the last practitioners in the tradition of Robert Bakewell.

Beyond the house, Lutyens also designed a stable block, converted into dwellings in 1983. A pair of cottages on the main road by Lutyens, harled and with battered walls, appears as a single cottage. The magnificent gardens, under the Players open to the public, were laid out by William Barrons Limited in the spirit of Gertrude Jekyll, if not actually to her design, in 1920. Listed grade II, they are amongst the very finest in the region.

The house and small estate passed, on W.G.Player's death, to Stephen Dane Player, his fourth son who died in 1979 when the house with 50 acres was sold to Lionel V. Pickering, the owner of Derby County F.C. Some remaining land is still in the hands the Player family.

Pevsner, 207; CL LIII (1950) 398; DLC 6-7/1972; PLAYER of Whatton Manor/BLG (1952) 2041.

EGGINTON HALL

Demolished

Egginton Hall: the dower house, Park Hill, c. 1900   *M. Craven*

Egginton was held at Domesday by Azelin under his probable relative Geoffrey Alselin, along with Etwall. It passed through an heiress to the Walkelins of Radbourne and thence came through another heiress to Sir William de Stafford of a cadet branch of the Staffords of Stafford and thus kin to the Gresleys and Longfords. Their heiress transmitted the main part of the estate to the Tinmores of Tinmore, Staffordshire, whence it came ultimately Lathburys. By this time – the late-fourteenth century – there was undoubtedly a seat at Eggington, although the de Staffords may have built one earlier. Miss E M Every in her notes, assembled at the beginning of the twentieth century from family papers and memories, records the filling in of a moat 'in the Park' in the very late-seventeenth century as a result of garden building.

Suffice it to say that by the time the Leighs (cadets of Adlington, Cheshire) had inherited from the senior line of the Lathburys – a junior line remained at Holme in the parish and later were at Horninglow, near Burton upon Trent until the twentieth century – a substantial mansion existed upon approximately the site on which the later house was built. This was described by the reticent Woolley as 'a good house' and passed in 1622 to Sir Simon Every, 1st Bt, of an old West Country family, when he married the Leigh heiress. Again, a junior line of Leighs remained in the parish for a while, but later removed to Lancashire.

The seat occupied by the Everys, which was taxed on 20 hearths in 1670, was burnt in 1736, at which time the estate extended to 3,200 acres, including much of Newton Solney. The fire cannot have been too drastic, as rebuilding was not treated with any urgency by the family; repairs no doubt sufficed. It was not until 1756 that William Baker of Audlem prepared plans for a new house which Colvin thinks were probably not put into effect, for in 1758-61 Benjamin Wyatt (1709-1772) began building, aided by his sons Samuel (1737-1807) and William (1734-1780). This work, it was long thought, formed the basis for the house which finally arose 1782-83 under the hand of Samuel Wyatt, who had aided his father at Egginton as a 21-year-old over two decades earlier. Yet amongst the family papers is a note in the hand of Sir Edward Every, 8th Bt (who had shortly before inherited from a distant cousin after living in relative if genteel poverty in Derby as the son of an innkeeper) reading: 'Ye old house pulled down...pd. Mr Wyatt £8 12s 7d ye 9th Febr. 1782'. The presence, however, of a very fine timber staircase with three turned balusters per tread and richly carved tread ends in the west vestibule as a secondary stair, rather suggests that Benjamin Wyatt's work was probably alterations, additions and repairs to the old house. Yet the new house appears to have been mainly of one build.

Wyatt gave it a nine-bay south (entrance) front of two storeys, with the central three bays breaking forward and characterized by a domed, top-lit bow containing a flying cantilevered Hoptonwood stone stair with a wrought-iron rail. The entrance was via a neo-classical Composite portico protecting a segmental headed doorcase, carved for £31 7s in 1782 by George Moneypenny of Derby; all the stone dressings were of Keuper sandstone. Above, the top balustrade was interrupted on the bow by a brick parapet with three *oculi* over the three bays. The facade was enlivened by sill bands with another band between the floors, and its length was emphasized by the addition of paired bows on the returns at both east and west ends. Those on the east flanked a pair of typical Wyatt tripartite windows, and on the opposite side flanked the subsidiary entrance – a Doric tripartite affair capped rather awkwardly by a full triangular pediment with a Diocletian window above.

To the north was a service wing, probably retained from the previous house, as was the elegant U-shaped brick stable block with round headed ground floor entrances and windows, central breakfront pediment with Whitehurst turret clock, and large square lantern above with ogiform cap.

Inside the house, the plasterwork was restrained, almost austere, being confined largely to the cornices, with the exception of the exuberance of the entrance hall. Several good fireplaces were reused from the previous house, although one or two rather exotic rococo French ones were imported later, too, and a particularly fine one with Blue John insets was carved by Moneypenny in 1783. At least one room was graced with late seventeenth century panelling of high quality, presumably surviving from the old house.

The 50-acre park, landscaped c. 1700 for Sir Henry Every by Lawrence Squibb of Derby, was re-landscaped with much new planting, and making dramatic visual use of the Dove which ran to the west of the house, and a lake and cascade were created. The latter was crossed by a very pretty *Chinoiserie* footbridge, later replaced by one supplied by Coalbrookdale and dated 1812, making it the eighth oldest iron bridge in Britain, decorated with pierced spandrels, a wiggly balustrade and cast-iron armorials. Although today much distressed – the balustrade has gone and the armorial plaques have been removed to another location in the village – it was spotlisted grade II* in 1990. The orangery, arbour and temple – all were eighteenth century – have gone. The great drawback of the park is that it was relentlessly flat, but contemporary views establish that its embellishment was highly successful, and it could well be the work of William Emes, who frequently worked in tandem with the Wyatts after the death of Joseph Pickford. An icehouse lurked in a plantation called The Triangle until World War One, when it was destroyed. A fine pair of Wyatt Lodges once graced the drive from Rekindle Street (now the A38). The estate was 3,200 acres in 1737.

Whilst the house was being rebuilt, the family removed to

91

Egginton Hall, c. 1900.   M. Craven

Rock House, Newton Solney, rebuilt in Gothick, quite probably by Joseph Pickford, before 1782. It thus formed a distant eye-catcher from the south front of the Hall, although a plantation intervenes today. It was sold off and replaced around 1839 by a villa of some charm, oddly still sporting a Gothic river front, but greatly simplified, being little more than an embattled curtain wall, but integral with the house. In about 1800, too, the dower house, a two-storey five-bay brick edifice was built, probably by Thomas Gardner of Uttoxeter, at Park Hill in Egginton parish, occupied by the Every's Mosley kinsmen in the years before Burnaston House *(qv)* was built. It was extended considerably in 1901 and after years of near dereliction, has been restored.

In the twentieth century, Egginton Hall was let quite frequently: to Captain Dugdale, for whom William Barron Limited did some work both in the park and to the gardens in 1908, after World War One by Major Frederick Gretton. Rapidly declining fortunes, however, caused the abandonment of the house after World War Two, and in 1955 the late Sir John Every pulled it down, removing to a fine late sixteenth century house in the village which he renamed The Cothay after Cothay Manor, one of the family's Devonshire seats. Here some pieces, like panelling were taken, and more ended up at The Wilderness, West Hallam, as a result of a sale at the Hall before its demolition, preceding which several attempts had been made to sell the house entire. Most of the estate, reduced to 2,234 acres by 1883 and 1,933 acres sixty years later, was also sold, the bulk of what remained being sold to the Durose family.

There were anciently three manors within the estate at Egginton, the result of the fragmentation following the five co-heiresses of the Staffords: Hargate Manor, Hardwick Manor, and Seymour's Place Manor. The latter is lost, but estate farms mark the sites of the others.

Egginton Hall was supposedly haunted by a one armed man who walked from the churchyard to the hall at midnight, the reason, apparently, why the widow of Sir Edward Every lived in the village, leaving the hall empty prior to World War Two. Interestingly, it was at about this time that the cedar tree by the library window fell. Legend had it that when this happened the family would lose the hall, and indeed, most of the estate, was sold not so long afterwards, and the hall demolished. The present Sir Henry Every lives in the village still, so the family connection there mercifully continues.

In 1994, the site of the hall along with 18 acres of the former park, was acquired by Derby-based property developer Kevin Ellis and his wife. He has since rather bravely built a new house on the site, in classical style, detailed to pay homage to its predecessor. Of brick with stone dressings, five bays by four with a first floor sill band and hipped roof behind a low parapet, the garden front is marked by a full-height bow. The entrance front has a muscular Doric

portico attached to a three bay breakfront under a plain pediment, the ground floor windows being set into a blind arcade. The architect was Adam Bench of Derek Latham & Associates of Derby. The remaining part of the stable block has been restored and work has begun on the restoration of the Coalbrookdale Bridge.

Colvin, 95, 1101, 1126; Pevsner (1953) 131; Woolley, I p.11; Lysons, V. 155; Pilkington (1789) 244; DAJ XVI (1894) 133; Hutton *et al* DBR 185 *Park Hill, Egginton* (Derby, 1995); EVERY MSS, DRO & in Derby Museum; DLC 3/74; AZELIN etc./DAJ XLIX (1927) 56; LATHBURY of Holme/V.1611; LEIGH of Egginton/*ibid.*; EVERY, Bt./BP (1999) I.1009-12.

ELVASTON CASTLE (II*)

Unoccupied

In 1461 Sir Walter Blount *(cf* Barton Blount) was granted the manorial estate of Elvaston, which included Ambaston and Thulston, previously held by the Frechevilles, to which family it had come from the Musards of Staveley. They had inherited it from Sir Thomas Hanselin, a lineal descendant of the Domesday tenant (if Rev. S.P.H.Statham's persuasive arguments concerning the Knight holding under Geoffrey Alselin, the tenant-in-chief, are correct), although his branch of the family had only acquired it on the death of Robert fitz William (great-grandson of Azelin, *cf* Egginton), Bishop of Worcester, in 1195.

It is known that the Blounts had a seat at Elvaston, for during the Wars of the Roses, and shortly after the grant, for it was sacked by a lawless bunch of adherents of the Longfords of Longford, led by members of the family. The elder Sir John Porte having purchased it from the Blounts, Lords Mountjoy, it was transmitted to Sir Thomas Stanhope of Shelford in the reign of Mary I, and the half-brother of his grandson Philip, the first Earl of Chesterfield, Sir John Stanhope, built a new house there dated 1633. This appears to have been the sort of H-shaped building with projecting straight coped gables typical of the area at this time, although being in lowland Derbyshire, it was of rich red brick with Keuper sandstone dressings. The gabled projections would appear, from surviving evidence, to have had canted two-storey end bays topped with a carved stone slate roof and containing 12-light mullioned and transomed windows, two lights being canted round the sides. The third floor above had (and still has) an eight-light window of the same type. Both the first and second floors were higher than the ground floor, so in this the house must have followed the pattern set by Hardwick and Chatsworth in having family and 'state' rooms above.

Subsequent work, represented by two surviving interiors on the south front, seems to have been undertaken shortly after the Restoration, causing tax to be assessed on 18 hearths in 1670, and again c. 1705 (date in drawing room). This seems to have involved the heightening of one ground floor room, and extending the south front, the house being set facing west. It also seems to have involved a dramatic remodelling of the gardens, tantalizing traces of which survive both in the documentary sources and on the ground; they appear to have included parterres, waterworks, including a canal and at least two long avenues. In view of the works carried out for their cousin, Lord Chesterfield at Bretby nearby *(qv)*, it may be that this undertaking was linked and therefore of considerable importance.

In 1742 the Elvaston Stanhopes were created *inter alia*

Earls of Harrington and at about this period more rebuilding seems to have taken place. Then or in the time of Charles, 3rd Earl, the north side appears to have been infilled between the seventeenth century central range and the extended east front with a five-bay, two and a half storey block; this also contained the staircase. There are two fireplaces of this period surviving too, although most of this range is plain, and was clearly intended mainly for additional accommodation and services. The next development was in 1812 when Benjamin Dean Wyatt was commissioned to design a new house, but contented himself with re-modelling the staircase in cantilevered Hoptonwood stone with a neo-Classical wrought iron rail and niches. Instead, a scheme by his father, James Wyatt, was produced a year later, being executed by Richard Walker, during 1815-29, after the former's death.

Wyatt's scheme was essentially a remodelling of the old house achieved by infilling the space between the projecting wings flanking the west front with a new great hall and throwing a gothick cloak around the remainder. The new west facade is of five bays and two storeys boasting a projecting porch with crenellations and angle turrets. The four-light mullioned and transomed windows have delicately worked cusped heads with hood moulds over, and the parapet is crenellated. The north-west projecting wing is arrayed to match, with a first floor oriel – of some sumptuousness – and angle turrets; the attic window is enclosed by bank niches. However, that on the south-west angle was originally left entirely as it had been in 1633. The Jacobean and Restoration east front, still gabled, was left alone at this stage. Thus in an engraving done in the 1820s, the facade looks strangely unbalanced, with a built-up wing on one side – ashlar faced in Keuper sandstone as was all the new build – and the other side left gabled and brick and enshrining the best Jacobean rooms, but with starkly differing heights. This phase also caused the eighteenth century north range to be gothicised.

The next phase began in 1836 when Lewis Cottingham was called in to rebuild and embellish the so-called Gothic Hall, now re-named 'The Hall of the Fair Star'. He is also said by most authorities to have rebuilt the east front, but from contemporary illustrations it is clear that this was not so. He also advised the 4th Earl on the design of the new and spectacular gardens he was about to lay out, and is thought now to have designed the Moorish Temple in the Alhambra Garden and in consequence, may be attributed with some of the other, relate, garden buildings. Illustrations of 1851 and 1857 make it plain that the east front was not rebuilt then, and it is likely that work on this aspect of the house did not begin until after the accession of the 6th Earl in 1862. A series of early photographs by Richard Keene of Derby make it clear that this work had been completed by the end of that decade at the latest. The new facade was nine bays wide with a taller centre section breaking forward between a pair of slim octagonal turrets, with others at the ends. The centre has a two-storey canted bay and the whole is crenellated, with the Earl of Harrington's arms at the centre atop the parapet dominating the rather less noticeable achievements of four related

dukes below, all carved by the talented Derby sculptor Joseph Barlow Robinson. The fenestration is of rectangular plate glass ensigned with cranked hood moulds, but the blank effect is relieved when the shutters within are closed, for their exterior faces are mirrored overall and overlaid with slender gothic tracery which shows up enchantingly amidst reflected light. On the north was provided a tall mullioned and double transomed window to light the staircase in the north-east angle and linked it to an impressive water-tower with crow-stepped battlements beyond which was a very pretty gothic outhouse; all the latter features were unceremoniously removed by the Derbyshire County Council in the later 1960s. The remaining question is: by whom was the east front re-built? The fact that J. B. Robinson boasted of his carving of the detailing in his *Catalogue of Works* gives a clue, for much of his work in the local area (his practice was virtually nationwide in its scope) was done in tandem with Henry Isaac Stevens of Derby, and certainly the east front at Elvaston is redolent of his style, although its monumental dullness might suggest a lesser hand.

Inside, the great hall was executed to Wyatt and Cottingham's design in a very impressive gothick, including a screen of four-centred arches, niches, fan vaulting and pendants, all gilded and painted in antiquarian style with Stanhope heraldry. The only incongruous note is the superb early eighteenth century marble fireplace, a legacy of a later phase of the previous house. Behind the hall lies the later eighteenth century staircase, with a door to the right of the foot of it to a room with a fine seventeenth century alabaster and painted fireplace and Jacobean panelling, enfilading through to the two late-seventeenth century or early eighteenth century rooms, one with cedar panelling with good bolection mouldings. In the angle between the great hall is the surviving low ceilinged parlour of 1633; above is a very fine closet of similar date, cunningly integrated into the master bedroom suite by Wyatt.

Beyond the house lies a stable block, built contemporarily with the south front, with central access and a pleasant square bell cupola and Whitehurst turret clock, beyond which are a Wyatt coach house, further offices, engine house, another "Moorish" temple and the buildings of the home farm, today run (reluctantly, one feels) as the Working Estate Museum by the County Council. The west boundary of this is screened by trees from the adjacent and very fine parish church. A pair of Gothic lodges, probably Walker's work, survive on the London Road.

Elvaston Castle, prior to reduction, 1964.   *J. Darwin*

93

The whole ensemble, however, is cemented aesthetically by the grounds and park of 198 acres, beyond which once lay an estate of 4,572 acres. Humphrey Repton was originally called in by third Lord Harrington to landscape the grounds, but was daunted by the unremitting flatness of the Trent Valley, and declined the commission. As a sop, he sent seven Wellingtonias to screen the park to the south. Shortly before Cottingham began work, in 1830, Harrington turned to the young and untried Scot, William Barron, who spent the next 20 years laying out the park, pleasure grounds and gardens. One of the glories of his work was the elaborate topiary garden to the west, almost destroyed by neglect but today restored in simplified form by the County Council. The whole of Barron's undertaking in tandem with the 4th Earl was of immense complexity and the 100 acres of gardens they produced was romantic, eclectic and virtually impossible of upkeep. The varied planting of tree specimens vies with Derby Arboretum in date. The gardens are deservedly listed grade II. Here, too, Barron pioneered his method of moving mature trees, a skill which stood him in good stead later, and indeed, his work at Elvaston enabled him to establish himself in business with his sons at Borrowash nearby, and he and his successors enjoyed a virtual monopoly of garden design well into the twentieth century, not only at country houses, but also in suburban villas and middling dwellings on the fringes of towns nation-wide. The topiary garden is embellished with another Moorish temple, like that to the north of the stables, a simple brick structure, neatly proportioned and apt. Other structures abound by the same hand, including the pump house with its Harrison of Derby machine. It is unclear who designed these: was it Barron, Cottingham or a third party? From 1839 the lake was added to the north and east of the house with a series of grottoes and rock-eyes beyond, smothered in rhododendrons. For all their stunning complexity, however, Barron's gardens at Elvaston must overlie the vestiges of a late 17th century garden of equal importance; before the one is ultimately (it is to be hoped) restored, the other must be properly investigated.

Part of Barron's gardens, c. 1868 by R. Keene.

M. Craven

Standing two thirds of the way down the tree-girt avenue from the west lodges is a final glory of Elvaston: the so-called Golden Gates. These most impressive iron gates are notable for their massive construction and were erected on the spot in 1819, having been looted from the vicinity of the Tuileries at the liberation of Paris in 1814. They were reputedly made for the Emperor Napoleon I. and were put up flanked by 15 foot high cast iron railings made especially in Birmingham, which terminate in huge piers made of large blocks of Chellaston alabaster, undoubtedly the most monumental exterior use made of this locally abundant and impressive material. Figures of Hercules slaying the lion top the piers and the whole was originally gilded. The alabaster itself may have come from an estate quarry at Ambaston, recorded as being open by Woolley a century before. Unfortunately, the gates were repainted blue sometime before White's Directory recorded the fact in 1857, and they remain largely of this hue today.

The estate retains numerous good buildings, including the school, Clock Farm – by Stevens (proof of his presence here) – Jacobethan with a prominent turret clock in the facade, Regency Thulston Grange and Elvaston House. The Grange (II) was built in the early years of the nineteenth century, a brick two-storeyed building under a hipped roof, plain and dignified. The rebuilt eighteenth century staircase is top-lit and there is a Blue John inlaid fireplace in white, probably Cararra marble in the manner of Richard Brown of Derby from Elvaston Castle. It was sold off in decay and has now been restored. Elvaston House, technically in the adjoining parish of Borrowash, was built beside an arm of the Derwent by a race and may have begun life as a mill house. Of seventeenth century origin, it was rebuilt at the start of the nineteenth century as a dower house, but was let to the Barron family from the 1860s, and was subsequently sold, by which time it had become Riverside House.

Before World War Two the Castle was occupied by the Harrington's kinsmen the Lillingstons, but during that conflict it was taken over by the young women of the Derby Training College for teachers. After they vacated the house in 1952, it was hardly used, and was ultimately put up for sale in 1963, some contents being sold at a sale 18-19/3/1964, the rest going to Ireland with the Harringtons. The purchaser was a gravel extraction firm, and the house and estate seemed doomed. However, after much local agitation, the Derby County Borough and Derbyshire County Councils jointly purchased it in 1969. They opened the first Country Park under legislation of 1968, and planned to establish a natural history museum and educational centre, but with local government re-organisation in 1974 Derby dropped out. The then County Council founded the Working Estate Museum, and began restoration of the fabric of the house with a view to opening it to the public. However, a change of control in 1981 froze that aspect of the plan, and the house has now entered its twentieth year of total neglect. The 388 acres of grounds acquired is still used as a pleasant country park, popular enough to be suffering from erosion from the number of visitors. In October 1999 the County Council suddenly decided to sell both house and park with no strings, but after much opposition, altered the terms to a lease; one of those involved in trying to re-acquire the site (and with the least detrimental plan) is the Earl of Harrington's grandson, Hon. William Stanhope, who is currently in competition with a timeshare company and others requiring huge enabling developments. Meanwhile, the Council has applied for a Lottery grant to restore the gardens to a manageable version of their original state. Both house and gardens, meanwhile, remain under dire threat.

Colvin, 271, 1016, 1120; Pevsner, 209-10; CL V (1899) 48-52, 803; DLC 12/62-1/63; Woolley 20, pp54-56; Pilkington (1789) II.102; Davies (1811) 274; Lysons (1817; Mundy Edn.) IV 158A-H; Barron (1852) 1-8, 71-77; Morris (1866-80) II. 21-22; Bulmer (1895) 742; Tipping, H. A. (c. 1908) I. 24-26; Myles (1996) 145-46; Anderson & Glenn (1997) *passim*; DRO Elvaston Deeds D518M, D2404; HARRINGTON, E/BP (1999) 1. 1320-22; MOUNTJOY, B/BDEB 54-56.

ERRWOOD HALL

Goyt Valley   *Very ruinous*

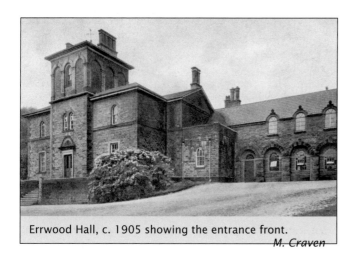

Errwood Hall, c. 1905 showing the entrance front.

M. Craven

Errwood Hall was probably in the most romantic location in Derbyshire, although for most of its existence, the house was located in Cheshire. Samuel Grimshawe, a Catholic Lancashire industrialist acquired the site, on the east slope of the then unspoilt Goyt Valley, and carved out a house platform. His seat, upon which he proposed to lavish much expenditure, was designed by Alexander Roos (1810-1881) possibly with advice from Alexander Beresford Hope, Hon PRIBA (1820-87) who had inherited Beresford Hall, Staffordshire, and some land in Derbyshire from his kinsman Field Marshall Viscount Beresford. His sketch design, which nevertheless bears a close resemblance to the house as built, bears the monograph legend 'Errwood, Cheshire, as not completed'. It was built from c. 1841 until 1845 with some work continuing until 1851 when Samuel Grimshawe died.

Errwood was Italianate with quirky Norman details. The entrance front faced east across the valley, with the garden front facing south. The latter, of two storeys, consisted of a three-bay centre, the lower storey consisting of a glassed-in loggia with round-headed terrace-depth windows, the centre effectively a door, with projecting pedimented bays either side with coupled sashes on the first floor over Venetian windows below. Built of rock faced and hammer dressed ashlar and coarse rubble of Millstone Grit sandstone (probably Rough Rock), the facade was embellished with a first-floor sill band and quoins. The entrance front was of three bays with segmental headed upper storey windows, the central bay rising through the eaves of the hipped roof and projecting as an Italianate tower with a blank arcade at the top punctuated by a single conforming window. Where this feature departs from the mundane is that a chimney stack penetrated the low pyramidal roof on either side. The apex of the roof was crowned by an elaborate wrought-iron weather vane. The entrance itself, beneath a paired window, was crowned with a stone tympanum bearing the carved armorial crest of the Grimshawes. Beyond and to the right was a lower seven-bay range with a five-bay blank arcaded centre, the arches rusticated, ending in a further more modest Italianate tower crowned with a belvedere; behind it lay the service accommodation. The west front, being overshadowed by the rising ground, was left plain. The stone was taken from an adjacent outcrop; the roof was slate.

It was originally intended that there should be a substantial apsidal Romanesque chapel on a mound to the south of the house connected to the west front by a steep covered way, and with a bell tower carrying a slim spire, the whole ensemble to lie on a massively constructed terrace punctuated by urn-topped buttresses, without doubt designed by Hope. However, the death of the elder Samuel Grimshawe meant that this work went unfinished, as S.D.Grimshaw, the son, seemed to lack his father's enthusiasm for building. Instead the chapel mound was adapted as a family burial ground, and a chapel was instead inserted into the upper storey of the north-east wing. Some impression of the interior can be gained from seeing the plaster reliefs after Canova, which were rescued from the house in 1930 and installed in Woodbank, Stockport, Cheshire, then recently converted into a Museum, and now offices of the local authority. The grounds, possibly also by Roos, who designed gardens in Scotland, were spectacularly planted with rhododendrons and serpentine walks creating a highly romantic aspect on the ground falling away from the fells above to the immature Goyt below with its ancient bridge. They were later opened to the public. There was also a private adit coalmine in the grounds which kept the house and neighbourhood supplied with fuel.

On the death of S.D.Grimshaw at about the turn of the century, the estate passed to his daughter's husband, H.R.H.Gosselin of Bengeo Hall, Hertfordshire, who assumed the additional surname of Grimshawe and died in 1924. His sister remained there until 1930 when she died and the estate was sold to Stockport Corporation. They let the house to the YHA until 1934, after which it fell gradually into desuetude, and the grounds rapidly ran wild.

In 1936 the area was transferred to Derbyshire, and in the 1960s the pretty Goyt was dammed and the Grimshawe's park was suddenly marred by a dreary and featureless sheet of water, now much given over to 'leisure'. The house itself was a picturesque ruin until the coming of the reservoir but thereafter was all dismantled except for part of the south front which was consolidated. The grounds have been controlled and turned into a series of trails for the edification of visitors, under the control of the Peak Park Joint Planning Board.

Watkin (1968) 189-90 & nn 51-2; Figueiredo & Treuherz (1988) 284; Hancock (1990) 15-29; Gow & Rowan (1995) 277-284; DLC 2-3/58; D. Misc. II 2 (1960) 241-4; GRIMSHAWE of Hutton Lodge/BLG (1921) 566.

ETWALL HALL (II)

Demolished

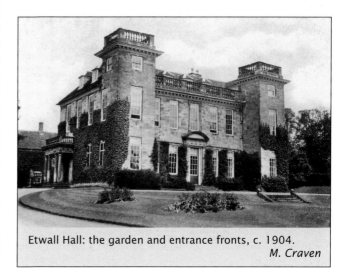

Etwall Hall: the garden and entrance fronts, c. 1904.

M. Craven

The early history of Etwall is full of complexity, and difficult to unravel. However, the main part of the manorial estate passed c. 1200 to a branch of the Riboeufs of Stretton-in-Shirland, and passed from them to a cadet branch of the de Etwalls, for Felicia, daughter and heiress of Richard de Riboeuf of Etwall (great grandson of Walter) married Robert de Ingram of Etwall; he held half a knight's fee there. Nevertheless, Felicia died without issue shortly before 1370, at which date the bulk of her inheritance was granted by trustees to the Abbey of Beauvale, Nottinghamshire, although a cadet branch of the Riboeufs continued at Etwall for some little time, perhaps on part or all of one manor. Under the Abbey, this moiety was held by the Babingtons. After the Dissolution, however, in 1540, it was granted by the Crown to Sir John Porte, son of Henry Porte, a Chester merchant with interests in Derby and nearby, and he built the first seat of which we know anything, fragments of which are believed to have remained in the fabric of the later building until its demise.

Etwall Hall from the north west showing the service wing, c. 1908.
                                                         J. Darwin

The heiress of Porte married Sir Thomas Gerard of Bryn, and his great grandson, Sir William Gerard, Bt, a Royalist, was forced to sell the estate to Sir Edward Mosley of The Hough, Lancashire in 1641, but he soon afterwards sold it on to Sir Samuel Sleigh, a Derby merchant of an old Hartington family, who was then a prominent Parliamentary supporter. He is said to have completely rebuilt the house shortly after acquiring it, using Keuper sandstone quarried from the slighted castle at Tutbury, which appears to have originated at Burton or Clifton. It is difficult to assess exactly what this house was like, but the unusual nature of the facade of the later seat points to the fact that it appears to have always had the two three-storey towers at the angles of the entrance front, for instance – these may go back to Sir John Porte's early Tudor house; possibly too, the range between was gabled, and the general shape was dictated by a house with central great hall having cross-wings at each end built by Porte. The house – like Elvaston – was taxed on 13 hearths in 1670, and Woolley, writing when its replacement was imminent, if not actually in train, called it, in his laconic way 'a good seat'.

Sir Samuel Sleigh – like many good rogues – lived a long life and married thrice; he also outlived his sons, and on his death in 1679 aged 76, the estate, along with Ash and Sutton-on-the-Hill, passed to James Chetham of Turton Tower, Lancashire, husband of his youngest daughter and co-heiress by his second marriage. His son, Samuel Chetham (1675-1744) decided to marry in 1713 to Mary, daughter and co-heiress of James Holt. With the promise of a much increased

fortune, Chetham immediately set about rebuilding his house. By 1713 Francis Smith of Warwick had begun work which continued, with gaps, until 1726.

The hall as he left it had a seven-bay entrance (south) front, the end bays consisting of the towers, which may well have been a feature of Sleigh's house for their fenestration showed clear signs of the first floor having been loftier than the ground storey, thus implying a typical Jacobean (or earlier) arrangement. The central five bays were almost certainly elements of a new two-storey centre – like the rest of this front in ashlared Keuper sandstone – all very plain and well proportioned and graced only with a central entrance with Doric pilasters supporting a frieze and segmental pediment, with a window in an eared surround above. There was a modillion cornice above topped by a balustrade, the same treatment being accorded to the towers, which were doubtless originally decorated with merlons or cupolas. Behind the balustrade was a highish roof with dormers. The west front was a three-bay extension behind the south-west tower, but latterly without the cornice and balustrade, possibly rebuilt about 1822, with a new entrance hall (replacing the old one in the centre of the south front) and entered through a substantial Doric porch with paired columns supporting a heavy frieze and entablature, with a balustrade over, probably reused from the 1713 build. The north side was of four widely spaced bays recessed back from the return of the west side, in brick with stone quoins, showing anomalous spacing and signs of older work. With its high hipped roof and lower service wing to the northwest, which looked all of a piece with it, there is a distinct impression to be gained of a build of about 1680; if so (and not Smith), being *retardataire* on a side of the house unlikely to be seen by visitors, no record of it has survived.

Inside there was a good seventeenth century staircase and contemporary panelling surviving from Sleigh's house. Early eighteenth century stucco work survived in the three 'best' rooms. A priest's hole was discovered behind the fireplace in the master bedroom when the house was being demolished. The entrance from near the church in the village was graced with a very fine pair of wrought-iron gates with overthrow graced by an armorial by Robert Bakewell at his best. After the demolition of the house and its replacement by a hideous comprehensive school, these were taken down and stored – or rather forgotten – in an outhouse. Here they were discovered in the late 1970s, and a vigorous campaign was mounted locally to raise money for their restoration. This was achieved, and they were restored by Mr Walker of Anslow, Staffordshire, and re-erected in front of Sir John Porte's delightful almshouses beside the church. The armorial is of Cotton with Sleigh in pretence, which they bore when found. Yet the Cottons did not come to Etwall until 1744, some time after the gates were made, which suggests that the armorial was altered after that date; in 1713-15 the arms should have been of Chetham with Sleigh in pretence. A further set of lesser gates and railings in the gardens appear to have been Bakewell's work (they have not survived except for a side gate now in Derby Cathedral), and the north end of the west front was linked to the stable block behind the house by a plain railing of spearheads punctuated by a pair of very plain wrought-iron gates hung between simple dignified stone piers perhaps the work of William and Benjamin Yates. These too appear to be lost.

The park was not overlarge, but pretty, and seems to have been tweaked into existence by intelligent use of existing landscape rather than landscaped formally; a railway line penetrated it, courtesy of the GNR in 1876, but has since been replaced by a by-pass and now numerous Portakabins, terrapins and all the paraphernalia of contemporary educational practice mar the setting.

On the death of Samuel Chetham, the house and estates passed to the husband of Mary, youngest daughter of Sir Samuel Sleigh by his third wife, Elizabeth, daughter and heiress of Rev. John Harpur, rector of Morley and a scion of the Harpurs of Littleover: Rowland Cotton, MP, of Bellaport, Shropshire. The last male heir of this family was William Cotton (1740-1819), certified a lunatic, and shut up in the house throughout his long life. On his death unmarried the estates were split between two of his three sisters and co-heiresses: Rebecca, who had married Richard Ward of Derby, grocer (a surprising match in view of the social sensibilities of the period, which may owe something in terms of possibility to the fact that Rebecca's mother was the only daughter of Daniel Webster, the Etwall farmer), and Elizabeth who married the Birmingham businessman, Joseph Green of Hall Green. The former's son, Rev. Richard Rowland Ward inherited Ash and Sutton (qv) and the latter gained Etwall, and their son assumed the surname and arms of Cotton in lieu of Green.

The last male heir died in 1894, leaving a sister and heiress who was also mad and confined to an institution, where she died unmarried in 1937. The heir was Brian Delves Broughton, but the house had been occupied since 1907 by Major Matthew Smith Dawson, JP, who died in 1940, whereupon it was commandeered by the military. In 1945 Dawson's kinsman Major Eric Beilby-Smith took over the tenancy, being followed by Captain Browning and finally by Reg Parnell, the Derby-born grand prix racing driver. He left in 1954, and it was purchased by the Derbyshire County Council who in 1955 destroyed it to build the Sir John Porte Grammar School (as it then was); why they could not have incorporated the house into the new school as they had at Tupton and Swanwick (qv) one cannot imagine. The loss of such an important and complex house was unforgivable.

Perhaps in reflection of its ultimate demise, Etwall Hall – which had a well-authenticated secret passage to the church,
bricked up in the 1890s – was much haunted. Quite apart from a large mulberry tree in the park which shed a branch whenever there was to be a death in the family, there was a 'green Lady' who was supposed to have been a suicide, and was accompanied by a classic irremovable blood stain on the floor of a bedchamber. The room in question was locked and the windows bricked up, so she must have been anything but a benevolent ghost; it is reported that soldiers billeted in the hall during World War Two would not sleep in this room. Another ghost opened and closed doors, and was believed in the village to have been the later nineteenth century butler who was allegedly pushed down the stairs and killed by the last male heir, Rowland Charles Hugh Cotton. The subsequent inquest found that although assisted in his downward course by the young prankster, he had in fact died from a heart attack. Cotton himself died in somewhat unexpected circumstances in 1894 aged only 25. Locals also say that when the house was being demolished the contractor's dog would not go anywhere near the site, a fact corroborated by other local dog owners. In view of the fact that the house never lay empty for any length of time, one wonders just how many of these tales arose out of the traumas of demolition combined with the propensity of the Cottons for bouts of insanity!

Pevsner (1953) 134; Colvin 887; Woolley 66 p.105; Henderson & Robinson (1979) 59f., 101; Smith (1990) 33, 123; Gomme (2001) 224-6, 528; CL V (1899) 656-9; DRO 286M/E 1-3; RIBOEUF/DAJ XLIX (1927) 246; PORTE/V.1569 & V.Staffs. 1583, 1663; GERARD,B./BP (1999) I. 1131-2; SLEIGH/FMG III 1070, V.1662; COTTON of Etwall/BLG (1937) 492; PARNELL/Craven (1998) 157.

EYAM HALL (II*)

Private residence

Eyam Hall: the entrance front.   *C.L.M. Porter*

Eyam Hall is a most interesting and engaging house set arrestingly in the centre of one of the most delightful and historic villages in upland Derbyshire. Most visitors appreciate its fitting presence, yet few know of its history; fewer still realize that it is still the seat of a very ancient Peak District family which has held it for somewhat over 300 years. The family is that of Wright of Great Longstone, descended from a twelfth century ancestor who was also the forebear of the Longsdons of Little Longstone (qv). Thomas, second son of William Wright of Great Longstone (qv) was settled at Unthank Hall (qv), and acquired Eyam by purchase after the Civil War and his son undertook an extensive rebuild of the modest house he found there (taxed on but four hearths in 1670) in 1676 – if a date on a rainwater head on the facade is to be believed. As his father had died three years earlier, this date seems plausible.

The estate at Eyam had long been held by the family of Stafford. Sometime before c. 1200, Richard de Stafford, believed to have been the third son of Hervey Bagot *alias* Stafford of Bromley, Staffordshire, acquired the estate. It was a large manor, and Leam (qv) early on became detached having been settled on Ingram, younger son of Richard de Stafford, and his granddaughter and heiress married a scion of the house of Morteyne (the Royal tenants-in-chief from whom the de Staffords held) who had taken the name of Leam. In 1308, Richard de Stafford and his wife, Isabella, daughter and heiress of his aunt by Richard de Eyam, had their marriage declared void on the grounds of consanguinity, thus disinheriting their son, who went on to found the house of Stafford of Tideswell. Eyam passed to Richard's uncle, Roger, of Bakewell, and his descendant, Humphrey, died in the sixteenth century leaving five daughters and co-heiresses, of whom four were married respectively to John Savage of Castleton, Rowland Eyre of Hassop, Francis Bradshaw of Bradshaw and Rowland Morewood of The Oakes (qqv). Part of the estate went to Bradshaw, and he forsook his residence at Bradshaw Hall, Chapel-en-le-Frith (qv) and rebuilt the old seat at Eyam, thereafter (confusingly) called Bradshaw Hall. His descendants lived there until 1735. Deeds held by the family make it clear that this house represents the Savile moiety, for Sir George Savile sold it in 1662/3 to John Wilson of Eyam who re-sold in 1671 to Wright, whose marriage settlement a year later refers to a 'newly erected messuage house'.

The present hall we know existed by 1670, and from an examination of its fabric it may reasonably be ascribed to the early seventeenth century in origin, if not a generation before. It remains to consider what kind of house Wright purchased.

The most revealing part of the fabric is the present east front, which has two different straight coped gables, and a gabled stair tower, clearly older. This has had its mullioned and transomed windows blocked and new ones inserted actually overlapping, and yet, even so, they do not relate to the Jacobean staircase within, which must accordingly be in its third position since this part of the structure was erected. This raises the question of whether it is the original staircase, much reconstructed, or one moved from elsewhere to replace what could well have been a stone one. Its pierced pendentives are set so low that they almost meet the finials on the newels, and the feeling is that it was fashioned for another, taller, building entirely. Could it have come from Bradshaw Hall? The south (garden) front would appear to have been of a piece with the later phase of the east (park) front and consists of three bays of three storeys with three and four-light mullioned windows with brief hood moulds; the majority of windows to the east, however, are mullioned and transomed.

The west (entrance) front is that most affected by the rebuilding of 1676: there are two projecting bays flanking a deeply recessed centre of two widely spaced bays with a crudely executed classical entrance between. Here the lower two floors have hood moulds extended into bands and four-light mullioned windows; the top storey had three-light windows with plain drip moulds, with three straight coped gables depressed into a modest parapet – one of the few concessions to the conventions of the age. Rainwater goods bearing the initials W/I E/1676 refer to John Wright and Elizabeth Kniveton, the son for whom Thomas Wright actually built the house and his wife, who would appear to have had some say in the conception of it, and almost certainly underwrote its cost. This front is ashlared in millstone grit sandstone, probably Shale Grit from Eyam Edge, as is the south, with larger blocks of the same stone to pick out the quoins, whereas the east, although of the same material, is coarse with dressed quoins. The south front also has similar gables to the west, but not over the earlier bays. The north-west projection of the west front would appear, therefore, to be new build, and beyond it lies a north range containing the kitchen, which is thought to have been added in c 1700 despite having extremely thick walls and being peppered with anomalies. Where it adjoins the east front there is a second staircase, also seventeenth century, almost as grand as the main stair.

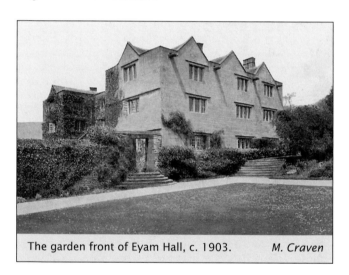

The garden front of Eyam Hall, c. 1903.   *M. Craven*

Inside one enters a wide low hall filling the whole of the recessed bay, and rather unusually laid with gritstone flags. The ceiling was once coffered but the plaster is mainly stripped away to expose the rough hewn beams, and there is a large stone vernacular fireplace. The main stair is reached through an arch in the south-east corner of the hall, very like the arrangement at Carnfield (qv). The south-west projection contains the parlour, with mid-seventeenth century panelling, and on the garden front is a plainer breakfast room, above which is the tapestry room, entirely lined with seventeenth century tapestries rather crudely attached one to the other and originally nailed to the wainscot beneath and said to have come from Bradshaw Hall nearby (qv). A good Restoration period chamber lies over the hall, and the second stair is reached from a landing off, behind the north-west projection. A series of crude outbuildings to the north have walls of coursed rubble with blocks of both Shale Grit and Carboniferous Limestone with (like the house) stone slate roofs.

The Wrights have owned the hall ever since, although they retreated to the West country for much of the nineteenth century, letting the Hall, and in 1990 it reverted to the Great Longstone branch of the family, and has recently been carefully restored and was opened to the public from spring 1992, forming a most worthwhile addition to the attractions of the village. The estate, regrettably, is now reduced to a few hundred acres, but at one time included a later nineteenth century villa in castellated style on the scarp to the east called Bretton Lodge.

Pevsner 213; Tarn (1971), 25; Lysons, V 162-3; Wood (1859) 37, 182-3; CL VIII (1906) 16 & 28/10/1993 pp.66-9; DLC 4/33 p. 25; STAFFORD of Eyam/DAJ XXIII (1901) 83f. & XXX (1908) 26f.; BRADSHAW-ISHERWOOD of Marple/BLG (1952) 1362; WRIGHT of Eyam/BFR 645.

FANSHAWE GATE HALL (II)

Holmesfield

This house is believed to have been quite a grand fifteenth century edifice which was dismantled, according to one account, in 1636, but more likely perhaps just after the Civil War and replaced by a much more modest edifice, somewhat akin to Cartledge Hall *(qv)*. The house is approached via two pairs of striking gatepiers the outer sporting balls on conical finials themselves resting on four smaller balls in the manner of a classical obelisk, the inner pair, later and rusticated, being topped by acorns, taken by some as a confirmation of the owner's Royalist credentials. The house is a pleasant, modest scale mid-seventeenth century L-shaped gabled small manor house, built not, as one might expect, out of the materials of its predecessor, but of coal measure sandstone rubble – probably Greenmoor Rock with coarse dressings of Crawshaw Sandstone from an adjacent outcrop – with low mullioned windows and a lower left hand gable between a more prominent one marking the wing which advances to the right. The majority of windows consist of two light mullions. Two rather odd earlier buildings also remain, facing north: one is a very tall four-storey structure built of rubble brought to course with single-light windows one above the other on the top three floors with a straight coped gable, and described in the DoE list as a dovecote. It has quoins on its north face only, and has all the attributes of a stair tower from a tall house, perhaps built aping the style of Robert Smythson, and perhaps originally with a decorative parapet. Beside it, separated by a few feet, is a lower building, two by two bays and two storeys, again with quoins and a straight coped gable. It has two-light mullioned windows, and could conceivably have been the kitchen wing of the larger house to which the taller building was once attached. These, then, are conceivably the remnants of the house built by the Fanshawes, although they might have been outbuildings *ab initio*.

The Fanshawe family came to this part of Holmesfield in the last years of the fourteenth century, for in 1411, Joan, daughter of John Fanshawe, senior, was admitted to one messuage and seven bovates at Holmesfield by Lady Alice d'Eyncourt, which latter family had held Holmesfield from 1086. In 1456, her nephew, John son of John Fanshawe junior had built his estate up further. In the sixteenth century, Henry Fanshawe became a Remembrancer of the Exchequer, acquiring extensive estates in Essex, on which his heirs settled permanently,

hence the ultimate abandonment and subsequent destruction, no doubt, of the family's Derbyshire seat. The next three generations were also courtiers, the last being raised to the Peerage of Ireland as Viscount Fanshawe of Swords (1661), as a reward for loyalty during the Civil War. It was probably Lord Fanshawe who actually dismantled the house at Fanshawegate, although they retained the estate. It had certainly gone by the time of the Hearth Tax.

Fanshawe Gate Hall, Holmesfield.   M. Ramsden

In 1716, the title became extinct, and the estate passed to T.E.Fanshawe of Great Singleton, Lancashire, whose descendant, Rev. C.S.Fanshawe (by inheritance a Baron of the Russian Empire) sold Fanshawegate to his kinsman Captain Basil Fanshawe (1857-1944) whose heirs thereupon sold up in Derbyshire. Since 1959 the house has been the home of Mr. & Mrs. John Ramsden who, with their son Mark, have done much to restore this attractive house to its former glory after two centuries as a tenanted farm.

Pevsner, 246; Jeayes (1906) No. 1405; Turbutt (1999) 926-8; DLC 4/98; FANSHAWE, V./BDEP 195; FANSHAWE of Dengie/BLG (1965) 736;

FENNY BENTLEY OLD HALL (II*)

Private residence

Fenny Bentley Old Hall with battlements, before the 1894 rebuilding.
C.L.M. Porter

What is today described as the Old Hall, and was for a long time formerly known as Cherry Orchard Farm, is a three-bay two-storey stone farmhouse dated 1680 with a single gable so fashioned as almost to be described as a pediment. Below a stone slate roof it has an attic cross window, the other windows being six-light mullion and transom ones. Attached to it is a squat and sturdy looking square tower, like the remainder of coursed carboniferous limestone rubble with quoins and dressings of Keuper sandstone, three storeys high but once possibly higher, and until the late nineteenth century, crenellated, supported on the west by a multi-stepped buttress. Inside it has a principal chamber on the first floor, approached through a doorcase with chamfered jambs from a stone newel stair. Beyond again is a crudish single-bay range of perhaps eighteenth century date. The tower, which has late seventeenth century mullioned and transomed windows in its south face at first floor level, is the remains of what the Lysons describe (on what authority is unclear) as 'once a large castellated mansion' which lay within a moat, traces of which are still visible to the north-east. A second tower is said to have once existed, and foundations, never adequately investigated archaeologically, were seen when the house was rebuilt in 1894, at which date the tower lost its original entrance and castellations. Its date is probably fourteenth century, although it may well have earlier origins.

From the mid-thirteenth century until at least 1364, this site was the seat of the Bentleys. The next positive thing known is that it formed the capital messuage of Thomas Beresford, who also held the adjoining estate of Newton Grange, both doubtless originally part of the manor. He died in 1473, leaving Fenny Bentley to his eldest son Aden, and Newton Grange to the younger, Thomas. Yet the lordship of the manor appears to have descended through the posterity of the elder brother of Thomas senior, until Olivia, daughter and heiress of Edward Beresford of Beresford Hall, Staffordshire, brought it to her husband, John Stanhope, and his daughter and heiress brought it to Charles Cotton, a son of Sir John, of Bedhampton; their son was the likeable intimate of Izaak Walton, who fell hopelessly into debt at which it was sold to the Jacksons of Stanshope (Staffs.). From this it is clear that John Beresford, father of Thomas of Fenny Bentley, must have held it by c. 1450, and the question arises: how did he come by it? His wife was Elizabeth, daughter of William Basset of Blore, Staffordshire, and the Bassets certainly had an estate at Fenny Bentley, even after this date. It is possible that she obtained Bentley and Newton Grange on her marriage, and that one of the unrecorded marriages of the Bassets was with a Bentley heiress. The alternative is that either the Bassets or the Beresfords purchased it.

In 1670, Mrs. Beresford paid tax on eight hearths, which may well represent the old seat, perhaps reduced, or a separate house elsewhere in the village. However, between that date and 1680, the Old Hall and part of the estate was purchased by the Recorder of Derby, Sir Simon Degge of Stramshall, Staffordshire, and his initials grace the same rain-water head on the seventeenth century portion of the Old Hall. It seems likely, too, that Degge destroyed the old moated seat, including, it is said, another tower. Degge's heir, Simon Degge, was living at the Old Hall in the reign of Queen Anne.

The Degges became extinct in the 1720s, and their portion was sold in 1724 to the Beresfords of

Compton, Ashbourne and Newton Grange (the Fenny Bentley branch having previously become extinct) and Richard Beresford lived at Fenny Bentley between c. 1786 and 1816 in a new seat, Bentley Hall, letting the Old Hall to the Waterfalls, tenants there for two centuries until succeeded by the Websters. After Richard Beresford's death, the property was sold to Field Marshall Viscount Beresford, a natural son of the Marquess of Waterford of a remote cadet branch of the family which went to Ireland in the seventeenth century; Lord Beresford also bought Beresford Hall and restored it. On his death, his heir, Alexander Beresford Hope, sold it to the FitzHerberts of Tissington who carried out the 1894 rebuilding.

Bentley Hall, built for Richard Beresford in the late 18th century.   M. Craven

Bentley Hall (II), the house built by Richard Beresford, is a late eighteenth century stone built house of two storeys and three bays, the central one canted; one can discern in it the influence of Joseph Pickford, who built Beresford's Ashbourne town house, Compton House in the 1760s although the roof has been altered. Lower wings on either side suggest an original intention to provide architectonic pavilions, either not completed, or subsequently rebuilt. It too became a farmhouse in the nineteenth century, inhabited by tenants of the Goodwin Johnsons of Callow Hall (qv), and has had several changes of ownership in the last two decades, changing hands in 1986 for around £200,000.

Pevsner, 215; Pilkington, (1798) II. 288; Lysons V. 48; Glover, II. 105; Hart (1981) 150; Emery (2000) 379-80; BERESFORD/Vv. 1569, 1611 & Beresford (1908) passim.; BERESFORD, V sub WATERFORD, M./BP (1999) II. 2949-2955; DEGGE/V. 1662 & Le Neve (1873) 231.

FOREMARK HALL (II*)

School

Foremark Hall, the entrance front in 1776.   M. Craven

The chief aspect which strikes one about Foremark Hall is its bulk which, in a house built in a low lying situation, is something of an achievement. It is ashlar Keuper sandstone from Weston Cliff, of two storeys upon a low rustic with a complex slated hipped roof which indents at the angles in order to accommodate lead covered cupolas set over the canted bays which mark the ends of the two main facades: the north (entrance) front, and the south (garden) front. The former, of nine bays, centres upon a giant Ionic pedimented portico approached by a pair of hemispherical steps up to the perron, and appears hunched, powerful; it grows upon one. Yet it has not always pleased everyone: Lord Torrington, visiting in 1790 described Foremark as 'of vile architecture and in a bad situation; in front there is a paltry pond with pitiful plantations'. He was an informed critic, but steeped in the neo-classicism of his age, not in the later Palladianism embodied in the house.

It was built by Sir Robert Burdett, 4th Bt, of Bramcote, Warwickshire, whose ancestor had acquired the estate by marriage with the heiress of the Franceys family, and the architect he chose was David Hiorne of Warwick who, with his brother William, had succeeded to the practice of William Smith the younger. Work began in 1759, but within months, the architect had died, leaving his clerk of works to carry on with building which was largely completed in 1761. That clerk of works was the young Joseph Pickford, fresh from an apprenticeship with his like-named uncle and guardian, who was contractor and foreman for Kent, Vardy and others. Much of the architectural language which Pickford relied on during the first decade of his independent career can be detected at Foremark, and indeed, some refinements in the design and detail of the house can be directly attributed to him. Fortunately Hiorne's engraved plan survives in *Vitruvius Britannicus* Vol V, and it can be compared with the finished house. Apart from the running together of the 'tea room' and its ante room on the west front to form a grand *salon*, the changes to the plan are in the details. The north front owes much in inspiration to Isaac Ware's Wrotham Park of 1754, but with the domed canted bay pavilions run together into the main block of the house instead of terminating three-bay wings. At Foremark there are sweeps curving forward from both fronts, but as extensions of the rusticated plinth, terminating in pretty, but rather inconsequential pavilions with niches topped by low pediments. The central block at Wrotham has an attic storey above the cornice, but at Foremark it is disguised within the balustrade. The garden front at Foremark omits the tetrastyle portico, replacing it with a very plain pedimented breakfront.

Inside the rooms are very spacious but a little disappointing. The stucco is Rococo but rather watered down, although the timber main staircase is pure Smith of Warwick. One enters through the portico into a *saloon* that runs right across the house with a screen of columns at either end and niches ensigning the facing marble fireplaces. The consequence of Pickford opening out the 'Tea Room' is that there are two large rooms running right across the house, separated by the dining-room and a staircase. Pickford opened out all the five ground floor bays to light his west room, which are shown as dummies in the *Vitruvius Britannicus* plan, as are the outer bays on the east front, along which were study, bedroom and dressing-room. The bedroom is lit by a Venetian window with a Diocletian over, very similar to the arrangement at the Hiornes' Kyre Park, Worcestershire (1754) and at Stivichall, nearby, the work of Flitcroft a year or two later. Pickford went on to make great use of this combination, but almost always – both as Vanburgh and Lord Burlington in the second decade of the century – under a pediment, the exception being at Ogston *(qv)* . The bedrooms on the first floor are *en suite* with dressing-rooms and sitting rooms on the east and west fronts, but plainer in the centre of the house. Below, the rustic contains much impressive vaulting and fine ashlared work, and achieves an almost Piranesian quality in low light. Sir Robert Burdett paid Thomas Chippendale a total of £1,206. 10s. 6d for furniture between 1766 and 1774.

Foremark: the garden front in 1991.   M. Craven

A Diocletian window beneath a pediment also characterizes the east lodge, which guards a fine wrought-iron gate with armorial overthrow made in 1913 by Taylor, Whiting and Taylor of Derby, and the park was an ancient one, but landscaped by William Emes from 1760, his first independent commission after resigning from Kedleston *(qv)*. As late as the 1950s there was an intact icehouse in the grounds, and the modest stable block – a well proportioned brick double pile building of two storeys with hipped roof – was built a generation before the rest of the house. This, then, for a time, marched with the previous house, a view of which came to light at a Christie's sale in May, 1998. This shows it to have been stone built and U-shaped with four gables, the central pair recessed over the great hall and divided by a chimney stack. The west cross wing terminated in a gable with six and three-light mullioned windows, whilst its counterpart on the east of the façade was clearly later with mullion and transom cross windows throughout. The west front seems to have had two further gables, with ball finials, like the others. The stables were on the same side, and the whole was set within a wall pierced by a pair of imposing later 17th century gatepiers from which one descended into the forecourt. Woolley described this house as "Large and convenient with a large well-wooded park and coney warren adjoining" and it was assessed for 24 hearths in 1662, probably the date it was rebuilt as it appears in the painting, for it was in that year that the new church, dedicated to St. Saviour, was built a few yards to the west of the house, "being rather of the nature of a chapel to the family" as Woolley put it. This replaced a then ruinous predecessor, not to mention another at Ingleby on the estate, the origins of which went back to 1272, and which was taken down and the materials dedicated to St. Saviour's. The present structure boasts three sundials, one dated 1650, no doubt from one of the chapel's predecessors, and the tower contains four bells by George Oldfield dated between 1660 and 1668. Inside there is a rather old fashioned arcaded and – oddly – glazed oak screen, an Early English font and a timber altar with a Hoptonwood top. A gallery was added in 1819. A pretty communion rail by Robert Bakewell graces the interior, just as a filigree iron screen, gates and overthrow by him enhance the approach from the house.

In 1910-11 William Barron & Sons laid out new gardens on the south side, which before overlooked but grass, and much improved that aspect of the house. In 1883 the estate ran to a considerable 5,923 acres. To the east of the house lies the model home farm ranged round a courtyard and perhaps originally by Pickford, and there is an interesting succession of glass houses dating from 1839 to c. 1910.

The estate was held directly by Nigel de Stafford in 1086, but found its way into the hands of a cadet branch of de Ferrers by the twelfth century, whence it passed via an heiress to Bertram de Verdon in the reign of Henry II. Sir Robert Franceys had acquired it – more likely by alienation than by inheritance – by 1387, and this family married the heiress of their Franceys kinsmen of Ticknall in the later sixteenth century, thus almost doubling the estate. The heiress of this union brought the seat to the Burdetts, and the eldest son, later the second baronet, took his forename from the surname of the Franceys family, although the conventionality of spelling has rather obfuscated the fact. In the 1790s, the diarist Rev. William Bagshaw Stephens, headmaster of Repton School, was tutor to the Burdetts and the Mundys, and recorded much of life there. Between the wars the family resided mainly at Ramsbury, Wiltshire, and it was sold to the Church Commissioners in 1940. During World War Two the army occupied the house, but afterwards it was let to Repton School – which must have pleased the frivolous shade of Stephens – as a preparatory offshoot, which it remains to this day. The baronetcy became extinct in 1951.

Beside the river on the estate are some curious caves, expanded into former habitations by human endeavor, called Anchor Chapel, although no reliable record exists of any anchorite having sojourned there. A charming painting by Thomas Smith of Derby, of mid-eighteenth century date, depicts members of the Burdett family enjoying a picnic on the riverbank before this place. Lord Torrington wrote of it: 'Keeping the hill top, I was soon directed to the rocks, called Anchor Church, above which, leaving my horses at the wicket gate, I walk'd thro' a small wood... and by a steep decent of turf steps, to this picturesque scenery of delight: and where, even, sequestration and anchoritism might appear happiness: of all men I shou'd prove one of the fittest for such a plan: my pleasures are few, and I cou'd catch and dress my fish.'

Indeed, the Burdetts seem much to have enjoyed entertaining *alfresco*, for they adapted the old Franceys seat of Knowle Hill as a summerhouse and banqueting house in the 1760s *(qv)*. Their agent, Robert Greaves was also provided with a fine villa at Ingleby Toft *(qv)* and they also had a handsome town house in Derby's Friar Gate, of similar date to Foremark, and perhaps, like Ingleby Toft, by the same hand. On the ridge behind the Hall, as a final touch of romance, lie the scattered tumuli of the Norse invaders, who are known to have over-wintered at nearby Repton in 873-74; it is worthy of note, perhaps, that Ingleby is a Norse place-name.

Colvin, 498; Pevsner, 217; Woolley 109 p.143; Gandon (1771) pls. 31-35; Lysons V 242; Burke (1853) II. 197; Cox (1875) 443; Tipping (1926) 87; Harris (1979) no.43; Saunders (1993) 17-18, 47-8, 50-1, 169; Gomme (2001) 461n.; CL LIV (1923) 214-20; RCHM(E) *Glasshouses at Foremark Hall* (Swindon 1997); Wilts. CRO Burdett MSS Accounts A1/1; FRANCEYS/V.1569. 1611; BURDETT of Bramcote, Bt./BP (1931) 411.

GLAPWELL HALL

Demolished

Glapwell Hall, c. 1920s

J. Darwin

102

Glapwell Hall was a rather rambling stone built house comprising work of several periods and well reflected its own history. A capital mansion was known upon the site, on the high Permian Magnesian limestone ridge just south of Bolsover, from the twelfth century, built by the descendants of Serlo, who held it from Hubert fitz Ralph. His grandson, Simon son of Serlo II styled himself 'de Pleasley', and it was his eldest son Serlo III who succeeded to Ashover. The third son William, succeeded to the Manor of Pleasley, founding the de Pleasleys and the de Birchills, and the second son, Hugh, came into the manor of Glapwell c. 1180 taking his surname from the place, and four sons left numerous descendants. He it was who we know to have had a seat there and probably founded the chapel which, in c. 1260, needed re-roofing. In 1481 the heiress of Glapwell brought the estate to the family of Woolhouse, and it passed from them to Samuel Hallowes of Dethick by marriage with Elizabeth, heiress of Thomas Woolhouse. Samuel was the grandson of Nathaniel Hallowes the notorious Derby MP, woollen draper, Mayor (in 1657) and Civil War *delator* whose exactions brought him three estates, and whose Commonwealth grant of arms was annulled at the Restoration. The family originally came from Youlgreave.

Hallowes it was who probably built the oldest part of Glapwell Hall to survive in the 1650s or '60s; it was taxed on nine hearths in 1670. This was the west front, built of coursed rubble (later stuccoed) of Permian Magnesian Limestone from an adjacent outcrop, consisting of a seven-bay range topped by three straight stone coped gables, the central one being wider than the outer pair, not dissimilar in overall style to the entrance front of Duffield Hall *(qv)*. The central entrance had a segmental pediment on modest brackets and the whole range was rather tall, of two storeys and attics, with a stone slate roof. The two bays beneath the end gables were strangely off-centre, and the fenestration was Georgianized sometime in the late eighteenth century. Before this, however, a handsome early eighteenth century range had been added – perhaps replacing a really much older wing – east-west behind the north end of the seventeenth century west front. To the east it had three bays and two storeys topped by a parapet with a hipped roof punctuated by tiny dormers above. An early eighteenth century two-storey north range (but of a separate build to the foregoing, one suspects, projected from the west front and was topped by a tiny cupola and a bell. Finally, in the 1870s, a new wing was added facing south behind the west wing. This had a two-storey canted bay with round headed windows, hipped roof and a single-storey reception room to its east. This had neo-Italianate Venetian windows rather in the style of Giles & Brookhouse of Derby as exemplified by their rebuilding of Rolleston Hall, Staffordshire, for the Mosleys. This part, of ashlared Permian Magnesian Limestone, also had a balustrade and ball finials. To the north-east, at the same time, a large conservatory was built.

In 1883 the estate in Derbyshire ran to 2,852 acres, but after World War One, T.R.F.B.Hallowes retired to Cadenham Manor, Hampshire and the house was let to one of the Gorell-Barnes's of Ashgate, Brampton. Hallowes's daughter and heiress married Benedict Hunt, and the estate was ultimately sold, the house being demolished in the late 1950s. All that remains is the eighteenth century stable block and a summer house of the same period (II), the latter very much a threatened building in the 1980s.

Lysons V 56; Tilley III (1899) 53; Darlington (1959) *passim*; WOOLHOUSE/V.1611; HALLOWES *formerly* of Glapwell/BLG (1921) 651; GORELL-BARNES *sub* BARNES *formerly* of Ashgate/*op.cit.*(1952) 118-9.

GRANGEFIELD

Trusley　　　　　　　　　　　　　　　　*Demolished*

Grangefield, Trusley; photographed by Edward Abney prior to 1851.　　　　　　　　　　*J. Stretton*

Some time between 1846 and 1848, Rev. Edward Abney, a Derby rector and photographic enthusiast, and W. H. Fox-Talbot, whose national photographic reputation is well known, were driving around the lanes of west Derbyshire looking for subjects to photograph with their Talbotype equipment when they happened on a timber framed farmhouse in the parish of Trusley, hoary with age, and over-large, perhaps, for its then use. This was Grangefield, dating from the 15th century with some later additions of the middle of the next century. It had a full height great hall, cross-wings at either end, that at the west having a second gabled range added, and a gabled full height porch, all of two storeys with attics. The windows were mullioned in timber, but some were latterly replaced c. 1800 with cambered headed three light affairs when part of the south front was skinned in brick, probably to prevent its collapse.

The estate, part of the manor of Trusley, had been given to the Abbey of Croxden by Robert de Beaufoy early in the 12th century, and at the Dissolution it was acquired by one Fitch, who had sold on to the Curzons of Kedleston from whom it was sold to the Kinardsleys (Kynnersleys) of Brailsford in quick succession before being acquired by the tenant, Charles Hope of Trusley, who married in 1561, but whose purchase was probably a decade or so later. He settled it on his younger son Robert, attested in possession in 1613, and from his grandson, another Robert, it passed by marriage (c. 1715) of his daughter Mary to Ralph Docksey of Snelston Hall. William Hope, a cousin, was described as of Grangefield on his burial in Derby in 1720, so he may have been a tenant. Certainly the house was let from Docksey's time, one of the reasons why it was never seriously rebuilt. Jane, the daughter and heiress of Thomas Docksey (and niece of David Garrick) married Samuel Harrison of Mayfield, Staffs., and the estate was split up and sold. The house and somewhat over 150 acres was purchased by Thomas Stretton, whose family farmed there for over a century, although the farm later became part of the Trusley Hall estate. Between 1846 and 1850 this venerable seat was dismantled and replaced by a post-Regency brick house of three bays and two storeys.

Lysons V. 281; Bagshaw (1846) 340; Cox III (1877) 336; Craven (1993) 14; HOPE/Hunter, FMG I. 323 & Glover, II. 585; DOCKSEY of Snelston/DAJ LXXII (1952) 69-71.

GRANGEWOOD HALL (II)

Netherseal   *Private Residence*

Grangewood Hall, 1900s.   *M. Craven*

This well-proportioned seat was built about 1821 for Capt. Thomas Mowbray, RN, then recently married, second son of George Mowbray of Ford Hall, Co. Durham, and he and his son George owned it until the latter's death in 1893. During the period 1850 to 1867, however, it was the residence of Stephen Lakeman and his son, Sir Stephen Bartlett Lakeman, a general in Turkish service married to a Phanariot Princess. It is of ashlar. Of two storeys with a band between, under a hipped slated roof, it has a three bay south front, the bays widely spaced and the central one breaking forward and containing a pedimented tripartite ground floor window. The east and west returns are bowed with the entrance tucked away rather inconsequentially behind the latter where the long service wing stretches to the north, itself greatly extended a generation or so later. Set in a small park opposite the Grange Wood, after which it took its name, it greatly resembles in style and detail Overseal Manor, little more than half a mile away, and without doubt by the same (unknown) hand. The bows containing but two windows in each, they are also reminiscent of The Firs, Derby, built at the same date by Rev. Edward Abney of Measham Hall, also nearby. The Firs, however, can be confidently ascribed to Richard Leaper of Derby, so he might have been involved at Grangewood also.

The modest estate had been carved out of the Gresley family holdings, and on the death of the second Mr. Mowbray it was sold to Zelie Colvile (nee de Previle), second wife of Maj.Gen. Sir Henry Colvile of Lullington Hall *(qv)*, also very close by, for eventual use as a dower house. However, she let it to Burton brewer Arthur Clay, and clearly found other accommodation when her husband died in 1907. Clay was followed by Maj. William Power between the wars, who was followed, as freeholder, by Nicholas Harrison of the Wychnor Hall (Staffs.) family and his widowed mother by 1952. Later it was acquired by narrow-tapes manufacturer Harry G. Bonas (1917-1983) and it is still with his family.

MOWBRAY/Burke AA 53-4; LAKEMAN/ Walford (1861) 585; COLVILE of Lullington/BLG (1952) 500-2; CLAY of Piercefield/*op.cit.* 462; HARRISON of Wychnor/ *op.cit.*1173; BONAS sub HOWE,E/BP (1999) I. 1465.

GREAT LONGSTONE HALL

see LONGSTONE HALL

THE GREEN HALL (II)

Ashbourne (Offcote)   *Private residence*

The origin of the freehold upon which Green Hall was built is obscure, except that by 1489 it had become the property of Thomas Hurt, who built a house thereon, shown in a curious map drawn in that year. His unrecorded wife may well have been an heiress of some Ashbourne family of note, and the Ashbournes themselves are possible. Hurt left four sons, the eldest inheriting Green Hall. His posterity remained there until the later seventeenth century.

By this time, the Hurts had built a late sixteenth century timber-framed house, part of which remains embedded in the fabric of the present structure. Most spectacular of these vestiges is what is called the old porch which betrays close studding, wind braces and a corniced sill behind which is a small two-light window. The sill is strongly moulded, as is a cross beam below. The roof also contains substantial amounts of earlier timber.

The heiress of Hurt married, in all probability, William Birom of Birom Hall, Lancashire and he appears to have settled there, for his sons were prominent in local affairs. In 1662, his grandson George lived there, with a son living of the same age. The latter's first cousin was Thomas, a Derby apothecary who served as Mayor in 1707 and died in 1714. The heiress of the younger George is said to have passed the house and modest estate to John Hayne, son of William, of Ireton Wood *(qv)*, but his four marriages are well documented, and the name Birom does not appear. Either it passed, in reality, by sale, or the Birom heiress married the father of one of John Hayne's brides.

John Hayne's homonymous son probably rebuilt the hall, and the date 1708 has been suggested, although the fabric also bears a datestone marked 'RH/1751'. The latter represents the probable date of the marriage of Richard Hayne (died 1787), grandson of the John of 1708, and Mary, daughter and heiress of William Newton of Brassington; doubtless some alterations were then put in hand at that time although it is difficult to say just what at this remove; most of the house looks all of a piece.

The rebuilding produced a most gracious, tall, gabled building of brick with stone dressings – probably of Keuper sandstone from an adjacent outcrop – which may represent the infilling between two wings of a U-shaped timber-framed house. The main east front has two straight-coped gables containing three storeys and two bays each with sashed fenestration ensigned by gauged brick lintels with stone keyblocks. The central bay is of two storeys, with segmental headed entrance and top parapet with balustrade and cornice. The whole lies between a pair of rusticated pilasters topped with ball finials. The frieze and cornice beneath the parapet bring these skilfully up to the height of another pair of rusticated pilasters at the angles. The south front has a further, plainer, gable set back with two bays, and there is a round headed staircase window to its right with an *oeuil-de-boeuf* above. A modern extension of one storey now marks this elevation. To the north is a stable block, probably contemporary with the house, although in a simple vernacular style, but modified with later cast-iron gothic windows.

The entrance front is so stylish that Professor Gomme has tentatively suggested Francis Smith of Warwick as the builder; another suggestion is Samuel Taborer of Normanton-by Derby and London, but as yet no records have emerged. John Hayne (died 1808), son of Richard, married Elizabeth, daughter of Anthony Bradley, an Ashbourne merchant, and left a daughter and heiress who died unmarried. His widow remarried J.G. de Burgh who

Green Hall, Ashbourne, 2001. *M. Titterton*

lived at Green Hall in the 1830s. Thereafter it passed to a kinsman, William Hayne, under whom Cockshutt Heathcote of Littleover was tenant until 1852 when there was a contents sale. He was followed by a Miss Trenbath in 1857 who ran a ladies academy there, but in 1858 the Hayne executors sold it. A Mrs. Swetenham was there in 1891, A.S.Freeland in 1908 and it was later let by a Mr Williamson, again as a school. After World War Two it was the seat of P.B.Balean who sold in 1965 to Mr Roger Stevenson. It is now owned by Mr and Mrs John Stevenson.

Pevsner 65; Henstock *et al* (1978) 9; Gomme (2001) 513; DAJ LXXX (1960) 124-128; DLC 1/1965; HURT/Glover, II. 5 & BLG (1965) 464; BIROM/V.1662; HAYNE/DAJ XCII (1972) 90-2, Glover, *op. cit.* 22, FMG III. 1015-6; BALEAN of Green Hall/BLG (1965) 35.

GREEN HALL

Belper   *Demolished*

Green Hall, Belper, c. 1900. *J. Darwin*

Belper had anciently been part of the manor of Duffield, and thus, since the fall of the Ferrers, Earls of Derby, part of the Duchy of Lancaster. Indeed, John of Gaunt (amongst other things, Duke of Lancaster) seems to have had a hunting lodge called Beaurepaire in the vicinity, from whence mutated the present name of the town. At the beginning of the industrial revolution the Derwent was perceived as a source of power, and it was Jedediah Strutt who acquired freeholds in the area and developed the town into a major centre of cotton spinning.

Having had three sons, Strutt found that somewhere was required for them all to live, and apart from houses in Derby he built Milford House *(qv)*. The son of William's brother George – George Benson – had Bridge Hill House built at Belper (since demolished), and Jedediah II had a new house built in Belper on the site of an older one called Green Hall.

We have, unfortunately no clues as to the nature of Green Hall prior to 1810, but it was doubtless a small stone built, probably Ashover Grit from the adjacent outcrop, yeoman's house with the usual straight coped gables, situated close to the centre of the village on land once perhaps associated with the manor house. The new seat was begun in 1809, the same year as Bridge Hill House was completed, and which it resembled. The architect was undoubtedly William Strutt FRS (1756-1830), Jedediah's multi-talented eldest son, whose architectural abilities are recounted in his obituary, from the pen of his youngest brother Joseph. Like Milford House, Green Hall was of two storeys under a hipped roof with a parapet and had a five-bay front with a pediment. The detailing betrays the hand of the amateur in the use of a blind arch into which the entrance was placed, and a depressed blind arch reaching up into the pediment containing the central bay which was incongruously ensigned with an old-fashioned segmental pediment. The placing of the entrance blind arch within the full height one owes much to the style of Pickford whom the young William Strutt must have known, as he lived in Derby at the same time and was assiduous in learning what he could from those best placed to advise him; both were friendly with Erasmus Darwin and with John Whitehurst. Strutt went on to design and build seven bridges over the Markeaton Brook in Derby (1785-89), including the allegedly 'very fine' St Peter's Bridge, several 'fireproof' mills (including a very tall and impressive one in Derby, where Osnabruck Square now lies), he took the credit for the concept of some of the design of Thomas Harrison's fine St Mary's Bridge across the Derwent there, and designed the Derby General Infirmary of 1806, although we know he employed Samuel Brown to make the drawings, and it is clear from photographs that the detailing and proportions are largely Brown's rather than Strutt's.

The only other façade which could be easily seen was the east, which was rather irregular, with a tall bay to the left pierced by a pair of tripartite windows in stone surrounds, connected to another bay breaking forward under a pediment with similar fenestration by a two bay section containing a loggia with entrance. A final bay beyond ended rather awkwardly all creating a disjointed effect. Much of the younger Jedediah Strutt's pleasure grounds also lay on the opposite side of King Street, here lying below the level of the house, and in August 1832 Strutt paid a local foundry £42 – 10s – 9d for a cast iron footbridge, very handsome with a moulded depressed Tudor arch over the street. This lasted until December 1867, when it was removed as an impediment to traffic.

The house was filled with gadgetry of the type pioneered by Strutt at St Helen's Derby: water central heating, hot piped water, patent ranges and improved plumbing and closets. All these owed much to Whitehurst's ideas, as published by him in the 1770s and employed by him at such places as Clumber Park for the Duke of Newcastle in the same era, and were probably transmitted to Strutt if not directly, then probably through discussions with Darwin. Unlike Milford House, the chimneys were prominent, and designed to obviate smoking fires, another subject on which Whitehurst wrote a treatise. The house was set in a small park attractively wooded, but upon which the town gradually was allowed to encroach, mainly from the best of motives and at the instigation of the Strutts themselves. Various members of the family lived there through much of the nineteenth century, but by 1888 it had been let to Miss Sophia E. Taylor who ran a preparatory school there which lasted until it was requisitioned in the Great War as a convalescent hospital, carrying on thereafter as a clinic. Other tenants followed until 1931 when the contents were sold and the house remained largely in institutional use until again requisitioned as an hospital during World War Two. Thereafter it was converted as flats but was demolished in 1958, the site today being – inevitably – a car-park, but the (converted) stables and a lodge house remain.

Davies (1811) 356; Glover, II. 118; Fitton & Wadsworth (1958) 250; Barrass (1994) 53; Jewell (1995) 65, 80; Craven (1996) 228-232; STRUTT/BLG (1952) 2441-2.

THE GROVE

Darley Dale   *Demolished*

This fairly substantial house would appear to have been built as a villa around 1820 for John Alsop of Lea Wood, a rich lead merchant of old local stock. As built it consisted of three storeys and three bays, embellished with an iron verandah, facing south west across the Dale, stone built, almost certainly the local Ashover Grit, with a long, lower, south east front and a service wing in the NE angle. It passed to Alsop's son, another John in 1831, but he died les than

The Grove, Darley Dale; the replacement house.
M. Craven

four years later when it passed to the grandson, John Alsop who, around 1839 greatly extended the house. He added lower, two storey two bay wings, set back a little, to SW front, embellishing the whole with a parapet and ball finials, and adding a pediment pierced by an *oeuil-de-boeuf* to the centre. Each two bay return was given a ground floor canted bay and a fine conservatory was added to the west end, too. The SE front at this time also acquired a prominent entrance bay, although the new hall lay some way from the stairs, which remained in their original position.

At rebuilding the ground floor of the original villa was adjusted to give a 33 ft. long library with billiard room behind. The new wings housed drawing room and dining room, both 30 ft. by 20. Unfortunately, there seems to be no other record, apart from a sale plan, of the interior. The stables, contemporary with the first build of the house, were situated to the south of the house and there was a new service court to the east. The pleasure grounds were attractively laid out and bosky, with 50 acres of parkland beyond.

In about 1848, John Alsop migrated to Australia, and the house was acquired by Rev. William Hiley Bathurst who, in 1863, inherited his family's Lydney Park estate from his brother Charles, and sold up, the new owner being Robert Pringle, fourth son of Alexander Pringle of Whytbank, in Scotland. He in turn sold the house to an opulent Manchester merchant, William Roberts in 1876, who lavished £3,000 on the church of St. Helen, nearby. However, in 1884 he decided to build himself a new house, and without delay pulled the old house down, its somewhat monumental replacement being finished by 1887. The stone is Ashover Grit, but not Stancliffe Stone, as the quarries were not re-opened until 1897.

It is not known who the architect for the new house was, although its appearance calls to mind Charles Matthew Hadfield or R. R. Duke of Buxton. It is a substantial building with a main block of three storeys with attics, mullioned and transomed windows, bands between the floors and prominent stacks, all irregular. A large single storey porch marks the SW angle somewhat in the mould of Buxton Winter Gardens, and a lower gabled range to the west completes the ensemble. The interior was brassily splendid, although a century of institutional use has toned it down considerably. Roberts never occupied his new house, for he died without moving in the year after aged 82. In 1889 it was sold at auction for £11,250 to William Atkins, who in 1891 opened it as the Darley Dale Hydropathic Institute, with piped water from Sharder Well and much sophisticated plumbing.

After the turn of the century, however, the spa was failing financially, and the buildings were taken over in 1904 by St. Elphin's School, formerly at Warrington, and it still occupies the site, large extensions having been added to the designs of Hadfield & Cawkwell in matching style 1967-75. Here Richmal Crompton, creator of 'William' taught classics for some years, before fame enabled her to escape.

Pevsner, 164; Glover II. 396; Bulmer (1895) 353; Barton (1993) 118; Tithe Award Map, Darley Dale (CRO); Sale catalogue 1876 DRO 216B/ES1/3(11); *Derbyshire Times* 29/7/1893; Research and printed notes courtesy Peter Atkinson, Esq.; ALSOP/Ince, Local MS 8022, Derby Local Studies Library; BATHURST *sub* Bledisloe, V./BP (1999) I.291-2; PRINGLE of Whytbank/BLG (1972) 734-5.

GROVE, THE

see OFFCOTE GROVE

HADDON HALL (I)

Nether Haddon   *Private residence; Open to the public*

Haddon Hall, the Upper Courtyard, c. 1908.   *M. Craven*

Haddon Hall, situated on a spur on the north bank of the Wye seems to be almost growing out of the landscape, its romantic outline set amongst trees creating a far more convincing and satisfying ensemble than all the contrivances of the Age of the Picturesque. Pevsner referred to it as '...the unreasonable dream-castle of those who think of the Middle Ages as a time of chivalry and valour and noble feelings. None other in England is so complete and convincing.' Celia Fiennes said of it, 'A good old house all built of stone on a hill.' The estate, part of the large Domesday manor of Bakewell, was held from the King by Ralph Avenel, son of William son of Avenel, and possibly by his father before him. His eldest son having been attainted c. 1195, the estate was forfeited and regranted by the crown to William, the next brother, whose son William left two daughters and co-heiresses, Alice, who married c. 1171 Richard de Vernon, and Elizabeth, who married Simon Basset. The former thereby came into Nether Haddon, where the hall stands. By the time Richard de Vernon inherited, there was some kind of a settlement at Nether Haddon, a small church with some Norman stonework, and a fortified manor house. Indeed, Vernon obtained permission from the Crown to fortify his house at Haddon with walls of 12 feet but without battlements. This work is today represented at the northeast angle by the so-called Peveril's Tower, a three-storey gatehouse with bastions and small two-light mullioned windows meanly piercing the forbidding walls at irregular intervals. Above the tower rises a thin stair tower, and there are today crow-stepped – rather Irish-looking – battlements put there in the fourteenth, not the twelfth century. The 12-foot wall may well have been one built around the outer bailey, for Dr Cox in the nineteenth century identified it surviving east of the chapel. The latter also contains Norman work, mainly a circular section pillar supporting a pair of earlier fifteenth century arches between the nave and the south aisle. The plain font, of similar period, confirms that this was once the extra-parochial chapel of St Nicholas, Nether Haddon. Today, it is almost 50 feet long with an unusually large (28 foot) chancel, a narrowed north and a south aisle. The south wall is thirteenth century with lancet windows, but the chancel and north side date from c. 1425 with the chancel side windows and bell turret added a generation or so later. The roof was rebuilt at a lower pitch in 1624, and the interior was fitted throughout with very fine timberwork: pews, rails, pulpit and desk, as the same date, all originally gilded fairly lavishly. There is still some good early glass (c. 1545) remaining, some fine monuments and painted fragments of murals of both fourteenth and fifteenth century date were revealed in 1858.

Whatever the extent of the twelfth century build, it would seem to have included at least part of the east front and possibly of the north – the cross-wing was not added until c. 1370-77. The centrepiece of this is the great hall to the right of the entrance from what later became the lower court, which passes through a square tower via a pointed arch. The previous great hall was probably to the south of Peveril's tower. This fourteenth century hall is almost entirely original, and is a very fine space indeed. The timber screen which supports a gallery over the screens passage with its three, four-centred arched doors (to buttery, kitchen and pantry) is later, c. 1450, and is decorated in a manner closely resembling contemporary church screens – crocketed tracery over blank panels – as is the panelling which is very early seventeenth century; otherwise it is admirable. The roof was renewed in the 1920s, however. To the north of the buttery and pantry, the kitchen is contemporary, and may have been free-standing originally. To the south is the parlour with great chamber above, rebuilt in the late fifteenth century

Peveril's Tower, c. 1875 (by R. Keene).   *M. Craven*

107

The building of the Great Hall marked the house's arrival at the single courtyard stage, which accords with the rise in status of the Vernons at this period. Their facility for marrying heiresses and the concentration of their estates in the immediate region continued the rise in their prosperity, and with it, the house continued to expand. Shortly after Dorothy, daughter and heiress of Sir George Vernon, 'King of ye Peake' married John Manners – according to popular legend after an elopement, although for what reason a bride should need to elope with so eligible a groom it is hard to imagine – a long gallery was built over pre-existing apartments along the south front, faced by an impressive and justly celebrated terrace making full and imaginative use of the rising ground. Beyond the cross-wing, on the same elevation, the Manners added the 'Earl's Apartments', for through John Manners, the Earls, later Dukes, of Rutland inherited the house. Like the long gallery, these employed canted bays in contrast to the Elizabethan south great chamber with its large rectangular mullioned and transomed west light. Below this is the parlour, the interior of which retains its painted ceiling decoration of red and white checks and various heraldic badges, crests and rebuses in squares. The cusped headed lights with their tall mullions are especially satisfying at the west end, contrasting startlingly with the rectangular Elizabethan window later installed above. The oak panelling is dated 1545, and the moulded beams were painted. The house is full of furniture of high quality matching the various periods of build, and there are both Brussels and Mortlake tapestries. Tax was assessed on 48 hearths in 1670, 34 years after the last building work had been completed – the access bridge from the road.

There are sixteenth century stables which one passes *en route* from the bridge to the present battlemented tower court entrance, and they are connected to the hall by a subterranean passage. The south garden, of which the terrace is part, is one of the many glories of the house, and with 346 acres of the park are rightly listed grade I. The Duke of Rutland's estate ran to 27,069 acres across the Peak in the later nineteenth century, and much had been acquired when various minor gentry families went under towards the end of the seventeenth century. The Birds of Youlgreave Hall *(qv)*, for instance, were glad to be able to sell their depleted estates to the first Duke in 1690 or thereabouts, remaining in their ancestral home for some generations as tenants, before becoming professional men in the nineteenth century; this pattern was repeated elsewhere in the same period.

The Vernons, too, had been very grand and had their attentions been paid at court as assiduously as they were lavished at home in building up the estate, they would have doubtless ended up in the peerage. As it was they chose to be

The Great Hall, c. 1890 and prior to restoration in the 1920s   *M. Craven*

backwoodsmen, and to good effect. Nor were they Vernons in the male line, for as early as the thirteenth century, they ended in an heiress who married a Francis from Cumberland, who took the surname of his arms of his benefactor. The raising of the Manners Earls of Rutland to a Dukedom probably saved this unique ensemble from despoliation – whether in the eighteenth century, which could have witnessed a 'Georganisation' like that at Longford by the likes of Pickford, who worked for members of the Duke's circle, or in the nineteenth century, when one could imagine Pugin or Salvin rebuilding it in some 'purer' form of gothic. As it was, the Dukes retired to Belvoir and other seats, leaving Haddon in the hands of cicerones who showed curious visitors its wonders, only appearing occasionally for shooting. No restoration was attempted until the Marquess of Granby, son of the 8th Duke, oversaw a careful campaign from 1920 to 1932, by which time the principles adumbrated by the Society for the Preservation of Ancient Buildings had been well learnt, and over the 12 years the house was gradually and most sensitively restored. In the event, little that could be called drastic was necessary, a telling tribute to the effectiveness of its construction.

One of the most important aspects of Haddon, which is still owned by the Duke of Rutland, the seat of his younger brother and open to the public, is that it grew up over 450 years as a loose continuum of construction, and then was left untouched for a very crucial 250 years. It thus has an integrity which few houses built over such a period can match. Further, it is entirely constructed – as one would, indeed, expect – from the materials which surround it: the walls of roughly coursed Carboniferous Limestone, upon which it stands, the dressings and much of the later walling and early ashlar is Ashover Grit from nearby Lees Moor, the stone slate roof also from nearby, the leadwork from the Vernon's numerous rakes and scrins under the limestone in the neighbourhood, and timber from the estate. Even the

The Long Gallery, c. 1897.   *M. Craven*

The garden and south front, 1988   *C.L.M. Porter*

glass was spun locally, courtesy of Bess of Hardwick's glassworks, set up for the benefit of Chatsworth, which lies over the hill in the next valley. Haddon is incomparably seated and timeless; it must constitute one of the finest ensembles in Europe.

Pevsner, 221; Lysons V. ccxxxvi-viii, 29; Burke (1853) I. 50; Cox II (1875) 87-94; Emery (2000) 383-91; DAJ XVIII (1896) 81-96 & XXII (1900) 3-4; CL IX (1901) 693-703, CVI (1949) 1651, 1742, 1814, 1884; *National Ancient Monument Review* I (1928) 96-103, 135-146, 150-5; *Arch. Journ.* 118 (1961) 188-98; *Builder* (1845) 237, (1851) 539, (1880) I. 611-13, (1884) I. 334; Carrington (1947) *passim*; Innes-Smith (1987) *passim*; VERNON of Haddon *sub* VERNON, B./BP (1999) 2884-5; MANNERS *sub* RUTLAND, D./*op.cit.* 2482-88.

THE HALLOWES (II)

Dronfield   *Golf Clubhouse*

The Hallowes sits well on a ridge on the edge of the small town of Dronfield its park now subsumed into a golf course. Built of coursed Coal Measure sandstone rubble (probably Silkstone Rock) with similar dressings, the house is basically a typical north Derbyshire H-shaped manor house with three straight coped gables on its main fronts and of two rather low storeys with attics. Indeed, it closely resembles Hassop Old Hall. Its elevations decorated with quoins, it has on the entrance front six bays, with three-light mullioned windows on the bays in the projecting wings, and two-light ones either side of the central entrance which is graced by an odd-looking segmental hood with side wings. The fenestration depends from a string course on both floors, although that above the first floor stops short of the angles.

If the same phenomenon was visible in that below one might postulate therefrom that the house had once been larger; as it stands it must merely represent slapdash builder's work. The attic windows are of two lights with brief hood moulds; the rooms behind them are also as high as those below, and the gables have blank *oeuils-de-boeuf* near the apices. Except at the ends of the facade, the gables are slightly depressed into a low parapet, suggesting a mid or late-seventeenth century date, and indeed, the fabric is dated 1657. The roof is of stone slate, almost certainly from Hallows Quarry listed by John Farey as in work in his survey of 1806-07. Yet inspection of the rather plain interior reveals that this date must represent an enlargement of the house, which appears originally to have been L-shaped, with the cross-wing on the west. The projecting range to the right of the entrance appears to be the only substantial piece of new build. The whole entrance front, therefore, would appear to have been skinned on to the older fabric to achieve the impression of unity, and only an irregularity in the roofline betrays the true story.

The estate had, in the Middle Ages, been that from which the later proprietors of Glapwell (*qv*) had derived their surname, although they had long since moved on and by the early Tudor period it was a seat of the Selioke family, also associated with Hazlebarrow Hall, Norton (*qv*), and who inherited it from the Salveins. Jane, daughter and heiress of Robert Selioke of Dronfield brought the house to Thomas Burton, who seems to have been the man who gave the house its present appearance. In 1670, Francis Burton was assessed on nine hearths, which seems to confirm this. Not long after his time the house was the seat of Andrew Morewood, younger son of Rowland, of the Oaks, and at least one further generation of his family appear to have lived there presumably as tenants. In the late eighteenth century, when the house appears to have been let, a large reception room was added to the west, of a single storey with a hipped roof behind a parapet. By the nineteenth century its ownership appears to have descended from the Burtons to the Lucas family of Chesterfield (to be distinguished from those of Dronfield) and let as a farm, declining ultimately into multiple occupation.

The Hallowes, Dronfield, 1982.   M. Stanley

In early 1933 it was sold to the golf club for use as a clubhouse, and the course was laid out, and it still fulfills this role to the present day, marred only by the loss of much of its original interior through being split up, and some unsympathetic fenestration.

Pevsner, 201; Lysons V 131-3; DLC 4/33 p. 25; SALVEIN & SELIOKE/V. 1569, DAJ XXXI (1909) 27-9; BURTON/ Glover II. 288; MOREWOOD/Glover II. 14-15.

HARDWICK HALL (I)

Ault Hucknall   *National Trust/Open to the public*

Hardwick Hall is one of the most spectacular houses in Derbyshire, and one of national importance. Yet its genesis was the result of trial and error on a colossal scale, and inevitably, at the heart of it lay that exceptional woman, Bess of Hardwick. Hardwick was part of the Manor of Stainsby, but in 1203 was granted to Andrew de Beauchamp. By 1224/1238 rights to a chapel there had been granted to Joscelin de Stainsby and it was in the hands of William de Stainsby by 1288 who held it from John de Savage of Stainsby, and it was held by his descendants until the time of his great-grandson, John in 1330. Soon after this, however, it passed to William Hardwick, fourth in descent from one Joscelyn de Havermere whose posterity were settled in the parish of Pattingham in south-west Staffordshire. One of the enigmas about the Hardwicks is the fact that their name corresponds to the place they acquired. This is presumably a coincidence, although Joscelyn married one of the daughters of Edmund d'Eyncourt in the very early twelfth century, and their association could conceivably have had a longer pedigree than would seem apparent. Another theory is that they took their name from Hardwick, Warwickshire, which place did have seated therein a family that took its name from the place. Yet the Hardwicks of Warwickshire seem to be a quite separate family from those of Pattingham, so the mystery remains for the time being.

The descendants of William de Hardwick, via his elder son (the younger is said to have remained at Pattingham and left descendants who still flourish) ended with the death of James Hardwick in 1581. He was the son of John, whose estate was very modest, by Elizabeth, daughter of Thomas Leake of Hasland (a cadet of the Leakes of Sutton Scarsdale, *qv*) who later remarried Ralph Leche of the family that had once held Chatsworth. James' heiresses were his three sisters of whom the eldest was Elizabeth (Bess). She had married at an early age Robert Barlow of Barlow, whose background was, like her own, decayed gentry. He died fairly young, leaving no issue, and she remarried Sir William Cavendish. As we saw earlier (*qv sub* Chatsworth) she ultimately married

Hardwick in 1868, by J.A. Warwick. In the foreground is Richard Keene with his daughters Eliza and Helen. Many of the early views used in this book were taken by Keene, who had a photographic business in Derby.   M. Craven

George Talbot, sixth Earl of Shrewsbury, and later acrimoniously parted from him. In April 1587, however, she obtained a legal ruling in her litigation with her husband which settled upon her a substantial income.

At this time she was living at Hardwick (which she had purchased in 1583 from her late brother's creditors), having broken with her son Henry, who supported Shrewsbury. It appears that the house had undergone some improvements at the hands of her thrice married neer-do-well brother, who had died childless and bankrupt whilst rebuilding it. It appears to have been a sixteenth century stone built house with close-set twin gables and a narrow recessed entrance between, probably L-shaped in plan. Bess's brother seems to have added an extension to the west, but not quite at right angles to the original build – an illogical proceeding but perhaps dictated by the nature of the ground at this point, or an eventual aim to completely replace it.

By July 1587, Bess had embarked on an ambitious rebuilding of the house and work continued until early in 1591. By that date, with a group of dedicated craftsmen working to Bess's own ideas, she had produced a vast edifice of three, four and five storeys, an irregular skyline and a south front of over 175 feet. It was set on Permian Magnesian Limestone which was oddly perhaps, only used for lime for the mortar, the structure being of Coal Measure sandstone throughout, the sandstone below the Clown Coal quarried from about halfway up the main drive. Permian Magnesian Limestone was used extensively at Bolsover Church, 13th century, and the Castle, c. 1613, and in many important buildings much further afield such as Southwell Minster and the Houses of Parliament, but Bess did not own the stone quarries on Bolsover Moor and the Coal Measure sandstone used to build her late brother's house was easily supplied. The prohibitive cost of transport was often the limiting factor in the use of stone from a distance of more than a few miles.

The main range of the ancestral home she raised in ashlar to four storeys, with the state rooms on the topmost, as at Chatsworth, kept the basic plan of the earlier building and its very low ground floor and three-light hooded mullioned windows. To its left she put in a new two-bay three-storey block with a depressed gable which followed the new orientation her brother had given his extension, although not set back. The return of this brought the building to a projecting external chimney breast, set in a wide gable that appears also to have had its basis in James Hardwick's new build. The return seems to have contained a staircase, explaining the offset fenestration on its south aspect. To the west again, Bess put in another gable, resembling that on the return bay to the east of the chimneybreast (itself gabled around it at the top), and with an attic window, of three storeys with an attic over a lower ground floor. As an afterthought (of which Bess appears to have had many – she must have been maddening to work with) she caused a tower with a balustraded top to be put in, absorbing the western half of the last-mentioned gable, of five storeys over a lower ground floor. This contained the main staircase, and to its west, at the end of the facade was a two-bay matching balustraded block of four storeys, again with the state apartments on the upper floor. In contrast to such a varied – and, indeed, confusing – facade, the north front was entirely flat and to this day looks very grim. The roof was of stone slate.

Inside there was much ornate, if rather barbaric, plasterwork and the great hall lay more or less in the centre of the house, behind the gable with the attached chimney breast, rising through two storeys. To its west was the buttery, and beyond the great stair the kitchen and pantry. Today, open to the skies and gutted, it represents a haunting sight, with areas of stucco and fireplaces seemingly floating

in space, attached to floorless walls, high up in the structure. Girouard highlights the similarities of Hardwick Old Hall to Worksop Manor, built by Lord Shrewsbury in the 1570s (whilst still married to Bess) but remarks on the lack of external ornament, in contrast to the Nottinghamshire seat, which is likely to have been the work of Robert Smythson, the builder of Longleat and Wollaton.

In November 1590, Lord Shrewsbury died, and the event vastly increased Bess' income. At the same time, it is clear that the building of Old Hardwick was leading her into some intractable problems, and she was faced with completing a house that would in all probability be unviable. Thus, almost before Shrewsbury's corpse had gone cold, she had started marking out a new seat, slightly to the north-east of the Old Hall. Nevertheless it was seven years before she was able to move in, and even then it was not entirely complete. In the intervening period she presumably resided in the completed part of the Old Hall.

The Old Hall at Hardwick, 1987.   J.A. Robey

Thanks to the survival of the building accounts, we are able to name the craftsmen who worked on this New Hardwick: John and Christopher Rodes, masons (who had worked at Wollaton), Henry Nayll and Richard Mallery did decorative stonework, as did William Gryffyn and James Adams, the former being responsible for the fine hall screen; Thomas Accres, who had been at Chatsworth and Wollaton too, carved the ornamental polished limestones (the 'marbles') especially the chimneypieces in the long gallery and elsewhere. Much of the stuccowork was done by Abraham Smith, especially the overmantels, which went with Accres's fireplaces. Pevsner calls it 'coarse, but jolly work' and its quality is indeed variable, although the overall effect inspires awe as indeed it was intended to. The source for much of the detail came from pattern books imported from the Low Countries and from Sebastiano Serlio's *Architettura*, plainly also a favourite source for the architect.

One serious problem is that the architect himself is not named as such in the accounts, although had Bess's correspondence survived for the 1590s, this lacuna would not have mattered. Girouard has established beyond any serious doubt that the gifted figure behind this quintessential house of prodigy was Robert Smythson, to whom the accounts do show a 20/- payment as 'surveyor'. He gave the exterior symmetry, unity, height and immense dash, in keeping with the character of its by now ageing proprietrix. To each smoothly ashlared elevation he gave much movement, and although the vast areas of fenestration – mullioned and transomed as in the Old Hall – suggests three storeys, there are four in places, with mezzanines being slipped in here and there to add drama to the spaces as well as convenience to the users. The movement in the facades is derived from the simple device of placing towers, a conceit deeply rooted in that neo-chivalric age, not at the angles, as one might expect, but half a bay in from them. This was enhanced by using not four towers, but six, by placing one further on each short side of the house along the centre-line, these sides being the north and south, for the house was orientated east-west with no central courtyard.

The classicism of Smythson's earlier buildings, where the storeys were marked by a progression of the Classical Orders and punctuated by correct friezes, is at Hardwick relentlessly stripped down, so that the floors are divided by an entablature and frieze, but with no pilasters, which are merely expressed, *in absentia* as it were, by the presence of these horizontal emphases. So powerful an effect did this device have on local masons and builders, that there was scarcely a manor house in the north and centre of Derby-

Hardwick Hall: the entrance lodge c. 1900   *M. Craven*

shire which did not thereafter sport unbroken string courses above the fenestration on each floor in imitation. The central two bays on each main front broke forward and were slightly canted and this, combined with the startling imbalance between glass and wall – one does well to note the old local rhyme: 'Hardwick Hall, more glass than wall' – gives the elevations their dynamism. Each tower, too, projects from the flat leaded roof to make an extra storey – containing banquetting houses, conceits, retreats or store-rooms – and each is lavishly crested with strapwork including Bess's cypher: E S. The remainder of the roofline is balustraded and punctuated behind with groups of stacks, and at the centre of the entrance front with Bess's armorial achievement. The entrance front also has a simple un-arcaded Doric loggia, echoed by a similar one on the east. Originally, it was intended that these should run right round the house at ground floor level, thus endowing it with a rectangular plan within which the angularity of the main build would come to rest. It may well be that the loggias were likely to rob the ground floor of too much light, and were thus dispensed with on grounds of practicality.

The interior, Girouard believes, was subject to a certain amount of alteration as building progressed; it is thought, for instance, that Smythson's original concept was for symmetry internally as well as externally. Hence the mezzanines to the south-east and north-east to allow for some service accommodation in the former and the height of the chapel in the latter. As at the old hall, however, the state apartments were on the very lofty top floor, with the apartments of Bess herself on the floor below. The most spectacular aspect of the former is the long gallery taking up the whole of the east front of the house, with the high great chamber behind it to the south-west, and the staircases which undulate almost throughout the entire house on various levels, emerging in the north and south towers. The centre of the house is occupied, as in the Old Hall, by a central hall going right across the two piles of the building, an arrangement which was then coming into fashion as being more practical than the old medieval great hall arrangement with all its asymetricality, formality and obsolescence. The hall still has a screen, however – monumentally architectonic – but as a frontispiece when entering the space behind, and not as a means of dividing access and service facilities. It is from either side of this hall that the two astounding staircases begin their dramatic rise through the house. Within, too, is that abundance of carved marble, ornamental and muscular plasterwork and carved timber for which the house is so memorable, combined with the tapestry and hangings

which so dramatically embellish the spaces within.

Outside, the house is enclosed by a courtyard guarded by strong ashlared walls topped with a riot of strapwork and obelisks, and at the entrance point, these walls cant outwards towards the visitor, (as at the angles), centred by a round arch decorated with an heraldic achievement, and housing a lodge. Like Bolsover, but on a less intimidating scale, these have something of the air of contemporary fortifications. To the south lie the ornamental gardens (listed grade I), and to the east the parkland is enclosed by a distant semi-circle of planting opening at its centre to an immense avenue. To the west, however, the park has the Old Hall as a most spectacular folly (it is today listed grade II*) beyond which it falls away very sharply to the valley below, now forever marred by the intrusive M1 motorway, also making a scar across the parks of windowless Sutton Scarsdale, as well as Bolsover and Barlborough. The park is 1,087 acres, and the estate in 1950 was 2,350 acres, somewhat more extensive than the pathetic 120 acres held under the manor of Staveley by John Hardwick in 1529, mineral dues notwithstanding.

At Bess' death in 1608, the estate passed to the Cavendish family, in the Earl of Devonshire's branch, regularly used as a second seat, and it was with their Ducal successors until the early 1953 when death duties forced the sale of the estate, and the gift of the house and park to the National Trust which opened it to the public. During the 400 years since it was begun remarkably little has been done to the house. Tax was assessed on a colossal 114 hearths in 1670, and 15 years later some small alterations were made by John Sturgess. The most radical alterations were those undertaken between 1820 and 1858 by the sixth Duke of Devonshire to his own designs, and mainly centred upon the staircases. He also added service accommodation to the north in matching style and rebuilt the stables. As for the old hall, this appears to have been only partly occupied when building ceased in 1591; the kitchens were apparently in use until about 1789, in conjunction with the use of the rooms immediately above as staff dormitories. Thereafter, the shell went into sharp decay, and has only been the subject of consolidation work over the last twenty eight years or so. In 1816 the so-called Giants' Chamber survived there, named from the huge classical Deities which decorated the fireplace. It then had oak pilastered panelling and arcaded stucco work above.

Numerous stories about Mary, Queen of Scots staying at Hardwick are to be discounted, along with those objects said in the nineteenth century to have been embroidered there by her; she died when the Old Hall was hardly started. Pilkington however, says: 'Wolsey stayed here a night *en route* from

York to his death at Leicester...', which suffers, as a story, from the same defect as that concerning Mary Queen of Scots: the house in the second quarter of the sixteenth century had hardly even benefited from the improvements of Bess' brother; there were many more comfortable seats available in the area than the Hardwicks' very modest one on a chilly hillside in north-east Derbyshire.

Pevsner, 229; Colvin, 903, 943; Pilkington (1789) II. 344-51; Lysons V. ccxxxviii, 190; Burke J. B. (1953) II. 65; Durant & Riden (1979, 1984) *passim*; Girouard (1983) 144-62; Cooper (1999) 124, 126, 137, 146, 168; DAJ XXV (1903) 103; DAJ CVII (1987) 44; CL II (1897) 434, 464, VIII (1900) 464-70, XIII (1903) 710, LVII (1925) 229, 320, 422, LIX (1927) 328, 499, 661, LXIV (1928) 806, 87,0, 904, 934, CXXII (1957) 346, CLIV (1973) 1786; *Builder* (1845) 237; University of Leeds MS 295 Vol. 242, N115.

HARDWICK MANOR

see EGGINTON HALL

HARGATE MANOR

see EGGINTON HALL

HARTINGTON HALL (II)

Youth hostel

Hartington Hall, the oldest continually operating youth hostel in the Peak. It has just had a £1 million refurbishment. *C.L.M. Porter*

Hartington Hall is the classic north Derbyshire manor house *par excellence*: stone built, gabled and H-shaped in plan, set on the fringe of a large village in breathtaking countryside. Yet its origins are somewhat obscure, and difficult to unravel. At the time of Domesday in 1086, the huge extent of Hartington was divided as two manors under Henry de Ferrers. In 1170, the southern manor was settled on the Minoresses (Poor Clares) of the City of London, and the hall was allegedly first built by them about 1350. The first tenant of whom we know was Richard Bateman, there by 1454, a member of a family from South Wingfield. His descendant in the fifth generation, Thomas Bateman of Hartington, whose grandfather seems to have obtained the freehold of the estate at the Dissolution, built the present house, which bears the date 1611.

The house could, however, have been built a generation earlier, for its asymmetrical entrance and hall and lack of string courses certainly suggest this. The south (garden) front of the house, which has two storeys and attics, has three straight coped gables with neat finials and low mullioned windows, of five lights on the ground floor, four on the first and of three in the attics. The central section is recessed and offset to the right, with the simple hooded entrance to the left with a single light above. The fenestration is topped by plain cranked hoodmoulds, and the Carboniferous Limestone walls are of rubble brought to course with Millstone Grit sandstone quoins and dressings; the roof is of stone slate. The interior still retains some early oak panelling, and the staircase is a plain one which goes some way to reinforce the suggestion that its date is earlier than 1611. There is also some good plasterwork of c. 1600 remaining inside. The west front was rebuilt in 1861-66, being extended to the north and later acquiring a two-storey canted bay in 1911. The architect was Henry Isaac Stevens of Derby. The additional accommodation was decorated with the sort of interior that provincial architects of that era believed reflected the Elizabethan Age: a little overscale compared to the low ceilinged accommodation of the rest of the house, yet essentially commodious and comfortable, with large carved oak chimney pieces and rather stiff stuccowork. This was carried out for Thomas Osborne Bateman, who also fitted contemporary stained glass containing the arms of Bateman, Osborne (of Derby) and Sacheverell (of Morley), the heiresses of which families his ancestors had married in their eighteenth century glory days. He was fifth son of Richard Thomas Bateman of Wheathills (Mackworth) and Derby, who had inherited the estate from his uncle Sir Hugh Bateman, Bt, in 1824. Sir Hugh, also of Morley Hall, which he had demolished, was raised to a baronetcy in 1806 with the unusual remainder in default of male issue to the heirs male of his two daughters in order of their birth. Sir Hugh was a direct descendant of the medieval Richard Bateman, although the Hartington property had been shuttled between branches of this prolific family in the intervening years on at least two occasions. T. O. Bateman's alterations included the provision of up-to-date service accommodation to the north and west, forming a courtyard with more outbuildings beyond. It is worth noting that in 1670 John Bateman paid tax on eight hearths; his kinsman more than doubled this total in 1866.

At about the turn of the century, the Bateman family left the house, and let it as a private hotel, although F.O.F.Bateman returned to it in 1910, putting in up-to-date plumbing, central heating, and even electric light the year following. In 1934, however, it was again let, this time to the Youth Hostels Association, the owner by 1939 being the mother of O.R.S.Bateman, who finally sold in 1948 to the YHA. It has remained a youth hostel ever since. It was, indeed, the first youth hostel in the country to have central heating and electricity.

Pevsner, 237; Tarn, (1971) 45; Bagshaw (1846) 363; Burke, J. B. (1852) I. 241; *Reliquary* XV (1874) 100; Cox (1877) II. 474; Bulmer (1895) 385; DAJ VIII (1886) 50; BATEMAN of Hartington/BFR 46; BATEMAN, Bt. *Sub* ST. AUDRIES, B./BP (1970) 2345.

HARTSHORNE UPPER HALL (II*)

Private residence

Hartshorne Upper Hall.   M. Craven

With Wakelyn Old Hall, South Sitch and Somersall Herbert *(qqv)* this house constitutes a small group of timber-framed manor houses in southern Derbyshire which, through the neglect or poverty of their owners, escaped rebuilding in brick. With the church and (much butchered) late eighteenth century public house, it makes a fine ensemble so close to the grim sprawl of Swadlincote and its associated settlements. The house is jettied, of two storeys plus attics, with extensive and charming herringbone work above the ground floor, which is merely close-studded and built on a massive stone plinth which in parts may pre-date the present structure. The building originally seems to have consisted of the longish range facing the road (west) with a cross-wing to the south. It had low mullioned windows and an old tile roof with one timber-framed and original dormer on the north return of the south wing. To the east once ran an eighteenth century service wing in brick with vernacular fenestration, but this was mainly demolished in the middle of the twentieth century. A slightly later gabled projection to the left of the entrance front was rebuilt in the nineteenth century in brick, since (rather misguidedly perhaps) painted white to match the infill of the remainder of the house.

More recently, however, a major scheme of restoration has been carried out, which has involved replacing much of the early twentieth century fenestration with modest casements to match the few surviving earlier examples, and the removal of the black tarring on the timbers to leave them again in their natural hue. On the debit side, the roof has been retiled rather too neatly, and the local planning authority allowed the insertion of miniscule dormers in the south front roof to no good effect at all; pressures from clients with a taste for home improvements to do such adventurous things to houses of this quality really should be resisted at town hall level. Nevertheless, the general effect on the house (and one might also except a banal flat-roofed loggia on the south front, too) has been beneficial, and the interior, with much excellent timber, including intact internal stud walls, panelling and a newel stair, has been allowed to speak for itself. There is a good wall in front of the house, a walled garden to the east and one or two surviving outbuildings of red brick. Charmingly, the bird house is timber-framed in black and white! One of the ground floor rooms contains a very fine late eighteenth century fire surround, possibly from elsewhere.

The background to the building of this house is more than usually complex, although we have Janet Spavold to thank for unravelling much of it. At the time of the Domesday Book there were two separate Hartshornes, both held by Henry de Ferrers in succession to one Aelfric; no one is named as holding from Ferrers, probably because both manors were waste. In c. 1160 it appears that one of the manors – probably the first mentioned in the Domesday account, being rather larger and richer – was granted to Bertram, son of Norman de Verdon by Robert Ferrers, Earl of Derby, one of whose daughters Bertram had married. At the same time we find two separate families – both called de Hartshorne and probably close kin – holding in the two Hartshorne manors under de Ferrers and their Verdon successors. Thus the Old Hall probably owes its origins to the Hartshorne family in some way.

John Benskin, a substantial yeoman had what we can now confidently call Upper Hall under Sir William Compton, who had purchased the relevant manorial estate from the Abells who had acquired it from the heirs of Hartshorne. Benskin or his successors had obtained the freehold by 1635, but by the end of the Civil War it had passed to a Mr Oldershaw (there were at this time Oldershaws in Derby, prominent Puritans, one of whom founded (with others) Plymouth, Massachusetts, USA in the 1620s) who may have obtained it through supporting Parliament in that conflict. In 1668 it was the residence of a Thomas Groome and was divided in 1672. By 1681 John Cantrell had bought it. Thus if Spavold's date of 1629 for the building of this house is correct, it was built by John Benskin, probably on the site of the manor House attested as being occupied by the Ireland family, the Hartshornes' heirs in 1504. At the same time the Benskins also obtained the tenancy under the Stanhopes (as ultimate heirs of the Meynells, who had married another Hartshorne family heiress), of Hartshorne Nether Hall. This house later passed with Bretby to the Earls of Carnarvon and the Wraggs but, we are told, the original building had been demolished in 1706 by the Stanhopes (then going through something of a mania for building) and replaced. Today only the rear part of Nether Hall, about which little is known survives, turned into an old folks' home after a Regency rebuild.

Hartshorne Upper Hall, (or Old Manor as it was called in the nineteenth century), however, descended from the heiress of Cantrell to William Bailey Cant, who died in 1800 leaving his estate, not to his heir, John Murcot, but to Lord Erskine, in recognition of his effective defence of John Horne Tooke, the radical, in 1794. No heir could take this sort of thing lying down, however, and a law case ensued – the costs dissipating much of the estate – won by Murcot, Cant's cousin. Thereafter it passed through many ownerships and vicissitudes to the twentieth century including further sub-division. It came on the market in June 1986 at £275,000 and again two years later at a somewhat reduced sum.

There remains one enigma: Woolley, writing in 1712 becomes expansive and says: 'Mr Cantrell, who has a good brick and stone house here called the Upper Hall... there is a capital messuage in Hartshorne called New Hall seat of the Benskins (purchased from Sir Henry Compton, KB). Benskin sold to Captain Thomas Colson whose son sold to Woolley.' As we have seen, Upper Hall is a timber-framed house, and not 'brick and stone'. This reference may refer to nearby Old Hall farm, which Spavold tells us was once the 'real old Hall'. The present Upper Hall then, is probably the New Hall, and Woolley's information may refer to part of its history, which has become detached from the canon as adumbrated above. One must also take account of the

'Manor House' dated 1677, also near the church. Fortunately, it does not completely contradict what has been set out, but constitutes one of several mysteries surrounding the history of the small estates in this ancient and fascinating parish.

Pevsner, 238; Woolley, 116, p.134; Spavold (c. 1988) *passim;* DLC 10/81 p. 72.

HASSOP HALL (II*)

Hotel

Hassop Old Hall: the south front, c. 1905.　　M. Craven

Hassop Hall is a much underrated and magnificent house, but like the family that built it, somewhat enigmatic. Hassop by the end of the thirteenth century had, with Tideswell, come into the hands of the Foljambes, who presumably acquired it (along with Tideswell and Wormhill) from the Daniels. On the death of Sir Godfrey Foljambe in 1388 his daughter and heiress carried it to a Yorkshire knight, Robert Plumpton, whose grandson of the same name sold it to Catherine, widow of Stephen, 11th son (as the old pedigrees allege) of Robert Eyre of Padley. It is also clear that Stephen Eyre had previously held Hassop under the Foljambes, and that it is likely to be true of his family before his time. Hence too the Eyre's celebrated 'severed leg' crest, which apes precisely the original crest of the Foljambes, but which the latter later relinquished when the Eyres became equally powerful in the area in the sixteenth century; needless to say that the Eyre legend that the crest was due to the loss of a leg at the Battle of Hastings by Truelove, their alleged ancestor, is so much eyewash!

It is likely that Stephen Eyre or one of his immediate predecessors built the first seat on the magnificent south facing slope on which its successor now stands. It was later replaced or radically enlarged perhaps in about 1600, although the only clues are a few surviving fragments of exterior fabric, especially on the east side, and some plasterwork in the hall. One clue is that when the north-west wing was

being demolished in 1955 a curious vernacular carved stone was found by Lady Stephenson, high up and facing inwards. It bears a crudely carved crucifix on three grieces with a figure on either side, that to the left being a bearded man in Elizabethan costume, and another to the right which is unfortunately worn away. Below is the date 158[?8]. The symbolism of the stone may well relate to the recusancy of the Eyres, and it is not without significance that their FitzHerbert kinsmen at Padley *(qv)* had suffered a raid by Lord Shrewsbury's men in that very year, during which the Padley Martyrs were arrested. Thus, some rebuilding after that date seems the more likely on this evidence. From what little can be gleaned from the remaining core of the old seat, map evidence (that of William Senior, 1618) and other fragments both extant and reported, the house seems to have been fairly large (tax was assessed on 20 hearths in 1670) with three storeys, and three steep straight gables and a two storey wing to the east with attics and containing the entrance and, possibly, the great hall of the previous house. The taller part had mullioned windows, the lower, three cross windows. Indeed, the east side rather suggests a further rebuilding, perhaps of the lower east range, in the 1630s. Although the Eyres were far from the circle of Lord Shrewsbury and the Cavendishes, it may in some way have aped the architectural style of such houses as Worksop Manor, as evidenced by a row of merlons along the parapet of the east return and deeper top-storey windows there. It was built of coursed Carboniferous Limestone rubble, with dressings of Ashover Grit, from which its replacement was fashioned.

In December, 1643, Hassop Hall was garrisoned for the King by Col William Eyre (1599-1650), several of whose kinsmen were also active Royalists and one of whom, buried at Great Longstone, was to pay for his zeal with his life. Eyre also had to compound for his estate for the colossal sum of £21,000, although so extensive and lead-rich was it that the sum was easily raised and the estate remained with his posterity. Indeed, it was the very wealth of the estate that allowed the Eyres to continue to flourish through an era of crippling recusancy fines, and, in about 1774, to completely rebuild their house.

This rebuilding, attributed in most sources, surely incorrectly, to around 1820, was carried out in ashlar, probably Ashover Grit from Ball Cross, with similar dressings, for Thomas, son of Rowland Eyre after his father's death,

South Front of Hassop Hall, c. 1910.　　M. Craven

probably in c. 1774 or a little earlier. Most of the surviving sixteenth century fabric remains on the north and east sides, but the main work was lavished on the long south front and the interior. This front is of seven bays with four full-height canted bays, placed slightly in from either end and alternately between, the intervening bays having ground floor niches with upper storey *oeuils-de-boeuf,* with the exception of the central bay where there is the former entrance, the aedicule of which has a triangular pediment on a simple frieze supported on Roman Doric columns. There are double bands between the storeys, a well moulded cornice and with parapet above, balustraded over the bays. The entire effect is like a vastly expanded version of the Grey House, Ashbourne, a building of 1763-64 firmly attributable to Joseph Pickford who, indeed, was working in 1774 for the Duke of Devonshire nearby at Chatsworth, and for the Barkers at Ashford *(qqv).* The general effect is rustic Palladian, and not at all Regency.

Yet there are features about this facade, which are not in the canon of Pickford's style, like the *oculi* although this feature can be found on the facade of the Assembly Rooms, Derby. Some of the anomalies, indeed, may stem from the shape of the previous house, which seems to have been rebuilt piecemeal, rather than have been taken down as a preliminary to rebuilding: the first floor even today is discernibly loftier, in good Elizabethan fashion, than the ground floor, whilst the second storey, had it been left to almost any provincial mason or architect of the 1770s, would have been lower. This may explain other features too, like the lack of a wide central bay with, say, a pediment, and even the canted bays may echo earlier features of a similar nature. Certainly it is not beyond the bounds of possibility that it could be Pickford's work, although an architect from Yorkshire (where the Eyres had estates) is perhaps more likely. Several names obtrude: John Platt had the black marble works at nearby Ashford from Henry Watson (who is alleged to have carved the drawing-room fireplace at Hassop, an ornate essay with Ionic columns and fine but busy frieze in Cararra marble) and worked at Sheffield for the Sitwells in 1777. He does not mention Hassop in his *Journal,* however, and the Sitwell family were politically the antithesis of the Eyres; this also rather tells against the involvement of Joseph Badger of Sheffield too, who was, however, born at Hathersage, in Eyre territory. Thomas Atkinson is a possible contender, however, for he worked for the recusant Cliffords at Tixall, Staffordshire and in Sheffield in 1776-77, and may have been close kin of the Thomas Atkinson who was a colleague and relation-by-marriage of Pickford's like-named uncle, the contractor of Horse Guards, in Whitehall; both had yards at Hyde Park Corner in the 1750s.

The interiors are peppered with fine neo-classical stucco ceilings, that in the drawing-room being especially fine, and is accompanied by shell-headed niches and carved overdoors. The study has another Pickfordian feature: a tripartite doorcase with glyphic frieze and (open) pediment. Outside there is some very fine wrought-ironwork by John Gardom of Baslow, including the graceful gates and a sophisticated icehouse also survives.

When Thomas Eyre died in 1792, the estate passed to his uncle, Francis, who had married Lady Mary Radcliffe, daughter and co-heiress of Hon. Charles Radcliffe, second son of the second Earl of Derwentwater, attainted for his part in the '15 and the '45. He had married Lady Charlotte Mary Livingston, daughter and heiress of the second Earl of Newburgh, a Scots title descendable to heirs general. When

the last Livingston Earl of Newburgh died, the grandson, Francis Eyre, assumed the title, although his mother's elder sister had married the Venetian Prince Guistiniani-Bandini and was thus actually entitled to it by primogeniture. What was then believed was that foreign nationals could not inherit British titles, and no one seriously challenged this through a succession of *soi disant* Eyre Earls of Newburgh to 1853, when the sister and heiress of Francis, *soi-disant* eighth Earl died. Thereafter, the Guistiniani-Bandinis finally established their claim and ultimately took British nationality, throwing into chaos the speculative claims of the Cadmans and Cloves's, near kin of the Eyres. The estate passed (not without litigation) to Col Charles Leslie, KH, 26th of Balquhain, County Aberdeen, husband of 'Lady' Maria Dorothia Eyre: the shenanigans concerning succession to both estates and 'honours' even included missing pages of the parish register and other real or imagined devices by which rival claimants attempted to block the good Leslie from taking possession.

By the time the Eyre line failed, more had been done to the

The former Dining Room decorated in neo-classical style in the late 18th century. Note the low ceiling reflecting the house's 17th century origins.   *Hassop Hall Hotel*

house, including the building of a fine ballroom with a shaped gable (built over a creamery and connected to the house by one of several subterranean passages) and spectacular stables and coach house in Carboniferous Limestone, all 1827-33 – hence the 1820 date usually attached to the entire house. The architect may well have been Joseph Ireland, who also built the superb, and arresting (in its context), Catholic Chapel at the end of the drive in the village of 1816-18. This is severe and correct Doric with a tetrastyle portico and ashlar cellared podium. Previously, the family had a chapel within the house, used until the Catholic faith was able to 'come out of the closet' in the early nineteenth century; Derby itself had finally acquired a chapel only three years earlier. The park is dramatic, although it is not known who designed it and the estate was of 4,875 acres in 1900. All was sold up, however, by Charles Stephen Leslie in 1919, the house and some land going to Col Henry Stephenson, later created a baronet, a Sheffield steel magnate. The Stephensons reduced the house in 1953 when the upper two storeys of the north west angle were removed and 1955 when four bays of the west wing, including two bays of early fabric, was shortened to effectively two bays, a very fine fireplace going to Field Head at Edale. In the 1820s, the entrance had been formed in one of the surviving west wing bays and the former entrance hall turned into a drawing room. At the beginning of the 1970s it was sold as a very sumptuous hotel.

To the south lies the stone gabled dower house, ('Dowager House', allegedly 1580) closely resembling the Hallowes, Dronfield (qv) but smaller, with two-light mullions throughout. It has since been sold as a separate freehold (in 1988) after some decades as three tenements, but has subsequently been redivided as 'prestige' dwellings. It appears to date from the 1630s, and is pretty, if rather close to the main road; it may have been let to the Townrawes in the nineteenth century. The gardens are also of high quality.

Pevsner, 239; Colvin, 528; Platt, J., *Journal, MS* transcription at Derby Museum; Lysons, V. 30; Pilkington (1789) II. 429; Davies (1811) 633; Meredith (1981) 267-8; DAJ XXXI (1909) & XXXII (1910), LXXXV (1965) 44-91; DLC 8/37, 10-11/68 & 5/81; *Bakewell Miscellany* (1/1978) 32-41; FOLJAMBE/BLG (1972) 338-9; EYRE of Hassop/ V.1662 & *sub* NEWBURGH, E./Lodge, *Peerage* (1852) 412; LESLIE of Balquhain/BLG (1937) 1360-2; STEPHENSON, Bt./BP (1999), V, 2696.

HAZLEBADGE HALL (II)

Bradwell   *Private residence*

What remains of Hazlebadge Hall is one cross-wing of two storeys only, dated 1549 with a straight uncoped gable. It is built of stuccoed, coursed Carboniferous Limestone rubble, with dressings of Millstone Grit sandstone, probably Shale Grit from an adjacent outcrop. The surviving fenestration suggests that originally the house was one of some quality, with a six-light mullioned window surmounted by one of five lights, with a niche bearing the arms of Vernon above, the date (1549), being placed between. The windows themselves have depressed arched heads and hood moulds. It is quite possible that the gable was once coped, but has since been altered; the roof is today slated. There are few signs of the remainder of the building, as the great hall and northern cross-wing were demolished a very long time ago to be replaced by a byre and shippon of probable early eighteenth century date with stone slate roofs. Inside little remains except some good moulded ceiling beams. It is significant as an early example of a house with a lobby entrance plan, a type that was still being built two centuries later, albeit in somewhat more sophisticated form, as at Youlgreave Old Hall (qv).

This house was by no means the first to have been built upon the site (or near it), for a branch of the Strelleys of Strelley Hall, Nottinghamshire, were resident there from c. 1199 when Philip, second son of Sampson Strelley of Strelley married Avicia, daughter and heiress of Richard son of Roger of Hazlebadge. He had previously been settled by his father at Brough Mill, nearby, and their second son, Robert de Strelley *alias* Molendarius ('Miller') remained at the mill, and may have been the first of a line there. The elder son was of Hazlebadge by 1252 and Philip, fifth in descent from him, died without issue in 1368, whereupon the estate was sold to the Vernons of Haddon. His brother, however, was of Brough, and his grandson, John, son of Hugh Strelley of Castleton was actually tenant of the Vernons at Hazlebadge around 1460, leaving a son, Robert, living 1483, after which we hear no more of them.

In reality it is likely that Robert Strelley was, like

Hazlebadge Hall, 1949.   *Derbyshire Life*

his father, tenant at Hazlebadge, for it was not until late in the fifteenth century that Sir Richard Vernon, third son of Sir William of Haddon, is found settled at the house. He died in 1517 leaving a natural son, another Sir Richard, progenitor of a line of Vernons at Hazlebadge and Tideswell, which ended around 1670 in Francis Vernon. Yet it is thought that he too had a son, John, then living, who was ancestor of the Vernons of Peak Forest who have posterity surviving in New Zealand today. If the interpretation of the hearth tax returns may be trusted (only one hearth taxed), then the house had been reduced as we see it today by 1670, despite the fact that the second Sir Richard Vernon had erected it but 121 years before. It would appear that this line of Vernons were also only tenants, for by the end of the seventeenth century, it had reverted, like Haddon itself, to the Dukes of Rutland. It was later tenanted by the Fox family from the later nineteenth century well into that following.

Pevsner, 242; Mercer (1975) 60, 65; *Nottinghamshire & Derbyshire Notes and Queries* II.11. (11/1895) 170; DAJ X (1888) 76; STRELLEY/DAJ XIV (1892) 72f.; VERNON of Hazlebadge/DAJ *op.cit.*71-75, XV (1893) 179-182, XIX (1897) 116 & XXII (1900) 26; MANNERS, *qv. Supra, sub* Haddon.

HEAGE HALL (II)

Private residence

Heage Hall in the 1860s/70s by R. Keene   *Derby Museum*

The rather irregular vestiges of a once larger house that is today Heage Hall seems to share something in common with the fragment of Hazlebadge: a single old cross-wing with later additions. In the case of Heage, the cross-wing is probably later rather than earlier fifteenth century in date, the few three-light mullioned windows having straight heads and hood moulds, and the house is all coursed rubble construction, of Coal Measures sandstone, probably Wingfield Flags, with similar dressings. At a right angle lies the entrance with a plain stone hood, set in a lower range which could conceivably contain even earlier work than the cross-wing, but which has undergone some drastic modifications since. Yet even this is a short piece, of but two bays with small mullioned windows, and is attached to an eighteenth century or early nineteenth century single bay, but reasonably commodious wing, much higher in contrast to that to which it is attached, but aggressively plain and vernacular, and which at some stage has had render spread over its random rubble walls. All the roofs are stone slated. Some evidence of its reduction in size lies in a number of old fireplaces carelessly left visible on two levels in a gable end at the right. This reduction in size might have been due to a serious fire suffered by the house at some stage in distant past (recalled locally as a folk-memory) although other work was done more recently. The house is said also to once have had a chapel, attested in 1343, but probably not that recorded as having been destroyed in a tempest in 1545, more likely to have been the local church. Inside there is a substantial close-studded partition to the north range, a large chamfered stone fireplace in the central room of the west range and a panelled bedroom. The barn and dairy in the yard beyond the house contain crucks, which are a feature said to have been also evident in the demolished range; indeed, the outbuilding may once have been an integral part of the building, which had eight hearths taxable in 1664.

The house, described by Woolley in his offhand way as: 'A good stone house', once had extensive grounds, ornamented by fishponds, but these are mostly now built over, having been alienated in the nineteenth century in small parcels. The house, the owners of which – in historical times at least – were a rum lot, is said to be much haunted. A bloodstained ermine embellished suit with brass buttons was found in a walled-off part of the demolished wing, and a headless woman – recalling a well known eighteenth century chauvinistic inn-sign – has been seen near the stream by the house. Further, the spectre of George Pole, an owner who was alleged to have been an amateur highwayman (debt seems to have pursued several families at the hall in times gone by), traverses the lane outside, accompanied by the rattling of harness. He is said, too, to have murdered his wife, who in her turn, had added to the cavalcade of spirits said to lurk around the environs of the seat. A piece of window glass, taken out at the turn of the century bore the scratched legend: 'Heureux en toi/malheureux en moi'; the handwriting was at the time authenticated by the British Museum as being likely of sixteenth century date. Doubtless the glass encapsulates yet another dolorous tale of tragedy and high romance!

The estate first comes into independent existence by 1403 when Sir Robert Dethick of Dethick and his only son, Thomas, were both killed in action at the Battle of Shrewsbury. The Dethick estate passed to Thomas Babington, husband of the knight's elder daughter, and Heage – then rendered *Heghedge* (High Heage) – to Henry Pole, married to the younger daughter. How it had come to the Dethicks, however, is quite unclear. Unfortunately, little is known of the early history of Heage, except that, as a parcel of the manor of Duffield, it passed from the de Ferrers, Earls of

Derby, to the Duchy of Lancaster c. 1268, being sold off by Charles I to Sir John Stanhope of Elvaston in 1629.

Henry Pole was a cadet of the Poles of Newborough, Hartington and Radburne, but his posterity signally failed to repeat the achievement of their forebears in marrying heiresses, and became impoverished. Hence the activities (or alleged activities) of George Pole of Heage (1604-74) as highwayman. His loot was alleged to have remained concealed within the house or grounds thereafter, the search for which rather blighted the existence of the family that followed the Poles. George was fifth in descent from Henry, and with the death of his grandson of the same name in 1681, the estate was split between his daughters and heiresses (married respectively to William Frith of Nottingham – the daughter and heiress of this match marrying Sir Charles Sedley of Nuthall – and Patricius Chaworth of Annesley). Edward, brother (and pious contrast) to the notorious George, was vicar of Youlgreave and Bonsall, and had posterity settled at Ashton sub Hill, Oxfordshire in the early eighteenth century.

The purchaser of the estate in 1681 was Thomas Argyle, probably a local yeoman, having married Elizabeth Swift at Duffield in 1668. The family were said to have come from Scotland with the Convenanter Army in the Civil War, but this should be viewed with scepticism, bearing in mind that a Thomas Argyle recorded in the central Derbyshire region as early as 1518. Thomas, fifth in descent, married Martha Haslam of Duffield there in 1779 (she was a member of the ironfounder Sir Alfred Seale Haslam's family, *qv* Breadsall Priory) but disinherited his elder son, Erasmus, being succeeded by his next son, Samuel, whose son George, having depleted his estate in defending lawsuits brought by the heirs of Erasmus (reduced to labourers in the parish by 1819), sold up in 1870, and his widow went to Langley Mill, where she became a draper. Their son moved to Derby, as did one of George's brothers. The other brother settled at Bent Farm, part of the estate at Heage, where he was succeeded by his son, John. Another earlier branch were tenants at Padley Hall, Ripley (*qv*).

A generation before 1870, however, the hall had been let to the Shores, claiming descent from a common ancestor with those of Norton (*qv*), who were millers at Heage Mill. They purchased the hall in due course, but the mill ceased to pay after the turn of the century, and they too were forced to sell, to Willoughby Lowe after World War One. Like the Argyles, the Shores' posterity remain fairly profusely in the area. The house was most recently sold to Mr D.Morton in 1979.

Pevsner, 243; Lysons, V. 140; Woolley, 54 p.88; Alcock No. 42; Shore (2000) *passim*; D. Misc. III.9 (1966) 676f.; DETHICK of Newhall/V.1611; POLE of Heage/*op.cit.* & Glover, II. 323; ARGYLE/D. Misc.*loc.cit.*; SHORE of Heage/DLC 10/81.

HIGHLOW HALL (I)

Private residence, B&B by prior booking only

A modest but wholly delightful and important manor house, probably of late sixteenth century date, set in breathtaking countryside high above Hathersage. It is irregular, with a bold canted bay to the left of the south front with a recessed bay to the right of it, breaking forward slightly beyond and ending to the right in a remarkably plain straight gable. The majority has a strongly crenellated battlement, with a band over the ground floor windows, which are generously proportioned two-light mullions on the ground floor with a three-light one above on the canted bay. Sitting slightly awkwardly and a little to the right of the centre of the facade is a low two-storey battlemented porch, also with a strong string course and a square headed entrance from which one rises up steps into the neat hall. The room over it is on a mezzanine level. The whole, in neat ashlar of Millstone Grit sandstone, probably Kinderscout Grit and Shale Grit from an adjacent outcrop (with similar dressings), is built on a stone plinth. The abrupt ending of the embattled parapet beyond the porch suggests strongly that it was intended to be carried on over the south-east corner. The lack of an obvious break may suggest that it was completed hurriedly by another hand. Likewise, the west return suggests an interrupted building scheme with the parapet carried round and ending abruptly, as does the first floor string course. The other elevations are plain, and much less architectonic, and an irregular projection at the northwest angle

but had a lesser grounding in the subtleties of classical Renaissance architectural practice, as the skinny ball-topped attached columns enclosing the courtyard arch suggest. The roofs are of stone slate.

In addition to the outbuildings, some at least of which are contemporary with the house, there is a pretty seventeenth century dovecote with a pyramidal roof, but with the openings now blocked. It is square, and could conceivably have been intended as a summer house or small banquetting house. The immediate environs also encompass a group of 20 tumuli. Whilst the house must once have been surrounded with pleasure grounds, 200 years of direct husbandry have obliterated most traces.

The estate was detached from the manor of Hathersage (held by the King in 1086) and was by c. 1350 in the hands of the Archers of Great Hucklow and Abney, established in the latter places by c. 1220 in the person of Thomas Archer. The last Archer, John, was of Highlow, and died after 1388 leaving two daughters and co-heiresses, of whom only the younger married: to Nicholas, son of Sir William Eyre of Hope. The estate remained with the senior (Padley) line of this important family, but was held under them by Richard, third son of John Stafford of Eyam *(qv)*, where he was succeeded by his son of the same name and grandson, John. At the close of the fifteenth century, it was granted by Robert Eyre II of Padley *(qv)* to his fifth son, Thomas and it was probably his descendant, Thomas, who built the hall. His grandfather, Thomas, had married twice, to a Reresby *(qv* Eastwood Hall) and to a daughter of Thomas Hardwick, a kinsman of Bess of Hardwick, and his mother had been a Saunderson of Tickhill, Yorkshire, firmly within the

Highlow Hall, c. 1901.   *M. Craven*

suggests an informal alteration of a later date or yet another remnant of a projected range, never built.

Inside, the hall has a moulded timber ceiling, an oriel, and a square framed open fireplace, which has suffered some mutilation in a later era. From the hall rises the staircase, a fine example of later seventeenth century date, of oak and with twisted balusters. It may have replaced a stone one in approximately the same position. In 1670, tax was assessed on nine hearths, which might suggest that a slight reduction in its size has since taken place, perhaps when it became a farmhouse in the eighteenth century.

The entrance to the courtyard is through an engaging triumphal arch, which must originally have borne an heraldic device, probably fretted out of stone, like a miniature version of those on the parapet of Hardwick. Indeed, the high quality of the south front – especially if it was originally intended to have been larger and symmetrical – strongly suggests that it was an early example of the type of small house pioneered by Robert and John Smythson in the wake of such grander projects as Hardwick and Oldcotes. If the date is slightly later that suggested by most commentators (including the Royal Commission on Historic Monuments) – say c. 1630 – then it might be possible to suggest John Smythson himself as the architect. Whatever the cause of the cessation of work, the mason who followed on was neat,

ambit of the Earls of Shrewsbury, thus making a connection with the Smythson group of houses plausible. Thus a probable chronology of the house may be discerned: the ambitious rebuilding was probably the idea of Thomas Eyre (1595-1633), on inheriting from his father Robert in 1628, and fortified by the inheritance of his wife, the daughter and heiress of William Jessop of North Lees *(qv)*. Unfortunately he died prematurely in 1633, leaving an eldest son, Robert, only an infant; it would have been at this moment when work stopped, unfinished. By the time he reached maturity, the Civil War was in progress, and when it ended he no doubt found it more convenient to retire to Holme Hall *(qv)* which he had acquired in the right of his wife, Anne Wells.

In the eighteenth century two brothers of this branch of Eyre married the co-heiresses of Archer of Coopersale, Essex, and Gell of Hopton, thus moving on to better things in the shape of more commodious houses in less bleak locales, and Highlow Hall was then reduced, and became a tenanted farm. The former branch – in accordance, some say, with a family curse – were forced to sell their estates under an Order in Chancery, and in 1802 Highlow passed to the Dukes of Devonshire. In the wake of this, the tenancy was held first by the Bagshaws and then by the Coopers; a postcard of the house dated in manuscript 26 September 1903 says: 'This is a view of the Hall where Willie Cooper lived'; it was at that time in the hands of Joel Cooper. This family was succeeded by the Wains, who farmed 900 acres of semi-moorland there in 1969, having obtained the freehold in the early 1950s, when the Devonshire estates were drastically reduced through death duties. Today it is owned by Mr & Mrs B. Walker.

Pevsner, 244; Tilley I (1892) 192; Jeayes (1906) no. 1225; DAJ XXIV (1902) 160-1; DLC 5/69; EYRE of Highlow/V. 1569 & *sub* ARCHER-HOUBLON of Hallingbury/BLG (1952) 1289 & *sub* GELL of Hopton/*op. cit.* 967.

HOLME HALL (I)

Bakewell   Private residence

Holme Hall, Bakewell in 1925.   *Derby Local Studies Library*

Holme lies just across the bridge across the Wye from Bakewell town centre, and was listed in the Domesday Book in 1086 as an outlier of the King's manor of Bakewell. In 1401, it was granted to Thomas, son of Godfrey Foljambe. A witness to the deed was one Roger de Holme, perhaps the Foljambes' tenant there. In 1536 it was held by one William Browne, yeoman. We are only really on firm ground when in 1626 one Bernard Wells, son of Thomas of Ashton-un-der-Hill, Gloucestershire, built himself the house which is still there to this day. It is not wholly clear why he came to Derbyshire, but we might suspect that it was a combination of lead extraction and the patronage of a great family, perhaps the Manners Earls of Rutland. At first glance, the house, very pretty in its riparian setting, looks for all the world like a miniature pastiche of Haddon Hall nearby. Yet that would be to underestimate it. Indeed, it shows signs of being perhaps another of John Smythson's small villas in Neoromantic style. Unfortunately, it has suffered repeated cosmetic rebuildings, which has obfuscated much of the evidence of its early history.

Its west (river) front was formerly the entrance, and is of three bays and two and a half storeys with a projecting porch, now blocked up and adapted. This, and the dressings, are of Millstone Grit sandstone, probably Ashover Grit from nearby Ball Cross. The top parapet is crenellated with mouldings very similar to those at Highlow, but with a central merlon, a favourite Smythsonian artifice. Small

finials of similar date mark the angles, and the roof is stone slate. The fenestration (where it appears to be original) is mullioned and transomed at ground and first floor levels, and mullioned above, but the porch, which is full height, is enclosed today by a pair of two-storey canted bays, also crenellated, which look nineteenth century. Here the windows at ground floor level reach to the terrace, and this may be the result of further Edwardian alterations.

The south front is of four bays, being part of the main 1626 build, which is constructed of roughly squared Carboniferous Limestone with Millstone Grit sandstone dressings, including quoins. Here there are three full storeys, containing what might be termed 'state rooms' necessitating a Smythsonesque change of levels at first and second floor. The fenestration is all of the cross type, and at bay three a new entrance was formed probably in the first decade of the nineteenth century; this is embellished with a four-centred arch under an angled hood mould and has a pleasing gothick fanlight. The hood moulds over the windows are continuous only over pairs of windows, a quirky arrangement. This front extends back into the masoned terracing – possibly contemporary with the house and punctuated by Renaissance arches and other details –by a further three bays, slightly lower, but in matching style. The fenestration here is entirely of paired lights under straight hood moulds, except for the window on the top storey, centrally placed, wide and deep with a cambered top, Edwardian in all probability. The north west range is in a similar form to the south, but plainer, and joins at right angles a three-bay, two-storey range with two-light mullioned windows which may, in origin, be earlier than the main part of the house, but perhaps rebuilt by Wells's heir, Robert Eyre, in 1658. This range has had rather French looking attic windows added consisting of *oeuils-de-boeuf* set in bulgy ogiform surrounds which rise from the curt parapet; they resemble similar ones included by Sir William Wilson in his unrealized design for rebuilding Melbourne Hall in the 1690s, and provide a jaunty counterpoint to the dignified ambience of the remainder.

Inside, alterations have removed most original features, but there is a fine oak staircase and gallery over the hall which occupies the easternmost canted bay; the other contains the great parlour. The SW range has a pair of quite large rooms on the ground floor, not quite aligned, and two smaller ones, the rearmost of the larger rooms having been once the kitchen (with smoke loft), that in front of it, a former hall (with surviving stone staircase off) adapted, Prof. Gomme thinks, as a winter parlour. The roof seems entirely a later eighteenth century rebuild, and '... under part of the property is a most valuable bed of chert ... the same vein of bed being now in actual workmanship in the adjoining estate to very great advantage'. The whole still sits in agreeable walled pleasure grounds.

On the death of Wells's son, Anne, the junior heiress, transmitted it to Robert Eyre of Highlow (*qv*), under which family it was tenanted by 1767 by the Twigges, *arrivistes* grown rich on lead. In 1802, however, the estate was sold by Order in Chancery (as was Highlow), and was bought by Robert Birch. The Birches sold in 1833 to one of the Barkers of Bakewell and was again sold before 1848 to John Hodgson. In 1854 it was in the hands of William Gisborne, a scion of a most distinguished Derby family originally

120

descended (on their own assertion) out of Hartington; it cost him £3,000. In 1879 it passed from Gisborne's widow to her second husband Benjamin Armitage, of a Mancunian manufacturing family, who carried out the Edwardian alterations; he used it as a summer residence. His son V.H.Armitage sold it to Col J.P.Hunt in the 1950s and it was last sold in April 1978 for £84,000.

Pevsner, 79; Tilley I (1892) 192; DAJ II (1880) 51 & VII (1885) 247; *Architectural History* XXXVIII (1995) 62-4; DLC 7/65; WELLS of Holme/V.1662; EYRE *sub* ARCHER-HOUBLON of Hallingbury/BLG (1952) 1289; TWIGGE/Glover II. 196; BARKER/FMG I. 214, III. 959 & 1040; GISBORNE/BCG (1891) 448 & Glover, II 246, 392; ARMITAGE/BLG (1952) 58.

HOLT HOUSE (II)

Two Dales   *Private residence*

Holt House, Two Dales, 1998.   M. Craven

Holt House, formerly The Holt, was built on a modest freehold portion of the former manor of Darley Nether Hall c. 1777-80, in fine ashlar of the very best Millstone Grit sandstone available in the county, Ashover Grit from Stancliffe Quarry; the plinth, however, is of coarse Ashover Grit from an adjacent outcrop. It succeeded a house called Toad Hole about which very little is known (unless the name derived from 'T'Owd Hall', referring to Darley Nether Hall i.e. the Old Hall corrupted in Derbyshire to T'owd, and which gave its name to a small hamlet to the west of the house). By the end of the seventeenth century, this moiety of the old manor had come by inheritance to a family called Watson, the heiress of which, Frances, married c. 1725 John Dakeyne, eldest son of Daniel, of Bonsall, grandson of Richard Dakeyne of Stubben Edge (*qv*), who had disinherited his eldest son, John, Daniel's father – a drastic method of showing parental disapproval seemingly rather popular in Derbyshire, as the experience of Sir John Rodes of Barlborough and Thomas Argyle of Heage (*qqv*) can testify.

John Dakeyne's elder son, Daniel (1733-1819) saw the benefits of the Sydnope Brook which flowed through his property, and in 1780 built a flax mill, at first worked by an ingenious hydraulic pump actuated by the considerable fall of the stream, and designed by himself. His teenage sons, James and Edward managed to improve this, and the Crown granted their father a patent on their behalf in 1795; later

the precocious pair went on to adapt one of the steam engines made in Derby by Thomas Gisborne's protege James Fox to great effect and in 1826 the mill was extensively rebuilt.

The third son, Daniel (1763-1806), was of a more cerebral bent and was a noted minor local poet and antiquary whose collections, at his premature death, found their way into the hands of his neighbour Sir Francis Sacheverel Darwin of Sydnope Hall (*qv*). Young Daniel it was who transported the Saxon cross shaft from Burley Fields nearby to the grounds of Holt House c. 1800, where it remained until transported to Bakewell churchyard in relatively recent times. The prosperity which Daniel *père* derived from his mills, however, persuaded him to set up as a banker as well, and the bank was (before its failure in 1801) for some years housed in his residence, Holt House. This was built in the c. 1780, to the design of an unknown architect, without doubt a local man, perhaps even Dakeyne himself. It has two storeys, the upper much less generous in height than the ground floor. The house was built on a rusticated plinth, and the west (entrance) front is of three bays under a parapet, moulded cornice and grooved frieze supported on skinny Ionic pilasters with very perfunctory capitals; these punctuate the angles (where they are paired) and the bays. The deep windows have plain surrounds and the entrance is almost without ornament, being reached via an elegant bifurcated sweeping stair to a high perron decorated with plain wrought-iron railings. The south front is of only two bays, and the angle pilasters here are single ones. To the east runs a later, lower service wing with a hipped roof, in contrast to that over the main block which is leaded and flat. This makes the combined north front the longest, which would seem incongruous.

The interior has restrained neo-classical plaster cornicing, but surprisingly little other ornament, but there is a very good walnut staircase with extremely slim balustrade. The dining room, however, sports a fine Hoptonwood stone firesurround inlaid with strips of Carrara marble inset with Ashford black marble, whereas the drawing room chimneypiece is of Carrara inlaid with Wedgwood type plaques.

The small and pretty park, enhanced by the agreeable setting, contains a gothick folly, probably the work of Daniel Dakeyne the younger, its date being c. 1800. The rear projection apparently dates from the same period, and was added to cope with the banking activities, originally conducted within the hall of the main house. The stables are also Gothick and are of one and a half storeys and with a 'datestone' proudly bearing the date 1416 – doubtless the work of the family antiquary!

Daniel Dakeyne was succeeded as proprietor of the works by his grandson, Daniel (the younger's) elder son Arthur (1801-1844), then aged eighteen. He was followed in his turn by his brother Charles who died childless in 1881 aged 79. It then passed to Rev. James Dearden Cannon of Peterhouse, who in 1862 had married Arthur's heiress Katherine. His brother Joseph Cannon (died 1899) ran the manufactory, by this time making a loss, closing it c. 1880. The last of the family to reside permanently (if briefly) at Holt House was Cannon's elder son, Arthur James Horatio (1863-1899), after which it was let on a sporadic basis. The house, 200 acre estate, the site of the mill and a quarry were sold by the Cannon trustees in 1924 to Austin Cookes with most of Two Dales, and thereafter the estate was gradually dismembered by sale, and much expansion of the village ensued. Cookes was succeeded by Edmund Hodgkinson on whose death the house and contents were sold in October 1932 being purchased by J. S. Wain. The house and park were purchased in 1965 by Nicholas Davie-Thornhill of Stanton-in-Peak, but was sold again in 1980, having been offered by the agents at £175,000. It was again for sale in June, 1988 at £375,000 and in 1994 with but 2.5 acres of grounds.

Pevsner 164-5; Glover, II. 364; DLC 1/68; DAKEYNE & CANNON/BFR (1896) 203-6; DAVIE-THORNHILL of Stanton/BLG (1972) 895.

HOMESTEAD (I)

Spondon   *Private Hotel*

The Homestead is one of six grade I listed buildings in the City of Derby, and is a very striking small seat erected by a rich tanner called John Antill – a member of a well established local family – in the early eighteenth century. It is dated 1740 IA on a rain-water head, but this date is not necessarily that of its building; it might be fifteen years or so earlier, indeed, it closely resembles Castlefields in style *(qv)*. The name of the architect is unknown, but its tall, four-square aspect might suggest someone like Richard Jackson, who did a very stylish job building the Derby Guildhall in 1731, and also built Walton Hall *(qv)*. Of three storeys and of brick with stone dressings, the entrance front is of five bays, the central one breaking slightly forward with rather busy quoins at the angles, of millstone grit sandstone, probably Rough Rock. There is a moulded cornice and coped top parapet, but the former is interrupted at the central bay to accommodate the top of a round-headed window with a broken pediment above. The entrance is a form of 'Venetian' with an arch with rusticated blocks and keyblock flanked by side lights ensigned with a triglyph frieze supported on Doric half columns. The fenestration has gauged brick lintels with stone grooved keyblocks identical to those on the Wardwick Tavern (formerly Alsop's Town House), Derby, datable to 1708. The entrance is reached up a flight of steps graced by wrought-iron balustrades with filigree lyre balusters, which can be confidently attributed to Robert Bakewell. The roof is tiled in slate.

The garden front is much plainer, but boasts a plain Venetian window to light the mezzanine on the main stairs. These, a very fine essay in timber, rise from the right side of the hall, which crosses the house in the usual manner. The hall ceiling, above the staircase, is decorated with superior plasterwork, some of the mouldings being identical with those in the bridal suite and staircase hall at The Friary, Derby and with the dining-room at 41 Friar Gate, and might suggest the work of one of the Denstones, father and son. The dining-room, left off the hall, is panelled throughout in contemporary style, as the old building manuals of the time suggest: panelling suffered least from the effect of tobacco smoke. Behind is the drawing-room, lit to the south by a recessed bay and graced by a Doric screen. Most of the original fireplaces remain, and the bedrooms are equally unspoilt except for the insertion of *en suite* bathrooms, done with as much sensitivity as one could expect, to some extent utilizing existing dressing-rooms. A pleasant, mainly Edwardian, stable block with pretty cupola and a coach house have been added to the east of the kitchen wing, itself of similar date and possibly the work of Alexander MacPherson of Derby. The whole is still set in attractive pleasure grounds, now regrettably hemmed in by the sprawl of unattractive post-war housing, built on the small park and part of the modest estate. Nice rusticated gate piers survive on Sitwell Street.

Homestead, Spondon, Derby, 1998   *M. Craven*

The builder, John Antill, is reputed never to have lived in the house, but his brother William did, until 1787. In that year it was sold to James Cade, who had married the daughter and ultimate co-heiress of the celebrated painter Joseph Wright of Derby (1735-1797) and the house was for very many years graced by several of his better pictures. The grandson of this match, Charles James Cade (1849-1917) was the last of the family to live there, moving away in 1911 and letting it to Sir Henry Fowler, Chief Mechanical Engineer of the Midland Railway, who removed to Spondon Hall *(qv)* in 1919 when it was offered for sale at what he considered to be too high a price. It was eventually sold in 1920 to British Celanese (Courtauld's) whereupon it became the residence of the site managing director Dr W.A.M. Soller. From the early 1950s, however, it was been reserved for the use of visiting dignitaries, having been recently and sensitively restored. In 1996 British Celanese was taken over, and the house was put on the market at £395,000, being purchased by Mr. & Mrs. A. Rutherford, who run it as a rather exclusive hotel and restaurant. The Homestead is of course doubly valuable as the only survivor of five minor country houses in Spondon Village: Field House *(qv)*, Spondon House, Spondon Hall *(qv)*, the Old Hall and the Grange having all gone over the past half-century.

Pevsner, 195; *The Cade Scrapbooks* MS 3 Vols., Derby Museum; Watson (1989) 43-4; Hughes (1997), 60-63; Chacksfield (2000) 39, 69; DLC 4/97; ANTILL/Derbyshire Family History Society, *Branch News* XLII; CADE/Derby Local Studies Library Box 57C; FOWLER/FD (1929) I. 708, WWD (1934) 69-70.

HOON RIDGE (II)

Private residence

Standing prominently on the low hills to the north of the road from Derby to Uttoxeter, this Arts-and-Crafts house, plainly influenced by the mature style of Sir Edwin Lutyens, makes an arresting site, with its prominent stacks, deep, sprocketed tile roof and pronounced eaves. Of harled brick, its south (garden) front is of five well-spaced bays and two storeys with a pair of prominent attic dormers, with others on east return and north. The end bays break forward under hipped roofs, that on the right being slightly more prominent and having a ground floor bow window. The narrower central bay breaks forward too, the first floor window aping an oriel over a door below, which gives access to the gardens from the dining room, the best proportioned room in a house where, generally, the interior spaces disappoint. The entrance is on the west under a wide protruding gabled bay, the main roof ridge forming a gablet above.

The hall itself is an odd space, L-shaped jinking to the left to gain access to the staff stair case, the main ascent being from an inner hall set rather inaccessibly behind the two reception rooms to the east of the garden front. Beyond the entrance is the service wing, which occupies the NW angle, but which was extended considerably in the 1970s when the house became a retirement home.

The house was built in 1907 to the designs of George Morley Eaton PRIBA of Derby on the site of Hoon Mount Farm, which it replaced, purchased from William Archer, and was set in over 800 acres of land. The client was Edmund Anthony Jefferson Maynard, JP, of a prominent gentry family from Chesterfield, who also had additional estates at Nether Padley, Matlock and near Chesterfield. Having had one of his three sons killed in action in the Great War and another having died young, the estate was sold on his death by the survivor, Capt. Anthony Lax Maynard, to Maj. Arthur Herbert Betterson. Most of the estate was disposed of in parcels, and in the 1960s it became a retirement home. It was sold, shorn of its stable block and cottages, with something over five acres of what were once notably fine gardens, for £395,000 in July 2000 and re-converted into a private house.

DM 5/11/1907; DET 28/10/2000; Information courtesy Mrs. I . M. Cook; MAYNARD/BLG (1952) 1749.

The south front of Hoon Ridge, 2000.   *Boxall, Brown & Jones*

HOPTON HALL (II)

Private residence

The Gell family are recorded as holding an estate at Hopton since at least 1327, and can be traced with varying degrees of certainty back to Robert Gyll, a juror at Wirksworth in 1209; his posterity grew rich on the proceeds of marketing lead. Ralph Gell, grandson of the Ralph recorded in 1327, who died in 1433, is designated in a charter as tenant in chief of Hopton. This fact raises puzzling issues, for the Gells claim to have married an heiress of a cadet branch of the de Hoptons who held the manor from c. 1200, it having been divided at some stage. It is clear, however, that the elder branch of de Hopton ended in an heiress who married Nicholas de Rollesley of the Rowsley family *(qv)* c. 1320, and that their heiress ultimately transmitted a portion of the manor to Sir William Kniveton. The congruence of date rather suggests that the de Hopton's heirs, the Rollesleys, sold up to the Gells in the mid-fourteenth century, and that the Gell's claim to a descent from the de Hoptons was a polite fiction. The Gells also claimed a wholly fictional descent from a Roman soldier called Gellius (a perfectly respectable Roman *gentilicium* as it happens). This came about in the late eighteenth century when Philip Gell unearthed a Derbyshire ware Romano-British pot during work to divert the road further from the front of the hall. In it was allegedly found a fragmentary inscription with the words: 'I F C / GELL / PRAE III COH / VI BRIT LEG' thereon. Even if the inscription had been earlier than the date of find, it does not stand up to critical prosopographical scrutiny; it makes a good yarn, however.

Clearly, a seat must have stood on or near the site of the present house for quite some time. The origins of the present house, however are said to lie in an H-shape manor house built in the later sixteenth century by Thomas, son of Ralph Gell who died in 1594. Yet there were but 13 hearths liable for tax in 1670, which although generous by some standards thereabouts, was not that many. The projecting wings of this house, between which was built a four-bay, two-storey infill topped by a giant segmental pediment in ashlar, are today brick, but contain fragmentary portions of stonework. The stone itself is Millstone Grit sandstone, probably Ashover Grit from either Alport or Kirk Ireton; the roofs are largely slate and old tile. The pedimented range has often been compared to that at Brizlincote Hall *(qv)*, yet it does not appear on a 1784 plan of the house and, with the two gabled bays either side of it, with their Venetian windows each awkwardly placed over simple sash, represents an infilling between two earlier projecting ranges. Indeed, from this plan, it is clear that the house had a great hall, entered by the east angle between the original south façade and the right hand gabled feature, suggesting the survival of a house dating from before the later 16th century. To the north were two projecting ranges, at least one of which was something of a tower, but gabled. In the 1670s, a two storey range was added to the west end forming a court on the south front and ending with a double gable with mullioned windows, the ground floor one also with a transom. The south façade had ten-light mullion and transom windows under a large pair of crow-stepped gables, with a smaller, plain one at the east end over the entrance bay. The east projection had a twelve light mullion and transom window on the ground floor.

The building programme which Philip Gell II (died 1795) initiated, probably immediately after this date, involved filling in the south front between the wings, with the easternmost one rebuilt to match a new one built contiguous with the 1670s range to the west, both being given paired Venetian windows under a Diocletian in the gable. At the same time, the entrance front was completely rebuilt in very plain style, two and a half storeys under a parapet, raised over the central three bays which broke forward slightly

The garden front of Hopton Hall, 1990.   M. Craven

from the two either side. The bay at the east end probably incorporated the 'tower'. The architect was very probably Thomas Gardner of Uttoxeter, for the entrance front is very much in his aggressively plain later style, although the Venetian windows on the south front seem rather slight for him. He certainly produced designs that were not proceeded with, and what was done may represent a scaled down compromise, for the treatment of the south gable ends certainly resembles the rebuilding he carried out for the Bill family at Farley Hall, Staffs., not long afterwards. The whole was done in brick, and stuccoed and grooved to resemble ashlar.

The next stage appears to date from c. 1820, when the central four bays on the south front were rebuilt with higher ground-floor rooms, and extended out slightly beyond the two 'Venetian' gabled ranges, the disparate heights being reconciled by a bold cornice over the first floor and the bold segmental pediment which is such a feature of the house today. At this stage, too a single sash replaced the ground floor Venetian window to the east, and a billiard room was provided in an asymmetrical single storey wing to the east beyond the gable. The lumpish, slightly Gothic porch appears to have been added to the north front around 1860, and at the turn of the 19th century, two pyramidally roofed projections in Arts-and-Crafts style were added either side of, and breaking markedly forward from, the entrance front.

Also in the 1780s the road was altered – leading to the discovery of the notorious Romano-British urn – and the crinkle-crankle wall with its curious 30ft high summerhouse was built. The latter is said to have been the result of Gell having told his workmen to keep building it upwards until he told them to stop; he then left for London, where he was delayed, returning to find that he had acquired a modest, if

windowless, brick tower with no floors! Set amongst the six sweeps of the garden wall, it makes, nevertheless, a fine sight, with its low pyramidal roof. The wall itself is of double thickness and warmed, as are the greenhouses, by heating flues. This method was also applied to the house, and the interior was redecorated. The front door has also a very fine fanlight above it, although the hall has been rebuilt – probably at the beginning of the twentieth century – using old and replica oak panelling; the staircase is entirely a confection of this period. One stunning piece was a fireplace with a six foot mantel shelf made entirely of Blue John, probably by Richard Brown of Derby; later this was removed during alterations of the Edwardian period (to be replaced by a 'Baronial' fireplace) and mounted on a neo-classical revival base to make an unique and agreeable side table. A turret clock by John Whitehurst III of Derby was fitted to the service wing shortly after Philip Gell died in 1842. Taller mullioned and transomed windows were also inserted in that part of the earlier house surviving at the west end of the garden front.

Although the house passed, with its estate – which stood at 3,744 acres in 1883 – through the Gells for over 600 years, all has not been plain sailing. When Sir Philip Gell, 3rd Bt, died in 1719, it passed to his sister Temperance, a lady of some munificence, who died unmarried in 1730, whereupon it all went to John, son of her sister Catherine who had married William Eyre of Highlow (qv). He assumed the surname and arms of Gell in 1730, and Philip Gell, who rebuilt the house, was his grandson. When he died, there was a sale of contents and he left the estate to his daughter and heiress Isabella who married William Pole Thornhill of Stanton Hall, Stanton-in-Peak (qv), MP for Derbyshire 1856-68, and they took the surname of Gell in 1828, but lived at Stanton and let Hopton. It stood empty, however, from 1849 to 1863 when Thornhill's heir, Henry Pole moved in, taking the surname and arms of Chandos-Pole-Gell.

Henry Gell died in 1902, and his son, Brig Henry Anthony Chandos-Pole-Gell did not live there long, being squeezed by rising costs. He let in 1904 to Philip Lyttleton Gell, eighth in descent from John Gell of Shottle, brother of Thomas, the father of the first baronet. This branch of the family had for some time been seated at Gatehouse, Wirksworth (qv) and their fortunes were in the ascendancy through diverse business interests. The lease of Hopton expired in 1918, when Gell sold up, the purchaser of the house and 800 acres being George Kay, a local colour merchant, who in 1926 sold on to P.L.Gell, the former lessee, but who died shortly afterwards, leaving it in turn his nephew P.V.W.Gell. He died in 1970, and his widow in October 1986, having adopted a philosophical attitude to the threatened encroachment of the Carsington reservoir – 'The park never did have a good lake!' Then, after three years of hesitation, Mrs Gell's two children, who were both settled in Worcestershire, decided to divide the house and contents. The former was sold to Mr Keck in October 1989 (qv Burnaston House), and the latter were disposed of in a great sale starting on 9 September that year, which included most of the furniture, and including all the relics of Sir John Franklin, the Arctic explorer, whose daughter was the mother of P.L.Gell. Much of the estate had been lost in 1978 to the Severn Trent Water Authority in order to be flooded for the vast reservoir then planned. The family retained the remainder, and the connection of this ancient Derbyshire family with their historic seat has been largely ended, to the benefit, mainly, of Messrs Sotheby. The house was sold again for £1.2M in April 1995. At the dawn of the twenty first century, with the blackest years for Country houses, between 1918 and 1979, past, Derbyshire can ill afford to lose any more historic estates; it is to be hoped that the break-up of Hopton will be the last such for a very long time.

Pevsner, 248; Colvin, 100; Woolley, 138, p. 205; Lysons, V. 297; DAJ XXVI (1904) 169; DLC 10-12/54, 8-9/62 & 9/80; Sotheby, Hopton Hall Sale Catalogue (sale 5-6/9/1989) pp.5-10; Derbys. CRO Gell MSS; Staffs. CRO, Bill MSS; CHANDOS-POLE-GELL/BLG (1937) 1823; GELL of Hopton/op.cit. (1972) 368.

HUNGRY BENTLEY HALL

see BENTLEY HALL

INGLEBY TOFT (II)

Private residence

Ingleby, a place endowed with a Norse name and Viking burials, is small, yet in 1086 was divided unequally four ways. Later, however, the manorial estate, perhaps held under the Earls of Chester by the Ingwardbys, was granted to the Priory of Repton in 1291. The heiress of Ingwardby married into the Abneys of Measham, and their seat at Ingleby was probably abandoned.

At the time of the building of the present Foremark Hall, however, a dower house was built in Ingleby, on an eminence below Knowle Hill *(qv)*, in 1760. The house is a square villa of brick with stone dressings of local Keuper sandstone, two storeys with attics and three by three bays. A cornice of curved modillions runs right round with a parapet above, upswept at the centre bay of the east (entrance) front which breaks forward, rising through both cornice and parapet to encompass an attic window and is crowned by a pediment: a very Palladian device. Behind the parapet the remainder of the attics are dormered in a slate mansard roof, the stacks above being grouped in four groups of four conjoined. The entrance is round-headed, rusticated and topped by a segmental pediment supported by Doric attached columns, flanked on either side by Venetian windows. The first floor windows have stone surrounds with triple keyblocks and the sills are supported on brackets. The remainder of the fenestration is plain, with gauged brick lintels. There are balls on the parapet at the angles.

The Venetian windows are echoed in the hall by a 'Venetian' screen separating the staircase hall, which is punctuated by Roman Doric columns. Beyond, there is a fine oak dog-leg staircase with three turned balusters per tread. Although dignified and seemly, this ensemble is, nevertheless, astonishingly small in scale. The south front contains the drawing-room, with a depressed arch two thirds of the way down, and a modest marble fireplace. That in the plainer dining-room is late Regency, in pencil-vein Sicilian marble. Here, however, the cornice is not a plain moulding, as in the drawing-room, but modillioned. Various brick outbuildings, including modest stables run, unusually, southwards from the west front. The whole is set in pretty pleasure grounds.

The architect was almost certainly David Hiorne of Warwick, whose design Pickford no doubt realized for the Burdetts, as at Foremark *(qv)*. Doubtless, Ingleby Toft (variously also called Ingleby House and Ingleby Hall) was also built by Pickford; the Venetian windows exactly match those at 44 Friar Gate, Derby, built a decade later. The doorcase is pure William Smith and thus surely David Hiorne, and replicates one at Kyre Park, Worcestershire. In the event, the house was not required for purposes of Dower when complete, and the Burdetts installed their gentleman-agent, Robert Greaves there, the brother of Joseph Greaves of Aston Lodge *(qv)*. He was very long-serving, and in the early nineteenth century was succeeded in his post and at Ingleby Toft by his son, R.C. Greaves. He was in turn succeeded by Col William Beresford, a kinsman, who had a lease with a generous acreage in the mid-nineteenth century. In the 1 920s it was the home of J.K. Ford of Derby, and it was sold off with a small freehold estate by the Church Commissioners after the Foremark estate was acquired by them in 1941. From the early 1960s it was the seat of the Notons and then the Wilds, but the land was progressively trimmed from it, until 1976, when A. Wild placed it on the market, it carried but 12 acres. It was sold in late 1979 to Mr & Mrs M. Harding , and they sold the house and garden only in June 1985 to the Drs J.R. Nash, who have tactfully restored this delightful house.

Ingleby Toft. *M. Craven*

Pevsner, 253; Woolley 108, p. 143; Lysons, V. 243; DLC 2-3/58; BURDETT, Bt./BP (1931) 411; GREAVES of MAYFIELD/BLG (1833/7) I. 306 & IV. 105; BERESFORD/ Beresford (1977) 47.

IRETON WOOD HALL (II)

Ireton Wood   *Private residence*

Ireton Wood is a small township within the parish of Kirk Ireton, which at the time of Domesday was an outlier of Wirksworth. The earliest mention of a family of any substance there is in a fine relating to one Henry Hervey of Ireton Wood in 1316. The first time we can be certain that the forerunner of the present house had come into existence is about 1630 when it was the seat (later taxed at four hearths) of one Thomas Catesby, perhaps a cadet of the gentle Northamptonshire family of which a homonym a generation before had been a leading conspirator in the

Ireton Wood Hall, c. 1912.   *M. Craven*

brick range of three bays, the entrance front having a projecting two-storey porch with ashlar (Millstone Grit sandstone) four centred arched entrance, sidelights, oriel window above, quoins and crow-stepped coped gable. A similar gable is to the left which has mullioned windows, and there is an octagonal two-storey tower with a tall spire, topped by a vane in wrought iron, probably by William Haslam of Derby. To the right of the entrance, there is no gable, but a ground floor canted bay topped by a pierced stone parapet. The end gable is also crow-stepped. One odd feature is that the fabric is composed of bricks set on edge. The roof, of Welsh slate, is oddly low-pitched, with two rows of four Tudor-style chimneys poking up behind it. The architect might have been H. I. Stevens of Derby; some detailing suggests his work, although the handling is in some ways awkward, when Stevens is usually more assured.

Henry Swingler doubtless found the house too small, and demolished most of the remaining seventeenth century work, replacing it with a large extension in a redder brick behind Leacroft's range. Although embellished with similar crow-stepped gables, this range has higher roofs, coarser detailing, and paired cambered headed plate glass sash windows, and dates from the 1890s. It was all set in a small but pretty park which, like that of neighbouring Blackwall Hall, takes advantage of the spectacularly hilly nature of the site. A service wing was also added to the north-east by the opulent Swingler.

One of the most striking features of Iretonwood is in fact at the entrance from the road. This has a pair of ashlar gatepiers in classical style having prominent caps with balls, set over a glyphic frieze. Hung between them is a very fine pair of wrought-iron gates indeed. Photographic evidence tells us they were made by William and Edwin Haslam of Derby (revivers of wrought-iron smithing there from c. 1848) using some pieces from a lost gate by Robert Bakewell, but with a good deal of their own work, too, characterized by scrolling work with repousse floral stops. This gate was once topped by an armorial: *a bend between two horses heads* (metal on colour); crest: *out of a coronet, a demi horse rampant holding between the hooves a cross crosslet fitchee;* motto: *'Fidelis usque ad mortem'* which has to date completely defied research. It originally photographed for Haslam when new, with the same piers, at an unknown location, but the gate was rescued in 1959 from beside the lodge at Barrow-on-Trent Hall *(qv; but the armorial does not relate to any of the families seated there)*, and was moved to Ireton Wood in 1959. It is listed II, but today the armorial has been replaced by a finial set on some rather awkward scrollwork.

Gunpowder Plot. The Ireton Wood Thomas was certainly styled "gentleman" and his widow, Elizabeth, quite possibly a local heiress, was living there at the time of the hearth tax assessment in 1670, seven years after her husband's death. The senior co-heiress brought it to Robert Mellor of Idridgehay, who let it to William, son of William Hayne of an Ireton Wood farming family, whose posterity went on to live at Green Hall, Ashbourne *(qv)*. In the eighteenth century, the house, was let to the Alsops, kin of the Mellors, the last of whom to live there being Robert Alsop 'Gent, and farmer' in 1829. Not so long after that, the house and estate were purchased by Frederick Richard Leacroft, son of Richard Becher Leacroft, a major landowner at Wirksworth and South Wingfield, but who lived at Wilderslow, in Derby. On his death, it passed to his brother, Rev. Charles Holcombe Leacroft, vicar of Brackenfield (1824-1899) better known to his parishioners as 'The Bishop of Brackenfield'. Having a vicarage, he let Ireton Wood Hall to Henry Swingler (1843-1906), son of Thomas, a Derby ironfounder. He was succeeded by his son, Norman Hugh Swingler (1879-1951), who seems to have acquired the freehold from the 'Bishop's' son, E.R.Leacroft of Rowberrow, Somerset, after 1925. It was sold in 1939-40, to Wilfrid Durose. Mr Durose died in 1971, and his widow in 1992. The house is now owned by their younger daughter, Carol, and her husband, Barry Sewards.

The present house was mainly built by F.R.Leacroft about 1865. To a very modest L-shaped seventeenth century house, probably built by Catesby, he added a two-storey

Woolley, 139, p.207; Bagshaw (1846) 368; Cox (1875) II. 499; Kelly (1908) 296; DAJ II (1880) 52 & XXV (1903) 204; CATESBY/Derby Local Studies Library, Ince MS 8022; MELLOR/Glover, II. 584; LEACROFT/V. Staffs. 1663 & Derby Local Studies Library, Box 57L; SWINGLER/ Walford (1909) 1062 & WWD (1934) 170.

KEDLESTON HALL (I)

Private residence/National Trust (open to public)

Kedleston Hall: the Francis Smith House, c. 1700.
Late Viscount Scarsdale

At the time of the Domesday survey, Kedleston was held by one Wulfbert under Henry de Ferrers. Yet by about 1100, it had come, perhaps by marriage, to Robert son of Hubert de Curzon, along with part of Twyford and Stenson, both linked by land holdings to Kedleston before 1066. Curzon was at the time seated at West Locking in Berkshire, but also acquired Croxall *(qv)* and built a seat there. Kedleston was later given to Alice de Somerville in dower by her son Richard Curzon of Croxall. It would seem that by this date a house had been built, as Kedleston had been granted to Thomas de Curzon by his brother Richard in 1198. From Thomas's son, Thomas, the place has descended since in unbroken male descent. When the Curzons of Croxall became extinct in the early seventeenth century *(qv)*, Kedleston became the seat of the senior branch of the family. The earliest house that is known about is one existing in about 1600, which appears to have been a standard late-sixteenth century H-shaped house of relatively large size. Certainly, 22 hearths were found taxable in 1664. By this date, however, the Curzons had gained hereditary honours from Charles I (whom, nevertheless, they failed to support in the Civil War,

allying themselves with Sir John Gell, their close kinsman); these consisted of no less than two baronetcies: one of Nova Scotia in 1636 and an English one granted five years later. The only relic of the earlier house appears to have been an oak settle of George II date incorporating five ornate mid-seventeenth century panels of mythological scenes and much other carving naming Sir John Curzon, 1st Bt., sold from Repton Hayes *(qv Repton Park)* in 1935, and subsequently lost.

Sir Nathaniel Curzon, 2nd Bt, at length decided on a new house, and this was designed and built by Francis Smith of Warwick from 1700 with further alterations of 1724 and 1727-34. The Smith house was one of his more opulent, and echoed Chicheley and Stoneleigh Abbey in having corner pavilions (as did contemporary Calke Abbey *qv*), a plan derived from Hooke's Ragley Hall, not far from Warwick. The house was in red brick with Keuper sandstone dressings, of two storeys and attics and nine by nine bays. The south front was entered via steps to a perron, thence under a triple arcaded loggia and so through the entrance, flanked by two recessed bays. The hall had two staircases off, the main one to the east, both in the pavilions. The other fronts all had five bays in the recessed centres, and the attics were set in the roof behind a parapet, the cornice of which was upheld by angle pilasters. The main entrance was to the north, and the hall on this side was larger than that to the south, with a pair of niches opposite the entrance; no doubt there was a wealth of fine stuccowork within. To east and west lay a picturesque assemblage of brick outbuildings, mainly of sixteenth and seventeenth century date. The house itself, being more compact than its successor, lay closer to the fourteenth century parish church.

Woolley is uncharacteristically forthcoming about the then new Kedleston: 'The house, having a large and well-wooded and well-stocked park, was built a few years ago, and is a very useful, noble pile of building of brick and stone on a little eminence which is pretty conspicuous. There may perhaps be some deficiency in the roof as some critics have reported, but the plan and two of the fronts are to be good building.' To complete the embellishment of the ensemble, Charles Bridgeman laid out new formal gardens and waterworks for Sir John Curzon, 3rd Bt., in 1722-26, for which James Gibbs designed the pavilions and, rather surprisingly,

The east front of Kedleston Hall, 1880s, by R. Keene.   *M. Craven*

a new house altogether! It was the death of Sir John, however, that prevented these from going ahead. It seems possible, in the light of Woolley's remarks that the house itself did have some serious drawback, otherwise why should Sir John allow himself to be talked into accepting a new design from Gibbs? However, he was succeeded by his brother, who appears to have had no such ambitions. He did, however, employ William Emes of Bowbridge Fields, Kirk Langley, from 1756 as gardener and to begin work on landscaping the park.

However, the fourth baronet died in 1758, and he was succeeded by Sir Nathaniel, 5th Bt, yet even before he died, things had begun to happen. The first was the arrival of James ('Athenian') Stuart, to produce plans for a new house, but he was soon ousted by Matthew Brettingham the elder, who (doubtless with the closest co-operation of his employer) staked out a vast new house, with central block containing state rooms, and four quadrants radiating therefrom, terminating in pavilions containing family accommodation, service accommodation, chapel and music rooms respectively in the north-east, northwest, south-west and south-east angles. Work began early in 1759, after Sir Nathaniel had first met Robert Adam, the family wing being started (and, indeed, completed) before the end of the year. The old house came down in two stages, in 1759 and 1761. Brettingham's assistant, Jason Harris, also began the Bath House in the Park, to service which a substantial inn was built to a design by Adam (but showing the unmistakable stamp of Brettingham in its facade) 1760-62. Indeed, whilst the family wing was building, Adam had made his first visit to Kedleston; yet he was not set on immediately, for although Brettingham was dispensed with before the end of the year, James Paine was brought in to continue the work. He produced a design for the entire north front, including three versions of the central block, one of which featured an Ionic hexastyle giant portico, a great hall and staterooms beyond. He completed the north-west pavilion early in 1760, but in April gave way grumpily to Adam who, as Paine had accepted Brettingham's wings but redesigned the centre section, accepted in his turn Paine's elevation, but neo-classicized it, moving it away from the Palladian detailing towards creating the ambience of the new language of classical architecture which Stuart and Revett had brought back from Greece.

In a sense, indeed, Curzon had turned a stylistic circle between meeting with Stuart in 1757 and employing Adam in 1760. Adam's north front was of a *piano nobile* built over a deep rustic with the top floor appearing as an attic storey. The whole was in ashlar, and the lowest storey was rusticated throughout. The stone was Rough Rock from Horsley Castle and Morley Moor, but the dressings are mainly of Keuper sandstone from Kirk Langley. The pavilions are each of five by three bays, beautifully proportioned, the central three on the front closer together, breaking forward beneath a pediment supported on Ionic half columns, and there are sill bands on both upper storeys. The quadrants, as well as the portico (which became Corinthian in Adam's scheme of things), are supported on arcading, and consist of five bays of one storey, with a single return bay flush with the pavilion adjacent, again divided by pilasters and topped by a plain parapet. The main block is of nine bays, with the windows of the *piano nobile* in pedimented surrounds balustraded at the sill, but Paine's lights to the three bays beneath the portico were replaced by tall niches with bas reliefs filling roundels above. There is a double band between the upper windows and the cornice and low, plain, parapet, and the portico is reached by a pair of dog-leg ramped staircases.

Whilst the north front is a magnificent facade, it is worth remembering that Adam, as so often in his *oeuvre*, was following and adapting the work of others; that this elevation is so impressive is a tribute to that special genius which he bore within him. Yet the south front was one he could tackle *ab initio*, and even without the intended wings (which it was decided not to proceed with on grounds of cost in 1764), it is the first great triumph of the neo-classical movement. Again nine bays, the central three are contained in a striking aedicule based closely on the Arch of Constantine at Rome, the arch itself blind and containing the entrance reached up a horseshoe flight of steps. The Corinthian columns support statues standing in front of a panelled parapet behind which rises the once five-stepped dome over the stunningly chaste saloon. The proposed wings were to have been single storey with five bays, the end and centre bays being recessed Venetian windows between tripartite ones separated by Ionic pilasters. A revised scheme envisaged losing the wings and sweeps, and attaching taller single-bay pavilions directly on to the main block. These were also to have had a Venetian window, with Diocletians both in the rustic and above the cornice, ensigned by Corinthian pilasters and with low pyramidal roofs. This addition of 1768 was to have contained a painted breakfast room and a bookroom, but in the event was also omitted, and the south front looks better for it.

It took until 1789 to complete the house, but the result was in many ways the greatest of Adam's works. The interiors were without exception stunning and original, enjoying a stylistic cohesion and a superfluity of excellency unmatched elsewhere. The great marble hall, which lies behind the north front is widely regarded as the finest Georgian interior in Europe, and although the point might be argued, its magnificence is beyond question. Not completed until 1778, its most striking feature is the double enfilade of seven and a half fluted Corinthian columns of red alabaster from Red Hill quarry, just over the border in Nottinghamshire, with a floor of Hoptonwood, highly polished. George Richardson adapted and supervised this work, although the original concept was (with the saloon beyond) Paine's. The stuccowork on the coved ceiling and walls is by Joseph Rose, and the overmantels are also by him, although the fireplaces themselves were executed by Joseph Pickford of Derby and carved by his friend and colleague, George Moneypenny. The cast-iron firebacks were obtained by Pickford from Francis Hurt's Alderwasley ironworks in 1775, and the firebaskets are after Adam's design. The niches in the hall contain antique sculpture by Matthew Brettingham junior, above which are *grisaille* panels of Homeric subjects after a scheme of Palladio. From the hall, one enters immediately into the rotunda which, being loftier, creates a stunning contrast to the cyclopean formality of the hall. The top-lit dome is coffered and large niches with shell heads (not dissimilar to the apse of the dining-room) occupy the spare space created by placing a round room behind a flat facade. The relationship between the two rooms was expatiated upon by Adam himself as being after the *atrium* and *vestibulum* of a grand Roman palace (presumably the Emperor Nero's *Domus Aureus*) in his book *The Ruins of Spalato*, and indeed, the fitting of the plan echoes Roman precedents exactly.

Each side of the two central rooms, there is an enfilade of lesser rooms (if that expression is really appropriate for such sumptuousness). The east and west fronts are of seven bays, and the former has a central Venetian window, lighting the drawing-room, which is approached via the music room, with its fine Schnetzler organ with Adam case, from the north. This window on the inside is carved in Chellaston alabaster, perhaps by Moneypenny or Richard Brown of

Above left: The Dining Room   *Derby Museum*
Above: The Rotunda   *Derby Museum*
Left: The Marble Hall   *M. Craven*

Derby, who produced a number of *objets de virtu* for the house in both Blue John and the lighter rusty-grained Chellaston alabaster. The fireplaces in both rooms are by Michael Spang and the furniture, as with much in the other staterooms, as supplied by John Linnell. Beyond the drawing-room is the more sombre library, with bookcasing by Adam made on site. On the west enfilade, the dining-room lies on the north front. The apse here, richly stuccoed, is to James Stuart's design of 1758 as modified by Adam, who designed the curving serving tables to fit. The painted ceiling is the work of three artists: Antonio Zucchi, William Hamilton and Henry Robert Morland, and four artists are represented in the wall panels: Zuccarelli, Snyders, Claude and Romanelli. The fireplace again is by Spang, with caryatids, and in Carrara marble in contrast to the enormous wine cooler in the apse, in Jasper, also to a design of Stuart's.

Thereafter one passes through the staircase hall (where the stucco work was done for Marquess Curzon in 1924), the state boudoir and into the state bedroom with its tester bed supported on posts in the form of palm trees, and its Blue John inlaid fire-surround, the mantel supporting a fine pair of obelisks in the same mineral, all by Brown. The boudoir is in fact more complex a space than the bedroom, as it lies adjacent to the wall of the saloon from which it is divided by a tripartite screen with a pierced segmental arch above the entablature perhaps again inspired by Diocletian's Palace at Split. The staircase itself has treads (unusually) of Ashover Grit from Stanton Moor.

Beneath the great hall is the so-called Caesar's Hall, which is aisled (now double aisled) and vaulted. From this leads the passages in the quadrants, one to the kitchens to the west, and the other to the family wing, within which are more fine,

but more restrained and intimate interiors, with good marble fireplaces by Joseph Pickford and George Moneypenny, who seems to have come from London where he encountered the former at Kedleston. Both were to contribute work on the detailing through to about 1778 on and off, and some of the garden buildings as yet unattributed may be by Pickford rather than George Richardson: certainly the south lodge might be as it closely apes the music room at Ashbourne Mansion *(qv)*. Moneypenny carved the decoration on several of Adam's garden buildings, including the fishing temple. Despite all this, Johnson, visiting in 1777, grumpily remarked that 'It would do very well for a town hall'.

The profusion of talent brought together by Adam to work at Kedleston was indeed a glittering array. Apart from Joseph Rose, Jason Harris and George Richardson, Joseph Hall of Derby was chief mason, and to help him with carving his fellow townsman Aeneas Evans (1728-77), and his kinsman Richard Brown. Hall's father, Elias, was also close kin to the Halls of Castleton who owned the Blue John mine there, and its availability to Brown enabled him to work with it freely. Matthew Boulton, also fleetingly involved providing ormolu door furniture, was deeply impressed by the Blue John, and thenceforth began to use it, mounting it in ormolu for candelabra, clock cases and pastille burners, in direct competition to the similar and equally fine products of Brown's works in Derby. Samuel Wyatt was there too, acting as clerk of works, and to him can be ascribed the vicarage of 1771-72, an unpretentious brick building with a pediment and blank arch containing part of its predecessor, built nearer to the house in 1761-62. He was succeeded by James Denstone of Derby *(qv Markeaton Hall)* who was sacked in

129

1771 by Curzon – since 1761 1st Lord Scarsdale – "for airing his Whiggish views", to be replaced by Pickford, who held the post until his own premature death in 1782.

The most important facet of this concatenation of talents was the effect of working under Adam or for Lord Scarsdale on an important group of Derby men: Pickford, Moneypenny, Hall, Brown, Emes, John Whitehurst and Joseph Wright. Wright painted Scarsdale's young son and was commissioned to do a landscape, whilst his childhood mentor and neighbour Whitehurst supplied at least two of his high-quality timepieces. It may be, too, that Whitehurst contributed to the hydraulic works needed by Adam to make the cascades operate successfully. An excavation by the Water Board in the 1960s revealed a buried hydraulic ram and conduits remarkably similar to those he installed for a similar purpose at Oulton Park, Cheshire for the Egertons a few years later, also in a park by Emes (who at Kedleston was displaced by Adam in 1760, but who conceived the lakes and cascades more or less as executed, working freelance until 1762) surrounding a house by Wyatt. It is not clear who put in the plumbing, either, but again, Whitehurst plumbed Clumber Park a decade later working with Stephen Wright, for the Duke of Newcastle, developing new and then revolutionary techniques. Yet from this time, Pickford, Moneypenny, Brown, Wright and Whitehurst either worked together or shared the same patrons, as did Benjamin and William Yates of Derby, who made the iron screen on the entrance front and gates at the North Lodge (by Adam, 1760-61) and went on to work with Pickford and Moneypenny at St Helen's, Derby in 1767. Another man who worked at the latter place with Pickford was the Derby *stuccadore* Abraham Denstone the younger. He also was working under Rose at Kedleston, and later went on to execute the ceiling at Derby Assembly Rooms (1773-74) to a design by Adam in a building put up by Pickford.

The stables were built by Samuel Wyatt, simplifying a design by Adam, in 1768, and this was followed by the bridge and cascade (1770-71), fishing temple and boathouse (1770-72), built concurrently with the lakes (completed 1775) and numerous other buildings which embellished the park. The ice house dates from 1759-60. Several of Adam's projected garden buildings were not, in fact carried out, including a 'Nabob's Palace', a quadrangular stable block with a 'fantastick' spire, a windmill, a Roman Milestone and a deer cote in the style of mosque. In the event, deer had to make do without this feature (unlike Sudbury qv) until the herd died out in 1842. The gardens (22 acres) and Park (494 acres) are today listed grade I. Beyond them, apart from the Kedleston Hotel (formerly Spa Inn, now much spoilt inside) lay a model farm by Adam at Little Ireton, once the seat of the Iretons and demolished by the third baronet in 1721 (qv), not executed as fully as intended, but impressive nevertheless with its stuccoed and pilastered elevations, oeuils-de-boeuf and a wonderful romantic dog-kennel nearby, although to whose design this last was built is quite unclear: it could easily be Pickford, no stranger to Gothick. The original village itself was cleared by Adam in order to make the park, and is now a scatter of largely nineteenth century cottages, a school and a sub-Wyattesque Smithy, outside the south lodge. The estate itself, incorporating Little Ireton and Farnah Hall (qv) was 9,606 acres in 1883.

In the eighteenth century, the Curzons produced a prominent younger branch, now represented by Earl Howe, and in 1898 George Nathaniel Curzon, the heir of fourth Lord Scarsdale, was created 1st Lord Curzon of Kedleston in the Irish Peerage. This was to enable him to become Viceroy of India (for which post a title was considered de rigeur), but at the same time to enable him to resume his career in the

House of Commons on his return. In 1911, however, he was further elevated (this time in the UK Peerage) as Earl Curzon and Viscount Scarsdale, the latter remaindered to the heirs male of his father. Ten years later, he was further created Marquess Curzon of Kedleston, with the Barony of Ravensdale (a place on the estate near Mugginton, once a Royal hunting lodge) with remainder to his daughters and their heirs male. That he narrowly missed becoming prime minister on the death of Bonar Law is said to have denied him a dukedom. On his death in 1925, he was succeeded as Baron and Viscount Scarsdale by his nephew, Richard, and in the Barony of Ravensdale by his elder daughter. Her nephew, Sir Nicholas Mosley, 7th Bt. (the eldest son of Lord Curzon's son-in-law Sir Oswald) is currently 3rd Lord Ravensdale. In 1979, Lord Scarsdale was succeeded by his nephew, Francis, who died in 2000.

The death of the 2nd Viscount, however, created a serious crisis for the future of Kedleston, for the sum of £2,500,000 was thereupon owing to the treasury in Capital Transfer Tax. The house and contents were offered *in lieu*, but it was not until 1984, after much uncertainty, that Lord Scarsdale was able to negotiate a satisfactory conclusion, and the National Trust took over the house with 300 acres of park and gardens, whilst the Curzons retained most of the remaining 5,700 acres of estate and the right to reside in the family wing. It is worth noting that the gardens were completely redesigned by Marquess Curzon from 1923, the work being carried out by William Barron and Son, of Borrowash. There were also extensive but mainly cosmetic additions and alterations made to the house, by S. G. Butler. The 12th century (and later) parish church which doubled for centuries as the chapel, was declared redundant in April 1983, two years after regular services ended.

That this superb house, contents and environs are happily preserved for the nation is a great tribute to the tenacity of Lord Scarsdale and the National Trust, for at the time of the crisis, it coincided with the possible break-up of Calke Abbey; and few then thought that both could be saved. That they were is a matter for a considerable rejoicing and in the case of Kedleston, a great tribute to the tenacity of the late Lord Scarsdale.

Pevsner, 25; Woolley, 95; Lysons, V. 194; Gibbs (1728) pl.LXX; Campbell IV (1767) pls. 35-51; Paine (1783) pls. 42-52; Cox (1877) III. 71-82; Hussey (1956) 70-8; Beard (1978) 8-10, 25; Harris (1987) *passim.*; Leach (1988) 89-91, 190-1; Saunders (1993) 66, 158, 173-4; Craven (1996) 72-83; Gomme (2001) 116-117, 532; CL (1901) 240-5, XXXIV (1913) 892-9, CLXIII (1978) 194, 262, 322; DLC 10-11/59; *Field* 13/8/84 p. 58-61; *Architectural History,* 40 (1997) 159-171; Kedleston Muniments (by kind permission of the late Lord Scarsdale, and with the considerable assistance of Mr. Leslie Harris); CURZON *sub* SCARSDALE, V./ BP (1999) II 2561-3.

KING'S NEWTON HALL (II*)

Private residence

King's Newton was originally part of Melbourne, and was early on divided into freeholds, spawning the gentle families of Wilne and Melbourne in the 15th century, and the rich yeoman families of Rivett and Hardinge in the sixteenth. The first member of the latter who comes to record is Nicholas Hardye a wealthy husbandman who in 1564 was granted the land in King's Newton which had been acquired from the dissolution of St Catherine's Chantry at Melbourne in

King's Newton Hall: the ruins of the old house c. 1895.
M. Craven

Edward VI's time by John Beaumont of Barrow, totalling about 46 acres. He also had land in Melbourne itself and an estate in Barton-in-Fabis, Nottinghamshire. His house was undoubtedly on the site of the present hall, and had two hearths, but eight rooms: hall, kitchen, bolting house, buttery, over parlour, servants' parlour, nether chamber and chamber over house. Thus it was probably a rather modest L-shaped house. His son, Robert, succeeded in 1582 and added a further parcel of freehold land before dying in 1596, being succeeded by his son Henry, the first of the family to describe himself a 'Gentleman'. His will (he died without issue in 1613) shows that the house had acquired a chamber built over the kitchen and a dairy, but was otherwise still served by only two hearths. His brother Nicholas inherited and added to his estate a portion of copyhold land held from the Earl of Huntingdon, the Lord of the manor, and his land totalled 108 acres or more on his death in 1631. However, his son Robert was but ten years old then, inheriting in 1642 when the Civil War had just broken out.

Robert Hardinge (the spelling of his name which he adopted) was closely linked to the Earls of Huntingdon, and was a prominent local cavalier, forming a friendship with his patron's dashing younger son, Lord Loughborough. Yet he managed to keep his estate intact and unencumbered during the republican period, marking the return of Charles II by building the arch over the local Holy Well in 1660. Two years later, his house was assessed at 11 hearths, and from the surviving fabric it is likely that he, rather than his father, built it, starting in 1660. It now had ten rooms on the ground floor, over cellars, and 13 on the floor above. Five of these, bedrooms, were designated by their colour schemes: yellow, white, green, red and blue. In its fabric, the house was of coursed rubble Millstone Grit sandstone (Ashover Grit from an adjacent outcrop), with distinctive fine and coarse banding. The plan was H-shaped, of two storeys and attics with cellarage at the front. The fenestration was of the mullion and transom cross type suspended from string courses on both floors, and this would tend to suggest a mid- rather than an early- seventeenth century date. The east and west fronts were of five bays, a pair of massive three-tiered chimney breasts being attached between bays two and three, and four and five; the symmetry thus achieved also points to a later date for its construction. Whether any fabric remained from the house standing in 1582 is unknown; if it was also stone built, it is possible, but if (as seems more likely) it was timber-framed, then it would have been entirely replaced.

The house must have undergone some rebuilding c. 1800, for the one surviving interior view shows 'pull-up' shutters to the windows, a later eighteenth century timber staircase with stick balusters and the diagonal fretted panelling, perhaps a survival from the sixteenth century house, cut down to dado level. The fireplace in the great hall had a bolection moulded surround but with an early Jacobean style adapted oak overmantel supported on later pilasters. Woolley in 1713 called it 'A good seat'.

Robert Hardinge was knighted for services rendered in the Civil War in 1674 and had a grant of arms based on those of the de Melbourne family whose adapted emblems he had disclaimed at the Visitation of 1662 and from which he claimed descent. He was succeeded by his son Robert (died 1709) and he in turn by his son, John, who made a prestigious marriage with Alice, daughter of Thomas Coke of Melbourne Hall (qv). Unfortunately they died without issue in 1729, and on his widow's death the estate (by this time several hundred acres in Nottinghamshire and Derbyshire) passed to the Cokes of Melbourne, who let it. We know that by 1729, the house had not grown, but had acquired a summerhouse. The Hardinge family survived in a cadet branch, descended from Gideon, brother of Robert (died 1709) who settled at Kingston upon Thames. His son, Robert, of Knowle Hill (qv), was MP for Eye, Suffolk, and this man's third son went to Ireland, being made a baronet in 1801 with remainder to his brothers and their issue male. His brother Henry became second baronet in 1826, and left three sons. The elder succeeded as baronet; the second, Capt George Hardinge, RN, became a naval hero, being granted a positive battlescene of a chief as augmentation to his arms (remaindered to his heirs male) and the third son, Field Marshal Sir Henry Hardinge was in 1846 created 1st Viscount Hardinge, and his descendant, another Field Marshal, Sir Charles, was in 1910 created 1st Viscount Hardinge of Penshurst.

The Cokes let the house to Francis, fourth son of John Mundy of Markeaton, and in 1757 he was succeed by his brother's son, Charles. In 1789 he in turn was followed by Edward Abney of Measham Hall, and then by William Jenney of the family later represented by the Harpur Crewes of Calke (qv), in 1835. Twenty-two years later it was in the occupation of Robert Green, but in 1859 an intense fire broke out and entirely gutted the house, leaving only the south, east and west walls standing to full height. Thereafter, it lay unoccupied for over 50 years, an ivy clad ruin.

Rescue came in the shape of a member of the Leicestershire gentry, George Ernest Paget, who engaged an unknown architect of strong Arts-and-Crafts inclinations to rebuild the house, almost certainly a Leicestershire man, perhaps Stockdale Harrison or even Ernest Gimson, who built or rebuilt several distinctive houses in the years up to 1908. The task was completed in 1910. The result was a house with a quite new ambience, although with a strong feel of the original. A new entrance was provided, with a low and wide four-centred arch fronting a recessed doorcase. New

Kings Newton Hall, c. 1914, as rebuilt.
M. Craven

131

windows were provided to match the old, the gables were raised in height and made more pointed, with small finals, additional ones being provided in the returns of the wings on the north (garden) front. The first floor string course was also removed and the centre of the west front endowed with a high window with two mullions and three transoms behind which lies the new staircase, an antiquarian design in oak; this bay is capped with new gable. New brick diamond stacks have been added on the slated roof. A datestone of 1560 can safely be disregarded. The pleasure grounds were laid out by William Barron & Son, and the Pagets had 40 acres of land with the house, which was sold on the death of Sir Cecil Paget's widow in spring 1979 to Mr Ernest Ottewell. The present opening of the courtyard is graced by a pair of fine wrought-iron gates in the Bakewell style, perhaps the work of Edwin Haslam of Derby. Lady Paget also commissioned the local sculptor Ronald Pope to execute a stone group, which was placed between the gates and the front of the house.

Pevsner, 259; Woolley 106, P. 141; Pilkington (1789) I.83; Lysons V. 83; Usher (1996) *passim.*; Melbourne Hall muniments; *Reliquary* I (1860-1) 16; HARDINGE, V./BP (1999) I. 1303-4; MUNDY *sub* CLARK-MAXWELL of Carruchan/BLG (1972) 636; PAGET, Bt./BP (1931) 1843.

KNOWLE HILL (II)

Ticknall　　　　　　　　　　*Landmark Trust property*

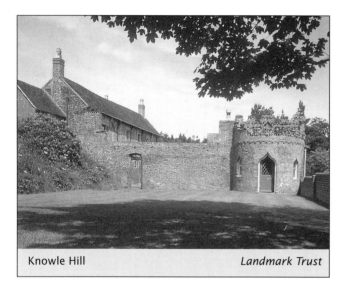

Knowle Hill　　　　　　　　　　*Landmark Trust*

In a very remote and unexpected place in the hills behind (that is, south of) Ingleby, lie the remains of the medieval seat of the Franceys family of Ticknall. In 1086, the King had sokeland in Ticknall, with part in Ingleby; Burton Abbey held some land there, and Nigel de Stafford had a manor with one carucate of soke in the jurisdiction of Repton.

Exactly which portion came to the Franceys family is not wholly clear; they inherited from a family called de Ticknall via the Beaufoys in the fourteenth century. Their house, at least by the time of its destruction, was 'very large and romantic' of timber-frame construction with gables, suggesting a sixteenth century date. It faced west on a bare ridge from which the ground fell gradually away towards Foremark. On the east side there was a ravine with a brook at its bottom, rising from the former home farm, now called Seven Spouts, after the spring which feeds it. This seat is associated with a romantic but entirely spurious 'severed

hand' legend, featuring a castle on the site (which never existed), a crusading husband (anachronistically called Sir Hugo de Burdett), a vile seducer and a tragic ending, the legacy being an alleged ghost.

In the late sixteenth century, the Franceys heiress married the head of the related house of Franceys of Ticknall, thus uniting the two estates, and the heiress of this marriage brought it to the Burdetts, who installed the Abells of Stapenhill as tenants. After the Civil War, the younger son of Sir Thomas Burdett 1st Bt, (a creation of 1618), Robert, briefly lived there before seeking his fortune in London and later in Ireland. It was then settled on Walter, third son of Sir Franceys Burdett, 2nd Bt, a barrister. He demolished the old house and rebuilt it nearer the edge of the ravine in an 'extraordinary mode of structure' regarded by his contemporaries as a 'curious house'. Unfortunately, there is little clue as to what it was like, nor why it was so extraordinary.

The next thing that happened was that Walter fell out with his family, and when he died unmarried, he left it to Robert Hardinge, MP, the son of Gideon Hardinge, (qv King's Newton) ancestor of the Viscounts Hardinge. On his death in 1758, it was repurchased by the Burdetts, who had commissioned David Hiorne of Warwick to build them a new seat at Foremark (qv). As a preliminary, they moved into Knowle Hill, and at the same time added a new range as well as commencing the landscaping of the park. The new range was built in the manner of a summerhouse literally on the lip of the ravine, a single storey to the west, and built on a substructure on the side where the ground falls sharply away. It is of five bays, of brick with Keuper sandstone dressings, and in gothick. The fenestration is ogiform in a simple moulding, and the interior doorcases within echo this. The main room, at the south end, had an Ashford Black marble bolection moulded fireplace (doubtless re-set from Burdett's house), stucco dado and glyphic frieze below the cornice; It was also once decorated in *trompe de l'oeuil*. It is quite possible that this range at Knowle Hill is the work of Joseph Pickford, then in full charge at Foremark. The use of local black marble for the fireplace is suggestive, as is the use of gothick, a style in which Pickford later worked.

As soon as Foremark was again habitable, in 1761, the old house at Knowle Hill was demolished, leaving only the summerhouse range and a timber-framed outbuilding parallel to the west, connected to form a courtyard by two walls. This range is, like the later range, of a single storey to the west (where it once faced the main house) and of two to the east, due again to the fall of the land. It is a timber-framed structure, plain, nogged with eighteenth century bricks and with a plain pitched roof supported on curvy brackets. It is of six bays, irregularly spaced, that nearest the south (on the east side) a door. The west side has but three bays, the central one also a door. The ground floor was formerly divided into two stables, once of four stalls each, with a brick floor, thus pointing to its original function. There are fragmentary remains of stone walling behind the brick towards the north end, and the ceiling beams are chamfered with scroll stops. Above there are four rooms with a passage along the two central ones on the west side, all floored in limeash. It would appear from an analysis of the fabric that the building is essentially seventeenth century, but reconstructed c. 1700. Today, the house platform of the original seat can be seen in the field in front of the existing structure, and a beech avenue leads towards it. The total absence of remains suggest that even Walter Burdett's house was perhaps at least partly timber-framed. The precisely rectangular field in which it stood was once walled about in stone (most of the eastern part remains) and the upper road, together with the straight canalized stream below the pond in the park suggest a mid-seventeenth century date for the site, doubtless imposed on an earlier layout.

The landscaping, extending to 44 acres, and carried out by an imaginative but unknown hand for Walter Burdett, made full use of the broken nature of the site, but it is clear that it was considerably re-ordered in the 1760s, when the function of the site changed, and that as William Emes was working on the park at Foremark, it is reasonable to suppose (in the absence of any direct surviving documentation relating thereto) that this ingenious and wildly romantic setting must be to a large extent to his credit; it must have been breath-taking once mature. It is undoubtedly the earliest Pictur-esque landscape in the area, if not further afield, making full use of the bosky chasm above which the house sits, and is akin to the 'Woodland Elysium' created for William Aislabie at Hackfall, Yorkshire if not closer in feel to that at Hafod. The chasm runs northwards towards the spreading flood plain of the Trent, visible in the distance, with Swarkestone Bridge just glimpsed to the north-east. This too is the panorama visible in Wright's painting of Peter Perez Burdett and his wife (of 1765), the cartographer leaning against a ruinous brick wall at the lip of the gorge. He is plainly conveying to those who looked at this stunning image that he is a Foremark Burdett (a fact that has yet to be proved) although he had not the affrontery to be posed before Foremark itself! Below the summerhouse range is a series of terraces, punctuated by ashlar niches, and opening therefrom on the uppermost, a brick passage, its walls lined with crevices to take sack bottles, expanding into a domed dining area underground. The DoE inspector who originally listed the structure suggested that this 'pos-sibly indicates the existence of a convivial society of some kind here'. In fact, the conviviality was that of Sir Robert Burdett, his family and extensive circle of friends, which, significantly, perhaps, included Sir Francis Dashwood of West Wycombe. Antiquarian style carved stone heads from this retreat survived 20 years ago in a rockery in Repton, and the whole park and lake at the northern end (now reduced to a soggy pond) encompassed 44 acres. Yet it may have been shaped on an earlier landscape, perhaps more formal, for Woolley says: 'Mr. Walter Burdett, an elderly bachelor... has made a very agreeable habitation... suitable to his humour and circumstances, where two Knowles or hills covered with woods and two pleasant valleys on each side, with two murmuring rivulets running along them, to which natural disposition he has added a great deal of art which renders it a most delightful place which, with his kind of hospitality, causeth it to be much resorted to.

Sic sciti laetantur Lares
Oh quis me geldis sub montibus Haemi
Sistat et ingenti ramorum proteget umbra'.

The question may well arise, then: is the subterranean dining cave, so typical of the later eighteenth century, and shades of Dashwood, the massive terraces and, indeed, the romantic parkland, the work of the plainly eccentric but likeable Walter Burdett? If so, then it must constitute an ensemble of even more importance than was previously perceived. Even if as we see it largely a creation of the 1760s, it is of no small significance. William Bagshaw Stevens, the wayward headmaster of Repton in the 1790s and tutor to the Burdett children was taken there for picnics and the Burdetts frequently resorted there on summer evenings in the years following.

By the 1900s it was reduced to a gamekeeper's cottage, but was used only intermittently after 1920, when the Burdetts moved permanently to their Wiltshire seat, Ramsbury. The last occupant was the eminent sculptor, Ronald Pope from 1943 to 1959. The house and park was sold to the Church Commissioners in 1942, and after 1960, the building fell swiftly into complete dereliction, the parkland became a wilderness, exuberantly overgrown and impenetrable, the lake diminished into an inconsequential, miry pond. The house was sold in 1978 for £8,000 for restoration, but little was done. Pressure (stimulated, it would be nice to think, by the account of the house in the 1984 edition of the present work) was brought to bear on national bodies, and in 1989 it was finally purchased by the Landmark Trust, who sensi-tively restored it (omitting the by then vanished tower, once china closets) from 1990 to 1993 under the direction of Rodney Mellville & Partners.

Pevsner, 341; Woolley 107, p.142; Britton & Brayley (1802) 402-3; Lysons V. 243; Davies (1811) 379-80; Bigsby (1854) 343; Hall (1863) 239-40; Bulmer (1895) 830; Galbraith (1965) 101; Haslam (1993) *passim.*; Usher (1993) *passim.*; DM 16/7/1758; DLC 1/56; FRANCEYS/V. 1569, 1611; BURDETT, Bt./BP (1931) 411; HARDINGE *sub* HARDINGE, V./BP (1999) I.1303-4.

LANGLEY HALL (II)

Kirk Langley   *Private residence*

Langley Hall, Kirk Langley, c. 1875, taken by R. Keene.
M. Craven

The history of Kirk and Meynell Langley is really rather complex, although some attempt at explaining it must be made in order to demonstrate why there are two seats in the village. At the time of the Domesday survey (1086) Lan-gley was held in chief by Ralph *fitz* Hubert, but we are not told who held it under him. By 1176 Robert de Meynell of Barlborough held it (or at least part of it) and 18 years later we find that Ralph fitz Nicholas held half a knight's fee there under the same Meynells and land in Killamarsh, also the patrimony of the Meynells. A suggestion is that Ralph may have married a sister of Robert de Meynell and that a moiety of Langley was settled on him. Ralph *fitz* Nicholas already held an estate at Thurvaston and was a member of the great Baronial house of de Stafford (*qv* Drakelow, Longford).

The moiety of Langley thus granted to the Fitz Nicholas family seems to have included the tenancy-in-chief for the daughter of the son of the grantee married Geoffrey de

Conquest, and the superior lordship, according to Rev. S.P.H.Statham, was held 'for a very long period' by their descendants, the Conquests of Loughton Conquest. A kinswoman brought the other half of this portion to the Lords Pipard, who held it until 1346, when it then passed to Sir Robert Twyford of Spondon, along with the estate of Thurvaston. It was probably this Sir Robert who built the house at Langley of which the vestiges were cleared away in two stages, in 1757 and 1834. Sir Robert's surviving son was rector of Mugginton from 1399, and left a natural son, Robert, who inherited all the estates, and on the death of his great-grandson, another Robert c. 1526, it all passed to the husband of his sister Ursula, Henry, second son of Peter Pole of Heage. Their great-grandson, German Pole, sold the estate in the sixteenth century to the Bassets of Blore, who also held the other original moiety, by now called Meynell Langley to distinguish it from the Twyford portion, called Kirk ('church') Langley.

From Robert de Meynell of Barlborough, eight generations of Meynells had held the other portion of Langley, along with Yeaveley, Winster and Tissington, and the marriage of Hugo Meynell with Joanna, daughter and heiress of Robert de la Warde of Lincolnshire brought about their adoption of the famous *vaire argent and sable* arms in lieu of a version of Longford with Ferrers-style horseshoes thereon. Ralph Meynell, who died in 1390 had a brother, William, on whom was settled the Yeaveley estate, and himself left four daughters and co-heiress, of whom three left issue, the elder taking Tissington, the youngest Newhall, and the third Meynell Langley. Her husband was Ralph Basset of Blore, whose descendant later purchased the other half of Langley from the Poles. Thence Langley was transmitted entire to Sir William Cavendish, 1st Duke of Newcastle KG, who married the heiress. However, his losses through his support of his sovereign during the Civil War forced him to sell it all in 1669 and it was purchased, appropriately enough, by Richard and Isaac Meynell, respectively sixth and seventh sons of Godfrey Meynell of Yeaveley, ninth in descent from William, brother of the last Meynell of Langley. The cost was £12,524 11s 6d. Richard died in 1716 without issue, and his brother's heiress sold it to her cousin Godfrey, grandson of Rev. Thomas Meynell, rector of Langley, and youngest brother of Richard and Isaac. The estate was re-divided on his death in 1758 between his sisters: Catherine, married to Alderman Gilbert Chesshyre of Derby and Dalbury, and Susannah, husband of Walter Lord of Little Chester, who got the present Meynell Langley estate.

Catherine Chesshyre's part was the old Kirk Langley manor house, apparently ruinous, and its immediate estate, although the remainder of the moiety had been sold off in freeholds at the time of the sale of the Duke of Newcastle. So inconsequential had the house become, even by Queen Anne's time, that Woolley did not even see fit to mention it.

Chesshyre died leaving a daughter and heiress who brought it to Robert Cheney of Ashford-in-the-Water (died 1809) for life only, for he was her second husband. In 1809 it passed to Rev. Henry Peach (1754-1833) of Derby, whose father had been Dorothy Chesshyre's first husband, having 'come from London' in the 1730s. Peach was a leading member of the prominent intellectual circle in Derby, being married to Mary Gretton, a niece of John Whitehurst FRS, and a friend of William Strutt, Joseph Pickford, and the Mundys. On his death, his son Thomas (1785-1874) relinquished the family town house in Full Street, Derby and from 1834 built a new seat at Langley which the family occupied down to 1956 when they removed to another house in the village. The house, now shorn of its estate, came shortly thereafter to D.F.Raybould of Derby, who sold it on

in April 1975. In 1993 it was the home of R. Grisenthwaite, Esq.

The house, partly demolished in 1758 was entirely replaced by Thomas Peach in 1833-34. It was medieval and largely built of Keuper sandstone, bearing a close resemblance to the surviving medieval wing of Norbury Hall (*qv*). A simple east-west range of brick with stone plinth and dressings had its great hall divided to create two upper chambers lit by a pair of 'three-light mullioned windows with four-centred heads to the left of a massive stepped chimney breast attached to the outer wall. To its right was a single two-light window. The end gable facing east was crow-stepped with a pair of cambered headed windows above a single one, all latterly adapted as sashes. To the west end had been added in 1539-41 by Sir William Bassett, a timber-framed and jettied range of three bays with small timber mullioned windows, including a door and, if the disposition of the fenestration is to be believed, the stairs. It would seem that when the original great hall was divided, this part was added to give access to the new first floor and to provide extra accommodation. An east range had also been added, running north, c. 1790 (doubtless as a replacement), with a single-storey brick portion punctuated by an archway into a rear courtyard and sporting a tripartite window between it and the medieval wing. A single-bay two-storey extension with a gable faced south on the same alignment, and was probably added in the seventeenth century. No record has survived of the interior. In 1670 it was taxed on eight hearths. It once (1498) had a domestic chapel of 28 x 20 feet, which went in the partial demolition in 1757. It was embellished with oak wainscot decorated with the armorials of the Bassets, a ceiling 'groined with oak in the gothic way' and a four-light east window. It also had a vestry, 'state room', lobby and stairs, no doubt giving access to a gallery.

Thomas Peach set about rebuilding on his father's death in 1833, and his architect was always supposed locally to have been A.W.N.Pugin, but proof is wanting and although interesting, the house shows little sign of so eminent a hand. Possibly it is the work of John Mason of Derby, who was associated with Pugin's Catholic church of St Mary, Derby, from 1838. Some parts of the old house remain within, including a medieval wall, and the south-east corner very much reflects the same portion of the house's predecessor, the east front being three bays, that to the north being set in a gable with a canted ground floor bay window. The south front, of two storeys and attics, is, like the rest of the house, of brick and local Keuper sandstone dressings, with five main bays. The narrow central bay breaks forward between a pair of octagonal angle buttresses which once rose up to the height of the gable finial as slim pinnacles (but have since been reduced) with the entrance between with a depressed pointed arch, and a single bay above, its window, like all the others, sashed and ensigned by a cranked hood mould. The outer gables are wider, with two bays under each, and the attic windows are simple vertical openings. The roof is of slate. An additional bay, probably later, sits uneasily on the left end of the facade which, with its quoins, centre-piece and sashes, has much charm but little scholarship. The rest, which included a water-tower, was mid-Victorian and the interior is largely a little plain and predictable. The remaining part of the service wing also seems to pre-date the main build, and may be seventeenth century work, but much has been removed. The whole is set on a ridge on the west side of the village and once was surrounded by an extensive and pretty park divided by the Meynells in 1757-58. The kitchen garden, now detached from the 1.60 acres surrounding the house, has a good eighteenth century crinkle-crankle wall.

Pevsner, 261; Woolley, 8 p.15; Lysons, V. 196; Notes courtesy D. F. Raybould, Esq.,MEYNELL/DAJ XLIX (1927) 302-16 & BLG (1965) 2012; PIPARD B./BDEB 429 & DAJ LVIII (1937) 57f.; TWYFORD/ DAJ XCIV (1974) 26-31 & XCVII (1977) 23-26; POLE of Langley/V.1569; CHESSHYRE/Derby Local Studies Library Ince MS 8022; CHENEY/BLG (1850/3) 87; PEACH/Walford (1871) 767 & *op. cit.* (1909) 858-9.

LEA HURST (II)

Lea   Home for elderly

Lea Hurst, c. 1950.   M. Craven

The deceptively large house was built on a portion of the moiety of the non-Domesday manor of Lea called Rolleston's Manor, the capital mansion of which is undoubtedly Lea Hall (*qv*). The core of this impressive house, of which Mrs.Gaskell wrote that 'it seems to be floating on air', is an early Jacobean building of Ashover Grit quarried from an adjacent outcrop. It faces almost north (as does Lea hall) and is of two storeys with a tall narrow projecting porch with an attic gable. The windows are mainly two-light mullions. The east end sports a wide gabled cross-wing containing two lower bays with again an attic, and windows similar to those on the main range with simple straight hood moulds. It is not wholly clear who built the house; was it a replacement for the then decaying Lea Hall? This is perhaps unlikely, as it passed at about the time Lea Hurst was built to the Peshalls, Staffordshire baronets and absentee landlords. In 1670 it paid tax on five hearths, and may have been the house of a yeoman farmer, Richard Marshall. Doubtless he was a tenant of the Peshalls. In 1648, the estate on which Lea Hurst stood was purchased (out of expropriation of the Royalist Peshalls' estates) by the puritan Spateman family, which lived at Road Nook Hall nearby (*qv*).

The house appears to have been let to Thomas Nightingale of Lea (1666-1735), a man who was the son of an Ashover smallholder, John Nightingale, and who started as a farm labourer to John Marshall of Lindway Lane Farm, Crich, quite possibly a kinsman of the former tenant of Lea Hurst, a fact which may have significance. He moved on to build a

modest fortune in lead smelting. This fortune was rapidly expanded by his second son, Peter, who later branched out into cotton spinning. He also married the co-heiress of Thomas Beighton of Wirksworth, another rich lead proprietor. In 1771 Peter Nightingale finally purchased the house and 1,381 acres of land, although his son, also Peter, removed to Rock House, Cromford (*qv*).

When Peter Nightingale II died in 1803, the estate and various industrial enterprises passed to his brother-in-law, George Evans of Cromford Bridge Hall (*qv*). His daughter and heiress, Mary had married William Shore of Tapton (of the Norton family *qv*) who died in 1822 leaving the Lea estate to his elder son William Edward Shore, who had assumed the surname and spurious armorial bearings of Nightingale in 1815. He immediately set about enlarging Lea Hurst as his seat in Derbyshire (he also owned Embley Park in Hampshire with 2,413 acres), to his own designs it is said, in 1822-23, and added to in the 1860s, probably by H. I. Stevens of Derby, who carried out Florence Nightingale's recommended alterations at the Derbyshire General Infirmary in Derby about this time. This effectively trebled the size of the house. A second, parallel range was added behind the old main range facing south of two bays, the west gable end having a ground floor canted bay topped by a balustrade. One attic dormer graces the roof, and beyond, in line with the original cross-wing, was a southward facing wing of two storeys and attics (due to the fall of the ground) effectively making the house cruciform in plan. This wing, like that to the west, sports a straight coped gable with a small finial. There is also a canted bay, in this instance of two storeys with classical fenestration topped by crenellations. A further wing extends to the east, of three bays and two gables over, with mullioned windows. This shows some signs of having its origins in the early eighteenth century. Beyond it is a lower two-storey range, again with a gable. To the north, another wing was added beyond the cross-wing, very low despite its two storeys, and perhaps adapted from a cottage or outbuilding of the original house. Sandwiched awkwardly between this and the seventeenth century cross-wing is a small domestic chapel with a decorated chancel window having a quatrefoil above a two-light mullion.

Inside, the spacious hall has a Hoptonwood stone staircase with an oak rail, and there is much use of oak for Jacobethan panelling and some reasonably exuberant plasterwork in the same style. The entire house is of ashlar Ashover Grit from an adjacent outcrop, with dressings similar. Most of the roof is, unfortunately, covered in concrete tiles.

At the time of the Regency rebuilding, the park was landscaped, making full use of the most spectacular natural topography to the south and west. There are several sets of rusticated stone gate piers scattered around it, with large ball finials, which look early eighteenth century. A pair of particularly satisfying wrought-iron gates open from the gardens to the park.

W E Nightingale died in 1874 leaving two daughters, the younger of whom was the redoubtable Florence, OM who died unmarried in 1910, who let Lea Hurst to Sir Joseph Lee. The estate was remaindered to Shore's sister and her husband, Samuel Smith and their son, William Shore Smith inherited Lea Hurst and Embley Park on Florence's death, and again, assumed the surname of Nightingale. His son and heir, Louis Hilary Shore Nightingale (1866-1940), left two sisters and co-heiresses, whose trustees sold the house with 395 acres in July 1946, and it was bought by the executors of Col. E S Holford in order to found a Florence Nightingale Memorial nursing home. This enlightened plan, however, ultimately came to nought, and the house was sold to William Bowmer of the Wheatsheaf, Whatstandwell for £7,000. He retained most of the land except the park, and transferred that and the house to the Royal Surgical Aid Society in 1951, who still run it as a home.

Pevsner, 196; Hall (1863) 81-4; *Nottinghamshire & Derbyshire Notes & Queries* IV. 7 p.105; D. Misc. IX pt. 5 (Spring 1982) 128-136 & IX pt. 11 (Autumn 1987); Derby Local Studies Library MS 3575; SPATEMAN of Road Nook/ V. 1662; NIGHTINGALE of Lea Hurst/FMG I. 142-3 & BLG (1937) 1685.

LEA WOOD HALL (II)

Holloway   *Private residence*

Lea Wood Hall: the garden front as built, c. 1900.   *M. Craven*

Lea Wood is perhaps the earliest domestic manifestation of the Arts and Crafts movement in Derbyshire and, if not wholly successful an essay in this style, is a striking building in an equally striking setting. It was built 1874-76 for Alfred M Alsop by W E Nesfield and Norman Shaw. The Alsops were descended from John, of Snitterton (died 1799), who had made a modest fortune in lead mining interests, and who left two sons, John, who took a lease of Lea Wood about 1800 from Peter Nightingale, and Anthony, barmaster of Wirksworth Liberty and occupant of Wensley Hall *(qv)*. John, of The Grove, Darley Dale *(qv)* died in 1831, being closely followed to the grave by his son, another John, four years later, and the latter's son migrated to Australia, leaving his property to his cousin, Alfred, the builder of the house. Alfred's father, Luke (died 1830) had married Lydia, daughter and heiress of Anthony Alsop of Wensley.

Most of Lea Wood Hall is built in coarse ashlar of Ashover

Grit as at Lea Hurst *(qv)* and is of two storeys. Its proportions are generally classical, yet the majority of the fenestration is mullioned and transomed, some in stone, others in timber, and its skyline, when built, was punctuated by lofty ornate stacks of grooved brick with moulded tops now, alas, wantonly truncated (no doubt to save on maintenance) to no good effect. The roof is attractively tiled. The south front also sports mathematical tiles, and there are full height canted timbered bays with hipped roofs and terracotta finials thereon: one at the SW angle, and another on the W. front. There are also plaster infillings with incised patterns and the whole sits beneath a high hipped roof.

The interior is well planned and decorated with Queen Anne Revival stucco, light oak paneling and some flamboyant chimneypieces. The grounds were landscaped by Arrow Smith of Tansley and in their heyday, with the intimate gardens (still with pre-Gertrude Jekyll formality) made a fine ensemble.

On A M Alsop's death, the house and grounds were sold to William Walker in 1891 and then to William Bennett Sudbury, son of an Ilkeston hosier and grandson to Alderman Francis Sudbury, one of the founding oligarchs of Ilkeston as a modern Borough. He was also kin to H. Tatham Sudbury, the noted Ilkeston architect of the early twentieth century. It was for sale with about eight acres for around £100,000 in July 1977, and again in April 1979 and 1981 before finding its present role.

Pevsner, 196; ALSOP/Derby Local Studies Library, Ince MS 8022 & D. Misc. IX 5 (Spring 1982) 128-36.

LITTLEOVER OLD HALL

Fire Service HQ

Littleover Old Hall is actually not so very old at all, having been erected in 1898 for a Derby contractor called Edward MacInnes, to designs by the capable Derby architect, Alexander MacPherson. Of brick with Keuper sandstone dressings, it is of two storeys with attics, quite large, irregular, with mullioned windows, some multi-transomed and mainly straight coped gables, although one prominent one on the east front is crow-stepped with a square paired stack projecting from it. The entrance front faces north and the porch, projecting quite dramatically to the right of the facade, has a small gable depressed into a high parapet over an upper chamber. The entrance itself is under a slightly depressed arch with a conforming hood mould into a galleried hall and an impressive billiard room is entered to the right from it via a staircase in oak, matching the panelling. To the left of the porch is a tall bay with an L-shaped range beyond. The south front is equally irregular with a canted bay of full height topped with a parapet and another small depressed gable looking rather like the coronet worn by Wonderwoman. To the left of it, a large Messenger & Company of Loughborough conservatory tucked skilfully into the south-west angle with the ballroom, is overlooked by two more disparate gables.

The remainder of the interior is rather predictable, with drawing, dining, music and morning rooms, but the grounds, laid out by William Barron & Son, were once attractive, although the former park began to be built over from the

Littleover Hall showing the south front in 1981. *D. Fraser*

1920s, which unfortunate development still continues, the demesne being overlooked by some particularly depressing mini-tower blocks set in a declivity south of the gardens beside a former beauty spot, The Hollow.

The estate at Littleover, an outlier of Burton Abbey's large manor of Mickleover in 1086, came in the fourteenth century to the Findernes, the heiress of which married Sir Richard Harpur of Swarkestone, by which match he inherited large estates in the Trent valley. Shortly afterwards, perhaps in the 1580s, his second son, another Sir Richard, was settled there, and presumably built a seat, unless the Findernes had already built one. Indeed, this is quite likely, for a fireplace and overmantel in Hoptonwood stone from the old Harpur seat survives in The Pastures *(qv)*, and although re-worked, would appear to be more Jacobean than Elizabethan. As Sir Richard only died in 1633, it is likely that he did build a new house. Unfortunately, we have no real idea of what this house was like except that tax was assessed in 1670 on 10 hearths and that Woolley later described it as 'A large old house and a good estate', set, according to Pilkington in a 'High and pleasant situation'. Hutton, writing in 1791, is more crushing: 'Nothing can be said in favour of this house except its antiquity: but everything may in favour of its situation, which is charming beyond conception'. Judging from the dimensions of the surviving fireplace, at least one room must have been reasonably lofty; perhaps a great hall. The house itself may well have been largely of brick with stone dressings.

The Harpur family continued at Littleover until the death aged 32 of John Harpur in 1754 when it passed to his sister's husband, Alderman Samuel Heathcote the younger, son of a like-named Derby municipal grandee noted for his Jacobite activities during the "'45". He unsuccessfully attempted to let it in 1760. Their son, Bache Heathcote, married the heiress of Josiah Cockshutt, builder of The Pastures nearby.

In the first decade of the nineteenth century, the Old Hall was rebuilt, reduced, and downgraded into a tenanted farm. All that was left was an L-shaped part, the south front consisting of a gabled cross-wing end-on and much rebuilt with irregular sash windows, and three bays of a range at right angles, refronted in Regency style with three bays and two storeys. The sashed windows had stone sill bands to relieve the brick of the remainder. T.Bache Heathcote removed to Rayleigh, in Devon about 1897, and sold it to MacInnes who pulled the old seat down 'Because dry rot had eaten so deeply into it'.

The present house, was tenanted during the 1920s by Arthur Manners, and sold, with 9.5 acres to Harold Walker, a wallpaper manufacturer from London, for £4,000 in 1934 after four years lying empty, and he brought in Barrons again to re-landscape the garden and grounds. During the Second World War, the stables and attached kennels were converted into a de-contamination centre in anticipation of gas attacks. In 1954 the house was sold for £12,500 to Rolls-Royce, as offices for their nuclear research programme, and new offices replaced the stable block. With the collapse of Rolls-Royce in 1971 it was sold by the liquidator for over £100,000 to the County Council for conversion to Fire Service HQ, when the authority managed to obtain consent for the development adjacent to The Hollow, previously denied to Mr. Walker for a far more modest affair! Today the house is disfigured by portacabins and a vast pylon bearing various aerials, satellite dishes, and so forth.

Woolley, 5 p.14; Pilkington (1789) II. 100; Hutton (1791) 300; Lysons, V. 228; DM 8/2/1760; Notes courtesy of the late Jim Walker; FINDERNE/*Reliquary* III (1862-3) 193-6 & DAJ CIII (1983) 91-7; HARPUR of Littleover/V.1662; HEATHCOTE of Derby/Heathcote (1899) 176-82; WALKER *sub* HIVES, B./BP (1999) I. 1416.

LOCKO PARK (II*)

Spondon   *Private residence*

Locko Park, Spondon, c. 1875 by R. Keene. *Derby Museum*

Spondon, of which parish and manor Locko was originally part, was held under the Ferrers at the time of Domesday, but seems to have become sub-divided later. Sometime after 1154 the Earl of Derby granted the advowson of Spondon church to the leper hospital of Burton Lazars, near Melton Mowbray, run by the Order of St Lazarus.

This grant was confirmed in 1180 and again by the Crown in 1200. It was followed by parcels of land granted by later Earls of Derby and by their successors, the Earls and Dukes of Lancaster. Consolidated, these formed an estate, which consisted of a manor in Spondon and that of (Over and Nether) Locko, a name thought by Dr Cox to derive from old french *lognes*: (rags) and *hay* (enclosure). Prof Cameron is inclined to think the first clement is from *Loca* (a lock), however. By 1296, a cell of Burton Lazars hospital had been founded at Locko, with its own hospital and chapel, all dedicated to St Mary Magdalene. After the foundation of the preceptory, most of the land was let: an estate in Upper Locko to the Sawley (or Sallow) family, and one in Nether Locko (with some land in Over Locko) to the Birds. Agnes, daughter of George Sawley, and heiress of his father Sir George, carried her portion to Thomas Pilkington along with Stanton-by-Dale, Sandiacre and part of Risley, later being sold to Faustinus Fielding. It passed from the latter's son, Anthony, to Alderman Edward Walker of Derby (mayor for the third time in 1681), whose heiress brought it to John Harpur of Littleover, who sold it to the Gilbert family.

The first Bird to settle at Locko was John, grandson of another John, who was MP for Derby in 1366 and 1377; the latter had an estate at Stanton-in-Peak, then sub-let to a branch of the Foljambes, which family also had a role in the confusing development of Locko: possibly when John became MP for Derby they swapped, for the Foljambes inherited yet another moiety of Locko from a family called Grene. Richard, younger son of this John, may have been the Richard Bird or Beard who founded the house of Beard of Beard Hall (*qv*). Another John, son of the first John recorded at Locko, was also MP Derby (in 1460), and his brother Ralph was settled at Over Locko. Woolley records a manor house there as late as 1713 with a small estate (probably that which came to the Harpurs) and a holy well dedicated to St Ann behind the house; it is not known precisely when it was demolished. Ralph's descendant, Thomas, living in 1611 left four daughters and co-heiresses whose progeny sold their fractions of this holding to the Gilberts. The Gilberts, previously of Barrow-on-Trent, came to Locko by sale, buying the Nether Locko estate from William Bird; Bird's widowed mother, Elizabeth Coke of Trusley, remarried William, father of the William Gilbert who purchased the estate.

Little is known of the Gilberts' house, nor is it known if it was on the site of, or incorporated anything of the old Lazar hospital, dissolved in 1539 and granted to John Dudley in 1544. His executors are believed to have sold to the Birds. Woolley wrote that Henry Gilbert (1659-1720) 'Has a very good stone house where (he) built a curious chapel of stone for the use of his family. . consecrated in 1673 . .' The house was taxed in 1662 on ten hearths, so was only of moderate size. Yet the chapel was (and is) a delightful classical building of two bays, in good quality ashlar of Keuper sandstone from an adjacent outcrop. The fenestration is round headed, with keyblocks, and the west entrance is similar, set under a large segmental pediment. Above is a blind balustrade carved with the words: 1670 DOMUS MEA VOCABITUR DOMUS ORATIONIS'. Inside there is much contemporary panelling and pews with a pretty carved pulpit and altar rail. The ceiling, also timber, is coffered, with pendentives at the angles and a group of plaster ones decorated with swags in

the centre, the remainder of the coffers being infilled with later stencilled decorations. This pretty building was the work of George Eaton of Etwall 1669-73, being consecrated 31 August of the latter year. The Gilberts were by marriage close kin of Shakespeare.

John Gilbert, son of Henry, sold the house and estate to Robert Ferne in 1721, and Ferne, no doubt succumbing to the sales pitch of the contractors in charge of building All Saints', Derby (1723-25) duly had Francis Smith of Warwick build him a new seat which was completed in 1737. This new house, contiguous to the north-east corner of Eaton's chapel, was of ashlar, Keuper sandstone again, nine by four bays and three storeys high, all under a parapet, balustraded over the bays. There are giant rusticated Tuscan pilasters at the angles, the windows have architraves and keyblocks and the parapet is decorated with urns. Within there is good, if perhaps rather predictable stucco, and a fine timber staircase off what was originally the hall, but the house was 'turned around' in 1853 and the space is now a drawing-room. This house and the estate were repurchased by John Gilbert before his death in 1773, by which time he had inherited the Thurgarton Priory estate in Nottinghamshire from his great uncle by marriage, John Cooper. His son, John Gilbert Cooper, later Gardiner (1751-1822), on his father's death, immediately sold it all again, this time to Richard Lowe (died 1785), fourth and surviving son of Vincent Lowe of Denby (*qv*), grown wealthy on the revenues of coal. On his death, it passed to the son of his aunt and heiress, William Drury, who adopted the additional surname and arms of Lowe by Royal Licence in 1790.

It is possible that the further alterations carried out by William Drury Lowe were actually begun by Richard Lowe. William Emes laid out the park (work continued by John Webb) and built the lake (fed by the stream from St Anne's Well, Over Locko Hall) in 1792, but the east Lodges look unmistakably like the work of Joseph Pickford, being neat pedimented buildings, with round headed windows set in blind arches – simplified versions of those he designed for Trentham, Staffordshire, in 1773. As Pickford died in 1782, the implication (given the attribution) is that work began a decade before. If the lodges are not by Pickford, they are either by Thomas Gardner (Pickford's former associate) or John Dodds who worked at Locko in 1792; the gothick icehouse may also be by the same hand. To balance the chapel, a drawing-room was added to the south-east angle of the Smith house in a convincing pastiche of the chapel's style, almost certainly by the same architect as was responsible for the lodges, and this too bore an inscription around the parapet: DOCTUS PHOEBI CHORUS ET MINERVIE LAUDES.

On the death of William Drury Lowe in 1827, the estate was inherited by his daughter and heiress, Mary Anne, wife of Robert Holden of Darley and Nuthall Temple (son of Pickford's client at Darley, *qv*). Their son added Drury to his name (before Holden) in 1853, whereupon he set about further improving the house at Locko. He called in Henry Isaac Stevens and enlarged the house greatly, latterly assisted by F.J.Robinson. The 18th century hall was floored over and decorative schemes were painted by Pietro Romoli, whom Drury Lowe had encountered on a visit to Florence in 1863, and who also decorated his Stevens-designed villa at Betws-y-Coed, Caerns. A *campanile* was added at the northwest angle, and a service court was made to the north of the Smith house, to which he added a Doric Portico in the south front. At the south-east angle, behind the new drawing-room, and running along the east front, he built a billiard-room and art gallery to display Drury Holden's extensive collection of Italian masters, all in a mild Italianate style with ceilings by

The Chapel at Locko Park, 1966. *Derbyshire Life*

Enrico Andreotti. The billiard room sports a particularly fine 18th century chimneypiece, probably from Nuthall Temple, Notts., and thus no doubt by Thomas Wright. The lavish dining room has a particularly arresting *palazzo* ambience, with more ceiling painting by Romoli, some *en grisaille* on medallions and modest *boiseries*. Although this range is always said to be Stevens's work, the bulk of it could be the work carried out by George Isborn a decade later, although the presence of a fine oak staircase by Joseph Barlow Robinson of Derby rather argues in favour of Stevens and Robinson.

The interior of the early eighteenth century part of the house was clearly re-done in the 1770s (Pickford again?), the drawing room especially, with richly carved dadoes and carved overdoors. However, the main staircase, re-built at its lower pitch, is of oak with two turned balusters per tread and carved tread ends, with a panelled and pilastered dado. Various parts of the house also have painting by C. di Baccivenuti, Stanley Payne, carving by J. B. Robinson, Edouard Lanteri, and Richard Brown of Derby.

Stevens was also responsible for the dignified west front, the triumphal arch and a free-standing tower with its John Smith turret clock to the west of the chapel. Another turret clock, believed to be by John Whitehurst the elder, graces the eighteenth century stable court to the northeast of the house. Whitehurst's nephew supplied a sundial for the kitchen garden terrace, an area graced with a mammoth and wonderfully architectonic glasshouse, built by Messenger of Loughborough in the 1890s, for William Drury Lowe, Drury Holden's son, who assumed the surname and arms of Lowe in lieu of Holden in 1884. He also laid out the formal gardens and arboretum at the same period with the help of William Barron & Son, who returned in 1918-24 to improve the gardens.

Locko is notable *par excellence* for the number of unrealised schemes drawn up over the nineteenth century.

These start with William Wilkins (1803), William Lees (1812), Brannah & Co. (a conservatory, 1844, probably built and replaced), through Alexander MacPherson of Derby (1883) to G.H.Morton and Arthur Edmund Street in 1895-96. On the death in 1993 of Capt P.J.B.Drury-Lowe, who made the house a noted venue for equestrian events, the house and 3,000 acre estate passed to his elder daughter and co-heiress, Lucy, Mrs. David Palmer.

Pevsner, 264-5; Colvin, 328, 607, 890, 1032; Woolley, 50, p.83; Cox (1877) III. 292-7; VCH (1905) II. 78; Craven, M. *Locko Park: A Survey* (Privately Commissioned, Derby 1993), *passim*; Gomme (2001) 165, 537; CL CXLV (1969) 1438, 1506, 1607; DAJ CXI (1991) 51-2; DET 24/7/1993; *Daily Telegraph* 2/8/1993; Nottingham University Library, Drury-Lowe MSS, Dr. A-P; BIRD/V. 1611; GILBERT of Locko/FMG III. 1028; FERNE/Derby Local Studies Library, Box 57F; LOWE of Denby/V. 1611 & *Reliquary* XI (1870-1) pl. xxxiv; DRURY-LOWE/BLG (1965) 1179; PALMER, B./BP (1999) II. 2188 & sub CHURCHILL,V/*op. cit.* I. 573.

LOMBERDALE HALL (II)

Youlgreave   *Private Residence*

The importance of Lomberdale Hall is that it was built – largely to his own designs – by the celebrated nineteenth century antiquary Thomas Bateman (1821-1861), and it still shows signs of his eccentric nature, despite his collections having been moved to the Museum at Sheffield in 1875 and 1893. Bateman was renowned for his – today highly unscientific – archaeology, which mainly consisted of opening every barrow, tumulus or other early feature he could find in Derbyshire, Staffordshire and Yorkshire, and magpying the finds away in cases at home, originally Middleton Hall *(qv)*, following in a more systematic way in the footsteps of his father, William Bateman, FSA.

Lomberdale Hall, 1997.   *M. Craven*

The house, built in 1844 about a mile SW of Youlgreave Church, of Carboniferous Limestone rock-faced ashlar, consists of a main five bay three storey range with a lower two storey one, irregular and receding, to the right. The main range is of two piles under a slated roof, partly obscured by a parapet set on a cornice of thinner ashlar with a grooved moulding, and all the angles terminate in what are effectively *antae* ending in tiny gabletted finials, whilst the gable ends themselves, mainly confined to the lower wing, are topped with thick two-dimensional trefoiled ones.

The fenestration may once have been sashed, but is now casemented and paned, set in rough architraves, with a course of similar ashlar strips between the ground and first floors, but here set on a flat band of Millstone Grit Sandstone. The lower wing also boasts some full height and canted bays, with a new entrance created, rather insequentially, in an angle under a flat entablature supported on a single rough pillar. This part is generally more architectonic, however and probably represents the "improvements" made in 1856-7, and Bateman may, on this occasion, have had the benefit of an architect rather than a skilled local mason to hand, perhaps, in view of the Bateman family's Mancunian connections, Richard Lane. Bagshaw recorded it as "A handsome stone mansion…in the walls of which at regular intervals are various grotesque and antique busts" and noted that Bateman had installed within it, along with the serried ranks of cases of antiquities, a tessellated pavement – presumably Roman, but not of Derbyshire provenance.

Although "strictly entailed" it passed at his death to his son, who quickly squandered his inheritance and sold the remaining collections to Sheffield Museum, that at Derby having pusillanimously turned them down – the beginning of an unfortunate habit. The house, spectacular setting and part of the estate, which was one with that of Middleton Hall *(qv)* were then sold to Thomas Walker, but by 1908 had been re-united with Middleton Hall by the Waterhouse family, who used it as a secondary residence. On the death of the long-widowed Mrs. Thomas Crompton Waterhouse in 1938 there was a contents sale, but her fifth son, Capt. The Rt. Hon. Charles Waterhouse took up residence there until his death in 1975. It was then acquired by the Stephensons from Hassop *(qv)* and is now the residence of Mr. Timothy Stephenson, the heir presumptive to the baronetcy.

Bateman (1855); Howarth (1899) v-vi; Hall (1863) 156, 283; Bagshaw (1846) 561; Bulmer (1895) 506; Youlgreave WI, *Youlgreave* (Bakewell, n. d.) 87; Bagshaw's Sale Catalogue 27-29/9/1938; BATEMAN/BLG (1894) 107-8; WATERHOUSE/*op. cit.* (1969) 863; STEPHENSON, Bt./ BP (1999) II. 2696.

LONG EATON HALL (II*)

Council offices

Long Eaton Hall, 1990.   *M. Craven*

Long Eaton Hall is a plain late eighteenth century gentleman's villa in brick with dressings of Crawshaw sandstone. The house is extremely plain, but what it lacks in ornament, it makes up for in the harmony of its proportions. Of brick with dressings of Crawshaw sandstone from Stanton-by-Dale, it has a main south (entrance) front of only three bays, two and a half storeys high with a modillion cornice and pediment over the central bay, which breaks slightly forward. There is a low stone parapet and a modest hipped tile roof behind. The west front is also of three bays, wider spaced, but with no movement in the facade. Although the east front is much shorter, it too is lighted by three windows, but beyond it lies a service wing, today much extended by its owners, the Erewash Borough Council. The entrance is through a pedimented tripartite stone doorcase, an almost exact replica of that provided at 41 Friar Gate, Derby (built 1769 by Joseph Pickford for himself), with the exception that the frieze of Freemasonic implements above the latter is, at Long Eaton merely chaste triglyphs. Above the entrance, the two windows are set in architraves, the one on the first floor eared; the remainder of the fenestration is plain under rubbed gauged brick lintels. The west front has, in the nineteenth century, acquired two dissimilar ground floor canted bays, which do nothing for that aspect of the building.

The entrance leads into an elegant hall from which rises a very fine well staircase of timber with three fluted balusters per tread and carved tread ends. The rail is ramped up at the angles, and although well made, the carpenter's pattern book must have been quite two generations out of date. The hall and stairwell are largely plain but sport an oak dado with blind fretwork and fairly lush cornices; both stairs and the latter closely resemble those at 27, Friar Gate, Derby, also a house attributable to Pickford and built in the same year as Long Eaton Hall: 1778.

Thus far, the hand of Pickford is plainly discernable at Long Eaton. In the former dining-room, opening off the hall to the east, is further proof: the room is finely proportioned and has a cornice from the same mould as Pickford's own dining-room in Derby. The fireplace is the crowning glory: of Carrara marble, it is inset with Blue John and very magnificently carved: certainly from the hand of George Moneypenny, Pickford's talented carver. It and the one at 41 Friar Gate are the only two Blue John embellished fire-surrounds to survive in buildings attributable to Pickford, although no doubt others once existed. This room was for many years the Council's the accounts office, the fireplace criminally obscured by the end of a payment counter, a situation now happily rectified. Opposite the dining-room is the morning room, separated from the drawing-room by the service staircase. On the first floor are two bedrooms and dressing-rooms, with a third large bedroom, perhaps originally a children's room.

Behind the house was once a quadrangular courtyard of outbuildings, coach house and stable, but these are mainly now removed. The whole is set in what were once pleasure grounds and a small park; now they are horribly municipalized and defaced by a closely contiguous superstore. The estate is quite built over, and has been since the mid-nineteenth century. An insensitive and frightful new development took place in 1988-9 right beside this pleasant house on the former west lawn. Clearly the Erewash Borough Council cares little for its few fine buildings, although the building was carefully restored in the 1990s, and now houses the bequest of paintings made by the original owner's descendant, Charles Sydney Howitt in 1921.

The house was built for Henry Howitt, a local landowner and farmer, whose ancestor, William, was taxed on four hearths in 1670 on approximately the same site. John's grandson sold up in 1839 in order to retire to Canada, and much of the modest estate was sold in parcels, which enabled modern Long Eaton to grow up around it. House and pleasure grounds went to the church and the building was used as a vicarage until 1873, when it was sold to Joseph Fletcher, a local lace manufacturer. His posterity sold it with about six acres to Long Eaton Urban District Council in 1921 for £14,000, and it has remained Council Offices ever since, and bears the Council's wartime Roll of honour on a pedimented plaque beside the entrance. Long Eaton UDC looked after it quite tolerably; it is their post-1974 successors who have proved themselves so unworthy.

Pevsner, 266; Colvin, 754; Woolley 26, pp.59-60; Reedman (1979) 49-51; Saunders (1993) 174; Matthew Constantine, Esq., pers. comm. 15/12/00; FLETCHER/ Fletcher (1957) Appendix.

LONGFORD HALL (II*)

Private residence

Longford Hall, with Pickford's alterations of 1762 (Keene, c. 1865).   M. Craven

The name Longford does not appear in the Domesday Book, but it is known that it grew out of a disparate settlement called Bupton, in which Henry de Ferrers's manors were held from him by the Saxon Elfin (ie Aelfwine) ancestor of the Brailsford family. Another portion was held by a family called FitzErcald, or more probably in the first years of the twelfth century or just before, by one Ercald, probably, like the earliest ancestor of the Okeovers and Knivetons, a man of Danish descent. Margaret, daughter and heiress of Ralph son of Ercald married Nicholas, son of Nigel de Stafford, bringing him an estate at Bupton. One son of this match was Ralph Fitz Nicholas, whose posterity held Langley (*qv*), the other was Nigel de Bupton who died in 1197, leaving a son, Oliver. The son of the latter, Nigel, was the first of this illustrious family to be called de Longford.

The family went on to great eminence in the county, although in the fifteenth century became very wild in the cause of the house of York, looting Elvaston Castle at one stage, the posse consisting of no less than six male members of the family! Sir Nicholas Longford probably built the

present house early in the sixteenth century. It consisted of two courtyards, two parallel ranges facing north and south being connected by a shorter range to the west and a cross range about two thirds of the distance towards the east, possibly leaving the entrance court open or screened. It was in brick with dressings of Keuper sandstone, probably quarried from Hollington or the Clifton-Norbury area but said to be from Uttoxeter. Each range was punctuated by four attached chimney breasts with tall stacks with gables between above two main storeys, the south front being 15 bays deployed in groups of three with quoins at the angles and on the chimney breasts.

The builder's brother, Thomas Longford, of Upton, Nottinghamshire, founded a branch (latterly called Langford) in that county, of whom George Langford of Nottingham, died 1715, is the last clear member. Another brother, John, was a Derby merchant, whose descendants held land at St Germans, Cornwall and Newton Solney about 1600, probably as heirs of Henry, brother of the first John, living 1521. There were two other brothers: Richard, of Mammerton, whose descendants were Longford farmers long after the main line died out, and William, whose heiress, Joan, married Sir Francis Gilbert of Youlgreave. The grandson of Nicholas Longford, another Nicholas, died without issue in 1610, whereupon the estates were sold by the then husbands of his two sisters, Francis Hastings of Cadbury, Somerset, and Humphrey Dethick of Newhall. This sale took place in 1622 and the purchaser was Clement, sixth son of Lord Chief Justice Coke, a Norfolk magnate whose descendants were raised to a baronetcy and later (twice) to the Earldom of Leicester.

Woolley says of the seat in 1713: 'A very large ancient seat... which (Sir Edward Coke) has very much improved, particularly by gardens and water courses'. This might suggest a garden in the style of Bretby (*qv*) and, given that Sir Edward (3rd and last baronet of Longford) had connections at Court, such is indeed possible. Subsequently the estate fluctuated between the senior representative of the Cokes and various cadet branches over the whole of its 300-year association with that family. An embellishment of 1737 was the installation of some very handsome wrought-iron gates to the gardens by Robert Bakewell of Derby, which Robert Coke ordered his agent, Mr. Wilkins, to have painted 'the same dark colour' as the palisading (into which they were set) 'For I like that colour much better than white for our works'. At the same time, and certainly in 1725, Samuel Taborer, also of Derby, was doing alterations here. In 1664, the Cokes had paid tax on a considerable 27 hearths.

On the death without issue of Sir Edward in 1727, the estate was left to Robert Coke to the exclusion of his senior kinsman, Sir Thomas Coke, subsequently created (in 1744) 1st Earl of Leicester, for whom Holkham Hall in Norfolk was then being built. The chief mason on his project was Joseph Pickford of Hyde Park Corner, uncle and guardian of the Derby architect of the same name, and indeed, the younger Pickford stayed at Longford in the earlier 1750s when visiting Fauld (Staffordshire) alabaster quarries to

In 1883, Richard Keene took this historic photograph of Longford Hall showing Emes's now vanished lake. *Derby Museum*

removed thence shortly afterwards to improve the landscape, a job which might well have been by Emes after his departure from Kedleston. This mill was damaged by fire some 30 years later and was rebuilt (it is said) by Sir Richard Arkwright, who apparently had a lease of it. It too is brick, quite tall with a double-recessed blind arch placed centrally. Pickford also provided a central pedimented stone doorcase at the entrance in the centre of the east front, which then still sported a great hall and a later tower, all lying behind Bakewell's gates which complete a dignified *cour d'honneur*. All the roofs are now slated.

Wenman Coke recommended Pickford to Lord Scarsdale and he perhaps in turn recommended Emes to Coke. Pickford went on to build the Derby Assembly rooms with recommendations from both parties who were major subscribers. Coke died in 1776, being succeeded by his son Thomas William Coke, who employed Samuel Wyatt to build a game larder, icehouse and conservatory, into which he put a magnificent Italian marble fountain, acquired on the Grand tour. He was later (in 1837) created 1st Earl of Leicester (of the second creation) and used Longford fairly extensively. He set about improvements to the house commensurate with his new elevated status, employing none other than Sir Francis Chantrey to put in and design ornate Neo-Grec plaster ceilings in some of the ground floor rooms, which Pickford had Georgianized but left relatively plain. At this time too the tower and great hall were demolished, the entrance front being reduced to a single storey. A four-bay brick conservatory was also added to the west end of the long south front and numerous other minor improvements made, work continuing until 1842. Early panelling was taken for re-use to Ingestre, but was burnt with that house in 1882.

From the mid-nineteenth century the house was used by younger sons: Hon E.K.W.Coke succeeding 1st Lord Leicester there and starting a successful cheese factory there in 1870, making Stilton. By 1883 the estate ran to 2,442 acres, but in 1920 it was all sold up, going to the Chesterfield born industrialist, Sir Charles Markham, Bt. By World War Two it was in the hands of H. Arthur Manners *(qv Littleover Old Hall)* and in his time, in 1942, the house suffered a serious fire. Edward Coke had made some effort to re-Tudorize the house, removing Pickford's ingenious flues and having groups of three brick Elizabethan-style stacks placed back on the chimney breasts. Markham had William Barron & Sons to redesign the gardens in 1924, widening the lake in the process. The fire, however, caused the abandonment of the house for a time, before the north range was almost entirely

select stone for his uncle to fit out the great hall at Holkham, Thomas Wilkins, junior, by then the Longford agent, being also agent for the quarries. In 1750 Robert Coke died childless leaving the estate to his sister's son Wenman Roberts, was by then already in residence at Longford, and he in 1759 also succeeded to Lord Leicester's Norfolk estates and assumed the surname and arms of Coke. In 1761, once he had completed Foremark *(qv)*, Pickford came to Longford, where he commenced the rebuilding of the house for Wenman Coke. He also married, less than a year later, Mary Wilkins, the agent's daughter, whose acquaintance-ship (and, no doubt, affections) he had gained during his visits some years before.

Pickford's brief was to turn the old early Tudor house into a convenient modern Georgian seat at minimal expense, a task which he set about with gusto. He removed the gables entirely, raising the walls to the height of their apices and inserting an attic half storey. Above this he placed a well-detailed triglyph frieze, cornice and balustrade which he decorated with balls and urns at the angles. He removed all the chimney stacks and incorporated the old breastwork into the balustrade, cleverly using them as small bays breaking forward at regular intervals. Likewise, he sashed all the windows and inserted a flat stone band above the ground and first floor ones, which he continued round the projecting chimney breasts. These were, however, not redundant, for Pickford built three free chimney stacks on the roof ridge of each range, connecting them to the tops of the old chimney breasts by terracotta exposed ducts; heaven knows if they drew adequately. The east ends were each of three bays but the balustrade stopped on the return facing the courtyard on both ranges, where the roof was eaved.

Pickford also built a large dignified stable block north of the house and east of the medieval church. This runs three sides round a courtyard open to the east and is of brick with stone dressings. It is of one high storey with attics except at the centrepiece, of three bays, which is raised another full storey and pedimented, with a Whitehurst turret clock in the tympanum. Each bay is set in a blind arch and the two end bays of each wing are also pedimented, a stone band running right round between the floors. Pickford was also probably responsible for the mill on the other side of Long Lane, the former Roman Road which marks the southern boundary of the park and first enclosed in 1258, near the village itself

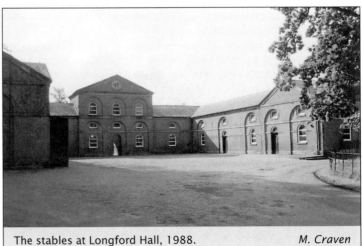

The stables at Longford Hall, 1988. *M. Craven*

demolished and the rest rehabilitated. Much of the park is now farmed, the lake has gone in favour of planting and the house and much of the estate were ultimately acquired by Mr D.Barnes, whose family still live there.

Pevsner, 268; Colvin, 753; Woolley, 87, p.125; Pilkington (1789) II. 264-7; Davies (1811) 412-3; Lysons, V. 199; Bagshaw (1846) 313; Bulmer (1895) 401; Jeayes (1906) No. 1557; Saunders (1993) 18-19, 51-2, 169; CL XVII (1905) 630; DLC 4-6/49, pp. 250-2; D. Misc. 7 pt. 4 (1975) 191-2; Northants. CRO Fermor H. Box K; Notes courtesy Brig. Arthur Trevor, DSO; LONGFORD of Longford/V. 1569, 1611; COKE, *sub* LEICESTER, E./BP (1999) II. 1671-4; MARKHAM, Bt./*op.cit.* II. 1864-5.

LONGSTONE HALL (II*)

Great Longstone   *Private residence*

Longstone Hall, 1987.   *M. Craven*

Longstone Hall is an example of that very rare Peakland phenomenon; a brick house. Only old Chatsworth, Parwich Hall and the Edensor Inn of the more substantial buildings compare in this respect. The bricks were made at The Willows, Great Longstone. Longstone Hall appears as a very four-square, tallish house of three storeys and three by three bays under a cornice and plain parapet with balls at the upswept angles. It is dated 1747, but looks a generation or so earlier. The stone quoins, cornice, blocking course and rusticated Tuscan entrance are all of Ashover Grit from Ball Cross quarry. The fenestration is in moulded architraves of the same material and the windows on the first floor appear to be somewhat taller than those below. This effect is more marked on the east front, mainly because the central first floor light was, from 1747 until early in the twentieth century, the front door, marked out by its bold moulding and depth. It formerly had a stone perron and a pair of sweeps up to it. The north side has been stepped forwards in two stages, and accommodates an earlier stair tower and some service accommodation and the west side is formed from the retained wing of the previous house, built of roughly coursed Carboniferous Limestone with dressings of Ashover Grit as the later build. This range ends in a gable with a ball finial, and contains (on the first floor) a panelled sitting room (lit by an eight-light mullioned and transomed window) oak wainscotted in Jacobean fashion, but with an

apparently earlier frieze of rather jolly looking writhing serpents.

It might be supposed that the house was built with a lofty first floor to make a *piano nobile,* and indeed, the main reception rooms of the house were so disposed until about 1960 when they were re-ordered on the ground floor, although not necessarily to good effect. In fact, close inspection of the fabric rather suggests that, far from 'closely resembling Eyam Hall' as most histories of the house aver, it was in fact a compact late Tudor or Jacobean tower house, with the main suite of rooms at first floor level as one would expect of such buildings. This impression is reinforced by the succession of seventeenth century fireplaces and the fact that the staircase – rebuilt in oak to a pleasing early eighteenth century pattern with three turned balusters per tread – ascends through the height of the house (on its north side) in what is in effect a tower in four stages, as at Tupton and Stydd (*qqv*). This staircase is lit throughout by a two-light mullioned window. In short, the house is clearly an eighteenth century recasing of a tower house built about 1600. In 1850 a wing of this earlier house – 'A beautiful old front so full of oriole windows...' – was taken down and replaced with the present service range, the oak wainscot being removed and stored for re-use by the agent, Robert Thornhill.

Inside, the hall runs right across the house to the foot of the staircase and has a two-compartment ceiling with sophisticated plaster mouldings. It is lined with re-positioned old oak panelling to half the height of the walls and is flagged in Hoptonwood stone. Opening from this is the present drawing-room, along the east front and dining-room opening to the west off the hall, containing a good gritstone bolection moulded fire surround with curt overmantel. The original drawing-room and dining-room are now occupied by the master bedroom and dressing-room with plaster cornicing which may go back to the time of the original house.

The grounds are mainly lawns, but with some gardens created in the present century with some flair, yet designed for limited upkeep. The walled kitchen garden now harbours the more prosaic tennis court and swimming pool. The modest park, now under cultivation, is gained from the road through a pair of ball-capped rusticated gritstone gatepiers with timber gates (perhaps later replacements for lost wrought-iron ones). A pair of this description are situated on the west driveway, and may have been (if not a second pair) moved from the south entrance. A courtyard to the west is formed of vernacular seventeenth century buildings with low three-light mullioned windows and stone slate roofs (those of the hall being leaded) built of limestone with gritstone dressings. To the north of this court is a larger detached range called the tithe barn, now converted as a large residence. It has a pitched tiled roof; its limestone walls have quoins at the angles and the central full-height opening, now rather predictably infilled with plate glass retained by treacle-coloured timber mullions and with staircase behind. Dove-holes mark the top of the walls in four levels. The restoration of this building, nevertheless, received a CPRE award and it is listed (II).

The builder of the eighteenth century house was John Wright, fifteenth in descent from John le Wright of Great Longstone, himself sixth in descent from the twelfth century originator of the family, Elias son of Matthew le Clerk, rector of Bakewell, common ancestor of the Wrights of Great Longstone, Eyam and Unthank as well as the Longsdons of Little Longstone (qv).

At the time of Domesday, Longstone was divided: part, later Great Longstone, was an outlier of the King's Manor of Ashford and part, now Little Longstone, was a manor of Henry de Ferrers'; Waltheof, who had early on held the former, was an ancestor of the Matthew mentioned above. The tower house was in all probability built shortly after he succeeded to the estate in 1605 by William Wright who died in 1656, leaving two sons. His great grandsons, the brothers Thomas and William, settled at Eaton Dovedale and Great Longstone respectively, the latter being left by William in 1711 to his third cousin once removed, John Wright of Eyam, who recased the house as we see it today at about the time of his marriage. On the death of his great grandson, William Henry in 1867, it passed to a nephew, George Thomas Wright, although in the intervening period it was let to Maj. William Carleil of Brosterfield from 1812, and his family lived there until 1870. The Wrights later resumed residence and the last of this distinguished family to live there was C.S.Wright, who sold it and retired to Eyam in the 1920s. It was then sold to Richard P. Goldschmidt, who set about removing the twin curving staircases leading to the former front door on the east, along with the stone perron, and moving the entrance down to the ground floor of the south front, initiating a process of lowering the accommodation completed around 1960 by the then new owner Francis, son of Sir George Kenning (1880-1956), the Clay Cross-born motor trade pioneer. It later passed to Francis Kenning's brother, George, who died in 1981. It was put on the market in May 1991 by his widow (who served as the first female High Sheriff of Derbyshire in 1988) but with planning permission for it to be divided.

The entrance front to Losehill Hall, c. 1912.   *M. Craven*

Designed by Charles Matthew Hadfield of Sheffield, and built in 1882, this rather uncompromising Jacobethan seat is of Carboniferous Limestone, cut to small flattish blocks brought to course with Millstone Grit sandstone dressings. It was built for a Manchester mill-owner, Robert Howe Ashton, a member of an old Castleton family, although the land on which the house was built is believed to have come to him through his marriage to Thomasina, daughter and co-heiress of Joseph Hall of Castleton, a kinsman of the eighteenth century Derby spar manufacturer Richard Brown and a member of the family associated with Castleton Hall (qv).

The house faces south across landscaped grounds with its service accommodation to the north, set on the lower slopes of the hill from which it takes its name. The south front is, like the entire house, irregular, of two storeys with attics, gabled and slate roofed. The west gable is larger than that set almost at the east end of this front, but has markedly less windows: two single ones with high transoms on the first floor over a single aperture made up of three similar lights, the upper floors having sill bands. The easterly gable has ten light mullioned and transomed windows of the same type on the main floors, with two bays between the gables, both of which break forward to varying degrees.

The east, entrance, front is essentially a south to north sequence of receding gables with miniscule finials, that to the left having a large canted ground floor bay, and that on the right being quite austere. Between is the angled, buttressed and balustraded entrance porch leading via a lobby to a full height gallery with stairs, lit beneath the gable with a Decorated Gothic window with hood mould.

The great hall is quite a noble space, with timbered roof, and with a gallery giving access to the bedrooms on the south side and ending in a short extension allowing the limitless views to the east to be seen through the great Gothic

The Oak Room, Longstone Hall, 1987.   *M. Craven*

Pevsner, 220; Lysons, V. 39; Tarn (1971) 29; Thornhill (1991) 14-16; WRIGHT of Longstone/BFR 645-7; CARLEIL/V. Yorks 1665, Walford (1861) 175 & (1871) 181; KENNING/BP (1956) 2537.

window. The stairs are oak, beautifully crafted in mid 17th century style with twisted balusters and ball finials on the newels. The remainder of the rooms have plenty of carved oak embellishments, including grand chimneypieces.

From his like-named father, a mine surveyor and lead proprietor, Ashton inherited a modest, but lead and fluor-spar-rich estate, to which his wife brought him more. On his death, his nephew and heir, Robert Howe Aspinwall decided to retain his own residence in the parish, the confusingly named Goosehill Hall, and sell Losehill, with its grounds and 25 acres, the buyer being Mansfield Brewery director Alfred William Chadburn, VD, JP.

In 1972 it was acquired by the Peak Park Joint Planning Board as the first residential study centre of a British National Park Authority, opened in the November of that year by HRH the Princess Royal. It has subsequently acquired various extensions, mainly to the west, and still competently sustains its role.

Information courtesy PPJPB and James Darwin, Esq.; ASHTON of Stoney Middleton/V.1662, Walford (1909) 35.

MACKWORTH CASTLE (II*)

Ruin

Mackworth Castle is the classic case of the castle that never was. From the road – a peaceful backwater east of the present Ashbourne Road, and once a Roman thoroughfare (part of Long Lane) – one sees a two-storey castellated gatehouse of later fifteenth century date, with bartizans at the angles and a central four-centred arch: plainly a gatehouse. Above the arch is a crocketed ogee moulding with three two-light mullioned windows above with once-cusped heads under rectangular drip-moulds. Beneath them is a simple string course, whilst above is a cornice sporting gargoyles beneath crenellations, one of which, between bays one and two, is adapted into a small octangular chimney with dwarf battlements, probably contemporary. The whole is well ashlared in Keuper sandstone from an adjacent outcrop. Four later and much rebuilt buttresses support this facade at regular intervals, but the returns are but a bay deep; the east side appears never to have been properly finished. Built out to the right is a pleasing two-storey eighteenth century cottage partly obscuring another original window and behind it a farm building of similar vintage, but extremely vernacular. A hooded fireplace is visible at first floor level.

Records mentioning the Mackworth family go back to the early part of the reign of Henry III, and most mentions of them consist of deeds enacted by or for the Touchet family, of Markeaton (qv), and indeed, the Mackworths appear to have been the hereditary stewards of that family. Thomas Mackworth, MP for Derbyshire in 1424 and 1429, was granted arms by John Touchet, Lord Audley; he died in 1445 having inherited in the right of his wife, Alice de Basing, the manor of Empingham, County Rutland, to which his posterity removed. Before then, Castle Farm, Mackworth probably marked the site of their house, doubtless timber-framed; two house platforms, in the field to its north are probably the

Mackworth Castle taken by R. Keene. Only a remnant now survives.   *Derby Museum*

remains of part of the complex. Henry, son of Thomas, outlived his son, who probably lived at Mackworth, and it may have been his son John (who died in 1489) that began work turning the old family home into an up-to-date stone manor house. Perhaps having built the gatehouse, he died, and his own son, succeeding to Empingham Hall as a minor, had no opportunity to continue the work. John Mackworth's younger brother Thomas, of Meole Brace, Shropshire, was ancestor of the present Mackworths, baronets, of Gnoll Castle. Fourth in descent from John was Sir Thomas Mackworth, created a baronet in 1619, a title which became extinct on the death in poverty of the 7th baronet, in 1803.

The first baronet's grandson, having lost all in the cause of the King during the Civil war, was forced to sell to the Curzons of Kedleston in 1655, by which time no mention of a house is made in the documents; doubtless it was dismantled for its materials. At some time in the eighteenth century, there appears to have been a rationalization of estate boundaries between Lord Scarsdale and F.N.C.Mundy of Markeaton under which the remnant of the Mackworth's estate appears to have returned to the ambit of Markeaton in return for land elsewhere. It passed from the Mundys to their heirs the Clark-Maxwells, who still hold it. Some restoration work is now urgently required.

Pevsner, 270; Woolley, 12 pp.17-8; Pilkington (1789) II. 111-3; Hutton (1791) 318-9; Lysons, V. 202; Lucas (1995) 54; MACKWORTH of Normanton, Bt./BDEB 331; MACKWORTH of Gnoll, Bt./BP (1999) II. 1811-13; CURZON *sub* SCARSDALE, V./*op.cit.* 2561-3; MUNDY *sub* CLARK-MAXWELL of Carruchan/BLG (1972) III. 636.

MAKENEY HOUSE

Hotel

This is the last Strutt family seat to have been built in Derbyshire, but has had a complex history. Around 1825 a villa was built for Anthony John Radford Strutt (1791-1875), son of Jedediah Strutt's second son, George Benson, called,

in the picturesque idiom of the day, Makeney Cottage, now Makeney Lodge. Perhaps the design was provided by Strutt's polymath uncle, William. Not far from this, but lower down, nearer the river, was another fairly substantial dwelling called Makeney House, the home of the Morley Park and Alderwasley ironmaster Charles Mold, who probably caused it to be built at about the time his partnership with his brother began in 1811. On the death of the brother, nearly forty years later, a series of legal disputes arose, and the house, on which there were two mortgages, was ultimately ordered to be sold. It was purchased in June 1856 by Strutt along with much of Mold's land, although he was unable to secure possession until August 1858.

At this juncture, Strutt appears to have commenced building a new seat for himself, which he called Makeney House, incorporating much of the Mold family home. It is possible that the architect was Edward Blore, who had designed his cousin Lord Belper's house in Nottinghamshire, Kingston Hall ten years before, but because later extensions have effectively masked this phase, it is impossible to be certain. The original house appears to have been as straightforward one of three full storeys, and forms the tallest element of the present house. As rebuilt it would appear to have been almost cruciform in plan, with a parapet with depressed gables, drip moulds over the windows and a two storey canted bay on the west.

Shortly after 1895, however, a new, long, double pile two storey range was then added towards the west ending in a pair of very plain gables, of six bays, punctuated by two chimney breasts and a full height bow with a hipped roof, with a new entrance created at the angle of the two ranges, the junction being marked by a tower with a gallery topped by a depressed ogiform cupola, very similar to that at Smalley Hall and Holbrook convalescent Home, thus the architect must have been Maurice Hunter of Belper. This expansion of the house took place as a result of the death in that year of Anthony Strutt, when it passed to his great-nephew George Herbert Strutt.

The house thereafter rather superseded Bridge Hill as the main residence of this branch of the family until 1935, when Arthur Strutt put it up for sale. It was bought by the Derbyshire County Council and the following year opened

Makeney House, c. 1904.

M. Craven

as the County Mental Deficiency Institution which, latterly under a more politically correct designation, it remained until closure in 1988. It was later sold and opened in 1992 as an hotel.

Giles (1993) 8; DAJ CVIII (1988) 87, 89-91; DM 9/11/1850; DRO C770c; PRO HO 151/2144/180v; MOLD/DAJ *op.cit.* 106-7; STRUTT of Bridge Hill/BLG (1952) 2441-2.

MAKENEY OLD HALL (II)

Private Residence

Makeney Old Hall prior to rebuildings, c. 1894. *M. Craven*

A rather modest, L-shaped yeoman's house of two storeys and attics, with straight coped gables and low mullioned windows with brief hood moulds, although some have been replaced by sashes. It was probably built in the late sixteenth century, and was certainly complete by 1614. Today, having been very thoroughly rebuilt in 1893, it is entirely of ashlar Ashover Grit from Duffield Bank, and the stone slate roof has given way to tile. Its owner at the time of its building was Richard Fletcher, whose heiress brought it to Vicesimus, youngest of the sons of Anthony Bradshaw of Duffield. His posterity were there until the early eighteenth century as gentlemen farmers in the original sense, but shortly afterwards the estate was acquired – no doubt by dubious methods – by John and Christopher Heath, sons of a Makeney copyholder, John (died 1765), latterly crooked Derby bankers. They went spectacularly bankrupt in March 1779, but not before one of their sisters had married a member of the dispossessed family: Vicesimus Bradshaw of Derby (the other was the mistress of Col. Revell of Carnfield, qv) who managed circuitously to re-acquire the property and under whose posterity the house was tenanted in the nineteenth century by the Bridges family. George Herbert Strutt bought it in 1893 and the rebuilding was almost certainly done by Maurice Hunter of Hunter and Woodhouse of Belper, who undertook almost all Strutt estate building work, Col. Hunter also doubling as agent. Strutt's tenant was, by a twist of fate, another Fletcher – Jonathan – who farmed there into the 1930s. For at least the last decade it has been the home of Mr. & Mrs. K. V. Gregory.

Lysons V lxxix; DM 1/4/1779, 24/3/1780; Sale Catalogue 1779 (DRO D3372 E25/1); BRADSHAW of Duffield & Makeney/DAJ XXV (1903) 13-72; HEATH/Derby Local Studies Library Box 57H; STRUTT of Belper/BLG (1952) 1362.

MARKEATON HALL (II)

Derby   *Demolished*

In 1086 Goscelin held Mackworth, Markeaton, Allestree and part of Kniveton from Hugh, Earl of Chester, this then being the latter's only Derbyshire holding, although it is believed that he had much more in the county prior to this. The estate appears to have been linked to the suburb of Wardwick, in Derby and its church of St Werburgh. There was also a church at Markeaton, but one hears no more of it after a while, and Mackworth Church was built by c. 1200, supplanting Markeaton, which may thereafter have become subsumed into the seat of Goscelin's descendants in the male line, the Touchets, as a chapel. Mention is made of a seat at Markeaton from very early in the twelfth century.

In 1405, John Touchet of Markeaton was summoned to Parliament as 4th Lord Audley of Heleigh, by virtue of his mother being the sister and heiress of the previous peer, Nicholas Audley, 3rd Lord Audley and 4th Lord Martin, and this situation continued until James Touchet, 7th Lord Audley, joined the so-called Cornish Insurrection of 1497 against Henry VII, as a consequence of which he was attainted, executed and had his estates forfeited the same year. It was not until 1512 that Henry VIII restored John his son in blood and honour, but the financial strain of those years, plus the cost of dancing attendance of the King at the Field of the Cloth of Gold forced the sale of the Derbyshire estates in 1516. George, great-grandson of John, Lord Audley, was active in Ireland and was created in 1617 Lord Audley of Orier and Earl of Castlehaven in the Peerage of that country, but his son was again attainted and executed in 1631. James Touchet, 3rd Earl, was restored in 1634, and the senior male line became extinct with the death of John Talbot Touchet, 18th Lord Audley and 8th Earl of Castlehaven in 1777. The medieval barony has since continued through female lines, but the Irish titles and this very ancient Derby family became extinct.

The purchaser of the Markeaton estates in 1516 was Sir John Mundy, of Checkendon, Oxfordshire, a goldsmith and Alderman of London, and Lord Mayor in 1522. He claimed a Derbyshire descent, the earliest member of the family having allegedly married Isabel, a daughter of Robert Eyre of Hope, whose grandson was granted an estate called Hawkesguard in Alstonefield, Staffordshire, before 1377. Of this family, Robert was returned to Parliament as a burgess for Derby in 1446. By his second wife, Juliana, daughter of William Browne, also Lord Mayor of London (1507 and 1513) and a man who also purchased a Derbyshire estate at (Stretton-en-le-Field), Sir John had six sons and four daughters, of whom the eldest, Vincent (later

Markeaton Hall: the garden front in 1961   *E. Saunders*

murdered), succeeded to Markeaton, whilst the Oxfordshire estates went to his daughter by his first wife.

Sir John Mundy appears to have built a new house at Markeaton. This was a largish building, very high indeed, an early prodigy house, for six bays reared high under three pointed gables above the ten small timbered gables ensigning the first floor, all set over a stone ground floor and basement. The west front seems to have been the main one, and a service wing of stone with a single gable was placed to the north. In front of this was a very extensive range of outbuildings, running equally, north-south before the house, being of timber framing over a stout stone plinth which was buttressed along its outside (west) side. To the north-west a separate stable court was built in similar style. Some stone

The old house at Markeaton Hall in 1753.   *Derby Museum*

plinthwork and a pair of buttresses still survive of this build today. How much of this lavish seat was incorporated from the house lived in by the Touchets is not known, however. The whole was walled about as was the immediate area of the house itself. Woolley described Markeaton as 'As an Ancient seat' and tax was paid on 11 hearths in 1662.

The Mundys were very numerous, branches becoming established at Allestree (and later at Shipley *qv*), Virginia, Darley Abbey, London, Bagshot, Quarndon, King's Newton *(qv)*, Rialton (Cornwall) and Alstonefield Manor. Of the senior line, Wrightson Mundy, seventh in descent from Vincent, became an MP, acquired a seat in Leicestershire, and thus enabled to move out, commissioned the replacement of his ancestor's old house at Markeaton. The new house was designed by James Denstone of Derby (1724-1780), son of that Abraham Denstone who executed the stucco work for the Derby Guildhall of 1731, and brother of the like-named man who was Joseph Pickford's *stuccadore*.

The house, finished by Denstone in 1755, faced east and west, like its predecessor. The east front was intended to be the entrance front, with five bays crowded under a pediment all between a pair of canted bays, the whole being of two storeys over a high basement. Either side of the central bay was a pair of entrance aedicules in Gibbs surrounds, the left one opening into a hall and the right hand one into a room with a corner fireplace with the secondary staircase behind. In practice, the arrangement was reversed, with the strange

pair of entrances being placed in the equivalent position on the west front, of nine bays, of which the central five broke slightly forward under a pediment containing an *oeuil-de-boeuf*. In this case one entered into the hall, the other door (to the left) bringing one into the staircase hall. The south front was of four bays with a canted full height bay to the south-east corner with central round headed windows as in those on the east front. A balancing canted bay graced the west end of the north front. The basement was arcaded and originally was to have had five bay wings either side of the main fronts, oddly without terminating pavilions, but this arrangement was mercifully not proceeded with. The house was in a particularly bright red brick with stone quoins and rusticated lintels, probably Rough Rock from Coxbench or Keuper sandstone from Bowbridge Fields. The house was topped by a cornice, parapet and bulgy urns at the angles and on the pediments.

The interior was quite striking, with especially fine stucco work, doubtless by Denstone's father (or brother), the best being in the music room, where there was a trophy of musical instruments as fine as any of its period. Some timber work and overmantels had been rescued from the old house, and the staircase was of cantilevered stone with wrought-iron lyre balusters by Benjamin Yates. Wrought iron was also used for delicate console tables in niches on the landing and in the hall. The drawing room was originally filled with Chinoiserie giltwood furniture in the manner of Thomas Chippendale.

Wrightson Mundy's son was Francis Noel Clarke Mundy (1739-1815), who, on his first wife's death, remarried his mother's cousin, Elizabeth Burdett of Foremark, in 1770. This appears to have spurred him on to embellish the house, for Mundy and his wife had set themselves up as serious patrons of the Whig intelligentsia, befriending or commissioning Joseph Wright, Erasmus Darwin, Richard Brown, John Whitehurst and others. He was known universally as 'French', she as 'The Duchess'. 'French' even indulged himself in a little poetry, his poem *Needwood Forest* receiving a delicate accolade from Anna Seward. Mundy also patronized Joseph Pickford, whom he employed to add a Grand Jury Room on to the Shire Hall during his high shrieval year (1772), and also to build an orangery and twin courtyard stable block, set off by a Palladian tower, for Markeaton Hall.

The latter was almost certainly built as a replacement for the early Tudor outbuildings and to some extent was built on their foundations. The orangery, south facing, is of nine bays, very striking, the end bays having Venetian windows in two-storey parapetted pavilions, the centre bay being a large French window with a segmental head projecting into a pedimented centrepiece. The intervening windows are also round headed, with an impost band in Keuper sandstone, and keyblocks, a feature which Pickford eschewed earlier in his career, but employed here, as at Ogston Hall. The roof today comes down over the cornice as eaves, but was originally set behind a parapet. The central pediment was once crowned by a beautiful weathervane by Benjamin Yates which vanished around 1970. The north facing side was plainer, but with a central brick Diocletian window much like that which graces the riding school at Calke. The west range ran from the orangery five bays to yet another pavilion, both having tripartite windows on this side and then ran north as a coach house with a central arch to reach the stables in the north court beyond. This last part was demolished by Derby Council in the 1950s, and the rest severely mauled.

At the same time as Pickford was building the orangery range (the east pavilion of which was fitted as a kitchen with the latest in ranges, built to the patent design of John Whitehurst, FRS, and connected to the basement of the Hall by a curving semi-subterranean passage) the park was being landscaped along the lines made fashionable by Lancelot Brown. The work was almost certainly undertaken by William Emes who from 1760 had a fine house, probably also by Denstone, and 63 acres on the estate called Bowbridge Fields (now Bowbridge House). The park covered most of the 185 acres of its medieval predecessor and included a serpentine lake (since widened for boating) a picturesque mill and cascade (which may have owed something to the hydraulic ingenuity of John Whitehurst), and wooded walks towards the boundaries, these last reached by a more formal one from the garden, running west. About 100 acres of the park is relentlessly flat, and in fact Emes did a good job creating the illusion that such was not the case.

Twenty years later, F.N.C.Mundy required more room in the house, and the four-bay, three-storey east extension was added in approximately matching style. It was probably the work of Samuel Brown of Derby, who also built Mundy's secondary seat, Wheathills, with Richard Leaper a few years later. This extension included a new east entrance with a distyle Tuscan portico with solid sides and a further cantilevered Hoptonwood stone staircase within, this time with cast-iron balusters of a strong scrolling vine design which crops up elsewhere in Derby and must be from an early local foundry. About a century later this entrance portico was replaced by a twin-domed glass affair by Messenger of Loughborough and was widely known thereafter by local people as 'Markeaton's Mae Wests'. The old porch was re-erected at the far end of the west walk where it remains as an eye-catcher.

The pets' cemetery in the park has an old gothic sandstone pinnacle set up as an obelisk; it may possibly be a fragment of the early house. Another embellishment was a marble fountain base from Venice brought back from the Grand tour by F.N.C.Mundy's son, Francis. This has a superstructure of Nuremburg ironwork and was set between the flights leading up to the perron on the west side of the house, but after 1964 was rescued and re-erected at The Rocks, Matlock Bath; it is now in Darley Park, nearby. Two superb cast-iron 'Warwick' urns by Handyside, the Derby founder, were erected at the top of the steps leading from the orangery to the park. These were removed 'for safe keeping' not long since, but are understood now to be missing.

The last Mundy, Francis Noel, died in 1903, and his widow remained at Markeaton until her own death in 1929: this was the formidable Emily Maria Georgiana, a grand-daughter of Lord Waterpark. On her death the whole estate of 2,765 acres reverted to Revd William Gilchrist Clark-Maxwell, grandson of Francis Mundy's sister Constance and W.H.Fox-Talbot, the pioneer photographer and a frequent visitor to Markeaton, where he interested another relative, Revd Edward Abney, in photography. Mrs Mundy had already, in her will, given the hall to the Derby County Borough Council '... for the purposes of an art gallery or museum or other municipal purpose of a similar character or as a recreation centre for the inhabitants of Derby' along with the 16 acres of gardens. Clark-Maxwell retained the estate but sold the park, totalling 211 acres, to the Council for £18,000. They then started out as they meant to go on by destroying the icehouse. Some of the conditions set out in Mrs Mundy's Deed of gift read: '1. Not to demolish or alter the mansion house during the lifetime of the grantor (Clark-Maxwell) without his consent and not to use the said house during such period for any other purpose than an art gallery or museum.'

Despite such good intentions, the house never really found a use before 1939 when it was commandeered by the Ministry of Defence for the billetting of soldiers, who grossly maltreated it. Minimal repairs were undertaken after the house was returned to municipal ownership after the war (1949) and all efforts to turn it into a gallery for the Borough's Joseph Wright paintings were defeated. In November 1964 this splendid house (as well as the late seventeenth century dower house) was carelessly swept away, one ancient Alderman declaring, during the debate that sealed its future, that it was a 'Shibboleth of the oppressive capital owning classes' and that it was better destroyed! All that remains are the neglected orangery (II), part of the stables, and a municipalized landscape studded with hideously utilitarian World War Two army buildings, disfiguring Emes's delightful park. It is truly a saga of which to be deeply ashamed, coming as it did within 18 months of the destruction of Darley Hall nearby by the same authority.

Pevsner (1953) 178; Colvin 300; Woolley 13, p.18; Pilkington (1789) II. 113-4; Hutton (1791) 316-7; Britton & Brayley (1802) 531; Davies (1811) 282; Neale (1824) I.; Cox IV (1879) 283-92; Saunders (1993) 67, 101, 173; DAJ XIX (1898) 93 & LI (1930) 115-140; DCR 20/12/1929, 21/3/1930; DM 4/4/1933; DET 25/12/1963, 1/1/1964, 1/2/1964, 6/2/1964, 27/11/1964; Derby Local Studies Library Mundy MSS Parcel 225 I-II; TOUCHET *sub* AUDLEY, B./BP (1970) 136-7, BDEP 535 & Darlington (1945) xxxii-xxxv; MUNDY/Vv. 1569, 1662 & *sub* CLARK-MAXWELL of Carruchan/BLG (1972) 636.

The Orangery/stables range and a (lost) Warwick urn of c. 1771, taken in 1967.   *Derby Museum*

MELBOURNE HALL (I)

Private residence

Melbourne Hall: the entrance front in 1980. M. Stanley

The ancient manor of Melbourne, a large one in the possession of the Crown in 1086, was early on granted to the Bishops of Carlisle, displaced from their see at regular intervals by the constant strife across the border between England and Scotland. Effectively, Melbourne was the seat of the Bishop. By the early thirteenth century, they had built a palace west of the church. To the south-east of the village lay an extensive Royal Park paled round over three and a half miles at a relatively early date, the remains of which are still visible in places. This was part of the lands attached to the large royal castle at Melbourne (qv) and which was ultimately sold to Sir Francis Needham in 1597.

The Bishop's Palace later was converted into a secular dwelling, called Beaulie Hall, demolished in 1821 and replaced by the plainish Regency Dower House. In 1629 a lease for three lives of the rectory and tithes of Melbourne was sold to Sir John Coke, Secretary of State to Charles I, younger son of Richard Coke of Trusley. He also purchased the former Royal Park from Sir Francis Needham at about the same time. At the expiry of the lease, the Cokes acquired the freehold of the former part of the property by Act of Parliament. Coke rebuilt a pre-existing house, perhaps a rectory, already made more habitable by Needham. This became a stone-built house of two ranges at right angles, of two storeys with attic gables, with some mullion and transomed cross windows. Little more is known about it except that portions of its fabric remain embedded in the present house.

Sir John Coke, although by then fairly aged, zealously supported the King during the Civil War, in stark contrast to his elder son and heir, also Sir John (1607-1650), who was a Parliamentary supporter and MP. In the event, by the Restoration, the younger Sir John's brother Thomas had died too, leaving the latter's son John in possession, but probably not resident in Melbourne, as his name fails to appear in the hearth tax records. He was succeeded by Rt Hon Thomas Coke, PC, who was Vice Chamberlain to Queen Anne and Teller of the Exchequer, who died in 1727. On inheriting Melbourne, he set about transforming it. His first move was to commission Sir William Wilson to design him a grand new house. In the event, this plan was not proceeded with, and looking at Wilson's clumsily drawn elevation, this need occasion no surprise. He proposed a long two-storey facade of 11 bays punctuated by a giant plain Ionic order with cross windows between. The wide central bay broke slightly forward under a segmental pediment, and two triangular pediments were each set one bay out either side of this. The attic storey, above the heavy cornice and frieze, was decorated with very French-looking *oeuils-de-boeuf* in curvy cartouches topped by statuary busts (bearing in mind that Wilson was first and foremost a sculptor). The entire facade as planned was to be almost 145 feet long.

In the event, Coke decided it would be safer to proceed piecemeal. William Gilks of Burton upon Trent began work improving the old house in 1706-08, returning to add to and recase the wing to the north in 1721-22. He was then replaced by Francis Smith of Warwick who in 1722 was building a now-vanished gatehouse drawn by 'Mr William Pickford an experienced man, to your honour's draft': in other words, Thomas Coke himself seems to have felt that he wished to design the improvements in outline, getting Gilks and then Smith to put his wishes into effect. A fragment of the ashlar gatehouse survives in an attic range (of brick) to the north. Smith also built a new east wing in 1725-26, all work being of two storeys with attics in coursed rubble of local Millstone Grit, equivalent to the Ashover Grit further north, but using Keuper sandstone from either Weston Cliff or Pistern Hill for the dressings and architraves.

Perhaps most significant was the transformation wrought upon the gardens, (listed grade I) beginning in 1699. Seventeen acres were laid out by George London and Thomas Coke, the contractor being William Cooke, the work reaching a climax in 1703. These gardens, running mainly south of the house to terminate in a semi-circular pond, were embellished with sculpture and ornaments. Lead statuary was made by John Nost (ordered in 1699), the very spectacular Vase of the Seasons being completed in 1705 for £100. Samuel Watson of Heanor also contributed two important vases. A further lead vase was added in 1989 to mark the association with the Australian City of Melbourne, thus keeping alive the tradition of beautifying the gardens, which are one of the few of this date to survive unchanged anywhere.

Most impressive of all has to be the wrought-iron arbour made by the Derby iron-smith Robert Bakewell, of 1708. Set on the far side of the pond from the house, terminating the vista therefrom, it is square in plan, set into a brick recess, topped with a dome and cupola, looking at once emphatic yet deliciously airy. There is much repousse embellishment, yet not too much, and as a first major work by this pupil of Tijou and Montigny, it is very impressive in its maturity. Bakewell was given the use of a modest house to the west of the hall, called Stone House (now commemorated by a plaque), where he had his forge. Once the commission was over (and relationships with Coke has somewhat cooled) Bakewell removed to Oakes's Yard, St Peter's Street, in Derby, where he continued his incomparable art until his death. He did, however, return to Melbourne in 1725 to make the terrace balustrade. Another Derby talent at work at this time was George Sorocold, the hydraulic engineer, and probable inspirer of Whitehurst in his own hydraulic endeavours more than a generation later. In 1703 he made the water supply work and created the ornamental pool beside which Bakewell's arbour stands. He also made the lake and the precursor of the famous Pool, itself created from the swamp-like morass of its neglected predecessor in 1820.

By Thomas Coke's death in 1727, the bulk of the works were complete, but his son and successor, George Lewis Coke, had not finished. Christopher Staveley of Melton was working on the interior of the house in 1740, and from then until 1744 William Smith of Warwick widened and completely reworked the south front, creating a wonderfully proportioned and cool facade of seven bays under a plain parapet with hipped roof behind. The central three bays break forward under a pediment adorned with a crisply carved armorial with a central entrance in a Gibbs surround, an artifice echoed in the ground floor window architraves; those above are in eared surrounds with keyblocks and sill brackets. There is also a plain band between the floors. William Jackson of Melton seems to have been the contractor for this work, done in near perfect Keuper sandstone ashlar work, and Joseph Hall the elder of Derby carved at least one chimney piece (for the great drawing-room, now the dining-room) and may have done other work.

Inside this part, there is a wide and light entrance hall (now

window was dropped to terrace level and made to open.

Lamb succeeded Coke in 1750, and died in 1768, being succeeded by his son, Sir Peniston, created in 1770 Lord Melbourne of Kilmore and 11 years later Viscount Melbourne, in the Irish Peerage. In 1815 he also received the UK barony of Melbourne of Melbourne, County Derby. He was succeeded by the 2nd Viscount, the eminent Prime Minister (with a short interruption) from 1834-41. His brother, a distinguished diplomatist, was created 1st Lord Beauvale of Beauvale, Nottinghamshire (another family estate, as was Over Haddon, Derbyshire) in 1839, inheriting his brother's honours in 1848, and dying six years later without issue when all the honours became extinct. His sister, Emily Mary,

Robert Bakewell's arbour taken in 1981.
Derby Museum

Taken by R. Keene prior to 1884: the staircase hall at Melbourne Hall.
M. Craven

not used as such) with a double depressed arched screen, beyond which rises the very fine timber staircase with one twisted and two turned balusters per tread and carved tread ends. There is fine, but restrained, plasterwork and plenty of good joinery. In the west wing, consisting of very early brickwork mixed with random rubble (probably part of Sir John Coke I's house), there is some Jacobean and later seventeenth century panelling, again from the early house. However, the wealth of Jacobean panelling and the exuberant overmantel in the present dining-room was brought in the nineteenth century from old Brocket Hall, Hertfordshire, by Sir Matthew Lamb, 1st Bt, the rich attorney who contrived to marry George Lewis Coke's sister and heiress. He had previously acquired Brocket, rebuilt for him by James Paine, and where Joseph Pickford of Derby appears to have built at least one pair of neo-classical lodges and to have done other unspecified work. Pickford also worked at Melbourne, refitting one reception room (which, is unclear) and working on the roof. In the nineteenth century, the deep *cour d'honneur* formed by the two projecting west wings, built by Francis Smith, was covered in to make a billiard room and occasional entrance. At the same time the library

passed the estates to Peter, 5th Earl Cowper, whose grandfather had been created a Prince of the Holy Roman Empire in 1778, probably as a result of the Archduke Leopold's affection for Countess Cowper, which was a deal closer than convention (or her husband) could stomach. It also ensured that Lady Cowper's two sons, Leopold and Augustus, could enjoy the same status that any other natural children of a Holy Roman emperor could expect. The 7th and last Earl Cowper died without issue in 1905, when the 3,700 acre estate passed via his sister, Lady Amabel Cowper to her husband, Lord Walter Talbot Kerr, a son of the Marquis of Lothian, and today it is the splendid seat of Lord Ralph Kerr, younger son of the present Marquis, his wife and family.

Pevsner 278; Colvin, 264, 410, 753, 865, 888, 903; Lysons, V. 209; Innes-Smith (1972) 24-27; Saunders & Usher (1987) *passim.*; Usher (1993) *passim.*; Gomme (2001) 241-3, 495-6, 538; CL LXIII (1928) 526; *Journal of the Georgian Group* 1988 pp.48-61; Melbourne Hall muniments, courtesy Lord Ralph Kerr; COKE/V.1662 & DAJ XI (1889) 54-67 7 XIII (1891) 143-4; MELBOURNE, V./BDEP 312; COWPER, E./ CP 394-7; LOTHIAN, M./BP (1999) II. 1758-64.

MELLOR HALL (II)

Mellor   *Private residence*

Mellor Hall in 1982.   M. Stanley

The early history of Mellor is a trifle obscure, but by about 1200 a family taking its name from the place emerge, the daughter and heiress of which, sometime in the thirteenth century, married Simon, third son of Sir Simon de Staveley of Staveley *(qv)*, and his grandson Robert adopted the surname of Mellor from the place, and no doubt established his seat there. Robert's son of the same name had two sons, Roger and a third Robert, who married the heiress of Robert de la Haye of Idridgehay and whose posterity settled there and later built South Sitch *(qv)*. The elder son, Roger, left three daughters and heiresses. The elder married Robert, fourth son of Sir John Radclyffe of Ordsall, Lancashire, KG; the younger, inheriting a sundered portion of the ancient estate, consisting of the subordinate manor of Bottoms Hall *(qv)*, transmitted it by marriage to William Stafford, a cadet of the house of Eyam.

The representative of the family at the time of the Civil War, Peter Radcliffe of Mellor had *(inter alia)* a daughter, Susannah (born 1644) who married James Chetham of Duffield, a merchant, and he purchased Mellor from his wife's brother, Peter (born 1638) in 1686. Anne, Peter's daughter and heiress, married John Horsfall of Melris-in-Craven; Radcliffe collaterals removed to Denton, Lancashire.

James Chetham decided to build a new house on a new site (a stone is signed I C/1691) the old Radcliffe seat being the site of the present Old Hall, taxed on five hearths in 1670; it was an L-shaped stone-built gabled house with mullioned windows. The new house was fairly up to date for so remote a part of England, although very provincial in expression, the main entrance front being constructed of fine ashlar of local Rough Rock with quoins of the same material. It is of two storeys and seven bays, the fenestration being of the cross type in thin architraves, now sashed on the first floor and all fitted with rather busy Victorian decorative glazing bars; keyblocks reach up into a band above both floors all under a hipped stone slate roof on a timber modillion eaves cornice. The central entrance has a bolection surround with a wide entablature on brackets above supporting a high-rearing swan-neck pediment enclosing a later Royal armorial. The lead rain-water goods either side of the central three bays are particularly fine examples of contemporary decorative plumber's work and even rival those at Calke in quality. Behind, the house is of coursed rubble, of Coal

Measure sandstone of a thin-bedded type, and is less regular, with a later projection. Decent outbuildings, in pleasant grounds, including a barn dated 1688, also survive. The interior is a little disappointing, having been 'modernized', probably in the early years of the nineteenth century. The hall and dining-room have oak wainscots and the oak staircase has twisted balusters.

Thomas Chetham of Mellor, who died in 1799, great-grandson of the builder of this unexpected and rather splendid house, never lived there, and in 1789 put it up for auction, but it failed to sell. In 1797 he sold part of the estate to Queen Anne's Bounty to augment the living at Mellor, and the remainder, with the house, went to its tenant, Ralph Bridge, whose son was farming there in 1816. By 1827 Bridge had sold to Thomas and John Moult (brothers claiming descent from the Palatine feudal barons de Montalt) of an old Chapel-en-le-Frith family. John son of Thomas Moult succeeded, his widow selling in 1890 to Jonas Craven, a Manchester businessman. By 1908 it was the seat of C.D.L.Greenhalgh, who put it up for sale in 1922, although he was still there in 1926. It was the property of Malcolm Norbury by 1931. The parish was transferred to Cheshire in 1935.

Pevsner, *Cheshire*, 279; Lysons, V., 168; Swann (1940) 23, 259; Walker & Tindall (1985) 157-8; de Figueiredo & Treuherz (1988) 255; BL Woolley MS 6670 f. 259; MELLOR/*Reliquary* VII (1866-7) & XII (1871-2); RADCLYFFE of Ordsall/BLG (1972) 738; CHEETHAM/BLG (1894) II. 1945; GREENHALGH/FD (1929) I. 1802.

MEYNELL LANGLEY (II)

Kirk Langley   *Private residence*

Meynell Langley Hall in 1984.   M. Craven

The early history of this portion of the historic Langley estate has already been to some extent reviewed *(qv)*. Robert son of Gilbert Meynell of Langley held a moiety there in the reign of Henry II, and Hugo, his descendant in the fifth generation married Joanna, daughter and heiress of Robert de la Warde. He was also, by an earlier inheritance, Lord of Tissington and Winster. His son, Sir Hugo de Meynell, KB, is said to have been created by Writ of Summons a baron in 1327; if so, it must have fallen into abeyance between the four daughters and coheiresses of his grandson, Ralph Meynell, on his death in 1390. The extensive estates were divided between these daughters: Tissington *(qv)* passed to

152

the husband of the eldest, Sir Thomas Clinton; Thomasina, the youngest, married Reginald Dethick, bringing him Newhall, and the Langley estate passed to Margaret's husband, Ralph Basset of Blore, who built a house here c. 1541 – with a chapel 28 ft. by 20 ft. with a groined roof – and whose posterity almost two centuries later purchased the other half of Langley from the Poles; the other girl died unmarried. The house, part of which had by then been abandoned, was taxed on 5 hearths in 1670. The Meynells repurchased the estate from the 1st Duke of Newcastle after the Civil War, and it was again divided in 1758 (the contents being put up for sale), Walter Lord of Little Chester acquiring Meynell Langley and demolishing the Basset seat and the chapel. His daughter and heiress brought it to her husband, Joseph Ward (a member of the same opulent mercantile family in Derby as Revd Richard Rowland Ward of Sutton-on-the-Hill *(qv))*. Their daughter and heiress, Susannah, married a kinsman, John Meynell of Anslow, Staffordshire (1727-1802). His father, Francis, a Derby apothecary, was fourth in descent from Francis Meynell of Willington and Yeaveley, whose nephew Thomas was Susannah's great-great-grandfather. John and Susannah built a new house at Meynell Langley, a simple five by three bay brick villa of the sort that Joseph Pickford excelled at, about 1770.

Once 536, now 120 acres, the park was landscaped, and as it abutted Bowbridge Fields, William Emes's residence, it is likely that he was responsible for its design. The park is rolling, with steep declivities, a small lake and well-placed planting. The house was modest, which caused Hutton to remark (in 1791) '. . some houses deserve a better situation: and some situations, like that of (Meynell) Langley deserve a better house'.

The next owner, Godfrey Meynell, resolved to improve this state of affairs (perhaps stung by Hutton's remarks!) and in 1806 began the expansion of the house to his own designs. This work included the present hall and cantilevered Hoptonwood stone staircase, top lit and with a gallery and cast-iron balusters. Opening off to the right of this delightful space is the library, the chief room to survive from the earlier build; apart from good later eighteenth century plaster cornices, the chief glory of this elegant room is the fire-surround, in Carrara marble inset with Blue John; it looks like the work of George Moneypenny. Further work was undertaken in 1818, extending the south (entrance) front to nine bays, and including the present drawing-room, delightfully light and with restrained Regency plasterwork and possibly the Derby brothers Thomas and Joseph Cooper were responsible for carrying out Meynell's designs, for the work resembles theirs at Parkfields, Derby, and elsewhere.

The resultant building was of brick and roughcast Keuper sandstone from Bowbridge Fields with stucco, but it still did not satisfy; in 1829, Francis Goodwin, then finishing the new County Gaol in Derby, was brought in to bring order to a slightly hotchpotch facade. He refronted it completely, removing the half storey of the 1770s house to make a long lowish two-storey front. Using fine ashlar from the same source as before, he stepped the facade out two bays in from either end, and the central three broke slightly forward again; the parapet was raised slightly over each advance, producing a harmonious massing. The entrance is graced with a portico supported on paired Greek Ionic columns, the entablature being carried over the flanking ground floor

windows. The west front, of three bays, Goodwin also ashlared, taking in the tripartite window installed earlier by Meynell at the western extremity. This front also acquired a canted ground-floor bay in the Victorian period, although the projecting ground floor tripartite window nearby looks like the Coopers' work. The east front has less fenestration and is stuccoed, and the slated roof is hipped.

The stable court is also mainly Goodwin's work, using those built in the 1770s as a starting point. It is faintly Italianate in flavour, ashlared, with a two-storey centrepiece of three bays over a Tuscan loggia *in antis*, flanked by paired round-headed windows in architraves. The lower flanking wings also have windows of this type, but single. Much of the rear of the house also reflects the earlier builds.

The Stable Court, Meynell Langley, c. 1910.   *M. Craven*

Later retrenchment had reduced the estate to 470 acres (three farms, one in hand) by 1982; two flats have been created in the house and three in the stable block. A pleasant stone Jacobean vernacular style lodge of c. 1860 graces the gates from the Ashbourne Road, behind which the Meynells still hold sway over a demesne which they have held (albeit with gaps) for nearly 800 years.

Pevsner,261; Colvin, 418; Hutton (1791) 319; Lysons, V. 197; Innes-Smith (1972) 96-7; DM 20/11/1758; DLC 5/63; Meynell muniments, information courtesy Godfrey Meynell, Esq.; MEYNELL of Meynell Langley/BLG (1965) 499; BASSET/V. Staffs. 1583; NEWCASTLE, D./BDEP 109.

MICKLEOVER HOUSE

Nursing home

Mickleover House, as extended, c. 1900.   *M. Craven*

Mickleover, historically lacking a major landowner, became split over time between a number of lesser lights. In 1789, Robert Newton, who owned the largest part, died, and his heirs, the Leapers, sold off some land including Mickleover Old Hall (qv) with over 100 acres. It was bought by Alderman Samuel Rowland of Derby, Mayor of the Borough four times between 1801 and 1827 and described by Glover as "an eminent agriculturalist and sportsman," the son of another Samuel Rowland (1720-94), a shopkeeper in Friar Gate Derby but who "discontinued business after his marriage and became a gentleman." The marriage referred to was to the heiress of John Hieron of Little Eaton, and thus the good alderman was thereby equipped with a good estate.

The house was built in 1821, and from the evidence of its detailing, it is clearly the work of Joseph Cooper of Derby, whose Parkfields (1823) it greatly resembles. As built it was five bays on the south (garden) front and four bays on the returns, two storeys under a hipped roof and stuccoed over in Brookhouse's Patent Roman Cement (manufactured in Derby) grooved to resemble ashlar. A pair of ground floor canted bays are almost certainly original. The hall, like all of Cooper's houses, is longish with a stone cantilevered staircase with attractive cast iron balusters from the Derby foundry of Messrs. Weatherhead, Glover & Co., later Handyside, which firm also made the cast iron sliding jalousies fitted to the windows, a refinement much utilised by Cooper. An elaborate peach house was provided to the SW, only recently removed.

To the east, and set back, were Rowland's hunting stables, consisting of a two storey five bay central block, the centre bay being higher and breaking forward, with a long, single storey range of loose boxes set at right angles. This was sold off in the 1950s and converted into a residence, but has recently been sold to a developer whose disastrous scheme to turn it into old persons' flats has unfortunately received planning permission shortly before the time of writing. A pretty single storey stuccoed gate lodge was built with antae at the angles, but this was given an Arts-and-Crafts gabled upper storey in the 1890s. The Old Hall (qv) was at this time used as the gardener's cottage.

Rowland died in 1830, and it became the property of one of his sons-in-law, Alderman John Drewry, the publisher of the Derby Mercury. He immediately set about enlarging it, presumably using Cooper again. He added a three bay extension on to the west end of the garden front, in exactly matching style, complete with iron jalousies, but breaking forward slightly. He also extended the new front by a bay to the west, including a large reception room on the SW angle. A new entrance was created on the west side, to which the original stone Tuscan projecting portico was moved.

By 1846 it was the residence of Moses Harvey, an associate of the Evans family (qv Darley Hall) in their cotton mill, and his family lived there until 1878, when it was purchased, less most of its estate, by Conrad Adolphus Wallroth. On his death at the turn of the century it went to Henry Charrington, of the brewing family, and a decade later to Alexander Preston-Jones. He sold in 1936 to Percy Caleb Cooper-Parry, an accountant, and after the Second War it was bought by Edward, the brother of Sir Clifford Gothard of Drakelow (qv).

He proceeded to undo Drewry's work by demolishing the

1830 extension, thus producing a more manageable home in the changed climate of the times. The portico was thereupon moved back to its original position in the centre of the south front. It later became an old folks' home, and although unfortunately unlisted it lies within a conservation area, which has twice saved it from the indignity of an enormous and inappropriate extension being added to the north side in lieu of the existing and original service wing. Nearly all the grounds have, unfortunately been built over.

Glover II. 594-5; Bagshaw (1846) 197-8, 199; Bulmer (1895) 780; DET 5/8/1999; ROWLAND/Glover, loc. Cit.; WALLROTH/Kelly, Handbook (1911) 1716; CHARRINGTON of Bures/BLG (1965) 441; GOTHARD/Kelly op. cit.(1970) 846.

MICKLEOVER MANOR (II)

Converted as dwellings

Mickleover Manor, c. 1870 showing the entrance front.　　J. Darwin

The manorial estate of Mickleover had been held until the Dissolution by the Abbey of Burton. Thereafter, and by a complex process, it had become divided, part going to Sir Thomas Gresham. He sold the land to William Gilbert, third son of Thomas Gilbert of Sileby, Leicestershire, a member of a very old family originating from Lullington, and later of Barrow-on-Trent. If there was a manor house at this date, a family must have held it as sub-tenants of the Abbey, and its successors; it is only their identity that remains obscure. Possibly the heiress of it married the father, Thomas Gilbert (whose wife is unrecorded), thus explaining his interest in it and, if indeed, this was so, his ability to pay Gresham's price. Unfortunately, absolutely nothing is known of any house, except that it cannot have been at all large, for Robert Newton paid hearth tax on but five hearths in 1670; this man's forebear, another Robert, had married William Gilbert's heiress.

The Newtons were cadets of the family of the Newtons of Horsley and Chaddesden, claiming descent from Welsh princely stock; they were kin to those of Duffield Hall (qv). They acquired an estate at Norton (qv) a generation later, and vastly rebuilt Norton House in the 1730s; consequently, they had not resided in the manor house at Mickleover since the beginning of that century, and the old house may well have been tenanted as a farm, a situation that still pertained in 1816 when recorded by the Lysons. It was doubtless timber framed, and Bulmer avers that it was cleared away when the present house was built, although on a slightly different site, perhaps that of the present stables.

In 1789, Robert Newton of Mickleover and Norton died 'Immensely rich and an old bachelor' leaving the Leapers, Derby bankers and tanners, as his heirs. John Leaper took the surname and arms of Newton, and in the second decade of the nineteenth century built a pretty Regency Villa, the Leylands, on the border between Derby and Darley Abbey to the designs of his youngest brother, Alderman Richard Leaper (1759-1838): an amateur architect of some distinction, tanner, and four-times Mayor of Derby. Yet this Villa soon became too small for the upwardly mobile Newtons, and Maj. William Newton (died 1854) decided to build a seat proper on his ancestral estate at Mickleover, raising money by selling his interests in Norton.

He is said to have selected Derby born Henry Duesbury as his architect, then completing the Derbyshire Lunatic Asylum in the parish, who is said by Pevsner to have built the new seat 1849-51, but he clearly was mixing the Manor (then Woodlands Hospital) with the nearby County Asylum (of which it was an annexe). But we get the impression that it was complete and inhabited by Charles Newton by 1857, when White's directory declares 'The ancient seat of the Newtons is a large handsome brick mansion...and contains upwards of seventy windows.' If such a house existed before, earlier directories such as Bagshaw (1846) would surely have mentioned it. Yet *The Builder* five years later tells us that the house was then 'in course of erection', which could, of course, represent a measure of hyperbole. Certainly, a design by Edward Blore was rejected. However, the house as built was designed by William Giles, of Giles & Brookhouse of Derby and the rainwater goods are all dated 1862. This anomaly has yet to be satisfactorily explained, and the muniments, still in the family's hands, are not currently available. The contractor was W. H. & J. Slater of Derby.

The brick house has Keuper sandstone dressings and in design is Jacobethan. The centrepiece of the south (entrance) front is a four-storey square tower topped by a plain parapet with very perfunctory crenellations on a simple roll-moulded cornice with gargoyles at the angles. There is a string course between each floor with mullioned and transomed windows on each except the uppermost, where the fenestration is without transoms has quatrefoil heads to the lights. A small square stair-turret echoing the form of the tower projects coyly above the parapet, and an angle buttress is stepped up the south-east corner. To the west of the tower are two gabled bays, one projecting beside it, and another beyond, rather more set back. Both have six-light mullioned and transomed windows with small stone attic lights consisting of a lozenge set within a circle in the gable ends. The gables are straight, coped with prominent kneelers and with small finials. The projecting bay has a ground floor canted bay window, whilst that in the other bay is effectively a French window. To the east of the tower, there are three, lower, floors the uppermost with gables projecting through the eaves of the slate roof. The west front of 11 bays boasts two further gables and a full height canted bay, and the short return has three gables. The service wing, to the east of the south front, is expressed in a large gabled range with two further two-storey bays to the east with a further range to the

north; the work was completed late in 1862.

Inside there is some good neo-Jacobean plasterwork, some considerable amount of oak panelling and a particularly fine timber staircase lit from a large multi-transomed west window. The pleasure grounds and small park, laid out by William Barron in 1861, were once 17 acres, walled round in brick but now reduced to seven acres. An original stable block survives.

On the death of Francis Curzon Newton (the Newtons had married the heiress of Curzon of Breedon and Lockington Halls, Leicestershire) at the end of World War One, the family removed to Lockington, and a preparatory school took a lease. Previously Sir Frederick and Lady Inglefield had rented it, and in 1915 had recalled William Barron & Son to re-landscape the gardens, but Lady Inglefield left on her husband's death in 1921. The school began in 1922, and in 1937 acquired the freehold, which had been sold by the Curzons; the 1,050-acre estate (which included Bearwardcote Hall) went to a number of other purchasers. After World War Two the school closed, and in the early 1950s the newly created hospital authority acquired the house and eight acres, transforming it into an institution of a residential nature which it remained until closure in 1989. The site was sold in 1990, when planning permission was sought to cover the majority of the remaining seven and a half acres of park with houses and flats. A local campaign was mounted to prevent this, on the grounds of over-development, and eventually a firm was found to build a limited number of houses on the north of the site and convert the restored house itself sensitively into residential units.

Pevsner 194; Woolley, 4 p.13; Lysons, V. 227; White (1857) 294; Cox IV (1879) 303 f.; Watson (1993) 16-19; *Builder*, 9/8/1862; DLC 8/37; DET 10/5/1993; GILBERT/V.1611; NEWTON/V.1662 and *sub* CURZON *formerly* NEWTON of Lockington/BLG (1972) 228; LEAPER/Glover, II. 592; INGLEFIELD/BLG (1952) 1342-3.

MICKLEOVER OLD HALL (II*)

Private residence

Mickleover Old Hall is one of a diminishing number of tim-

Mickleover Old Hall showing the entrance front in 1989.　　M. Craven

ber-framed buildings in Derby, and one of very few former country houses in the county to enjoy this pleasing and vernacular form of construction. Yet Mickleover Old Hall is a late example of the genre, being dated on the upper storey bressumer of its delightful gabled two storey porch '1648/ NISI DOMINUS FRUSTRA'. Indeed, strictly speaking, and despite its grand title, it is strictly the house of a rich yeoman rather than that of a country gentleman, for was it built neither by the Lord of the Manor (an absentee at that time) nor by the chief landowner, Edward Newton, whose family had but recently inherited the main estate at Mickleover from the heiress of the long-established Gilberts. The Gilberts had a seat of their own in the village, near the church close to the present manor.

Mickleover Old Hall is box framed double pile house on a stone plinth infilled with brick nogging using stretcher bond, of two storeys and attics, gabled and with a huge brick chimney breast attached to the north side. The south front is very traditional and twin-gabled in appearance, but the twin pile plan was bang up to date for the period. The house was quite probably thatched originally, but is now roofed in old tile, and the original timber mullioned windows were replaced in the nineteenth century with stone mullions with cast-iron frames as part of a refurbishment of c. 1840 said to have cost £900.

Essentially, the ground plan shows four rooms per floor, anticipating in its (approximate) symmetry the practice of later in the seventeenth century. Inside, a fine hall reveals a pleasing oak staircase with turned balusters, later than the house, looking c. 1695 in style (its attic pitch is of an earlier kind altogether). This suggests that the increasing prosperity of the owners led to a refurbishment at about this time. Only the drawing-room retains its original oak panelling, although the bedrooms were so lined in the late 19th century, too. The surviving panelling is inscribed: C/R A/1655 which is most valuable, for it confirms the local legend that the house was built for 'A Cromwellian Officer', a man, pious enough, moreover, to place the words in Latin over the entrance from the opening lines of the Vulgate Ps. 127. It has a pleasant garden and a pair of brick ball-capped gatepiers of eighteenth century date. It also suggests the date at which the house was finally fitted up.

The builder was Captain Robert Cotchett (1611-1657), eldest son of William (1585-1635), himself son of John, first of the family to live in Mickleover. Three further generations are recorded in All Saints' Parish, Derby going back to the late fifteenth century. Cotchett was commissioned as a Captain in Gell's Regiment at Derby in 1642, and later supported the foaming radical Thomas Sanders of Little Ireton. Mary, his first wife, had died shortly after their marriage in 1632, and he remarried Ann, whose initial appears on the panelling. Their children, the eldest son, Thomas, a prosperous lawyer, inherited, and his like-named son allied himself with the young John Lombe in 1702 in their unsuccessful attempt to throw silk thread in the 'Old Shop' at the Derwent's edge in Derby, but he went bankrupt within a few years, and on his father's death in 1713 probably sold up. Thomas, senior, it was who paid tax on seven hearths for the Old Hall in 1670, and on his death, it was bought by the Newtons and absorbed into their estate, becoming Cedars Farm.

In about 1790 it was purchased by Alderman Samuel Rowland of Derby who was slowly building up an agricultural estate in the area. His successor John Drewry later 'repaired and beautified' it, renaming it The Cedars, later Cedar Lodge. This was because the old Gilbert house (qv) had become the Old Hall, inhabited by a farmer called John Gregory in 1846. These works probably account for the

change in the fenestration. He moved out when he had completed Mickleover House (qv) when it became the gardener's cottage. By 1846 George Coxon, farmer, a tenant of the Harveys, inhabiting it. Thereafter, and right up to World War Two, it was an adjunct to Mickleover House. More recently it has changed hands on a number of occasions.

Pevsner, 194; Woolley 4, p.13; Bagshaw (1846) 197; Bulmer (1895) 780; Reade IV (1923) 76-7; Hutton (1991) 21-2, 38, 40, 51, 55; Watson (1993) 14-15; Derby Civic Society *Newsletter* no. 55 (1989) 6-7; Hutton DBR (1989) No. 59; NEWTON, ROWLAND see Mickleover House.

NETHER HALL

see HARTSHORNE UPPER HALL

NETHERSEAL HALL

Demolished

Netherseal Hall, before final rebuilding, 1859.   RCHM(E)

It has been suggested by some commentators that Robert de Seyl who held the whole of Seal (then in Leicestershire, the transfer to Derbyshire was later, in 1889) at the time of the Domesday Book was the son or at least heir of Wideline, who held that place in 1066. Be that as it may, Seal descended to Ralph Seal (to modernise the spelling) great-grandson of Robert, on whose death without issue, the manor (belonging to Henry de Ferrers in 1086) was split between his sisters and co-heiresses, married respectively to William de Wivell and William son of Roger de Stretton, of the Stretton-en-le-Field family (qv). At least two of the Seals were household officers to various Earls of Derby, Robert, uncle of Ralph, being constable to the Earl in 1178. He founded a branch of the family later Coventry merchants, from whom descended Revd Richard Sale (1545-1626) rector of Weston upon Trent and ancestor of the Sales of Shardlow, Willington, Barrow and Derby.

William de Stretton released his rights in Netherseal to William de Ridware of Hamstall Ridware (Staffordshire). and *jure uxoris* of Boylestone. He was also seneschal to the Earl of Derby. Netherseal passed to his elder son Roger by 1254 and Agnes, daughter and heiress of his descendant in the fourth generation, Sir Walter de Ridware, brought it in marriage to William Cotton by about 1400. It would have appeared to have been alienated about 1507 when the senior line of Cotton ended in four sisters and co-heiresses, after which there is a period of obscurity until the manor and estate were purchased by Gilbert Morewood about 1620. Morewood, second son of Rowland Morewood of The Oakes, (qv) and uncle of the first Morewood of Alfreton (qv) was a rich young London merchant and, like the Mundys of Markeaton (qv), the Brownes of Stretton-en-le-Field and the Moores of Appleby (qv), decided to invest in a country estate in this area. Although the Seal family had undoubtedly lived at Netherseal, the Ridwares and Cottons both had seats elsewhere, and the manor may well have been without a capital mansion at the time Morewood purchased it.

Gilbert Morewood soon rectified the omission, however, immediately building a high ashlar seat of seven by two bays (but with two modest wings to the east) which faced east-west beside the church. Like a simplified version of Tupton Hall (qv) it was of three storeys over a high basement, but without any of the odd changes of level which characterize Tupton. The windows were all of the cross type with string courses above each storey except the basement, that over the ground floor windows being cranked down over the modest front door which was approached up a flight of steps. The flat lead roof lay behind a plain parapet but was adorned by two groups of stacks aligned with the facade and pierced by an arch. It was set in a pleasantly undulating park.

Morewood died in 1650 leaving only daughters, of whom the youngest, Frances, brought Netherseal Hall to Sir Thomas Gresley of Drakelow, 2nd Bt (qv) who died in 1699, leaving it to his second son Thomas, who had in any case been inhabiting it since reaching his majority. His grandson, Thomas (also rector of Netherseal) died in 1785, having added a brick four-bay, two-storey range with a pitched roof to the north, effectively extending the west front, except that it was set slightly back and screened by trees. He also was probably responsible for the pretty octagonal domed projection which was built remarkably close to the house just left of the entrance. He also planted the grounds 1756-9.

Thomas's son, William (1760-1829) was also rector, and about 1810 seems to have had the house sashed throughout, work which had the effect of masking the high basement, the windows of which appear to have been blocked in. He married twice, the eldest son of his first marriage succeeding as 9th baronet, where-upon the house passed to his younger half brother, Revd John Morewood Gresley, rector there and ultimately ancestor of the 13th and last baronet. He was succeeded in rectory and es-tate by the younger son of the 9th baronet, Revd Nigel Gresley (father of the great locomotive engineer, Sir H.N.Gresley). He set about expand-ing the house on a large scale about 1860. The west front was extended towards the north by two further bays, the end one of which broke slightly forward before meeting a new west wing of four widely spaced bays and three storeys under a cornice and dwarf parapet. The parapet of the main west front was taken down and replaced by a curious array of six shaped gables with blank cartouches in them, looking for all the world as if Sir William Wilson at his most dire had been unleashed on the house nearly two centuries before, especially as they failed to match the spacing of the bays. These gables ran round the short south front also. The new wing extended three bays to the West as well. A boxy porch was added at the same time which sat rather unhappily with the little octago-nal structure. The house was let from some time in the nineteenth century to the Robertsons of Chilcote, who left in 1904. The eldest Gresley son rebuilt it yet again in 1908-11 with the help of Sir Reginald Blomfield. He removed the lowish upper storey from the new wing, replacing it with a plain ashlar parapet, and provided the far end bay with a two storey canted one. In the angle of the two ranges he removed an entrance in a two-storey, three-sided projection built about 1860, which involved converting the oak panelled hall behind.

The original hall had long since been converted into a sitting room, and the former entrance into a French window. The grounds were also laid out afresh and simplified. Yet within a few years, pecuniary pressures forced Gresley (who died in 1938) to move away, and by 1914 the house was unoccupied, although a little later Col K.C.Brazier-Creagh was the tenant. When he left, however, the fortunes of the house of Gresley were in severe decline, and, failing to find a tenant or a buyer, the house, contents and estate were offered at auction in 1927. The house failed to sell and was purchased separately by E. J. Manners of Netherseal Old Hall (qv)who appears ot have occupied it for a time before pulling it down in 1933; the site is now built over. The parish was transferred to Derbyshire in 1897.

Woolley 126, p.165; Nichols (1804) III.iii.993; Fellows (1985) 169; Sale Catalogue, 7/5/1927, Burton Library; D. Misc. (1975) 152; SEAL sub SALE formerly of Aston Rowant/BLG (1952) 2229; MOREWOOD/Glover, II. 14-15; GRESLEY, Bt./BP (1970) 1172-3.

NEWTON OLD HALL (II*)

Newton-by-Blackwell   *Private residence*

Newton Old Hall, Blackwell.   *Derbyshire County Council*

From Cragg Lane, the entrance front of this complex and attractive house gives the appearance of being as one of very modest dimensions. A pair of early eighteenth century gatepiers with ball finials support a very pretty vernacular wrought-iron gate and frame a lowish two-storey range with three bays of low mullioned windows of four lights under a straight coped parapet with finials. At first glance it all looks thoroughly Cotswolds Arts-and-Crafts, and there is, indeed, reason to suppose that this façade was once gabled, but was rebuilt in the early twentieth century. The stone, coarse ashlar, is Coal Measure sandstone, probably Top Hard rock, the dressings, coarser, possibly being of Crawshaw sandstone, the roof is stone slates, but inside there is much evidence of an earlier, timber-framed structure. This part is dated 1690, and the string course over the four bays of ground floor windows is extended over the modest entrance with its simple chamfered surround. The east front is of two bays, and appears to have been reskinned at about the same time as the entrance front, although the parapet does not extend round it. The north front has a gable at each end, that on the right projecting, the range separating them having been raised, presumably in 1690, thus making the gables asymmetrical. The fenestration here is sparse, irregular (due in part to the presence of the staircase within) and of two-light mullions. The right gable also contains evidence of earlier work, this time in stone, but it is very difficult to interpret. The north front seems to be an amalgam of at least three straight-coped gables all run together, although some work may be early twentieth century, as some of the high quality rain-water goods are dated 1909. This front masses to a third storey between two sturdy stacks originally issuing from the apices of two separate superimposed gables, taking the form of another gable, and all forming the return of the right gable of the east front.

The house, therefore, may have begun as an L-shaped one incorporating a timber-framed predecessor to which subsequently has been added further gabled projections to the north and east, the angle between them subsequently infilled. All was once set in a miniscule pleasure ground, but this is now broken up by later stone boundary walls.

The inside of the house is today devoid of much of the decorative timber-work it must have once had. Nevertheless, there are two original stone fireplaces, and several seventeenth century doors and two early eighteenth century ones. The most interesting features are recurrences of studding in the upper storeys, a magnificent timber roof, showing much evidence of the earliest phase of building, not to mention *ad hoc* later adaptations to cope with extensions, and the staircase. This is oak, with twisted balusters running between moulded ball-capped newels, and runs to the top of the house with no diminution of quality; it would appear to have been installed in the 1690 rebuild, and to have supplanted an early steep and crude affair at the other end of the house.

The inhabitant of this house in 1670 was probably John Brook

with four hearths taxable in 1670, and the owner was the Molyneux, Bts, of Teversal (a creation to a cadet branch of the Earls of Sefton's family of 1611), Sir John Molyneux being the owner in 1710 and joint Lord of the Manor (of Blackwell) with Gilbert Holles, Earl of Clare. The division of the manor (held by one Ralph under Ralph *fitz* Hubert in 1086) seems to have occurred by the fifteenth century, Sir William Holles having acquired one moiety (Blackwell itself) from the Longfords before 1590, and the Molyneux having acquired their share (Newton) from the Babingtons at an unknown date.

Sir John Molyneux, 1st Bt, was seated at Haughton, Nottinghamshire, but appears to have over-reached himself financially, and was forced to mortgage Haughton and Teversal, building himself a modest Jacobean twin gabled seat at Newton, doubtless that occupied by Mr John Richardson, his agent, in 1670, taxed on seven hearths. It had a chapel beside it, built 1696, but destroyed c. 1860. On the death without issue of the 7th and last baronet in 1812, the estate passed to Lord Henry Thomas Howard (later Molyneux) brother of the 12th Duke of Norfolk, from whom it passed in 1830 to the Earls of Carnarvon. They sold to William Downing, junior c. 1857 who had been tenant since c. 1840 and whose heirs sold to the Adlingtons of Skegby, who demolished it about 1900. George Booker was the last tenant. Newton Old Hall, on the other hand, was probably the Molyneux seat's predecessor renovated as a subsidiary house. In practice, it was tenanted almost constantly up until the 20th century but amongst its most illustrious occupants was William Strutt, father of the famous Jedediah, the spinning entrepreneur (*qv* Green Hall, Belper) who was, indeed, born and bred here. William appears to have shared it with his brother, also Jedediah, the latter's son and heir, Thomas, leaving, at his death in 1790, a small charity at Blackwell, administered by a local butcher, but which was extinguished with the latter's untimely bankruptcy in 1818.

The staircase, Newton Old Hall, 1916.
M. Craven

Joseph, the eldest son of William (Jedediah was the second son) died in 1794, leaving his son Statham Strutt as tenant, but on his death, the representation of the senior line of Strutt devolved on to Martha, his sister, married in 1792 to Joseph Chamberlain of Lacock, Wiltshire, who was the ancestor both of Rt Hon Joseph and of Sir Austen Chamberlain of the illustrious Birmingham family, although members of the Strutt family seem to have continued in occupation as tenants until about 1840. At the time of the 1670 hearth tax, however, John and Richard Strutt were both living in houses taxed at one hearth each; could this represent two halves of this house at that time? It remained a tenanted farm for some time further, but in 1892 it was the home of a collier and was described as in tumbledown condition. Early in the 20th century, the Earls of Carnarvon sold the freehold to a Mr Salmon, who renovated it and whose widow was in occupation in 1925. It was for sale by auction in July 1979, and changed hands again in 1981 for

£55,000, shorn of all but a small garden. Mr. & Mrs. J. M. Radford owned the house in 1995.

Pevsner, 291; Glover, II. 123; DAJ XIX (1897) 104; DLC 3/81; MOLYNEUX, Bt./BDEB 360; CARNARVON, E/BP (1999) I. 505-7; STRUTT of Newton/Derby Local Studies Library, Ince MS 8022 & *sub* Ward, *sub* BELPER, B./BP (1999) I. 249-50 & *sub* CHAMBERLAIN of Highbury/BLG (1965) 336.

NORBURY HALL (I)

Private residence, partly open by appointment

original west windows and later fireplace – may replace a half-timbered first attempt on the part of his father. The hall's undercroft is still intact, retaining an original stud wall and approached via a segmental-headed fourteenth century doorway at the south end, over which once must have run the external staircase by which one reached the hall proper. To the north was probably a timber-framed solar cross-wing, perhaps added a little later, but long since gone and unrecorded; a blocked doorway in the hall points to its existence, however.

The fenestration on the east side is of square mullioned lights, perhaps somewhat later, and some early heraldic glass (as well as more figurative seventeenth century pieces) has been reset in them. Also on the east side (where the

The 13th century north wing of Norbury Hall.   *J. A. Robey*

Norbury Hall (or Manor, as some call it) is in reality two houses: an astonishing medieval survival forming a north wing to the present house, and an exquisitely preserved and magical sixteenth century one built at right angles, refronted about 1680, and quite unravaged. For 570 years it was the seat of the senior line of the FitzHerbert family, and was in their possession for a further two centuries.

The medieval wing appears to have been begun after 1252 by William FitzHerbert, 5th of Norbury, doubtless replacing an earlier timber affair; in that year he obtained free warren in the parish. The lower courses of what is in essence a classic semi-defensive 'upper Hall' house must date from this period, as above the string course the ashlar, of Keuper sandstone from an adjacent outcrop, becomes more even and the three lights on the west front are in the Decorated style with trefoliated heads and two lights, and were probably the work of Sir William's like-named son around 1305. The present upper part of the hall – the great chamber, with its two fine

undercroft is hidden by higher ground, in this case the churchyard) is the later side hearth with its stone chimney and original capping: a miraculous survival. The roof is built of re-used timbers on two king post trusses. It is strapped onto fifteenth century moulded tie-beams which once carried the cross beams of a panelled ceiling. At least one empty mortice for a wall post brace suggests that the tie-beams may have come from the Tudor house which was replaced by the present one. At the time of the building of the Tudor house, an extension was added to the medieval hall to connect it thereto.

The estate had been long held under the Prior of Tutbury by the FitzHerberts, William fitz Herbert (almost certainly to be identified with the son of Herbert, an opulent Derby merchant recorded in an early Darley Abbey charter) having been granted the tenancy by the Priory in 1125; it had come to the canons late in the eleventh century from Henry de Ferrers who had obtained it from the King in 1081; it may previously have been the Earl of Chester's. In 1448, however, Nicholas FitzHerbert managed to acquire the freehold by way of a land exchange and his son Ralph seems to have had the confidence to have enlarged the house between 1473 and 1483. This seems to have also been a largely stone house, with accommodation facing south at right angles to the original upper hall, and including a new great hall (with rooms over) probably facing west, thus forming a three-sided courtyard with the original build and closed off to the north by the now vanished solar and outbuildings. Some ancient fabric does, indeed, survive at the north-west corner of the present house. Later evidence also establishes that there was an oriel window. The house also contained fine stained glass, including more heraldry and a series of roundels depicting the months of the year, of which half a dozen survive, reset.

The Victorian Hall at Norbury, c. 1895, now demolished.   *M. Craven*

Later, the house fell into desuetude, for by the marriage of Sir Thomas with the heiress of Sir Arthur Eyre, this branch of the FitzHerberts acquired the grander Padley Manor *(qv)*, and removed there, Sir Thomas FitzHerbert later being arrested by Lord Shrewsbury's agents in 1581 as a recusant, dying in the Tower in 1591. This misfortune was followed by retrenchment next at Norbury, and there is much evidence of alterations there in the 1620s, including herringbone panelling, identical to that once at Babington House, Derby (of 1626) and Tissington (1610). The drawing-room overmantel and the panelling in 'Sir Anthony's study' (in the early, north-west, angle) are also of this date. However, more disasters befell through championship of the King during the Civil War by Sir John FitzHerbert, who fell in his Sovereign's cause at Lichfield 13th January 1649, already bankrupted by fines and exactions.

His heir, William FitzHerbert, inherited a 'ruinous' seat at Norbury, but a forebear had married the daughter and ultimate heiress of Humphrey Swynnerton of Swynnerton Hall, Staffordshire, a house also severely damaged during the Civil War, in 1643. Hence, he came to Norbury, which was put into repair for him. Basil FitzHerbert, his son, made haste to rebuild Swynnerton Hall after the Restoration. Having removed there, he then turned his attention to rebuilding Norbury, taxed on 18 hearths in 1664, as a secondary seat. We shall never know how the medieval range survived – perhaps it had utility as a store, but the later great hall was demolished and most of the south range. Later fifteenth century timbers, indeed, were used in a new roof on the old upper hall, and other moulded beams of the period survive in the replacement south range built in 1680. This is of brick (laid to Flemish bond, unlike those parts which survive from the 1473 build, which are in English bond) and of two storeys with attics in a hipped old tile roof. Of eight bays, the fenestration is of the cross type, but in timber; there are quoins at the angles, and the entrance is off-centre at the fifth bay, giving a felicitous but essentially vernacular look. The north front has two straight coped gables in projections, joined at a later date by a low two-storey range with service accommodation. Several two-light mullioned windows survive to the north and west from the previous house, and although much has been re-used from it inside, it was largely re-planned. The staircase is of oak, with turned balusters and flat capped newels, very simple and attractive.

From sometime in the middle eighteenth century, it was occupied by tenant farmers, called Maskery, who were there until the late nineteenth century. The FitzHerbert family, however, had less and less to do with their Derbyshire seat. Thomas FitzHerbert (1746-1781) married Mary, Mrs Thomas Weld (of Lulworth) and daughter of Walter, second son of John Smith of Acton Burnell, Shropshire, who, after his death, contracted a marriage (invalid under the terms of the Royal Marriage Act) with George, Prince of Wales (later George IV) in 1785, in her own drawing-room. Mrs FitzHerbert's descendant, Basil FitzHerbert, married Emily, daughter of Lord Stafford. This was a title created by Writ in 1640 in favour of Hon. Sir William Howard, KB (with precedence to 1547) by virtue of his marriage with a daughter of the last peer of the Stafford family, but not his heiress, as the true heir was deemed (quite irregularly) to be unfit to succeed to the peerage through abject poverty; yet, but for an attainder of 1521, the poor man was *de jure* 9th Duke of Buckingham and 15th Lord Stafford of the creation of 1299! Thus Basil FitzHerbert's son succeeded as Lord Stafford, a title which the family still enjoy.

It was Basil FitzHerbert who sold part of the estate, including land opposite the present Hall (on the other side of the road), to S.W. Clowes. He pulled down the old vicarage, which stood there, and commenced to build a large house. This was designed by Giles and Brookhouse of Derby and built in 1871-74. The west front resembled their Broomfield Hall *(qv)* consisting of a pair of wide canted bays linked by a single one, with round headed plate glass windows set in rectangular aedicules, rather like a large suburban villa, with hipped roofs over the bays. The building was of brick with horizontal banding of local Keuper sandstone, every four courses giving an arresting effect if nothing else and a large airy iron-framed conservatory stood at the south-west angle. The south front was long and irregular, of eight bays, with ugly stone dormers in a faintly Lombardic style. The entrance was at the west end, with a buttressed gothic door with a mullioned light over the arch and above an oriel, with lights which faintly echoed those on the medieval range over the road. The centre of the front had a projecting ground floor bay and there was a conical capped turret at the south-east angle. There was also a squat Italianate tower behind the south front and a forest of studiedly odd chimneys above the slate roof. No one could have called it beautiful and it had, indeed, all the characteristics of a monstrosity. The grounds were laid out by William Barron & Son 1871-74 and in 1881, Clowes also acquired the old

160

hall (as it had become known) from the FitzHerberts, and used it as service accommodation after the Maskerys left, connecting his property either side of the lane by a rustic bridge, since removed. According to Bulmer's *Directory* of 1895 it had been 'Recently restored and is intended for a museum'. Whether this represented restoration of the medieval wing, more general work, or just good intentions is not clear, for by and large the main house continued to gradually decay until 1964, when it was sold to the late Marcus Stapleton-Martin. He restored it painstakingly with the help of Lawrence Bond, and later, Rory Young, who built the pretty muniment room in the garden south-west of the house, into which some more pieces of old stained glass were put. All new stonework is Keuper sandstone from Hollington Quarry (Staffordshire). There is also a pretty octagonal fishing temple below the house on the Dove. The Clowes house was, perhaps mercifully, demolished in 1960.

Mr Stapleton-Martin, his restoration completed to the highest standards, died unmarried in 1988, leaving the hall to the National Trust, and today their tenants are Mr and Mrs C. F. M. Wright. Mr Wright, like his predecessor, has a blood line from the FitzHerberts of Tissington, cadets of those of Norbury, which makes an entirely fitting link to take this delightful and important seat into the twenty-first century. The medieval part is open to the public by prior appointment.

Pevsner, 290; Woolley, 93, p. 130; Bulmer (1895) 441; Bowyer (1953) 49, 54-59; Emery (2000) 425-7; DAJ VII (1885) 221-59 & XIX (1897) 94; CL 3/5/90; FITZHERBERT of Norbury *sub* STAFFORD, B./BP (1999) II, 2679-84; CLOWES of Norbury/BLG (1952) 474; MARTIN of Norton/*ibid.* (1972) 615; WRIGHT of Butterley/*ibid.* (1952) 2800-1.

NORTH LEES HALL (I)

Hathersage   *Holiday let*

It is very difficult to establish the precise origins of North Lees; at the time of Domesday, Hathersage, a very large parish with four manorial outliers, was split into two manors under Ralph *fitz* Hubert. These were held in the twelfth century by the Hathersage family, the heiress of which married William de Withington, of Withington, Lancashire, whose son Matthew took the surname and arms of Hathersage before his death in 1216. On the death of his son, they were split between the families of Goushill and Longford, the latter retaining theirs until their extinction in 1610. Thereafter it appears to have passed in due course to the Pegges who sold it in 1705 to the Duke of Devonshire. The Goushill manor was sold, on their extinction in the fifteenth century, to the Thorp family, whence it came to the Eyres, being retained by their heirs, the Archers of Coopersale, as late as 1816. The place of North Lees in all this, lying as it does in Hathersage Outseats, is unclear; before 1431 it was held by the Leghs, from whom it passed to the Swiftes. Their heiress brought it to the Wykersleys, likewise a Yorkshire family, from whom it descended to William Jessop of Broom Hall, near Sheffield, who built the present house. It is also worth noting that, between the mid-fifteenth century and 1530, the estate was held from the Swiftes by the same Eyres who held the Goushill moiety of one of the Hathersage manors.

Jessop, a man associated with the circle of Lord Shrewsbury, decided to demolish the medieval house except for its great hall, perhaps, adapting other portions into outbuildings, for north of the site crucks remain in a barn, and there are remains of a dwelling attached which, with the barn, would have formed a range of six or seven bays. Parts of these may even go back to the days of a tenant of the estate called Alexander de North Lees, living in 1306. The new house was essentially a hunting lodge, a neat High House of three and four storeys over a basement and built of coursed Millstone Grit sandstone rubble, probably Shale Grit from an adjacent outcrop, with similar dressings. The roof is leaded and flat. The way in which the floors are combined has been described by Girouard as '. . . typically Smythsonian ...' and

North Lees Hall, c. 1901.

M. Craven

in this connection the association is reinforced by the decorative merlons, which cap the parapet. The south part, of a single bay, is of three storeys over a basement, the latter having single lights immediately beneath the chamfer of the plinth, and a string course runs above the generous six-light mullion and transom window above. Two similar windows mark the floors above again, and in effect three chambers are stacked the one on top of the other, all very bright, being lit by ten-light mullioned and transomed windows to the east and six-light ones to the west, the latter being curtailed by the wide chimney breast which runs up the central side of the west front. Beyond it there are four rooms, one per floor, but meaner than those to the south. They are lit by very plain four-light mullioned windows. To the north-east corner is the stair tower, rising an extra level to give access to the leads and crested by merlons identical with those of the main parapet, all typical of the medievalizing influence of Robert Smythson.

Inside, there are plainish stone fireplaces and in the southern rooms, exuberant Sheffield School plaster ceilings, one of which includes the crest and motto of the Jessops as well as the date 1594, the crest of the Rodes's of Barlborough and other mottoes as well. The original service wing appears to have been a timber-framed structure, perhaps not on the footprint of the one which replaced it after 1646: a low, two-bay two-storey structure in stone with a gabled stone slate roof. The outermost bay is a small projecting gable, and a tall stack rises against the end to the east. There are vestigial remains of a pre-Reformation chapel in the grounds, which betray some irregularities due either to traces of formal gardens (in which case they would be of paramount importance and worthy of archaeological investigation) or of later agricultural activities. The setting generally, however, is glorious and very sequestered.

Under the Jessops, the house was tenanted by Richard Fenton, a notorious south Yorkshire recusant, and before him (and indeed, before the building of the present house) a family called Smith were there, whose heir Fenton was. In 1615, the house and small estate passed to the Savages of Castleton, but was sold about 1646 to John Greaves, of Beeley Hill Top (qv) who probably built the service wing and was assessed for tax on four hearths in 1670. From Greaves it passed to William Saville whose heirs, the Gilberts, disposed of it in 1734 to the Staleys of Conksbury. From them it passed to the Holworthys of Brookfield Hall, into the estate of which the house was incorporated (qv) about 1825-30. Their heiress was the niece of Joseph Wright of Derby, ARA, on whose death it was purchased by the Cammells of Norton (qv). During most of the time from the sale by the Greaves family, it was tenanted, the Eyre family (in a remote cadet branch) returning from 1750 to 1882. By the turn of the century, the lower rooms had become a grain store, and half the lights in all the large windows at the front of the house had been blocked in stone, probably to avoid the effects of window tax, a situation which remained until Lt-Col G.G.Haythornthwaite purchased it from the Coal Board, to which the Cammells had sold the Brookfield estate. He restored it in 1965 and installed a tenant. In 1971 it was acquired by the Peak National Park who retained the tenants but sold it on to the Vivat Trust in 1985 and a further more scholarly restoration was undertaken 1986-88. Since then it has been available for short lettings mainly for recreational purposes.

Even in the nineteenth century, its *genius loci* inspired its inclusion in *Jane Eyre*, albeit with its identity slightly blurred.

Pevsner, 291; Lysons, V. 177; Meredith (1981) 8; Girouard (1983) 125-6; Cooper (1999) 196; Reliquary IX (1869-70) 201-6; DLC 12/60 & 1/61; SWYFTE *sub* CARLINGFORD, V./BDEP 523; EYRE of Crankhill/V. 1662; FENTON/BLG (1968) 198; SAVAGE of Castleton/V. 1662 & DAJ XX (1898) 47-51; SAVILLE/V.1662; CAMMELL of Norton/BLG (1952) 353.

NORTON HALL (II)

Flats

Norton Hall, 1982.   M. Craven

Sir Francis Chantrey, Norton's most famous son, once described the present hall as 'A packing case with windows', a description little far off the mark, for the house is not particularly well proportioned and is softened by little detailing. It was 'lately rebuilt' when the Lysons wrote the Derbyshire volume of their *Magna Britannia* in 1815-16, and is said to have been completed in the former year. An alternative date of 1793 seems possible, however: the Lysons could have been recording alterations. It was in fact built by Samuel Shore (1738-1828) perhaps to a design by Woodhead and Hurst (if the 1815 date is right) or William Lindley of Doncaster if 1793; the former were the successors of the latter. It is built in fine ashlar of Coal Measure sandstone, probably Grenoside Sandstone or Greenmoor Rock, with a slate roof. If the Lysons are correct in saying that the house is a rebuild, then the early eighteenth century west range of its predecessor was probably incorporated and to some extent dictated the proportions of the remainder.

The seven-bay, two and a half storey south front has a three-bay breakfront under a rather skimpy pediment, bands between the floors, quoins at the angles and keyblocked architrave surrounds to the fenestration. The tetrastyle Doric portico is *in antis*, and there is a top cornice and dwarf parapet. The two bays at the south-west angle and five bays of the west front would therefore comprise the surviving range of the previous house which was proportioned and detailed approximately as now, if a surviving engraving is to be believed; the bands go along this, and all the other detailing survives, repeated from the south front. The east side is also of five bays, but set closer together, and undoubtedly constitutes new build. A lower, two-storey service wing to the north also appears to be an eighteenth century recasing of the earlier and similar five-bay one, probably added in the early eighteenth century.

Shore's father of the same name had inherited the house from Edmund Offley (died 1754, only three years after his own father, Joseph), whose heiress, Urith, he had married. The Shores, Sheffield bankers, were Unitarians, and had a chapel in the house until they built anew one in the village in the 1780s. They departed for the West Country towards the end of the nineteenth century, selling the house and part of the estate (of which 28 acres then lay in the West Riding of Yorkshire, but now regrettably all in that ever-expanding county) to the Cammells of Brookfield Manor (qv), Sheffield steel magnates, who in the twentieth century let to William Frederick Goodliffe. It was purchased after World War One by another steel man, Col B.A.Firth, whose eldest son, Mark, left it to the City of Sheffield in 1932, its parkland now forming part of Graves Park. The park, which may have been one of those landscaped by the north Derbyshire clergyman, Revd Christopher Alderson (who later worked for the Prince Regent), stretched west and north from the house, which is situated immediately west of the historic parish church. The estate in 1883 was 4,888 acres. The interiors are today rather plain, including the original staircase, but excluding an oak panelled room in the manner of Sir Christopher Wren.

The manor and estate came to the Shores, by a long series of successions going back to Ingram, founder of the de Alfreton family, whose posterity brought it to William de Chaworth, who is recorded as having a park at Norton in 1330. The Chaworth heiress brought it to John Ormond, and on his death in 1487, a part each was inherited by the husbands of his two daughters and heiresses. From one it passed to Jerome Blythe of Birchet, a hamlet in the parish, from the Eyres of Offerton. His grandson, Charles Blythe (1599-1645) sold his Norton manor to John, son of Ralph Bullock of Unstone (qv) in 1622, thereby re-uniting the two, for Robert Bullock had purchased the other portion in two moieties in 1572 and 1585, and John acquired these too. His son, William Bullock (1616-1666) left the estate encumbered, and it was sold to Cornelius Clarke of Ashgate, from whom in 1696 it passed to Robert Offley and hence, ultimately, to the Shores.

The house known to precede the present edifice appears plainly to have been of three builds: to the east of the south front was a low, two-storey gable with a long, multiple-light mullioned window on the upper floor beneath a small attic light. The four bays adjoining were of three and four storeys beneath a parapet, the first floor being the tallest. The three bays reading from the right as one faced it were approximately symmetrical the second bay being fairly deeply recessed. The fourth, SW bay, contained an extra storey, and there was a band between the first and second floors and an odd gabled belvedere on the roof with the stacks behind. It is tempting to see the gabled range, as part of a house built by the *arriviste* Anthony Blythe (died 1601) who, although counting some distinguished ecclesiastics amongst his kin, was descended from a scythesmith in the parish. The remainder looked as if it was built in the 1630s, if not somewhat earlier, and may represent a perhaps a stylish rebuilding attributable to John Bullock, aping the type of house built by the Smythsons, and it is directly comparable to Tupton Hall (qv). It must have been quite large: 18 hearths were taxed in 1670.

Later, before c. 1780, the SW bay was rebuilt with but three floors, but increased in width to two bays and given a top balustrade which ran round along the five bay west front, the rest of the south front being given string courses between the floors and regularly sashed, all in the manner of Smith of Warwick and thus probably done c. 1710-20 for Robert Offley (previously of Norwich) in typical provincial baroque style.

The present house was, when built, fitted with a patent central heating 'stove' and system by Charles Sylvester after the principle of that installed by William Strutt, FRS, in St Helen's House, Derby, to a design of his own but based on ideas published by John Whitehurst in a treatise of the 1770s. It does not appear to survive, although a long westward extending conservatory of mid nineteenth century does. In 1932 it was converted into a hospital, which role it filled until the 1990s, when it was disposed of by the Health Authority and converted into flats.

Pevsner (Yorkshire, W.R.) 478; Sylvester (1819) p.x; Bagshaw (1846) 656; Armitage (1910) 53; Robinson (1957) 89; De ALFRETON/ DAJ XLIX (1927) 283-91; CHAWORTH, B./CP II. 214-5; BULLOCK/V. 1569; BLYTHE/V.1569; SHORE of Norton/BLG (1875) II. 1257; CAMMELL *formerly* of Norton/*ibid.* (1937) 323; FIRTH of Norton/*op.cit.* 789.

ADDENDUM

CARNFIELD HALL

From Mr. J. Cartland

The south wing of Carnfield Hall has fifteenth century features and woodwork, which may suggest that the work done there in the 1560s was an addition to an existing house by Thomas Revell, the grandson of Hugh Revell, (Thomas married Anne Eyre of Holme Hall, Chesterfield). Also, some work was carried out on the house in 1627-8 and a new staircase tower of three storeys with an oak staircase built on the old west front. Robert Revell's alterations of the 1690s appear to have had the effect of turning the back of the house into the front, thus to face a (then) newly laid out avenue. The front doors of Carnfield and Calke Abbey contain very similar work and – as the Revells and Harpurs of Calke were cousins, and work to Calke was carried out shortly after that at Carnfield – it is quite possible that the same builders were utilised.

Carnfield and 700 acres passed to John Eardley Wilmot following the death of (the illegitimate) Tristram Revell in 1797, with one half of the Hall let to the estate's agent William Wilson (who had also served as agent to the Revells). His son, Richard, who acted as the Wilmot family solicitor was also to live in the hall and indeed purchased the whole estate in 1834 after Wilmot had fallen into financial difficulties. It seems the purchase (£18,000) had been made with money from Richard's father-in-law, a Chesterfield lawyer and thus Carnfield remained in family hands even after Richard Wilson was arrested for debt in 1840. He died in Derby prison later that year whereupon his daughter, Isabella, and son-in-law Thomas Radford of Smalley Hall took possession. Their son, Vaughan Hobbs Radford, inherited and proved to be a much loved squire. Upon Hobbs Radford's death in 1912 the estate was to be sold by Melville Watson, estate agent, but rather unusually he ended up buying it himself and even more unusually he was murdered by a disgruntled tenant in June 1914, bringing to an abrupt halt a series of admirable restoration works that he had instituted. His widow lived on in increasing poverty until her death in 1949, whereupon Mr Noel Darbyshire took possession, but the house had subsidence problems and was abandoned for many years, though a garden centre was established adjacent to it in the 1970s.

In 1987, the current owner Mr James Cartland acquired the Hall and instituted a series of renovations, the house opening to the public in 1990. In the nick of time the house has been brought back to life and is now kept in excellent condition.

THE GREEN HALL, ASHBOURNE

From Mr. J. Stevenson

John Hayne's son, also John, may have rebuilt The Green Hall as early as between 1690 and 1700. The 'RH 1751' upon the fabric of the building is a most interesting and large coloured brickwork inscription which may be seen upon the stable block. A nineteenth century engraving of the house shows string courses above each pair of windows, though these were removed in the 1950s. Since the Second World War, the Hall has been owned by P.B. Balean and Roger F. Stevenson. It is now owned by Mr & Mrs John Stevenson (no relation to R.F. Stevenson).

HIGHLOW HALL

From Mr. B. Walker

In 1996 Mr & Mrs Barrie Walker purchased Highlow Hall from Mr Philip Wain (who had purchased it from his father, Mr Tom Wain, two years previously). The entrance arch to the house carries a 'heraldic device' which is in fact a fleur de lys, this feature had been lost for some time but has now been replaced by the current owner.

A drawing of c. 1710 (found in the roof of Hassop Hall but now safely archived in Sheffield Museum as part of the Bagshawe papers, MS 779) depicts Highlow Hall; this was possibly by John Eyre. The drawing shows that the house was originally much larger with both a north and south wing. The dimensions of the north wing were 30' x 20', a fact the present owners discovered by actually digging up the foundations which were found to correspond very closely to the measurements noted upon the drawing. The south wing featured a south facing gable which had a door on to the garden. Both the north and south wings were demolished at a time presently unknown and the outer wall of the north side was partly rebuilt to give the plain aspect that now exists. The little 'L' shape on the north wing was formed purely to allow a return on the Tudor stairs for access into the old solar, which is above the Great Hall. Originally these stairs would have given access into the north wing. This can be verified by studying the north wall which is not tied to the ashlar facings of the façade.

The fireplace was originally in the middle of the Great Hall. Entry to the house was gained directly into the Great Hall opposite the stairs (these gave access to the south wing which was much smaller than its eventual replacement, the current structure).

The new north wing was formed by demolishing the old wing down to about 8ft from the foundations or at a lower window head level (there must have been a lower ground floor – possibly kitchens or cellars), then back-filling part of the lower floor and building upon it a much larger new wing. The roof of this new wing was much higher than heretofore and extended over part of the old Great Hall; this necessitated building a wall in the hall to carry the roof. This wall formed a hallway into the house and also had the effect of putting the fireplace into the corner. The said extension of the roof also necessitated the cutting back of the battlements, as can presently be seen.

These alterations gave the then owners three south facing bedrooms with fireplaces (all have which have been restored). The large hall fireplace was blocked up and a door cut into the back giving access to the rear of the house. The Great Hall was converted into a kitchen complete with a large stone sink under the window. Those 'improvements' have, thankfully, been removed, the fireplace and the chimney restored and the Hall returned to an older and more authentic appearance, albeit smaller due to the newer wall.

At the same time as the demolition of the wings part of the ground floor was filled in and the garden level lifted, thus obscuring some of the lower windows. The present owner found one of these windows, which was below ground level and has restored it; it now forms part of the house wine cellar.

By and large the gardens are much as they were in c. 1710. Apart, that is, from the sycamore avenue which extended into what is now a field. The pond at the end of this avenue is now not much more than a bog, but fortunately John Eyre (or whoever did the 1710 drawing) put in fairly precise measurements on all aspects of the house which made identification very simple, (for example during recent garden renovations parts of the old south facing porch were discovered). The Hall's 'Dovecote' may well in fact never have been a dovecote, as no dove needs 6ft x 4ft openings! We may never know exactly what this building was for, but a planned programme of excavation to include going through a now concreted floor may yield results.

BIBLIOGRAPHY

Notes:

Sources are expressed in the notes in the usual way with the following exceptions: Burke's genealogical publications – abbreviated as set out below; Colvin's *Dictionary of British Architects,* 3rd Edn. [Colvin + page], GEC *Complete Peerage* [CP + vol. + page], Glover's *History and Gazetteer of the County of Derby* 1st edn. 1829/31 [Glover + Vol. + page], Hunter's *Familiae Minorum Gentium* [FMG + Vol. + Page], Lysons' *Magna Britannia* Vol. V *Derbyshire* [Lysons V + page], Pevsner's *Buildings of England* series [Pevsner + page] for Derbyshire and [Pevsner + *County* + page] and the various Heralds' Visitations, which are given as [V. + year] for Derbyshire and as [V. + *County* + year] for others.

For the convenience of the general reader, references to Pevsner and Colvin precede all others in the notes, followed by non-genealogical works, then references to magazines, journals, newspapers etc., then by primary sources, followed by genealogical references in the order that the relevant families occur in the article to which the notes are attached. Where possible, in this respect, the most accessible sources are given for those wishing to go into more detail; they are not necessarily the most accurate accounts. Burke's publications, for instance, are not to be relied on for earlier ancestries in editions preceding the Great War, and cannot be taken as truly scholarly until the 1960s; however the 1999 *Peerage and Baronetage* is a model of genealogical probity.

MS sources, public and private, are listed under each article where they have a bearing by location and reference.

ABERG, F. A., (Ed.) Medieval Moated Sites, CBA Research Report No. 17 (London, 1978)

ABRAHAMS, S., A Short Account of the History of Sydnope Hall & Darley Dale (Darley, 1978)

ADAM, W., The Gem of the Peak (Derby, 1840)

ADAMS, N., A History of Walton-on-Trent (Walton, 2000)

AIKIN, J., A Description of the Country from Thirty to Forty Miles Round Manchester (London, 1795)

AIRS, M., The Tudor & Jacobean Country House – A Building History (Godalming, 1998)

AITKEN, M., et al., Smalley Remembered (Heanor, 1990)

AITKENHEAD, N., and STEVENSON, I. P., Geology of the country around Buxton, Leek and Bakewell. (London HMSO, 1985) Mem.Br.Geol.Surv.

ALCOCK, L., NW, CBA Research Report No. 42 CC.

ANCIENT MONUMENT SOCIETY Journal (Since 1956)

ANDERSON, M. & GLENN, J., Elvaston Castle, A Report for the Architectural Association (Boston, Lincs., 1997)

ANDREWS, M., Long Ago in Peakland (Nottingham, 1948)

ANON, An Account of Beauchief Hall (Derby, 1829)

ANON, The History and Topography of Ashbourne and the Valley of the Dove (Ashbourne, 1839)

Architectural History Journal of the Society of Architectural Historians (London, from 1957)

ARKELL, W. J., Oxford Stone (London, 1947)

ARMITAGE, H., Chantry Land (London, 1910)

BAGSHAW, S., Directory of Derbyshire (Derby, 1846)

BAGSHAWE, M. B. T. & INNES-SMITH, R. S., Oakes Park (Derby, 1976)

BARLEY, M., The English Farmhouse and Cottage (London, 1961)

BARLOW, Sir M., Bt. Barlow Family Records (Derby, 1932)

BARRON, W., The British Winter Garden (London, 1852)

BARRON & SON LTD., A List of some of the Principal Works (Derby, n.d. [c.1929])

BARRY, C. et al, Report of the Commissioners on the Selection of Stone for the New Houses of Parliament (London, 1839)

BARTON, D. A., Around Matlock (Matlock, 1993)

BATEMAN, C., A Descriptive and Historical Account of Alfreton (Derby, 1812)

BEARD, G., Craftsmen and Interior Decoration in England 1660-1820 (London, 1981)

BEARD, G., Decorative Plasterwork in Great Britain (London, 1975)

BEARD, G., The Work of Robert Adam (London, 1978)

BEMROSE, H. H., The House of Bemrose 1826-1926 (Derby, 1926)

BENNETT, J. D., The Vanished Houses of Leicestershire, (Leicester, 1971)

BERESFORD, Col. M.de la Poer, The Book of the Beresfords (Chichester, 1977)

BESTALL, J. M. (Ed. Fowkes, D.V.), A History of Chesterfield, Vol III (Chesterfield, 1978)

BIGSBY, R., Historical and Topographical Description of Repton (London, 1854)

BLANCHARD, Dr. I. S. W. (Ed.) The Duchy of Lancaster's Estates in Derbyshire, DAS Record Series, Vol. 3 (Derby, 1967)

BLORE, T., A History of the Manor...of South Wingfield 2 Vols. (London, 1793)

BOSWELL of Auchinleck, J., Life of Samuel Johnson 2 Vols. (London, 1905)

BOWYER, L. J., The Ancient Parish of Norbury (Ashbourne, 1953)

BOYES, M., Allestree Hall (Derby, 1982)

BRADBURY, E. & KEENE, R., All About Derbyshire (Derby, 1884)

BRIGGS, J. J., History of Melbourne, (2nd edn., Derby, 1846)

BRISCOE, J. P., Nottinghamshire and Derbyshire at the Beginning of the Twentieth Century (Brighton, Briscoe 1901)

BRITTON, J. & BRAYLEY, E. W., The Beauties of England & Wales Vol. III (London 1802)

BRUNSKILL, R. W., Illustrated Handbook of Vernacular Architecture (London, 1971)

BRUNSKILL, R. W., Brick Building in Britain (London, 1990)

BULMER, T., Directory of Derbyshire (London, 1895)

BURKE, J. B., Vicissitudes of Families (3rd series, London,1863)

BURKE, J. B., Visitation of Seats...of the Noblemen and Gentlemen of Great Britain & Ireland (2 Vols. London, 1852-3)

BURKE, J. B., Visitation of Seats...(Second series, 2 Vols. London, 1854-5)

BURKE'S PUBLICATIONS:

Title etc.	Abbreviation
Colonial gentry (2 Vols.1891, 1895)	BCG
Distinguished Families of the USA (1939)	DFUSA
Dormant & Extinct Baronetcies (1838)	BDEB
Dormant & Extinct Peerages (1883)	BDEP
Family records (1897)	BFR
Irish Family Records (1976)	BIFR
Landed Gentry (18 Edns., 1833-1972)	BLG (+date)
Peerage & Baronetage (107 Edns.1826-1999)	BP (+date)

BURTON, I. E., The Royal Forest of the Peak (Bakewell, 1967)

BURTON, W., The Description of Leicestershire (London, 1622)

BYARD, M., The Story of The Hayes in Swanwick Rev. Edn. (Alfreton, 1998)

BYNG, Hon. J., (afterwards Viscount Torrington), The Torrington Diaries, Ed. Andrews, C., 4 Vols. (London, 1934-8)

CALENDAR OF PATENT ROLLS, 1232-1509/1547-1578, 68 Vols. (London, 1891-1982)

CAMPBELL, C., Vitruvius Britannicus Vol. IV (London, 1767)

CAMDEN, W. Britannia, (London, 1637)

CAMERON, K., The Place Names of Derbyshire, 3 Vols. (Cambridge, 1959)

CHACKSFIELD, J. E., Sir Henry Fowler (Usk, 2000)

CHISHOLM, J.I., et al Geology of the country around Ashbourne and Cheadle (London, HMSO 1988)

CHOLERTON, P., Chaddesden (Stroud, 1999)

CHRISTIAN, R. C., Butterley Brick (London, 1990)

CHRISTIAN, R. C., Derbyshire (London, 1978)

CLAY, J. W., The Extinct and Dormant Peerages of the. Northern Counties of England (London, 1913)

CLAY, R. M., Samuel Hieronymus Grimm of Burgdorf in Switzerland (London, 1939)

CLEMENSON, H. A., Diminishing Derbyshire Estates, in Geographical Magazine, 11/1980.

CLIFTON-TAYLOR, A., The Pattern of English Building (London, 1972)

CLIFTON-TAYLOR, A. & IRESON, A. S., English Stone Building (London, 1983)

C[OKAYNE], G. E., The Complete Peerage, 15 Vols. (London, 1910-1959,1982, 1998)

COLVIN, Sir H. M., Biographical Dictionary of British Architects (3rd edn. London, 1995)

COLVIN, Sir H. M., Calke Abbey (London, 1985)

COLVIN, Sir H. M., The Country Seat (London, 1970)

COOPER, B. & COOPER, N., Transformation of a Valley (London, 1983)

COOPER, N., Houses of the Gentry 1480-1680 (London, 1999)

CORNFORTH, J. & WALL, C. St. Q., Sudbury Hall (London, 1978)

COTTON, C., Wonders of the Peake 2nd Edn. (London, 1683)

COULSON, C. L. H., A Handlist of English Royal Licences to Crenellate 1200-1578 (Unpublished MS 1982)

COUNTRY LIFE (London, from 1897)

COX, J. C., Notes on the Churches of Derbyshire, 4 Vols. (London, 1875-8)

COX, L. J., Over the Hills to Calke 2nd Edn. (Derby, 2000)

CRANE, A., The Kirkland Papers 1753-1869 (Ashby-de-la-Zouche, 1990)

CRAVEN, M. A. J. B. A Derbyshire Armory Derbyshire Record Society vol. XVII, (Chesterfield, 1991)

CRAVEN, M. A. J. B., John Whitehurst, FRS (Mayfield, Staffs., 1996)

CRAVEN, M. A. J. B., Richard Keene's Derby (Derby, 1993)

CRAVEN, M. A. J. B., The Derby Town House (Derby, 1987)

CRAVEN, M. A. J. B., The Illustrated History of Derby (Derby, 1988)

CRAVEN, M. A J. B., The Illustrated History of Derby's Suburbs (Derby, 1996b)

CRAVEN, M. A. J. B., & STANLEY, M. F., The Derbyshire Country House 2 Vols (Matlock, 1982, 1984)

CRAVEN, M. A. J. B., & STANLEY, M. F., The Derbyshire Country House New & Rev Edn. (Derby, 1991)

CROFTS, J., & READ. J., Footsteps Through Smalley (Smalley, 1995)

CUTTS, C. G., History of Thornbridge Hall (Ashford, 1986)

DARLINCTON, R. R. (Ed.), The Glapwell Charters (Kendal, 1959)

DARLINGTON, R. R. (Ed.), The Darley Cartulary, 2 Vols. (Kendal, 1945)

DAVIES, D. P., A View of Derbyshire (Belper, 1811)

DEBRETT, People of Today (London, 1992, 2000)

De FIGUEIREDO, P. & TREUHERZ, J., Cheshire Country Houses (Chichester, 1988)

Derby & Chesterfield Reporter [DCR + date]

DERBY COUNTY BOROUGH COUNCIL Official Opening of the Municipal Airport, Programme 7 June 1939 (Derby, 1939)

Derby Evening Telegraph [DET + date]

Derby Mercury (Derby, 1732-1929) [DM + date]

Derbyshire Advertiser [DA + date]

Derbyshire Archaeological Society, Journal, (Derby, from 1879) [DAJ + no + date]

Derbyshire Life & Countryside, (Derby, from 1921) [DLC + month + year]

Derbyshire Miscellany Journal of Local History Section of the Derbyshire Archaeological Society (Matlock, from 1957) [D. Misc. + Vol. + Part + year]

DEVONSHIRE, DUCHESS OF, The House, A Portrait of Chatsworth (London, 1982)

Dictionary of National Biography (Reprinted in 2 vols., Oxford,1979)

DIXON, P., Wingfield Manor, A Brief Guide (1995)

DRAKE, B. M., Electric Lighting in Country Houses in Country Life 14/10/1899

DURANT, D. N., Bess of Hardwick (London, 1977)

DURANT, D. N. & RIDEN, P. (Eds.), The Building of Hardwick Hall Pt. I, (DRS IV, Chesterfield, 1980)

DURANT, D. N. & RIDEN, P. (Eds.), The Building of Hardwick Hall Pt. II, (DRS IX, Chesterfield, 1984)

EDEN, R. A., et al, The Geology of the Country Around Sheffield (London, 1957)

EDWARDS, D. G. (Ed.), Derbyshire Hearth Tax Assessments 1662-1670 (DRS VII Chesterfield, 1982)

EDWARDS, D. G., The Hunlokes of Wingerworth Hall 2nd Edn. (Wingerworth, 1976)

EGGLESHAW, P., et al., Around Old Heanor (Heanor, 1982)

EISENBERG, E., Wingerworth Manor & Estate (Derby, n.d.)

EMERY, A., The Greater Medieval Houses of England & Wales Vol. 2 (Cambridge, 2000)

ENTWISTLE, R., Holymoorside Past and Present (Shirland, 1976)

FAREY, J., A General View of the Agriculture and Minerals of Derbyshire 3 Vols. (London, 1811)

FEARNEYHOUGH, H. W., Chaddesden – A History (Derby, 1991)

FELLOWS, R. A., Sir Reginald Blomfield (London, 1985)

FERREY, E. B., South Wingfield Manor (London, 1876)

FITTON, R. S. & WADSWORTH, A. P., The Strutts and the Arkwrights 1758-1830 (Manchester, 1958)

FLEMING, L. & GORE, A., The English Garden (London, 1979)

FLETCHER, S. B., The Fletcher House of Lace (Derby, 1957)

FORD, T., A History of Chesterfield (Chesterfield, 1839)

FORD, T. D. Blue John (Ashbourne, 1999)

FOX-DAVIES, A. C., Amorial Families (London, 1905, 1910, 1929) [FD + date]

FRANKLYN, J., The Gentleman's Country House and its Plan, 1835-1914 (London, 1981)

FRASER, W., The Parishes of Swarkstone and Stanton-by-Bridge (Burton-on-Trent, 1944)

FRASER, W., Field Names of South Derbyshire (Ipswich, 1947)

FRITH, J. B., Highways and Byways in Derbyshire (London, 1920)

FROST, D. & SMART, J. G. O., Geology of the Country North of Derby (London, 1979)

GALBRAITH, G. (Ed.), The Diary of William Bagshaw Stevens (Oxford, 1965)

GAYRE, R., The Armorial Who is Who (London, 1978)

GEORGIAN GROUP Journal (London, from 1990)

GIBBS, J., Book of Architecture (London, 1728)

GIBSON, W. et al, Geology of the Southern Part of the Derbyshire and. Nottinghamshire Coalfield (London, 1908)

GIBSON, W. & WEDD, C. B., Geology of the Northern Part of the Derbyshire Coalfield (London, 1913)

GILES, J. A., A History of Milford & Makeney (Milford, 1993)

GIROUARD, M., Robert Smythson and the Elizabethan Country House
(2nd Edn. London, 1983)

GIROUARD, M., The Victorian Country House (London, 1979)

GLOVER, S., Directory of Derbyshire (Derby, 1827-9)

GLOVER, S., History and Gazetteer of the County of Derby, 2 Vols. (1st Edn. Derby 1829/31; 2nd. Edn. Derby 1831/33)

GLOVER, S., Notes on the History of Derbyshire (Derby,1842)

GLOVER, S., The Peak Guide (Derby, 1830)

GOMME, A., Catton Hall & The Genesis of Sutton Scarsdale in Colvin, Sir H. M., The Country Seat (London, 1970)

GOMME, A., Francis Smith of Warwick (Donnington, 2001, forthcoming)

GOW, I & RONAN, A., The Scottish Country House (Edinburgh 1995)

GREEN, A. H. et al, Geology of the Carboniferous Limestone, Yoredale Rocks and Millstone Grit of North Derbyshire (London, 1887)

HALL, I., The Auld Hall & The New Hall in Bulletin of the Buxton Archaeological & NH Soc. I (1986)

HALL, S. T., Days in Derbyshire (Derby 1863)

HAMILTON, J., The Misses Vickers (Sheffield, 1984)

HARRIS, J., The Artist and the Country House (London, 1979)

HARRIS, J., The Design of the English Country House 1620-1920 (London, 1985)

HARRIS, J., William Talman (London, 1982)

HARRIS, L., Robert Adam and Kedleston (London, 1987)

HARRISON, J., Some Account of the History of Normanton-by-Derby Duplicated MS (Normanton, c. 1958)

HART, C., North Derbyshire Archaeological Survey (Chesterfield, 1981)

HARTLEY, M., Sutton-on-the-Hill, 2nd Edn. (Sutton, 1998)

HASLAM, C., Knowle Hill, An Interim Report (Shottesbrooke, 1993)

HEATHCOTE, E. D., An Account of Some of the Families Bearing the Name of Heathcote which have descended out of the Co. of Derby (Winchester, 1899)

HENDERSON, J. B. & ROBINSON, E. R., The Etwall Heritage (Ilkeston, 1979)

HENSTOCK, A. et al., A Georgian Town, Ashbourne 1725-1825 2 Vols. (Ashbourne, 1989, 1991)

HENSTOCK, A. et al., Victorian Town (Ashbourne, 1978)

HERRMANN, L., Paul and Thomas Sandby (London, 1986)

HEWETT, C. A., English Historic Carpentry (Chichester, 1980)

HIGGINBOTTOM, M. & THACKER, T., The Story of Swanwick Hall (South Normanton, 1971)

HIGGINSON, M., The Friar Gate Line (Derby, 1989)

HILL, O & CORNFORTH, J., English Country Houses, Caroline 1625-1685 (London, 1966)

HIPKINS, F. C., Repton and its Neighbourhood (Repton, 1899)

HOLDEN, W., The Derbyshire Holdens and Their Descendants (London, 1930)

HOLME, C., The Gardens of England in the Midland and Northern Counties (London, 1908)

HOLMES, M., The Country House Described (London, 1986)

HOSKINS, W. C., The Making of the English Landscape (London, 1955)

HOWARD, M., The Early Tudor Country House (London, 1987)

HOWE, D., The Story of Holbrook (Cromford, 1986)

HULL, E., Building and Ornamental Stones (London, 1872)

HULL, E., The Triassic and Permian Rocks of the Midland Counties of England (London, 1869)

HUNT, B. J., West Hallam Heritage (Ilkeston, 1978)

HUNTER ARCHAEOLOGICAL SOCIETY Transactions

HUNTER, J., Familiae Minorum Gentium, 4 Vols. (Harleian Society, Vols. XXXVII-XL, London, 1894-6)

HUNTER, J. Pedigrees (Harleian Society, Vol. LXXXVIII, London, 1936)

HUNTER, J., South Yorkshire (London, 1828)

HUSSEY, C., English Country Houses, Mid-Georgian (London, 1956)

HUTTON, B et al., Derby Buildings Records (Derbys. Archaeological Society Architectural Group)

HUTTON, B., Historic Farmhouses Around Derby (Cromford, 1991)

HUTTON, B., Houses and Everyday Life in Weston-on-Trent (Weston, 1994)

HUTTON, W., History of Derby to the Year 1791 (London, 1791)

IBBETSON, P., The Gardens of Shipley Hall (Matlock, 1986)

INNES-SMITH, R. S., A Derbyshire Guide (3rd Edn. Derby, 1991)

INNES-SMITH, R. S., Haddon Hall (Derby, 1987)

INNES-SMITH, R. S., Melbourne Hall (Derby, 1968)

INNES-SMITH, R. S., Notable Derbyshire Homes (Derby, 1972)

JACKSON-STOPS, G., Sudbury Hall (London, 1987)

JACQUES, A. S., Melbourne (Derby, 1933)

JACQUES, D., Georgian Gardens: the Reign of Nature (London, 1983)

JEAYES, I. H., Derbyshire Charters (London, 1906)

JEFFERY, J. et al., Kilburn in Morleston (Kilburn, 1994)

JENNINGS, J. R. G. et al., Belper (Belper, 1981)

JEWITT, Ll., The Ceramic Art of Great Britain (London, 1883)

JOHNSON, R., A History of Alfreton (Ripley, 1968)

KELLY'S Directories of Derbyshire (London, 1877,1903/8/12/25/28/32/36/41)

KELLY'S Handbook Of the Official, Titled and Landed Classes (London, 1890, 1911, 1924, 1939, 1970, 1976)

KERRY, Rev. C., History and Legends of Smalley (Derby, 1905)

KETTLE, P., Oldcotes (Cardiff, 2000)

KETTLE, P., The Sutton Scarsdale Story (Chesterfield, 1988)

KILBURN, T., Joseph Whitworth – Toolmaker (Cromford, 1987)

KING-HELE, D., Erasmus Darwin, A Life of Unequalled Achievement (London, 1999)

KIP, J., Nouveau Theatre de Grande Bretagne Vol. I (London, 1715)

KITCHING, C., Squire of Calke Abbey (Cromford, 1995)

KITCHING, C., William Astbury's Repton Diary (Repton, 2001)

LEACH, P., James Paine (London, 1988)

LEE, S. T., The Story of Stanley (Stanley, 1968)

LEES-MILNE, J., English Country Houses, Baroque 1685-1715 (London, 1970)

LELAND, J., Itinerary of a Tour Through England and Wales, Leland 1545 (Oxford, 1710)

LE NEVE, P., Pedigrees of the Knights, Created between the Years 1660 and 1714 (Harleian Society Vol. VIII London, 1873)

LOCKER-LAMPSON, G., Life in the Country (London, n.d. [1945])

LUCAS, R., The Manor of Markeaton, Mackworth & Allestree 1650-1851 (Derby, 1995)

LUGARD, C. E., The Saints and Sinners of Ashover (Leicester, 1924)

LYSONS, S. & D., Magna Britannia, Vol. V., Derbyshire (London 1816)

McARDLE, P., The Story of Barlborough Hall (Rotherham, 1979)

MADAN, F. C., The Gresleys of Drakelow (London, 1899)

MANTELL. K. H., Haddon Hall (Derby, 1987)

MERCER, E., English Vernacular Houses (London, 1975)

MERCER, E, STRANGE, P. & HAWKINS, R., Somersall Herbert – The Hall Report to West Derbys. Dist. Council (1979)

MEREDITH, R., Farms and Families of Hathersage Outseats (2 parts, Rotherham, 1981,1983)

MERRILL, J. N., Famous Derbyshire Homes (Clapham, Yorks., 1973)

MOORE, A., A Son of the Rectory (Gloucester, 1982)

MOORE, P., The End of an Era (Snelston, 2000)

MORLEY Village History Committee, History of the Parish of Morley (Ilkeston, 1977)

MORRIS, C., (Ed.) The Journeys of Celia Fiennes (London, 1949)

MORRIS, F. 0. (Ed.), A Series of Picturesque Views of the Country Seats of Great Britain &.Ireland 6 Vols. (London, 1880)

MORROW, E., Willington Memories (Lancaster, n.d.)

MOWL, T., & EARNSHAW, B., Trumpet at a Distant Gate (London, 1985)

MURRAY LESLIE, I., Rosser & Russell Ltd. (London, 1974)

NEALE, J. P., Views of Seats...6 Vols. (London, 1818-23)

NICHOLS, J., The History and Antiquities of the County of Leicester, 4 Vols. In 8 (London, 1795-1811)

OAKES, T. H., A Short History of Riddings (Ripley, 1890)

PAINE, J., Plans, Elevations, etc...2 Vols. (London, 1767, 1783)

PALFREYMAN, A. F., Excavations at Park Hall, Mapperley, Ilkeston & District Local History Society Occasional Paper No 2 (Ilkeston, 1970)

PAYNE, C. J., Derby Churches Old & New or, Derby's Golgotha (Derby, 1893)

PEAK PARK JOINT PLANNING BOARD, Building in the Peak (Matlock, 1973)

PEVSNER, Sir N., Buildings of England
Cheshire (London, 1971)
Derbyshire (London, 1953)
Derbyshire, 2nd Edn., revised Williamson, E. (London, 1978)
Leicestershire, (London, 1970)
Yorkshire, West Riding (London, 1967)

PHIPPS, J., The Style of Joseph Pickford MS MA Dissertation (De Montfort University, Leicester, 1992)

PILKINCTON, J., A View of the Present State of Derbyshire, 2 Vols., (Derby, 1789)

PORT, F. R., The Family of Port (USA, 1969)

[PYE, H. J.] Anon., Clifton Camville (London, 1892)

PYM YEATMAN, J., The Albinis of Derbyshire (Birmingham, 1907)

READ, A. L., Johnsonian Gleanings 11 Vols. (London, 1908-52)

REEDMAN, K., The Book of Long Eaton (Buckingham, 1979)

REEDMAN. K. et al., Around Old Heanor (Heanor, 1981)

REDMAN, N., An Illustrated History of Breadsall Priory (1998)

REID, P., County List of Houses Destroyed in Great Britain and Ireland, Vol. 1 (1981)

Reliquary, The, Ed. Ll. Jewitt (Derby, 1860-92)

RENN, D. F., Norman Castles in Britain, 2nd Edn. (London, 1973)

RIDEN, P., The Butterley Company1790-1830 DRS XVI (Chesterfield, 1990)

ROBERTSON, C. L., Historical Rooms from the Manor houses of England 2 Vols. (London, 1929)

ROBINSON, J. M., The Latest Country Houses (London, 1984)

ROBINSON, J.M., The Wyatts, An Architectural Dynasty (Oxford, 1979)

ROBINSON, P. M., The Smiths of Chesterfield (Chesterfield, 1957)

ROYAL COMMISSION ON HISTORIC MANUSCRIPTS The Tutbury Cartulary (London, 1952)

ROYAL COMMISSION ON HISTORIC MONUMENTS Historic Buildings Reports (York & Swindon, various dates)

RYAN, S. D. M., A Short History of Foremark (London, 1965)

SALTMANN. A. (Ed.), The Kniveton Leiger, Derbyshire Arch. Soc. Record Series, VI. (Derby, 1971)

SALTMANN, A. (Ed.) The Cartulary of Dale Abbey Derbyshire Arch. Soc. Record Series II (Derby, 1966)

SAUNDERS, E. J., Joseph Pickford of Derby (Stroud, 1993)

SAVE, The Vanishing Houses of England (London, 1982)

SCOTT, J., SMITH, J. H., & WINTERBOTTOM, D., Glossop Dale, Manor & Borough (Glossop, 1986)

SHARPE, J. M., The Design of the Derbyshire Country House (Unpublished MA thesis, de Montfort Univ., Leicester, 1986)

SHAW, G., A Brief History of Eckington (Eckington, 1984)

SHAW, G., People and Places of the Eckington District (Eckington, 1985)

SHAW, S., The History and Antiquities of Staffordshire, 2Vols. (London, 1798, 1801)

SHEPPARD, C. B., Pinxton Porcelain (Sutton-in-Ashfield, 1996)

SHORE, I (Ed. GADSBY, G.,) The Haunted House (Loughborough, 2000)

SILVESTER, C., The Philosophy of Domestic Economy (London, 1819)

SINAR, J., & HUGHES, R. G., Derby and the Civil War (Derby ,1971)

SITWELL, Sir R. S., Bt., Renishaw Hall & the Sitwells (Derby, 1985)

SLATER, J. Directory of Derbyshire (1862)

SLEIGH. J., A History of the Ancient Parish of Leek, in Staffordshire , 2nd edn. (Derby, 1883)

SMITH, A. Etwall (Derby 1990)

SMITH, B. M., Padley Chapel (Hathersage 1991)

SMITH, E. G. et al, Geology of the Country Around Chesterfield, Matlock and Mansfield, (London, 1967)

SPAVOLD, J., Hartshorne Manor (Derby, n.d.)

SPEED, J., The Theatre of the Empire of Great Britain Vol. I (London, 1670)

SPENCER-SILVER, P., Pugin's builder (Hull, 1993)

SORRELL, D. S., Vernacular Architecture of Duffield Frith (Unpublished MS, Derby Museum 1972)

STAFFORD, J. W., A History of the House of Stafford of Botham Hall (1906)

STANCLIFFE ESTATES CO, LTD., Illustrated Catalogue (Darley Dale, 1913)

STANLEY, M. F., The Stone Slates of Derbyshire, (forthcoming)

STANLEY, M. F. The Building Stones of Dale Abbey. Report to Derbys. County Council for Dale Abbey Conservation Area (unpublished, 1977)

STANLEY, M.F. Carved in Bright Stone. In Parsons, D. (ed) Stone quarrying and building in England AD43-1525 (Chichester, 1990)

STANTON, P., Pugin (London, 1971)

STAPLETON-MARTIN, M. B. B., The Medieval Hall at Norbury (Ashbourne, 1973)

STRONG, Sir R., BINNEY, M. & HARRIS, J. The Destruction of the Country House (London, 1974)

TARN, J. N.., The Peak District National Park: its Architecture (Bakewell, 1971)

THOMPSON, F., A History of Chatsworth (London, 1949)

THOMPSON, L., A History of Tapton House (Cranleigh, 2000)

THOMPSON, L., Memories of Tapton House School (Cranleigh, 1999)

THOMPSON, M., The Construction of the Manor at South Wingfield, Derbyshire in Siveking, G., (Ed.) Problems in Social and Economic Archaeology Part IV (London, 1976)

THOROLD, H. C., The Shell Guide to Derbyshire (London, 1972)

THOROTON, R., History of Nottinghamshire, Ed. Throsby, J. with additions, 3 Vols. (London, 1797)

THORPE, F. S., The Heritage of Loscoe & Codnor (Loscoe, 1990)

TILLEY, J., The Old Halls, Manors and Families of Derbyshire, 4 Vols., (Derby, 1892-1902)

TIPPING, H. A., English Homes, Period 6, Vol. I (London, 1926)

TIPPING, H. A., Gardens Old and New 3 Vols. (London, n.d. [c.1908])

TOMLINSON, T., North Lees Hall (Hathersage, n.d.)

TOYNBEE, P. & WHIBLEY, L. (Eds.,) The Correspondence of Thomas Gray 3 Vols. (1935)

TUDOR, T. L. New Light on Duffield Church, (Derby, 1939)

TURBUTT, G., A History of Ogston (Ogston, 1975)

TURBUTT, G., A History of Derbyshire 4 Vols. (Cardiff, 1999)

TURBUTT, G., The Hospitaller Order of St. John...in Derbyshire History (Cromford, 1999)

USHER, H., Castles in the Air (Derby, 1997)

USHER, H., Knowle Hill 2nd. Rev.Edn. (Ticknall, 1993)

USHER, H., The Hardinges of King's Newton (Derby, 1996)

USHER, H., & SAUNDERS E. J., Melbourne Hall & Estate & The Royal Park at Melbourne (Melbourne, 1987)

USSHER, R., A History of the Parish of Croxall (1881)

VICTORIA HISTORY OF THE COUNTIES OF ENGLAND. Derbyshire, 2 Vols. (London, 1905)

VISITATIONS OF THE HERALDS
  Derbyshire 1569, by William Flower, Norroy.   [V.1569]
  Derbyshire 1611, by Richard St. George, Norroy. [V.1611]
  Derbyshire 1634, by Richard St. George, Norroy. [V.1634]
  Derbyshire 1662, by William Dugdale, Norroy.   [V. 1662]

WAIN, H., A Brief History of Bretby (1964)

WALFORD, E., County Families of the United Kingdom (London, 1865, 1871, 1909)

WALKER, J. S. F. & TINDALL, A. S., The Country Houses of Greater Manchester (Manchester, 1985)

WATKIN, D., Thomas Hope and the Neo-Classical Idea (London, 1968)

WATSON, J., British and Foreign Building Stones (Cambridge, 1911)

WATSON, S., A History of Mickleover and Littleover (Derby, 1993)

WATSON, S., Spondon – A History (Spondon, 1989)

WATSON, W, The Strata of Derbyshire (Sheffield, 1811)

WHATMORE, A. W., Leicestershire and Rutland Sites and Notes and Queries (Leicester, 1861)

WHITE, T., Gazeteer of the County of Derby, (London, 1857)

WHITEHURST, J. An Inquiry into the Original State and Formation of the Earth 2nd Edn., London, 1782.

WHO'S WHO IN DERBYSHIRE (Derby, 1934)

WILLIAMS, G., Report on Manor House Farm, Hasland (1962)

WILSON, M. I., The Country House and its Furnishings (London, 1977)

WOLFE, J. & GANDON, J., Vitruvius Britannicus Vol. V (London, 1771)

WOOD, M., The English Medieval House (London, 1965)

WOOD, W., History & Antiquities of Eyam (Sheffield, 1859)

WOOLLEY, W., History of Derbyshire Ed. Glover, C & Riden, P. DRS VI (Chesterfield, 1981)

WORSLEY, G., The 1740s, The Lost Decade in the Journal of the Georgian Group (1991) 21-26.

WORSLEY, L., Bolsover Castle Conservation Plan (London, 1999)

WRIGHT, S. M., The Derbyshire Gentry in the Fifteenth Century DRS VIII (Chesterfield, 1983)

YHA Hartington Hall (London, n. d.)

YOUNG, J., Alabaster (Matlock, 1990)

YOULGREAVE WOMENS' INSTITUTE, Some Account of Youlgreave Middleton and Alport, (Bakewell, 1931)

INDEX